The Sopratos

Other *Pearls Before Swine* Collections

Da Brudderhood of Zeeba Zeeba Eata
The Ratvolution Will Not Be Televised
Nighthogs
This Little Piggy Stayed Home
BLTs Taste So Darn Good

Treasuries

Lions and Tigers and Crocs, Oh My!
Sgt. Piggy's Lonely Hearts Club Comic

THE SOPRATOS

A Pearls Before Swine **Collection by Stephan Pastis**

Andrews McMeel
Publishing, LLC
Kansas City

Pearls Before Swine is distributed internationally by United Feature Syndicate, Inc.

The Sopratos copyright © 2007 by Stephan Pastis. All rights reserved. Printed in the United States of America. No part of this book may be used or reproduced in any manner whatsoever without written permission except in the case of reprints in the context of reviews. For information, write Andrews McMeel Publishing, LLC, an Andrews McMeel Universal company, 4520 Main Street, Kansas City, Missouri 64111.

07 08 09 10 11 BBG 10 9 8 7 6 5 4 3 2 1

ISBN-13: 978-0-7407-6847-7
ISBN-10: 0-7407-6847-6

Library of Congress Control Number: 2007925341

Pearls Before Swine can be viewed on the Internet at
www.comics.com/comics/pearls.

These strips appeared in newspapers from October 31, 2005 to August 6, 2006.

 ATTENTION: SCHOOLS AND BUSINESSES

Andrews McMeel books are available at quantity discounts with bulk purchase for educational, business, or sales promotional use. For information, please write to: Special Sales Department, Andrews McMeel Publishing, LLC, 4520 Main Street, Kansas City, Missouri 64111.

To my nieces and nephew—
Elenique, Kalianthe, John, and Stephanie

Introduction

Being a syndicated cartoonist means getting a lot of e-mail.

There's the praise, which is great. There are the strange requests, which are even better. And then there are the rip-snorting angry folk, who are the best.

The praise generally follows a familiar pattern. They like a certain character or a certain strip. They liked one of the books. A husband and wife want me to know they speak to each other in Crocodilese ("Hulloooo zeeba neighba!"). I especially love it when someone tells me they go around quoting a line from the strip to their friends. I don't know what it is about cartoonists, but I think we all harbor a secret desire to write a line that makes its way into popular culture.

The strange requests are even more interesting. An example of a common one is this:

> "My wife and I are celebrating our tenth wedding anniversary on Friday. If there's any way you could mention it in your strip, that would be great. Nothing big. Maybe just a small 'Congratulations Cliff and Marianne' in the corner of one of the panels."

Everyone seems to want to see their name in the strip. And a lot of people want me to name one of the characters after them, or think I already have. This leads to some funny e-mail:

> "My name is Bob. I wrote to you about a year or so ago. Anyways, I saw that in the comic yesterday you named one of the dead crocodiles 'Bob.' I assume that was supposed to be me?"

There have also been some people who wanted me to send them a drawing of one of the characters in a specific pose that they could get tattooed upon their body. Or art to decorate their child's nursery. Or a character that they could use for their school mascot.

Then there's the most common request, people who want me to send them an original strip, some of whom offer to pay and some who don't. In either case, I always have to decline. I've only sold one strip, and it was for charity. I don't know why, but it just feels wrong to sell a strip, a bit like selling one of your kids.

Then there are the people who want me to draw them a sketch or send me their books to sign. I always feel terrible having to say no to such simple requests, but when you multiply that request by the hundreds, it can take up your whole drawing day.

The most entertaining of these requests are the demanding ones. Here's an example:

"I'd love it if you could draw your characters for my husband. Just the pig, the mouse, the goat, and maybe a few of the crocodiles (oh, and he loves the duck also). In terms of personalizing the sketch, my husband loves hunting, golf, the Minnesota Twins, and Ford Mustangs. Also, he's been a member of Rotary for twenty-one years. It would be great if you could work that in. If possible, I'd really like the drawing by Saturday, so I can give it to him for Father's Day."

But the best of the best, the crème de la crème, are the complaints.

First, there are the just-plain-hate-filled folk, who load their e-mail with lots of exclamation points and keep hitting the "CAPS LOCK" button.

"You think you're funny, but you're NOT!! You SUCK!!! Your comic has never made me laugh! Not even close! And you can't draw worth SH*T!"

When I'm bored, I will sometimes send those people the following:

"Dear *Pearls* Fan,

Thank you for your kind words. Your support of *Pearls* is appreciated. Unfortunately, due to the overwhelming popularity of the strip, Mr. Pastis cannot respond to each and every one of his fans personally, but he's glad to hear you enjoy the strip."

More than not, that will trigger a follow-up e-mail. Those look like this:

"&$%@ you, you #&$@#*. I am NOT a fan of your @*&@ing comic. And DON'T SEND ME YOUR %#*#ing FORM E-MAILS."

This of course means I have to send him the same response a second time.

Then there are the more specific folk. These people write when a particular strip or series of strips has angered them. Ohhh, there've been a few of these.

Off the top of my head, and in no particular order:

* Greek people (upset at being depicted as dirty restaurant owners)

* Parents of kids with ADD (angry at my saying they shouldn't be drugged)

* Palestinians (angry at the Jerusalem bus strip)

* Bisexuals (furious that I called a lonely man who would date people of either sex a "desperasexual")

* *Family Circus* fans (angry over any number of things I've done—depicting the kids as grown-up alcoholics, having Dolly say, "I love my dead grandpa," or having the kids shelter Osama Bin Laden for a week)

* Family members of people suffering with Lou Gehrig's disease (angry at Pig for saying how coincidental it was that a guy named Lou Gehrig died from something called "Lou Gehrig's disease.")

* George W. Bush supporters (mad that I had Rat writing him a letter saying that if he was going to bomb all 192 countries, he'd better pick up the pace)

* Homosexuals (mad that Rat called Pig "a fairy")

* *Baby Blues* fans (deeply offended that I would show their favorite characters being babysat by Rat, who sat alone at their kitchen table doing tequila shots)

* Turkish people (apoplectic over my naming a llama "Ataturk," a former leader of Turkey. This one even triggered a letter from the Turkish ambassador to the United States.)

* Nuns (angry that I referred to a nun getting an enema)

* Abraham Lincoln supporters (offended that I showed Lincoln saying, "I need to see another play like I need a hole in the head.")

Add to these the more general never-ending complaints about having the characters swear, drink, smoke, and shoot guns, and it's easy to see:

I've got the greatest job in the world.

—Stephan Pastis
Creator, *Pearls Before Swine*

Panel 1: DO YOU REALIZE THAT ALMOST NO ONE KNOWS THEIR NEIGHBOR ANYMORE?. WE DON'T TALK TO EACH OTHER... WE DON'T VISIT EACH OTHER... NOTHING...

Panel 2: ..EXCEPT FOR ONE DAY OF THE YEAR ...TODAY... AND WHAT DO WE DO ON THIS UNIQUE DAY?... WE KNOCK ON OUR NEIGHBORS' DOORS... ...AND <u>THREATEN</u> THEM.

Panel 3: DING DONG DING DONG DING DONG HEY, DUDE, TRICK OR TREAT ALREADY.. C'MON, OPEN YOUR DOOR!!
HE'S NOT HOME...LET'S EGG HIM.
...I LOVE HALLOWEEN.

10/31

Panel 4: HI THERE, PIG...WHAT'S WITH ALL THE PARTY STUFF?
IT'S FOR MY NEW FRIEND, WILLY THE BALLOON DOG.....IT'S HIS BIRTHDAY AND WE'RE HAVING A PARTY!

11/1

Panel 5: WOW...AND YOU EVEN GOT RAT TO COME?
YES, I CAME. I'M NOT A JERK **ALL** THE TIME, YOU KNOW. I EVEN GOT THE L'IL GUY A PRESENT.
OH, WILLY, LOOK!! IT'S A...
POP

Panel 6: ......CACTUS.
WHOA...HOW DID *THAT* HAPPEN?

Panel 7: WHAT'S THE MATTER WITH YOU, PIG?
I GOT A NEW BALLOON ANIMAL, TIMMY THE DOG, BUT TIMMY HAD THIS SLOW LEAK AND I DIDN'T THINK HE WAS GONNA MAKE IT, SO I GAVE HIM TO RAT.

Panel 8: WHY'D YOU GIVE HIM TO RAT?
BECAUSE RAT SAID HE'S A TRAINED BALLOON ANIMAL DOCTOR AND HE KNOWS HOW MUCH TIMMY MEANS TO ME, SO I'M REALLY HOPING HE CAN —

11/2

Panel 9: BAD NEWS......TIMMY HAD AN ADVERSE REACTION TO THE SCALPEL.
TIMMY!!
...WE DID EVERYTHING WE COULD.

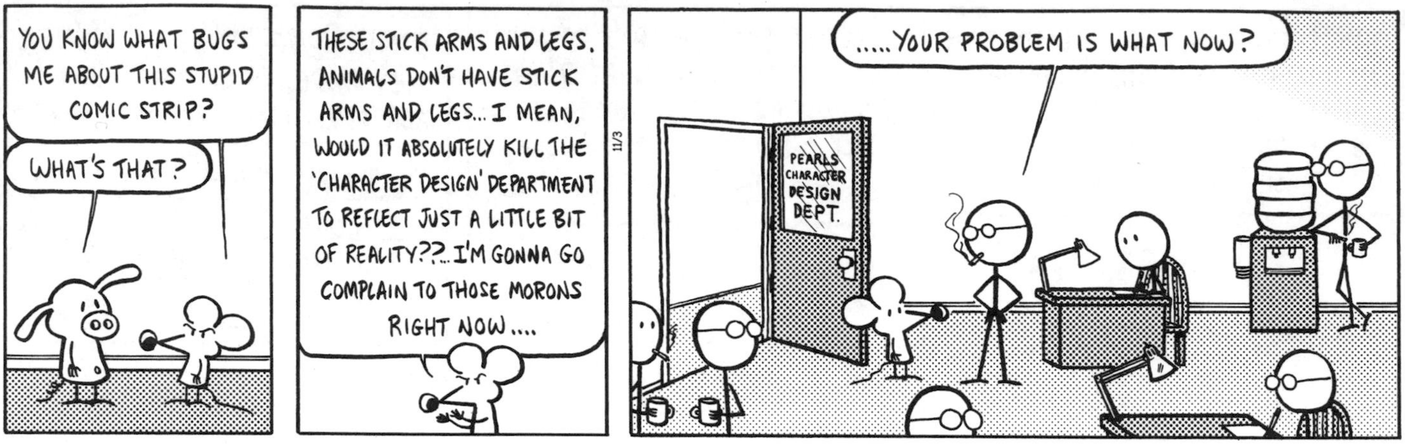
YOU KNOW WHAT BUGS ME ABOUT THIS STUPID COMIC STRIP?
WHAT'S THAT?
THESE STICK ARMS AND LEGS. ANIMALS DON'T HAVE STICK ARMS AND LEGS... I MEAN, WOULD IT ABSOLUTELY KILL THE 'CHARACTER DESIGN' DEPARTMENT TO REFLECT JUST A LITTLE BIT OF REALITY??.. I'M GONNA GO COMPLAIN TO THOSE MORONS RIGHT NOW....
11/3
PEARLS CHARACTER DESIGN DEPT.
.....YOUR PROBLEM IS WHAT NOW?

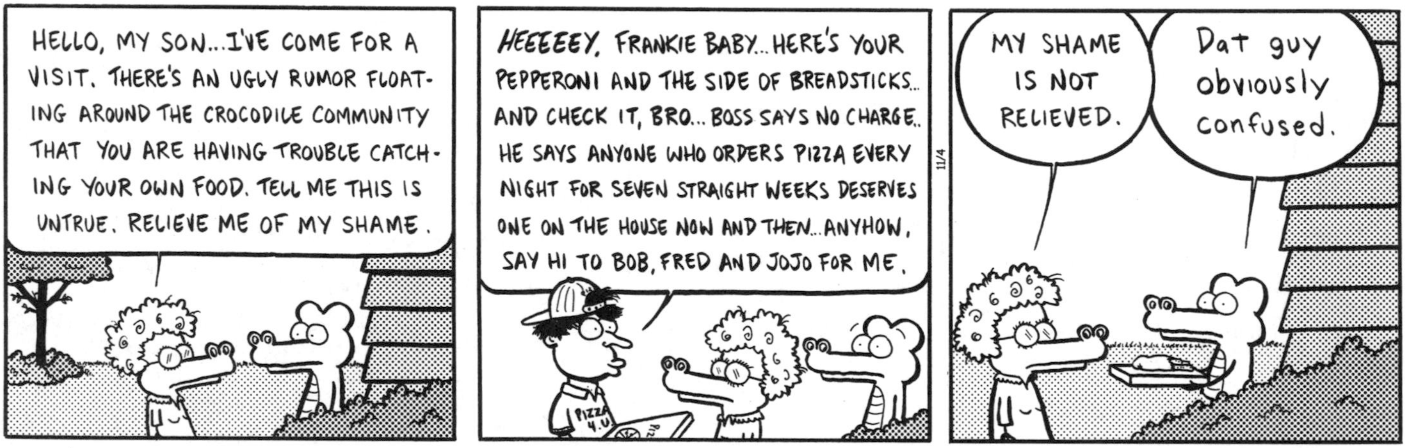
HELLO, MY SON...I'VE COME FOR A VISIT. THERE'S AN UGLY RUMOR FLOATING AROUND THE CROCODILE COMMUNITY THAT YOU ARE HAVING TROUBLE CATCHING YOUR OWN FOOD. TELL ME THIS IS UNTRUE. RELIEVE ME OF MY SHAME.
HEEEEEY, FRANKIE BABY... HERE'S YOUR PEPPERONI AND THE SIDE OF BREADSTICKS... AND CHECK IT, BRO... BOSS SAYS NO CHARGE.. HE SAYS ANYONE WHO ORDERS PIZZA EVERY NIGHT FOR SEVEN STRAIGHT WEEKS DESERVES ONE ON THE HOUSE NOW AND THEN... ANYHOW, SAY HI TO BOB, FRED AND JOJO FOR ME.
PIZZA 4 U
11/4
MY SHAME IS NOT RELIEVED.
Dat guy obviously confused.

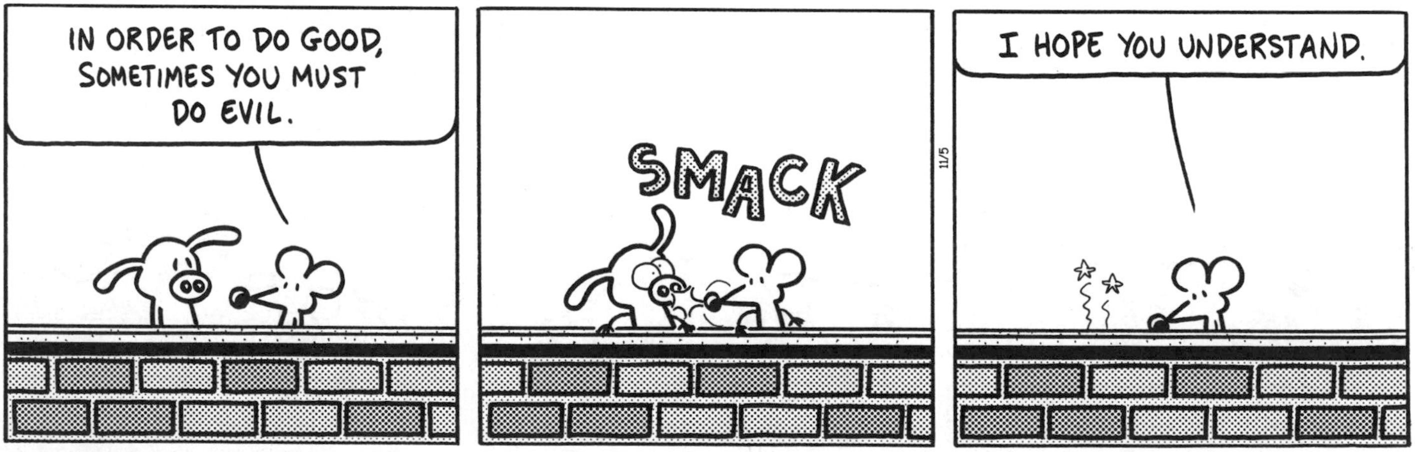
IN ORDER TO DO GOOD, SOMETIMES YOU MUST DO EVIL.
SMACK
11/5
I HOPE YOU UNDERSTAND.

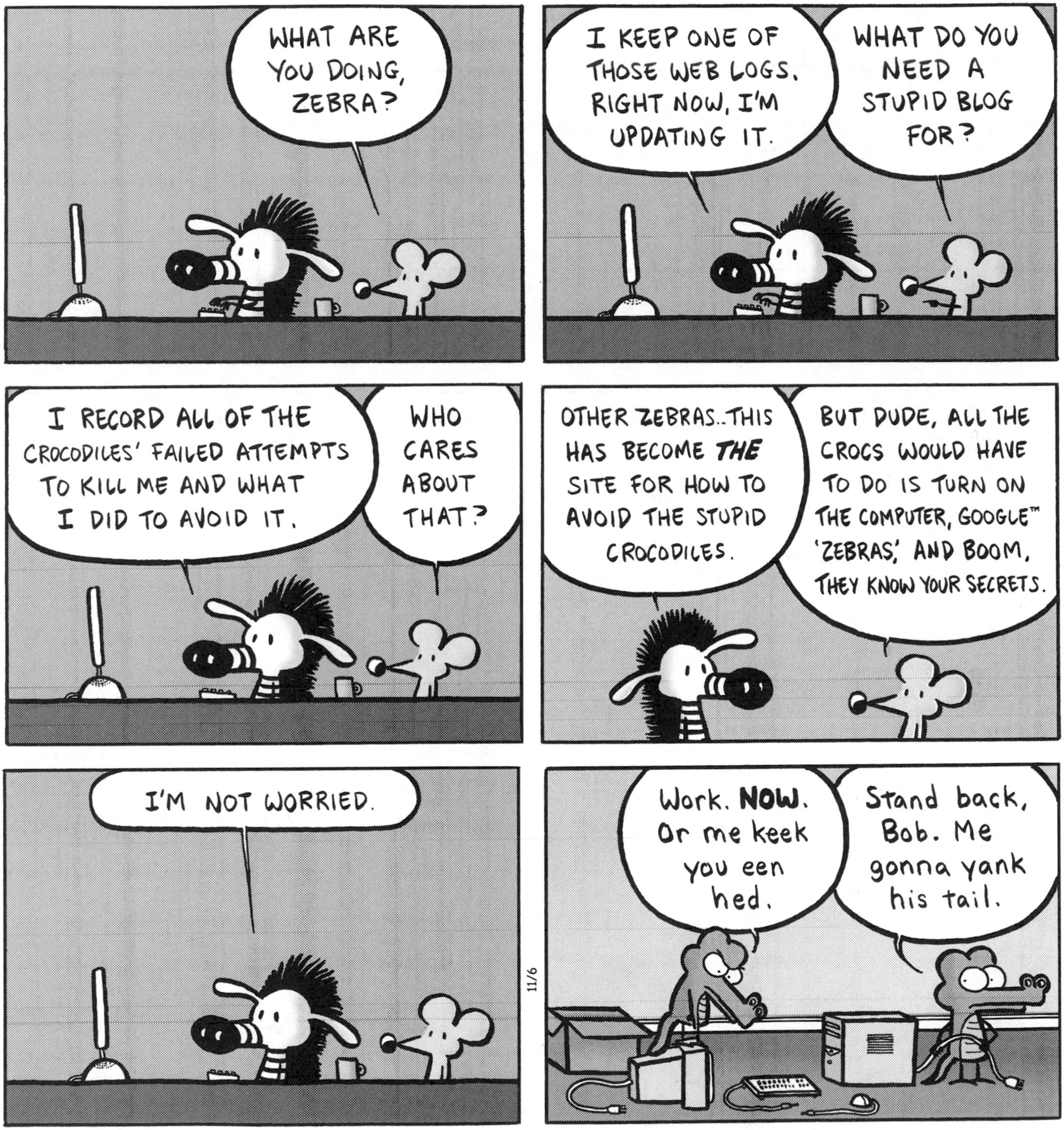
WHAT ARE YOU DOING, ZEBRA?
I KEEP ONE OF THOSE WEB LOGS. RIGHT NOW, I'M UPDATING IT.
WHAT DO YOU NEED A STUPID BLOG FOR?
I RECORD ALL OF THE CROCODILES' FAILED ATTEMPTS TO KILL ME AND WHAT I DID TO AVOID IT.
WHO CARES ABOUT THAT?
OTHER ZEBRAS...THIS HAS BECOME THE SITE FOR HOW TO AVOID THE STUPID CROCODILES.
BUT DUDE, ALL THE CROCS WOULD HAVE TO DO IS TURN ON THE COMPUTER, GOOGLE™ 'ZEBRAS,' AND BOOM, THEY KNOW YOUR SECRETS.
I'M NOT WORRIED.
11/6
Work. NOW. Or me keek you een hed.
Stand back, Bob. Me gonna yank his tail.

Panel 1:
HEY RAT... WANT TO PLAY WITH MY VIKING ACTION FIGURINES?

YEAH, DUDE... I LOVE VIKINGS. WANT ME TO SET UP A TOWN FOR THE GUYS TO BURN AND PILLAGE?

Panel 2:
I'M SORRY. MY VIKINGS DON'T BURN AND PILLAGE.

WHAT DO YOU MEAN THEY DON'T BURN AND PILLAGE? **ALL** VIKINGS BURN AND PILLAGE.

Panel 3:
MY VIKINGS COLLECT DAISIES AND WRITE THEIR INNERMOST THOUGHTS IN A DIARY.

VIKINGS DO NOT WRITE THEIR INNERMOST 6#6A#6A THOUGHTS IN A 6#A6#A# DIARY!!!!

Panel 4:
Today I heard a naughty word.

Panel 5:
"LITTLE MISS MUFFET SAT ON A TUFFET EATING HER CURDS AND WHEY. ALONG CAME A SPIDER WHO SAT DOWN BESIDE HER AND FRIGHTENED MS. MUFFET AWAY."

Panel 6:
"THEN MUFFET WENT BACK AND CHECKED HER GUN RACK, GRABBING A .357. FINDING THE SPIDER, SHE SAT DOWN BESIDE HER AND BLEW THAT POOR SUCKER TO HEAVEN."

Panel 7:
THE UNCUT VERSION.

Panel 8:
Hullo, zeeba neighba... Leesten... Me want say sorry for tings we does and geeve you nice paypahweight as token of new-found frensheep.

TA-DAAA!!!

Panel 9:
...MY COUSIN'S SKULL.

Panel 10:
Sorry. Me no have time to shop.

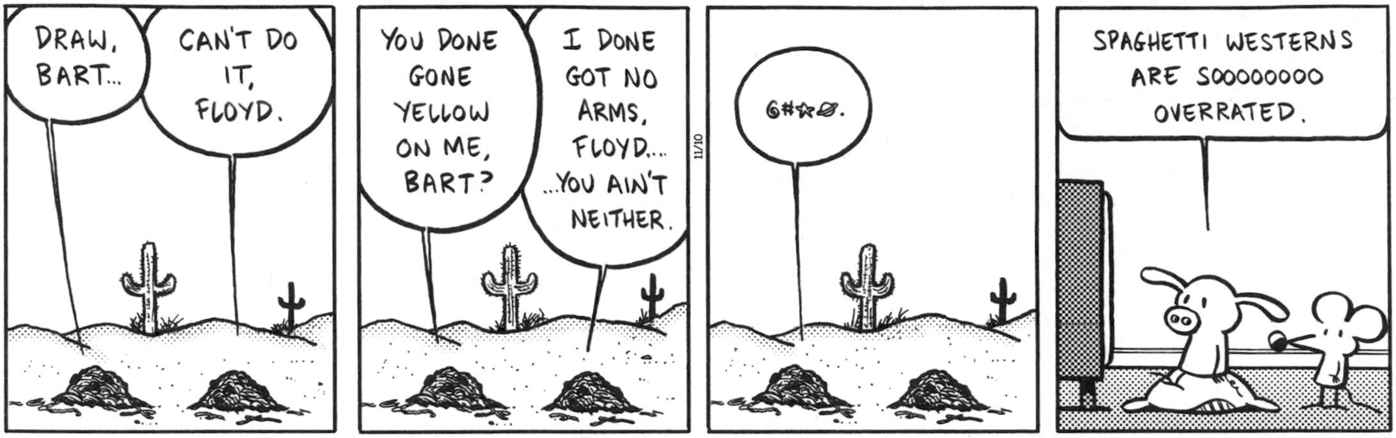
DRAW, BART...
CAN'T DO IT, FLOYD.
YOU DONE GONE YELLOW ON ME, BART?
I DONE GOT NO ARMS, FLOYD... ...YOU AIN'T NEITHER.
11/10
SPAGHETTI WESTERNS ARE SOOOOOOOO OVERRATED.

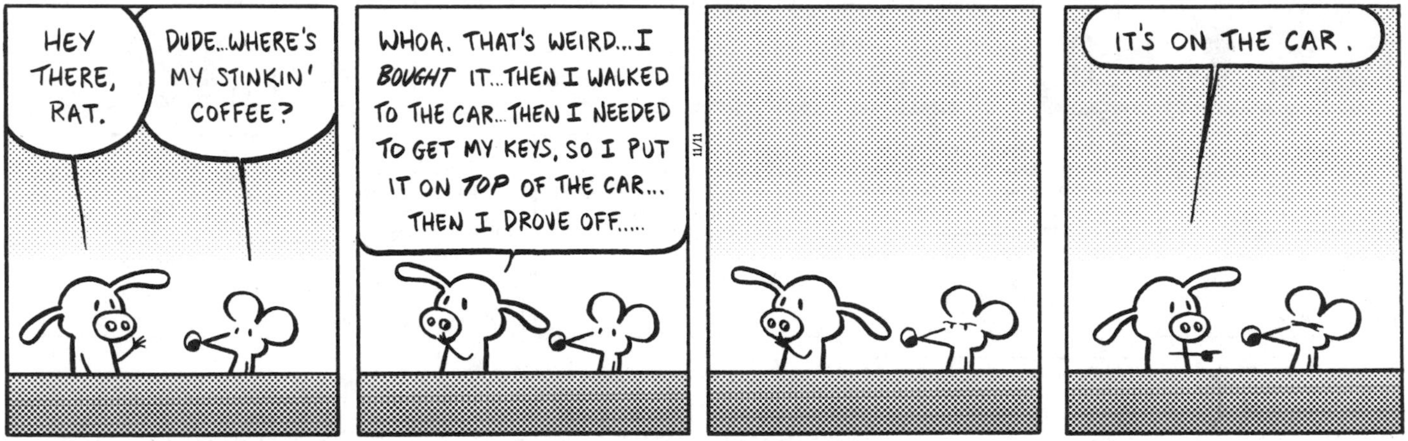
HEY THERE, RAT.
DUDE...WHERE'S MY STINKIN' COFFEE?
WHOA. THAT'S WEIRD...I BOUGHT IT...THEN I WALKED TO THE CAR...THEN I NEEDED TO GET MY KEYS, SO I PUT IT ON TOP OF THE CAR... THEN I DROVE OFF.....
11/11
IT'S ON THE CAR.

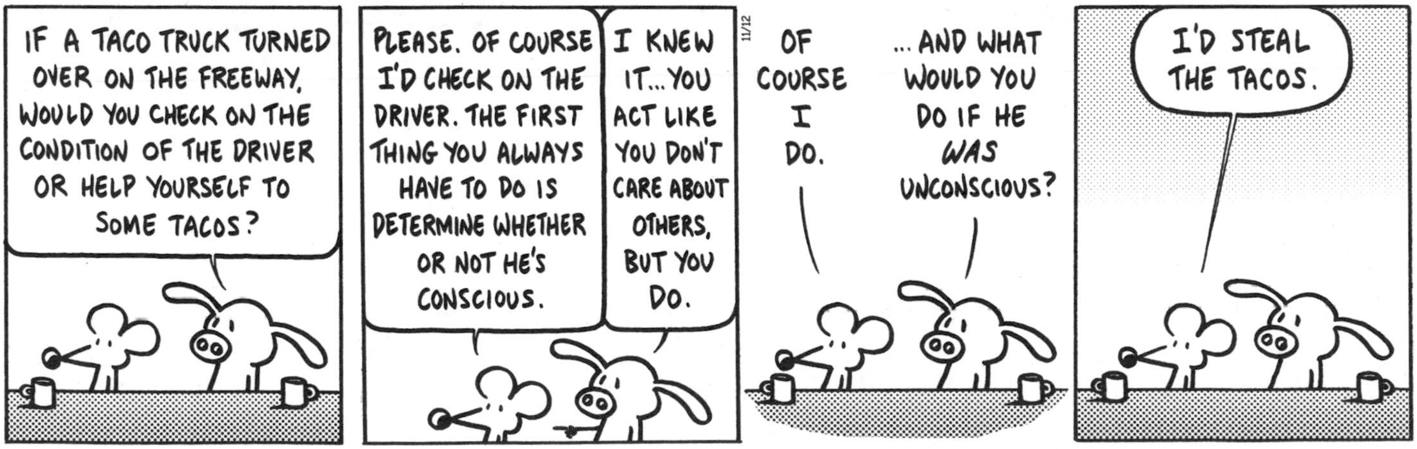
IF A TACO TRUCK TURNED OVER ON THE FREEWAY, WOULD YOU CHECK ON THE CONDITION OF THE DRIVER OR HELP YOURSELF TO SOME TACOS?
PLEASE. OF COURSE I'D CHECK ON THE DRIVER. THE FIRST THING YOU ALWAYS HAVE TO DO IS DETERMINE WHETHER OR NOT HE'S CONSCIOUS.
I KNEW IT...YOU ACT LIKE YOU DON'T CARE ABOUT OTHERS, BUT YOU DO.
11/12
OF COURSE I DO.
...AND WHAT WOULD YOU DO IF HE WAS UNCONSCIOUS?
I'D STEAL THE TACOS.

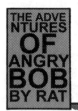

THE ADVENTURES OF ANGRY BOB BY RAT
Angry Bob was angry.
TYPE TYPE
"I will attend the flower show at the County Fair," thought Bob. "Flowers will make me happy."
TYPE TYPE
Angry Bob went to the flower show and noticed this year's theme: "All Praise Be to the Fairies."
TYPE TYPE TYPE
"I like fairies," Bob thought to himself. "This is a solid, well-chosen theme."
TYPE TYPE TYPE TYPE
Walking the show, Bob saw fairies on the walls, fairies on the gazebos and fairies floating from the rafters. And Bob saw a large fountain in the center of the room.
TYPE TYPE TYPE
Termed "The Fountain O' Hope," it was crowned by a granite fairy clothed in Cupid's garb, complete with bow and arrow.
TYPE TYPE
Bob grew romantic. He stared at the red-haired woman next to him and grabbed her arm. "Here is a penny, ma'am. Although I am a stranger to you, I ask that you join me in casting a penny into the Fountain O' Hope."
TYPE TYPE TYPE TYPE
Reluctantly, the woman took the penny, flicked it into the water and quickly walked away, which Bob did not see, because he had closed his eyes and knelt by the fountain.
TYPE TYPE
"I wish that this beautiful woman will see fit to marry me," he whispered to himself, casting his penny into the Fountain O' Hope.
TYPE TYPE TYPE TYPE
As Bob heard the penny's splash, he experienced a euphoric rush of hope. "My gosh," Bob uttered, "This penny worked. I feel it. I believe in this Fountain O' Hope! I believe in this Cupid Fairy!" And so Bob rose.
TYPE TYPE TYPE TYPE
And lost his balance.
TYPE TYPE
And crashed into the large fountain.
And toppled the Cupid Fairy.
Who fell arrow-side down atop Bob.
Who drowned.
In the Fountain O' Hope.
TYPE TYPE
WHOA WHOA...YOU ALWAYS SAY YOU LIKE TO END ALL THESE STORIES ON A HOPEFUL NOTE, BUT BOB'S DREAM DIDN'T COME TRUE...YOU NEED TO END WITH A DREAM COME TRUE.
The red-haired woman returned to the Fountain and saw what had happened. "My dream came true," she muttered.
TYPE TYPE TYPE

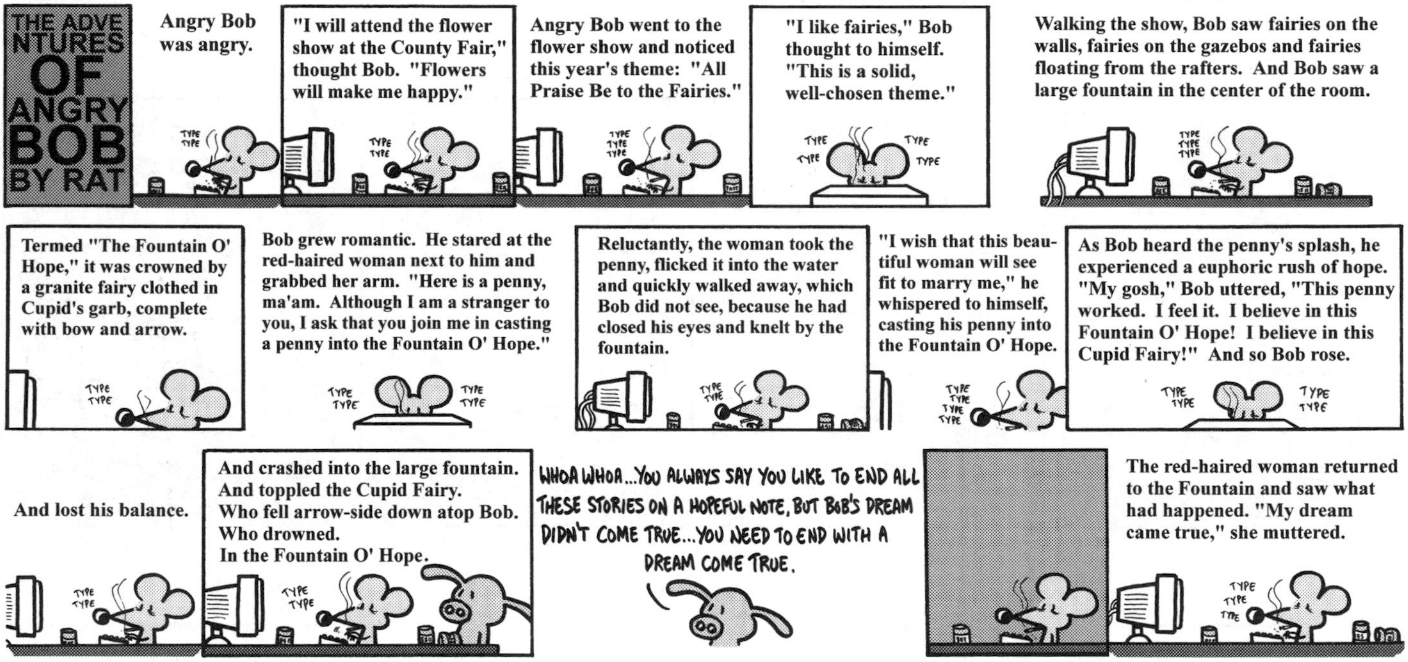

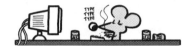

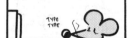

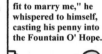

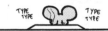

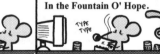

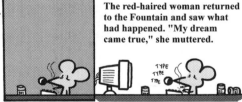

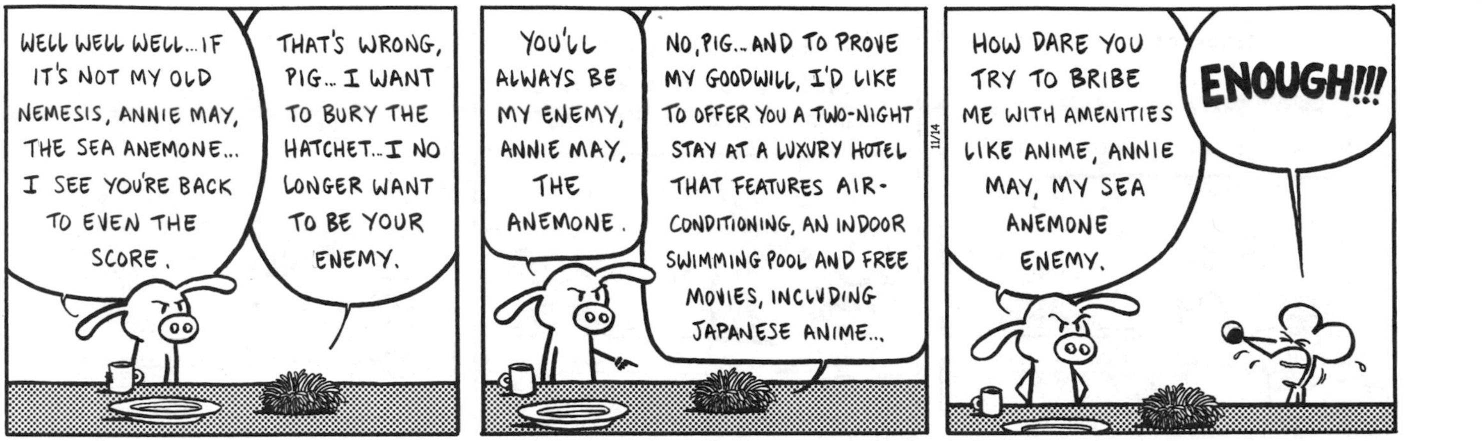
WELL WELL WELL... IF IT'S NOT MY OLD NEMESIS, ANNIE MAY, THE SEA ANEMONE... I SEE YOU'RE BACK TO EVEN THE SCORE.
THAT'S WRONG, PIG... I WANT TO BURY THE HATCHET... I NO LONGER WANT TO BE YOUR ENEMY.
YOU'LL ALWAYS BE MY ENEMY, ANNIE MAY, THE ANEMONE.
NO, PIG... AND TO PROVE MY GOODWILL, I'D LIKE TO OFFER YOU A TWO-NIGHT STAY AT A LUXURY HOTEL THAT FEATURES AIR-CONDITIONING, AN INDOOR SWIMMING POOL AND FREE MOVIES, INCLUDING JAPANESE ANIME...
11/14
HOW DARE YOU TRY TO BRIBE ME WITH AMENITIES LIKE ANIME, ANNIE MAY, MY SEA ANEMONE ENEMY.
ENOUGH!!!

"Pearls Before Swine" creator, Stephan Pastis, is taking today off to spend time with his wife at home. Creative control of today's strip has been passed to Rat, who has promised said creator that he will avoid any and all offensive material that could trigger reader outrage. We join the strip in progress.

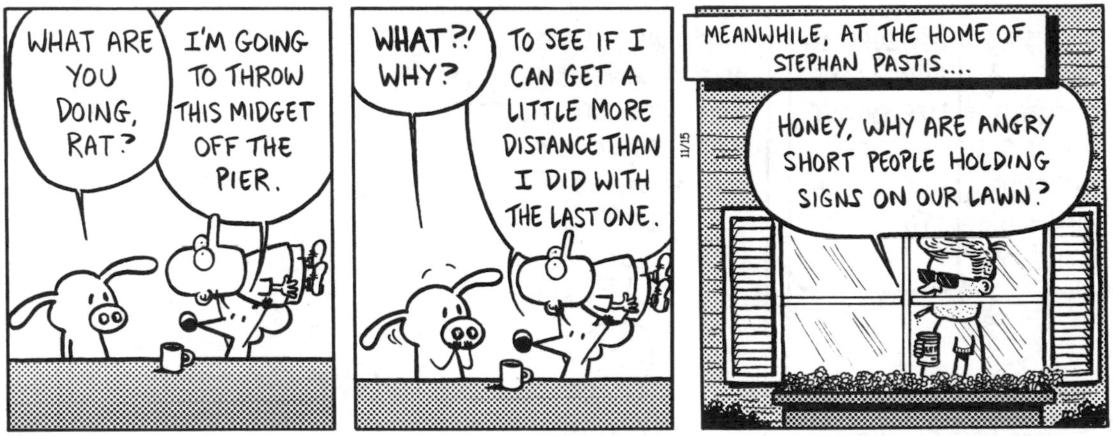
WHAT ARE YOU DOING, RAT?
I'M GOING TO THROW THIS MIDGET OFF THE PIER.
WHAT?! WHY?
TO SEE IF I CAN GET A LITTLE MORE DISTANCE THAN I DID WITH THE LAST ONE.
11/15
MEANWHILE, AT THE HOME OF STEPHAN PASTIS....
HONEY, WHY ARE ANGRY SHORT PEOPLE HOLDING SIGNS ON OUR LAWN?

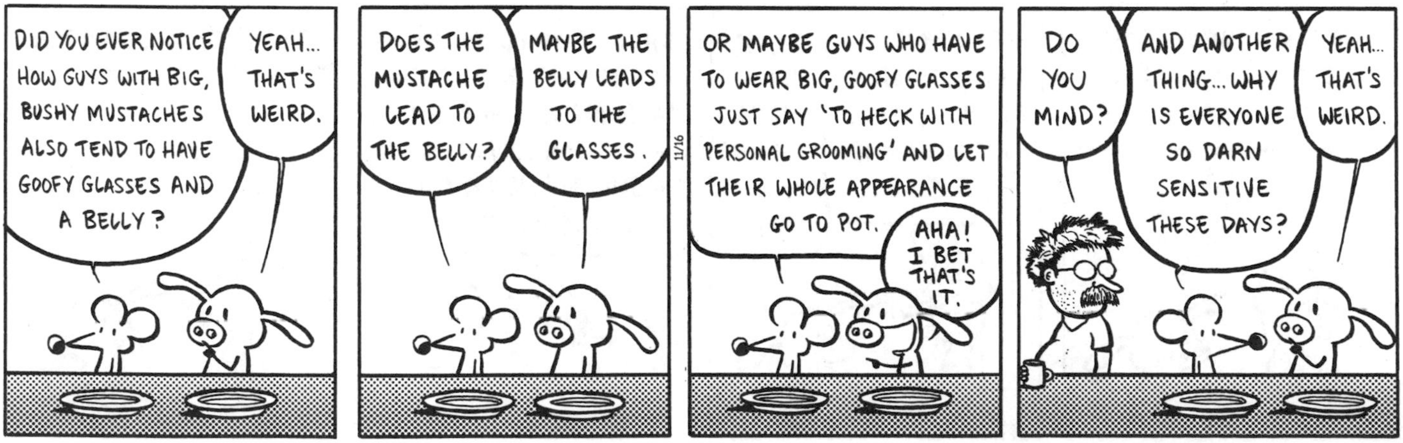
DID YOU EVER NOTICE HOW GUYS WITH BIG, BUSHY MUSTACHES ALSO TEND TO HAVE GOOFY GLASSES AND A BELLY?
YEAH... THAT'S WEIRD.
DOES THE MUSTACHE LEAD TO THE BELLY?
MAYBE THE BELLY LEADS TO THE GLASSES.
11/16
OR MAYBE GUYS WHO HAVE TO WEAR BIG, GOOFY GLASSES JUST SAY 'TO HECK WITH PERSONAL GROOMING' AND LET THEIR WHOLE APPEARANCE GO TO POT.
AHA! I BET THAT'S IT.
DO YOU MIND?
AND ANOTHER THING... WHY IS EVERYONE SO DARN SENSITIVE THESE DAYS?
YEAH... THAT'S WEIRD.

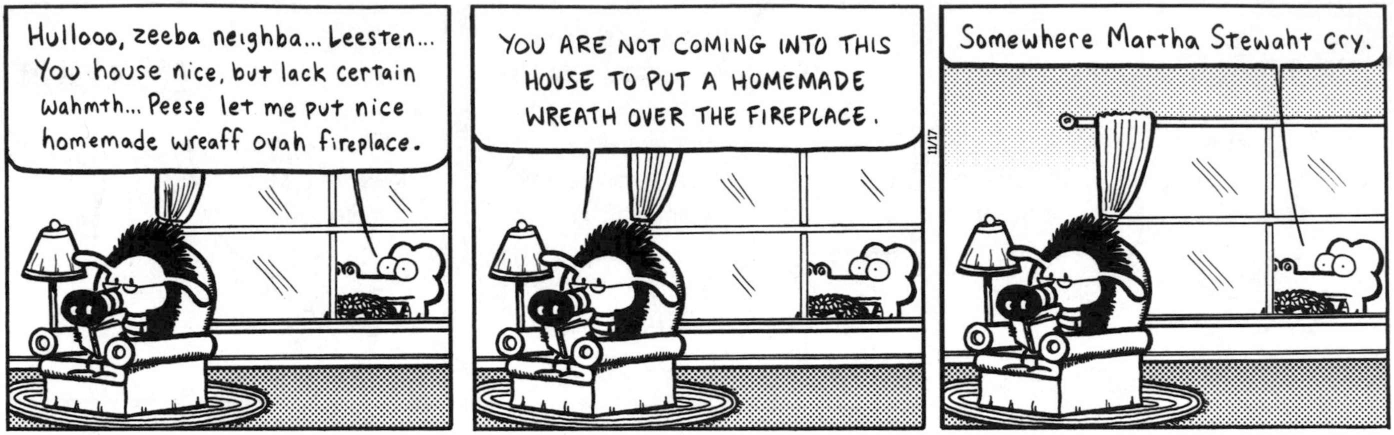
Hullooo, zeeba neighba... Leesten... You house nice, but lack certain wahmth... Peese let me put nice homemade wreaff ovah fireplace.
YOU ARE NOT COMING INTO THIS HOUSE TO PUT A HOMEMADE WREATH OVER THE FIREPLACE.
11/17
Somewhere Martha Stewaht cry.

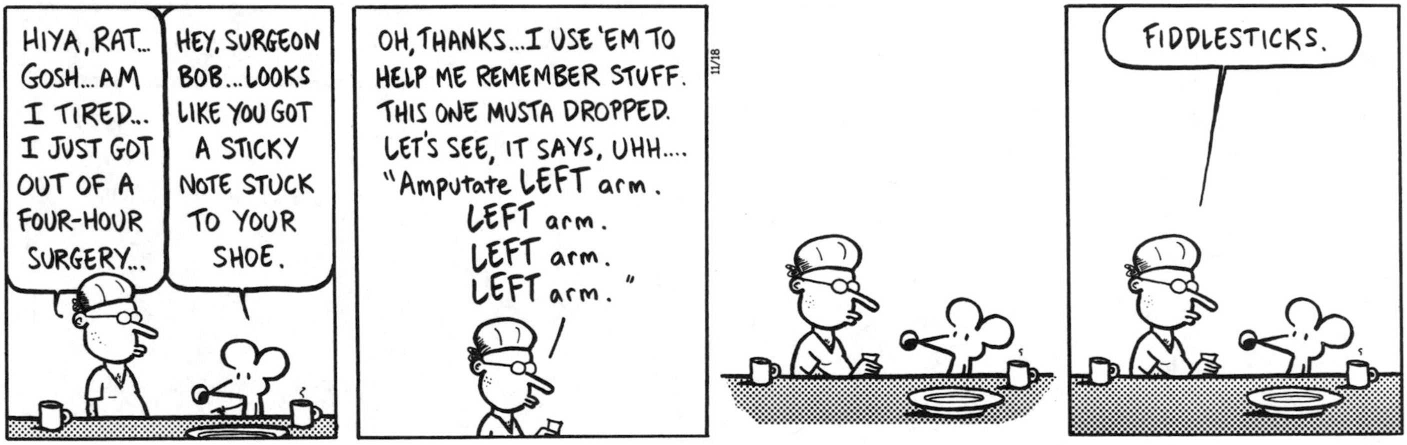
HIYA, RAT... GOSH... AM I TIRED... I JUST GOT OUT OF A FOUR-HOUR SURGERY...
HEY, SURGEON BOB... LOOKS LIKE YOU GOT A STICKY NOTE STUCK TO YOUR SHOE.
11/18
OH, THANKS... I USE 'EM TO HELP ME REMEMBER STUFF. THIS ONE MUSTA DROPPED. LET'S SEE, IT SAYS, UHH.... "Amputate LEFT arm. LEFT arm. LEFT arm. LEFT arm."
FIDDLESTICKS.

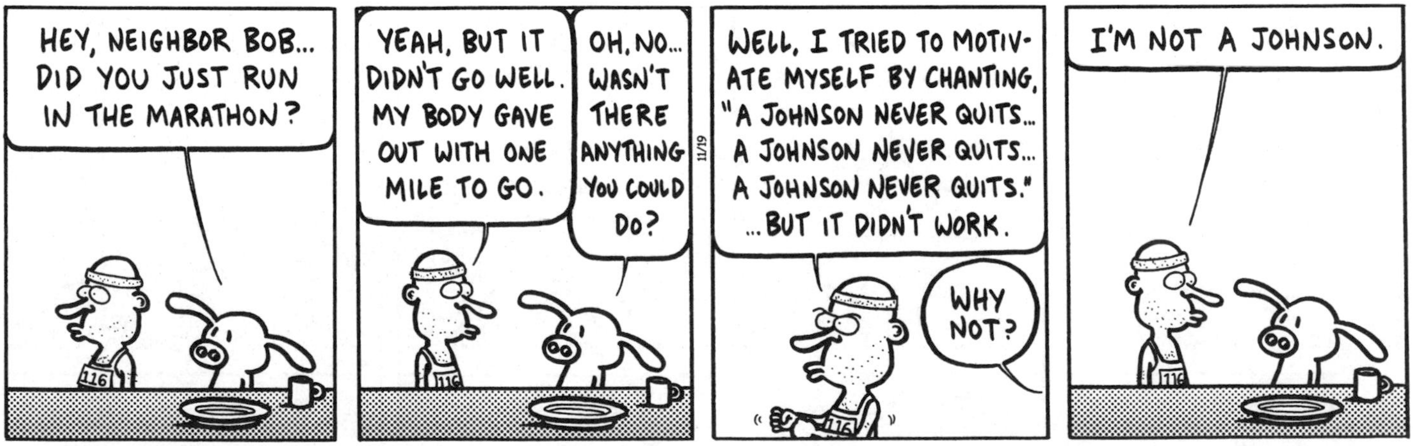
HEY, NEIGHBOR BOB... DID YOU JUST RUN IN THE MARATHON?
116
YEAH, BUT IT DIDN'T GO WELL. MY BODY GAVE OUT WITH ONE MILE TO GO.
OH, NO... WASN'T THERE ANYTHING YOU COULD DO?
11/19
WELL, I TRIED TO MOTIVATE MYSELF BY CHANTING, "A JOHNSON NEVER QUITS... A JOHNSON NEVER QUITS... A JOHNSON NEVER QUITS." ...BUT IT DIDN'T WORK.
WHY NOT?
I'M NOT A JOHNSON.

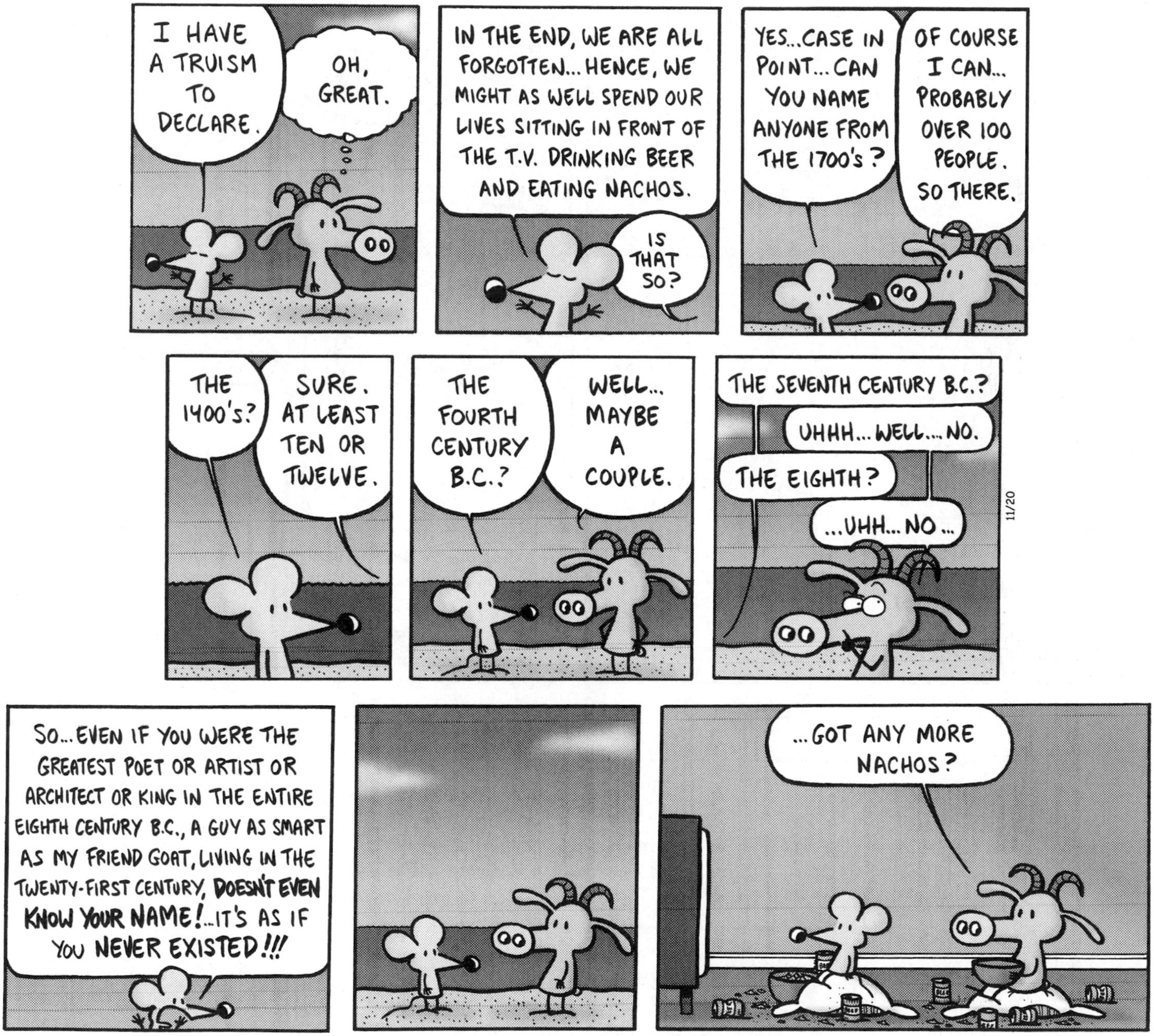
I HAVE A TRUISM TO DECLARE.
OH, GREAT.
IN THE END, WE ARE ALL FORGOTTEN... HENCE, WE MIGHT AS WELL SPEND OUR LIVES SITTING IN FRONT OF THE T.V. DRINKING BEER AND EATING NACHOS.
IS THAT SO?
YES...CASE IN POINT... CAN YOU NAME ANYONE FROM THE 1700'S?
OF COURSE I CAN... PROBABLY OVER 100 PEOPLE. SO THERE.
THE 1400'S?
SURE. AT LEAST TEN OR TWELVE.
THE FOURTH CENTURY B.C.?
WELL... MAYBE A COUPLE.
THE SEVENTH CENTURY B.C.?
UHHH... WELL... NO.
THE EIGHTH?
...UHH... NO...
11/20
SO... EVEN IF YOU WERE THE GREATEST POET OR ARTIST OR ARCHITECT OR KING IN THE ENTIRE EIGHTH CENTURY B.C., A GUY AS SMART AS MY FRIEND GOAT, LIVING IN THE TWENTY-FIRST CENTURY, DOESN'T EVEN KNOW YOUR NAME!...IT'S AS IF YOU NEVER EXISTED!!!
...GOT ANY MORE NACHOS?

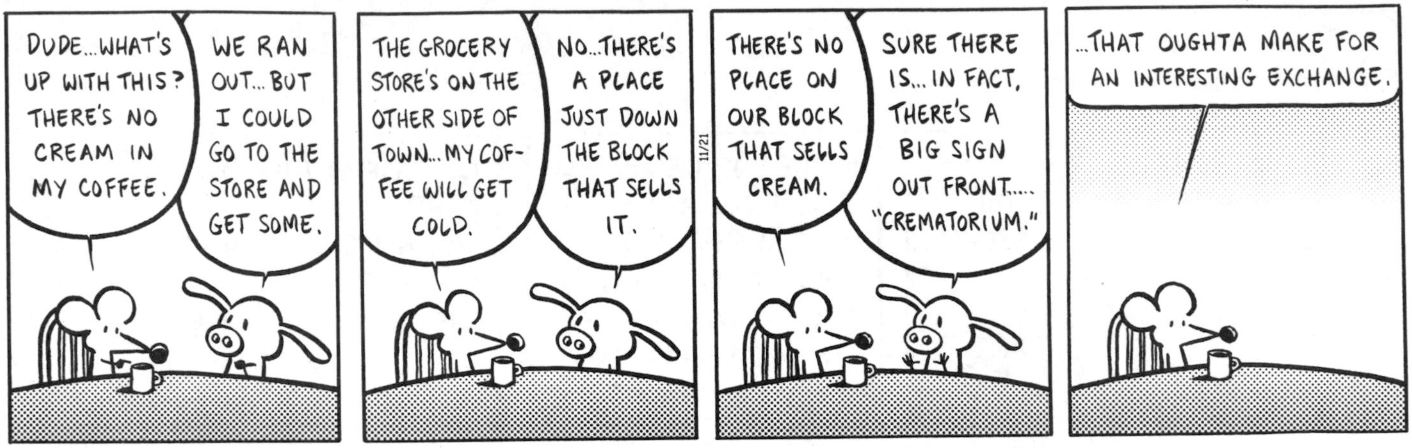
DUDE...WHAT'S UP WITH THIS? THERE'S NO CREAM IN MY COFFEE.
WE RAN OUT... BUT I COULD GO TO THE STORE AND GET SOME.
THE GROCERY STORE'S ON THE OTHER SIDE OF TOWN... MY COFFEE WILL GET COLD.
NO...THERE'S A PLACE JUST DOWN THE BLOCK THAT SELLS IT.
11/21
THERE'S NO PLACE ON OUR BLOCK THAT SELLS CREAM.
SURE THERE IS... IN FACT, THERE'S A BIG SIGN OUT FRONT..... "CREMATORIUM."
...THAT OUGHTA MAKE FOR AN INTERESTING EXCHANGE.

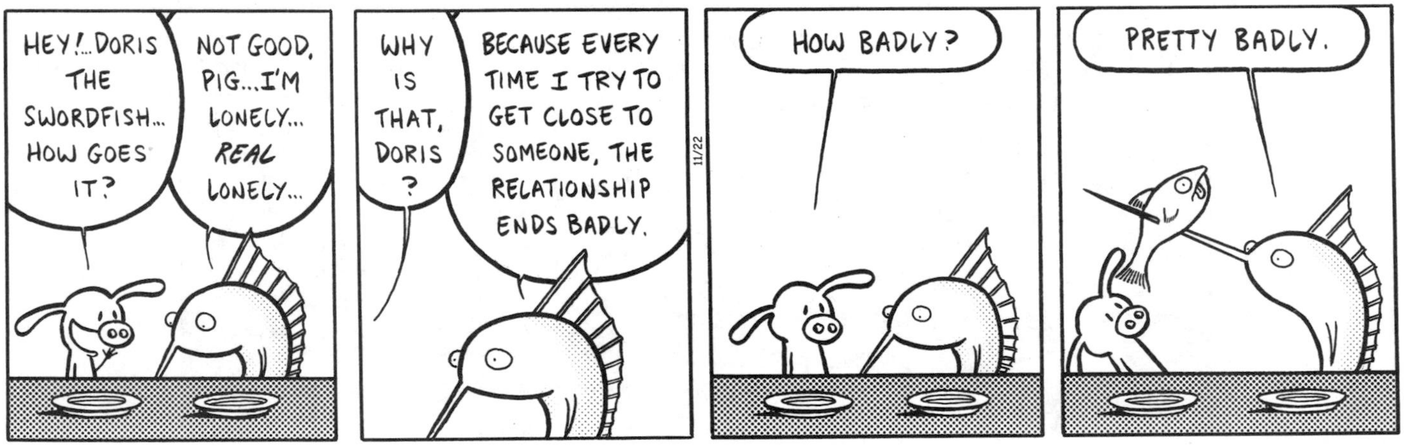
HEY!...DORIS THE SWORDFISH... HOW GOES IT?
NOT GOOD, PIG...I'M LONELY... REAL LONELY...
WHY IS THAT, DORIS?
BECAUSE EVERY TIME I TRY TO GET CLOSE TO SOMEONE, THE RELATIONSHIP ENDS BADLY.
11/22
HOW BADLY?
PRETTY BADLY.

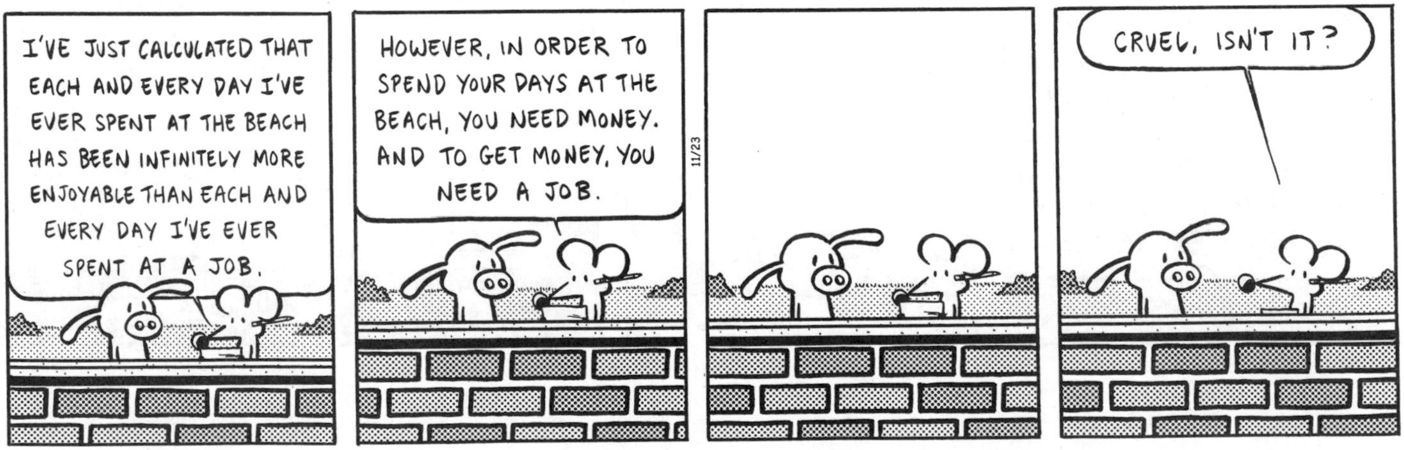
I'VE JUST CALCULATED THAT EACH AND EVERY DAY I'VE EVER SPENT AT THE BEACH HAS BEEN INFINITELY MORE ENJOYABLE THAN EACH AND EVERY DAY I'VE EVER SPENT AT A JOB.
HOWEVER, IN ORDER TO SPEND YOUR DAYS AT THE BEACH, YOU NEED MONEY. AND TO GET MONEY, YOU NEED A JOB.
11/23
CRUEL, ISN'T IT?

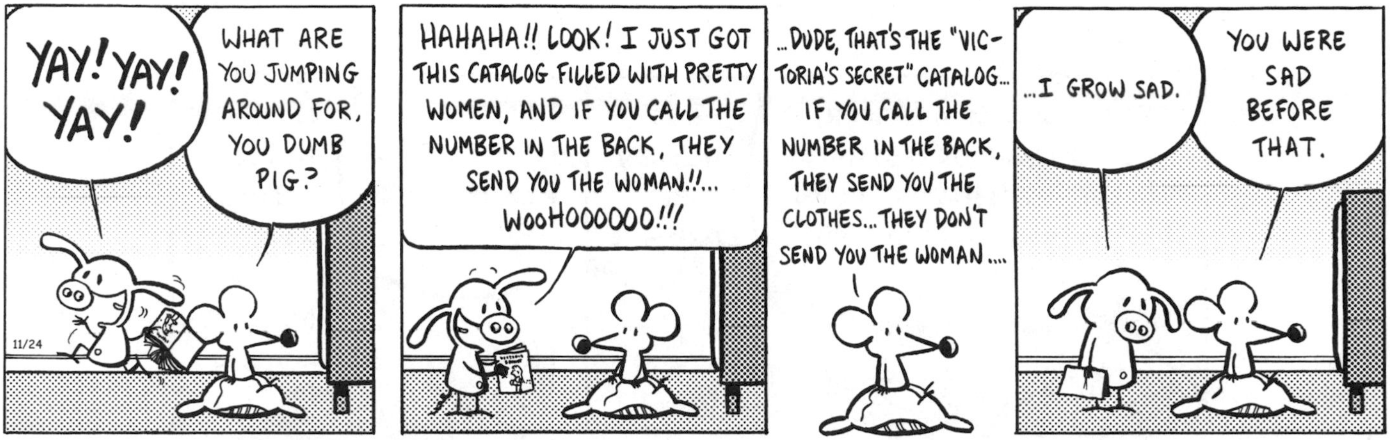
YAY! YAY! YAY!
WHAT ARE YOU JUMPING AROUND FOR, YOU DUMB PIG?
11/24
HAHAHA!! LOOK! I JUST GOT THIS CATALOG FILLED WITH PRETTY WOMEN, AND IF YOU CALL THE NUMBER IN THE BACK, THEY SEND YOU THE WOMAN!!... WOOHOOOOOO!!!
...DUDE, THAT'S THE "VICTORIA'S SECRET" CATALOG... IF YOU CALL THE NUMBER IN THE BACK, THEY SEND YOU THE CLOTHES... THEY DON'T SEND YOU THE WOMAN....
...I GROW SAD.
YOU WERE SAD BEFORE THAT.

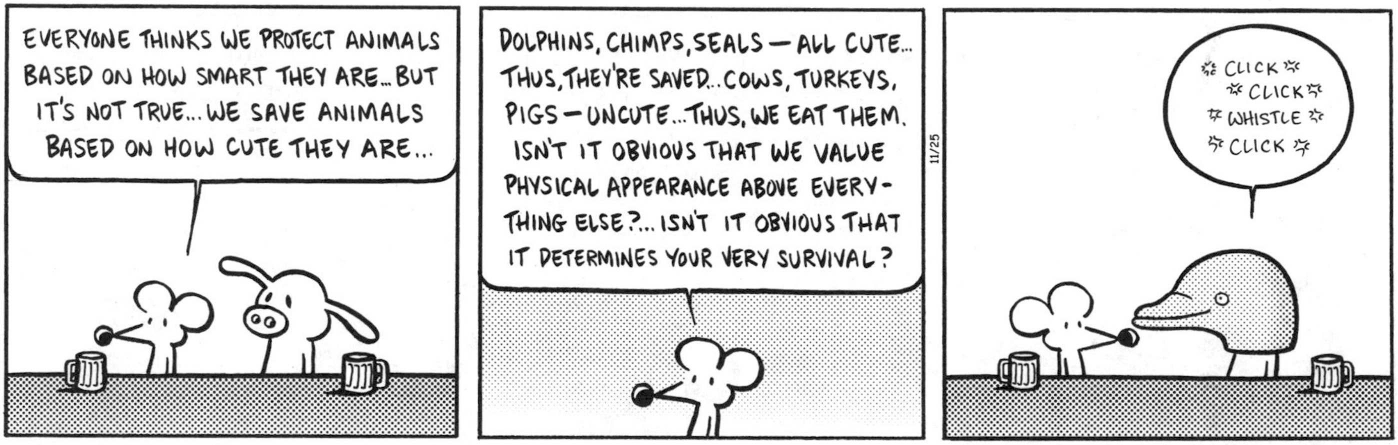
EVERYONE THINKS WE PROTECT ANIMALS BASED ON HOW SMART THEY ARE... BUT IT'S NOT TRUE... WE SAVE ANIMALS BASED ON HOW CUTE THEY ARE...
DOLPHINS, CHIMPS, SEALS — ALL CUTE... THUS, THEY'RE SAVED... COWS, TURKEYS, PIGS — UNCUTE... THUS, WE EAT THEM. ISN'T IT OBVIOUS THAT WE VALUE PHYSICAL APPEARANCE ABOVE EVERYTHING ELSE?... ISN'T IT OBVIOUS THAT IT DETERMINES YOUR VERY SURVIVAL?
11/25
CLICK CLICK WHISTLE CLICK

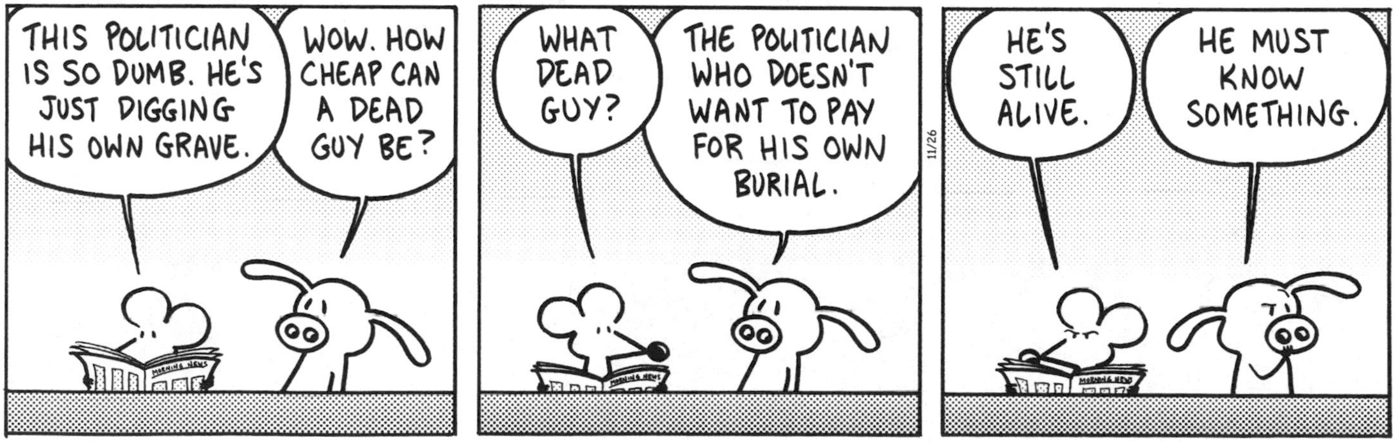
THIS POLITICIAN IS SO DUMB. HE'S JUST DIGGING HIS OWN GRAVE.
WOW. HOW CHEAP CAN A DEAD GUY BE?
WHAT DEAD GUY?
THE POLITICIAN WHO DOESN'T WANT TO PAY FOR HIS OWN BURIAL.
11/26
HE'S STILL ALIVE.
HE MUST KNOW SOMETHING.

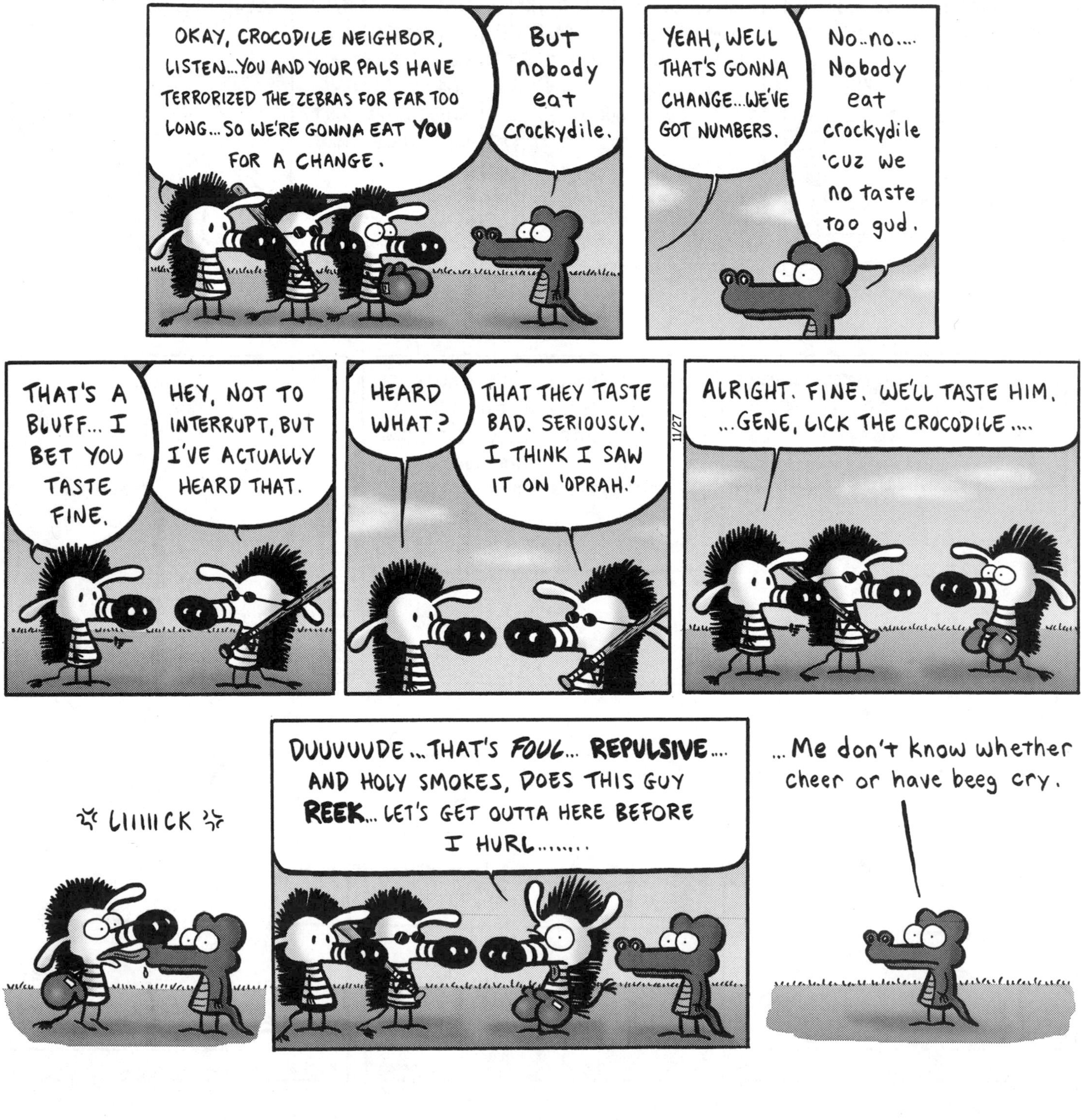
OKAY, CROCODILE NEIGHBOR, LISTEN...YOU AND YOUR PALS HAVE TERRORIZED THE ZEBRAS FOR FAR TOO LONG...SO WE'RE GONNA EAT **YOU** FOR A CHANGE.
But nobody eat crockydile.
YEAH, WELL THAT'S GONNA CHANGE...WE'VE GOT NUMBERS.
No..no.... Nobody eat crockydile 'cuz we no taste too gud.
THAT'S A BLUFF... I BET YOU TASTE FINE.
HEY, NOT TO INTERRUPT, BUT I'VE ACTUALLY HEARD THAT.
HEARD WHAT?
THAT THEY TASTE BAD. SERIOUSLY. I THINK I SAW IT ON 'OPRAH.'
11/27
ALRIGHT. FINE. WE'LL TASTE HIM. ...GENE, LICK THE CROCODILE....
LIIIIICK
DUUUUUDE...THAT'S *FOUL*... **REPULSIVE**.... AND HOLY SMOKES, DOES THIS GUY **REEK**... LET'S GET OUTTA HERE BEFORE I HURL.......
...Me don't know whether cheer or have beeg cry.

Panel 1: DUDE, I SAW THE MOST AMAZING SHOW LAST NIGHT. IT WAS ALL ABOUT CARRIER PIGEONS. PEOPLE ATTACH THESE MESSAGES TO THEIR LEGS AND SOMEHOW THESE BIRDS ARE ABLE TO LOCATE THE INTENDED RECIPIENT HUNDREDS OF MILES AWAY.

Panel 2: BUT HOW DO THEY DO THAT?

NO ONE REALLY KNOWS. IT'S ONE OF THE GREAT MYSTERIES OF THE UNIVERSE...

Panel 3:

...SECOND HOUSE ON THE LEFT.

11/28

Panel 4:

SOMETIMES I THINK THE WORST OF ALL SINS IS TO HAVE POTENTIAL AND THEN SQUANDER IT... DON'T YOU THINK?

I'M SORRY. I DIDN'T HEAR YOU. I WAS TRYING TO MEMORIZE A FAMOUS POEM.

Panel 5: OH YEAH? ...WHICH ONE?

"BEANS, BEANS, THE MAGICAL FRUIT... THE MORE YOU EAT THE MORE YOU ——" UHH...WAIT A MINUTE... HOW'S THAT THING END?

Panel 6:

IT DOESN'T SOUND LIKE POTENTIAL IS AN ISSUE FOR YOU.

AWWW, NUTS.... HOW COULD I FORGET MY FAVORITE ROBERT FROST POEM??

11/29

Panel 7:

HI, THERE.... I'M FROM THE CABLE COMPANY... I'M HERE TO DISCONNECT YOUR SERVICE.

WHY ARE YOU DOING THAT?

Panel 8:

IT APPEARS YOU'VE BEEN LETTING SOME OF YOUR FRIENDS CUT INTO YOUR CABLE LINE AND STEAL THE SIGNAL. THAT VIOLATES OUR TERMS OF SERVICE.

BUT I DIDN'T LET ANYBODY DO ANYTHING. ...I WOULD NEVER LET A FRIEND STEAL THE SIGNAL.

11/30

Panel 9:

Sopranos best show EVAH.

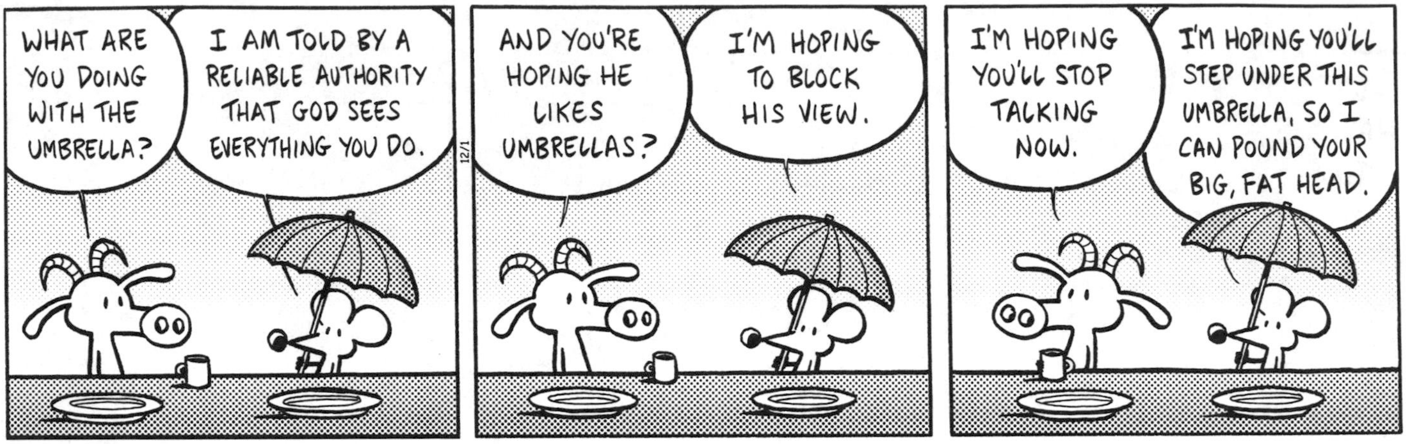
WHAT ARE YOU DOING WITH THE UMBRELLA?
I AM TOLD BY A RELIABLE AUTHORITY THAT GOD SEES EVERYTHING YOU DO.
12/1
AND YOU'RE HOPING HE LIKES UMBRELLAS?
I'M HOPING TO BLOCK HIS VIEW.
I'M HOPING YOU'LL STOP TALKING NOW.
I'M HOPING YOU'LL STEP UNDER THIS UMBRELLA, SO I CAN POUND YOUR BIG, FAT HEAD.

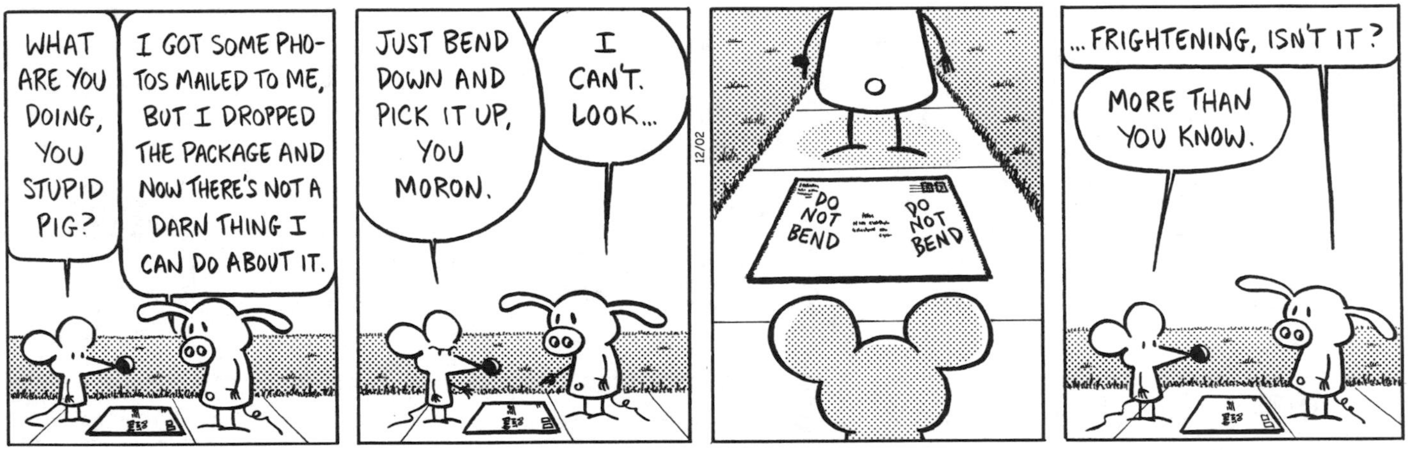
WHAT ARE YOU DOING, YOU STUPID PIG?
I GOT SOME PHOTOS MAILED TO ME, BUT I DROPPED THE PACKAGE AND NOW THERE'S NOT A DARN THING I CAN DO ABOUT IT.
JUST BEND DOWN AND PICK IT UP, YOU MORON.
I CAN'T. LOOK...
12/02
DO NOT BEND
DO NOT BEND
...FRIGHTENING, ISN'T IT?
MORE THAN YOU KNOW.

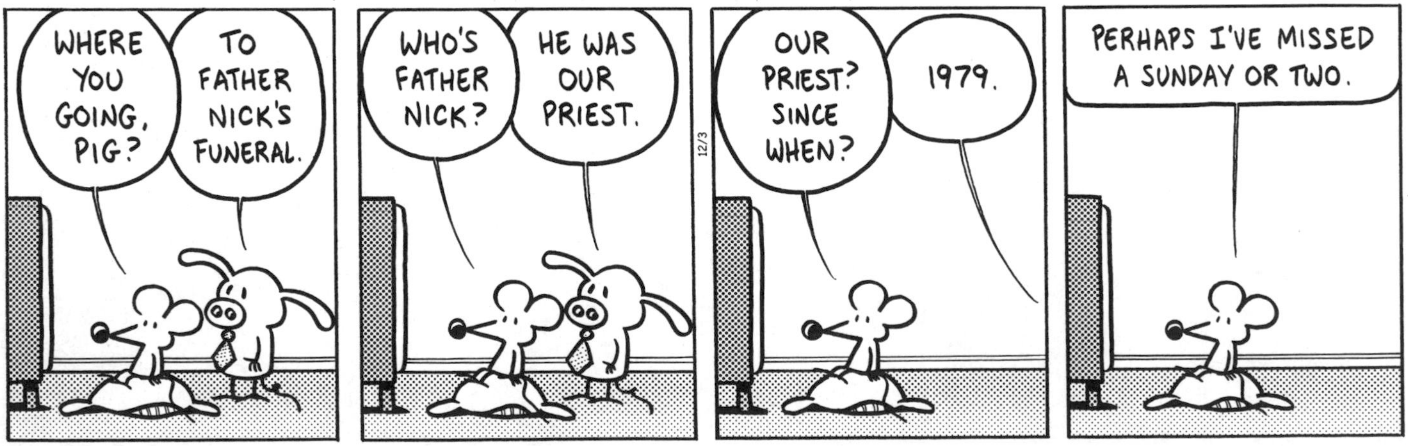
WHERE YOU GOING, PIG?
TO FATHER NICK'S FUNERAL.
WHO'S FATHER NICK?
HE WAS OUR PRIEST.
12/3
OUR PRIEST? SINCE WHEN?
1979.
PERHAPS I'VE MISSED A SUNDAY OR TWO.

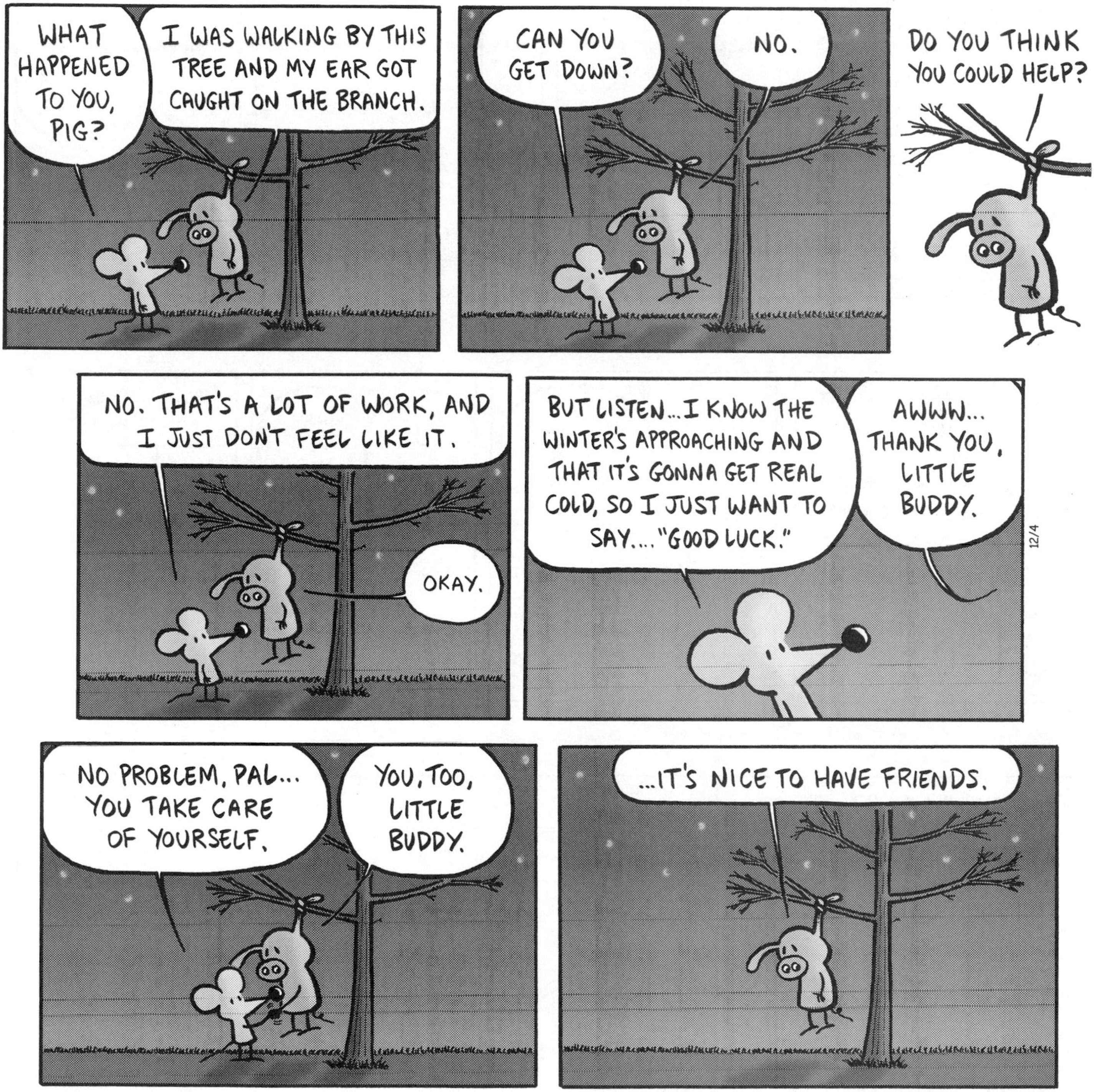
WHAT HAPPENED TO YOU, PIG?
I WAS WALKING BY THIS TREE AND MY EAR GOT CAUGHT ON THE BRANCH.
CAN YOU GET DOWN?
NO.
DO YOU THINK YOU COULD HELP?
NO. THAT'S A LOT OF WORK, AND I JUST DON'T FEEL LIKE IT.
OKAY.
BUT LISTEN...I KNOW THE WINTER'S APPROACHING AND THAT IT'S GONNA GET REAL COLD, SO I JUST WANT TO SAY...."GOOD LUCK."
AWWW... THANK YOU, LITTLE BUDDY.
12/4
NO PROBLEM, PAL... YOU TAKE CARE OF YOURSELF.
YOU, TOO, LITTLE BUDDY.
...IT'S NICE TO HAVE FRIENDS.

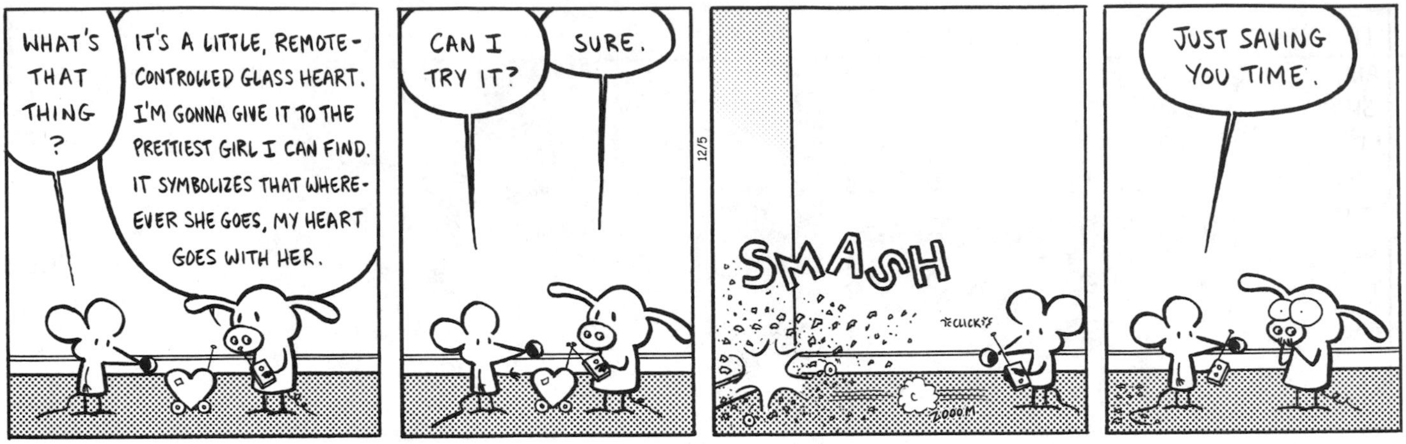
WHAT'S THAT THING?
IT'S A LITTLE, REMOTE-CONTROLLED GLASS HEART. I'M GONNA GIVE IT TO THE PRETTIEST GIRL I CAN FIND. IT SYMBOLIZES THAT WHEREEVER SHE GOES, MY HEART GOES WITH HER.
CAN I TRY IT?
SURE.
12/5
SMASH
CLICK
ZOOOM
JUST SAVING YOU TIME.

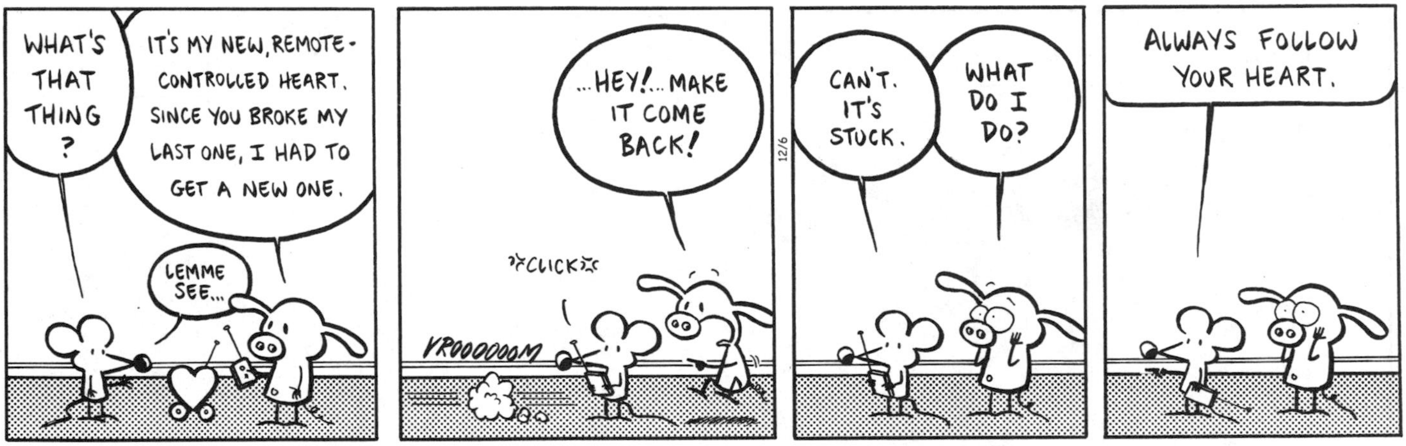
WHAT'S THAT THING?
IT'S MY NEW, REMOTE-CONTROLLED HEART. SINCE YOU BROKE MY LAST ONE, I HAD TO GET A NEW ONE.
LEMME SEE...
...HEY!... MAKE IT COME BACK!
CLICK
VROOOOOOOM
12/6
CAN'T. IT'S STUCK.
WHAT DO I DO?
ALWAYS FOLLOW YOUR HEART.

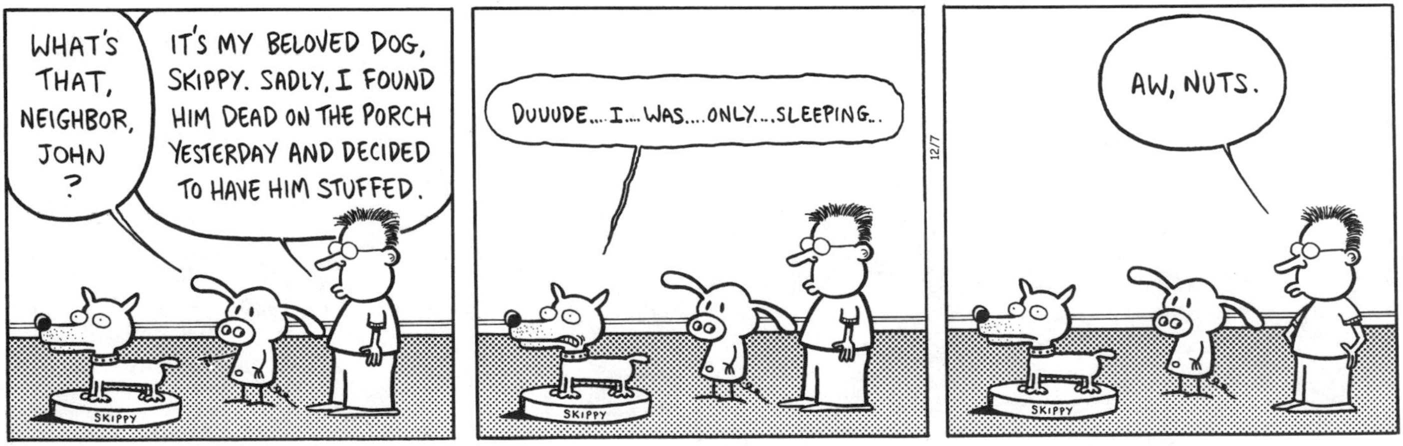
WHAT'S THAT, NEIGHBOR, JOHN?
IT'S MY BELOVED DOG, SKIPPY. SADLY, I FOUND HIM DEAD ON THE PORCH YESTERDAY AND DECIDED TO HAVE HIM STUFFED.
SKIPPY
DUUUDE.... I.... WAS.... ONLY.... SLEEPING..
12/7
AW, NUTS.

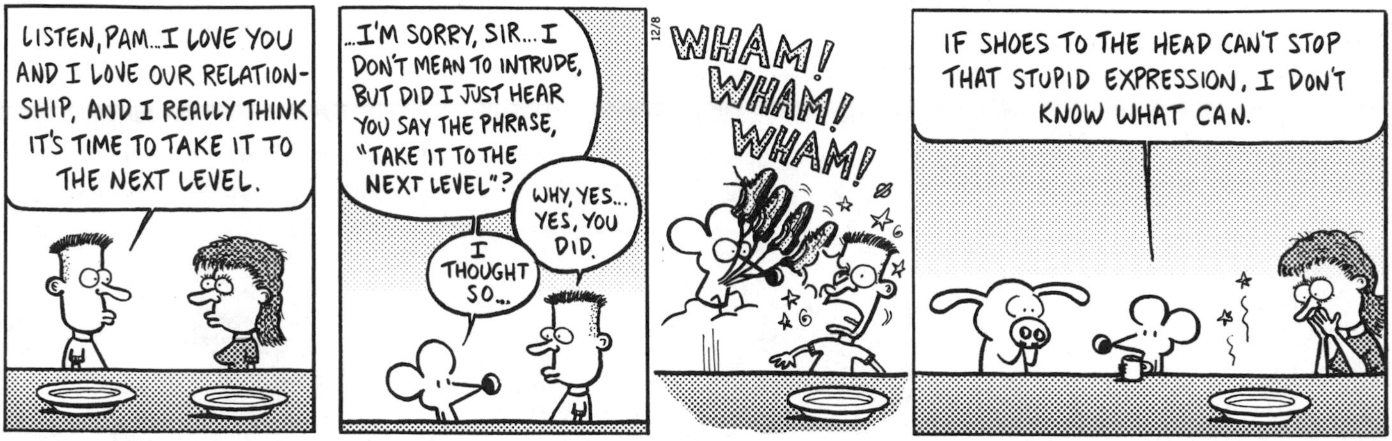
LISTEN, PAM...I LOVE YOU AND I LOVE OUR RELATIONSHIP, AND I REALLY THINK IT'S TIME TO TAKE IT TO THE NEXT LEVEL.
...I'M SORRY, SIR...I DON'T MEAN TO INTRUDE, BUT DID I JUST HEAR YOU SAY THE PHRASE, "TAKE IT TO THE NEXT LEVEL"?
WHY, YES... YES, YOU DID.
I THOUGHT SO...
12/8
WHAM! WHAM! WHAM!
IF SHOES TO THE HEAD CAN'T STOP THAT STUPID EXPRESSION, I DON'T KNOW WHAT CAN.

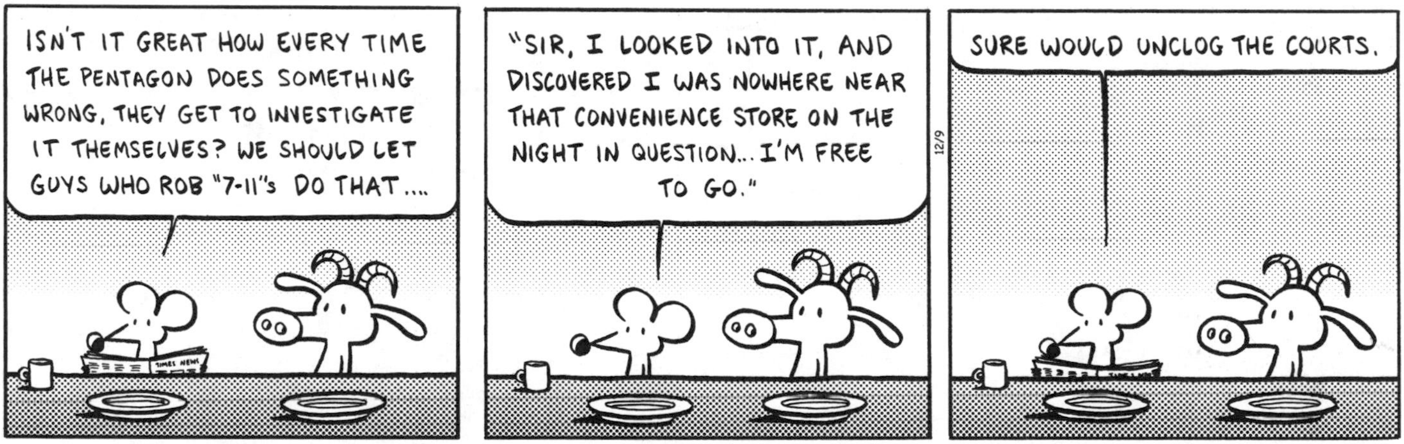
ISN'T IT GREAT HOW EVERY TIME THE PENTAGON DOES SOMETHING WRONG, THEY GET TO INVESTIGATE IT THEMSELVES? WE SHOULD LET GUYS WHO ROB "7-11"s DO THAT....
"SIR, I LOOKED INTO IT, AND DISCOVERED I WAS NOWHERE NEAR THAT CONVENIENCE STORE ON THE NIGHT IN QUESTION... I'M FREE TO GO."
12/9
SURE WOULD UNCLOG THE COURTS.

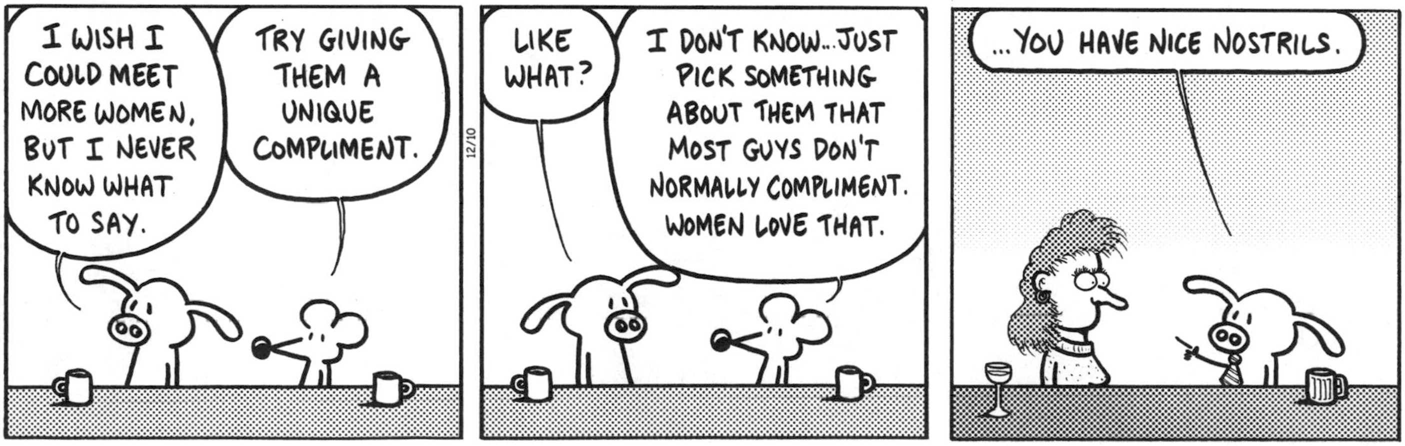
I WISH I COULD MEET MORE WOMEN, BUT I NEVER KNOW WHAT TO SAY.
TRY GIVING THEM A UNIQUE COMPLIMENT.
12/10
LIKE WHAT?
I DON'T KNOW...JUST PICK SOMETHING ABOUT THEM THAT MOST GUYS DON'T NORMALLY COMPLIMENT. WOMEN LOVE THAT.
...YOU HAVE NICE NOSTRILS.

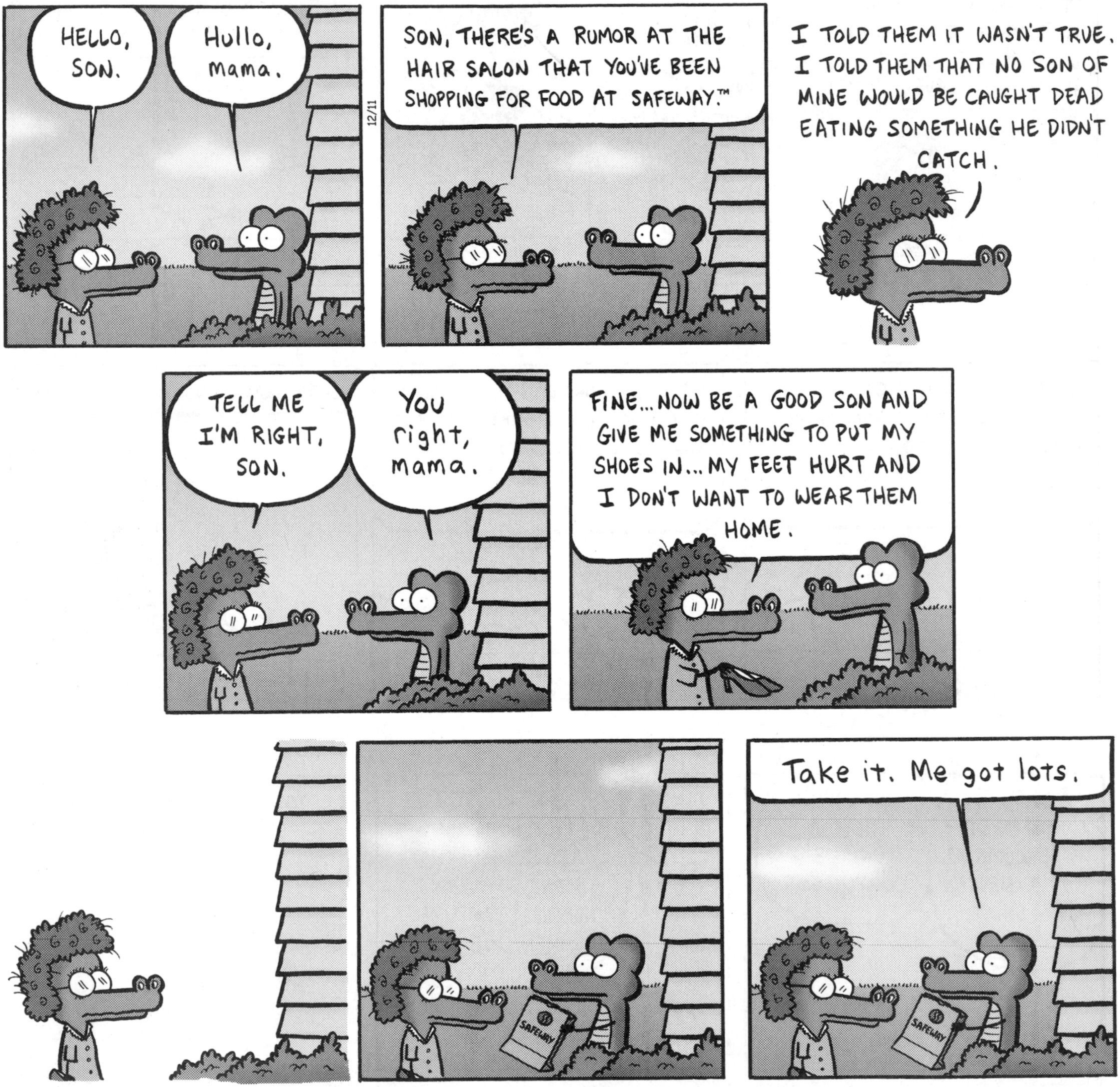
HELLO, SON.
Hullo, mama.
12/11
SON, THERE'S A RUMOR AT THE HAIR SALON THAT YOU'VE BEEN SHOPPING FOR FOOD AT SAFEWAY.™
I TOLD THEM IT WASN'T TRUE. I TOLD THEM THAT NO SON OF MINE WOULD BE CAUGHT DEAD EATING SOMETHING HE DIDN'T CATCH.
TELL ME I'M RIGHT, SON.
You right, mama.
FINE... NOW BE A GOOD SON AND GIVE ME SOMETHING TO PUT MY SHOES IN... MY FEET HURT AND I DON'T WANT TO WEAR THEM HOME.
SAFEWAY
SAFEWAY
Take it. Me got lots.

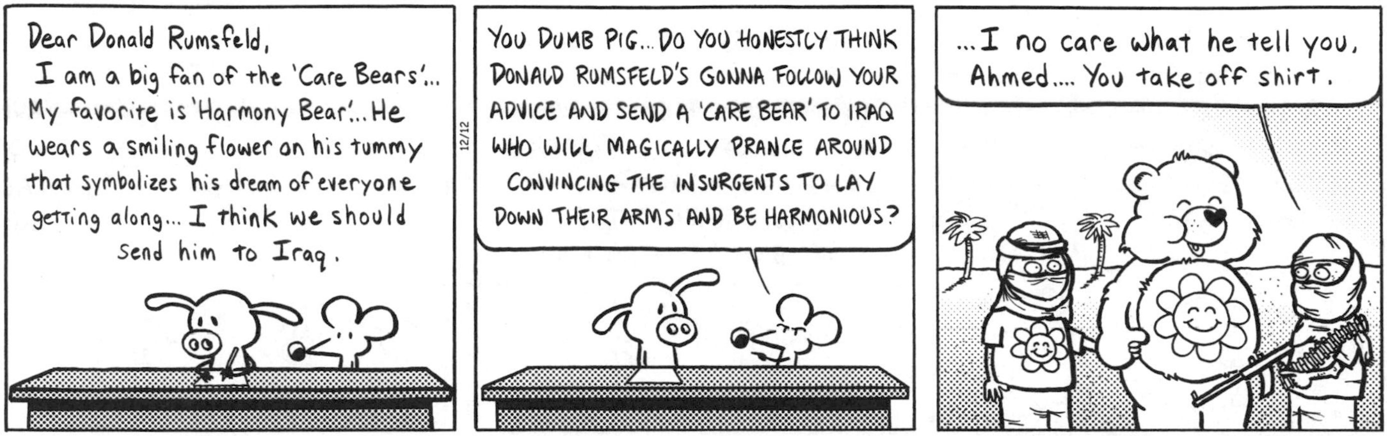
Dear Donald Rumsfeld,
I am a big fan of the 'Care Bears'... My favorite is 'Harmony Bear'... He wears a smiling flower on his tummy that symbolizes his dream of everyone getting along... I think we should send him to Iraq.
12/12
YOU DUMB PIG... DO YOU HONESTLY THINK DONALD RUMSFELD'S GONNA FOLLOW YOUR ADVICE AND SEND A 'CARE BEAR' TO IRAQ WHO WILL MAGICALLY PRANCE AROUND CONVINCING THE INSURGENTS TO LAY DOWN THEIR ARMS AND BE HARMONIOUS?
...I no care what he tell you, Ahmed.... You take off shirt.

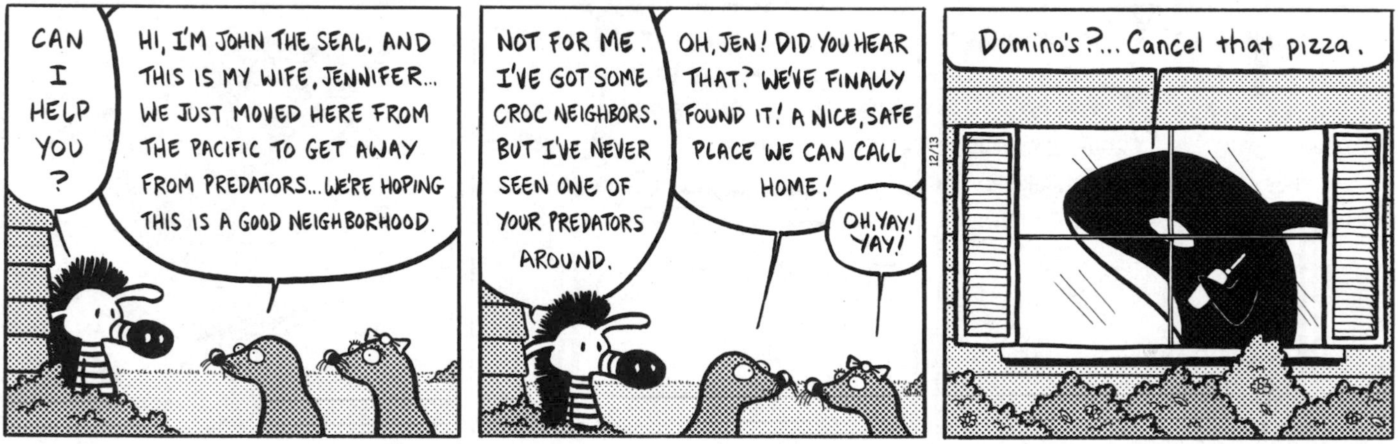
CAN I HELP YOU?
HI, I'M JOHN THE SEAL, AND THIS IS MY WIFE, JENNIFER... WE JUST MOVED HERE FROM THE PACIFIC TO GET AWAY FROM PREDATORS... WE'RE HOPING THIS IS A GOOD NEIGHBORHOOD.
NOT FOR ME. I'VE GOT SOME CROC NEIGHBORS, BUT I'VE NEVER SEEN ONE OF YOUR PREDATORS AROUND.
OH, JEN! DID YOU HEAR THAT? WE'VE FINALLY FOUND IT! A NICE, SAFE PLACE WE CAN CALL HOME!
OH, YAY! YAY!
12/13
Domino's?... Cancel that pizza.

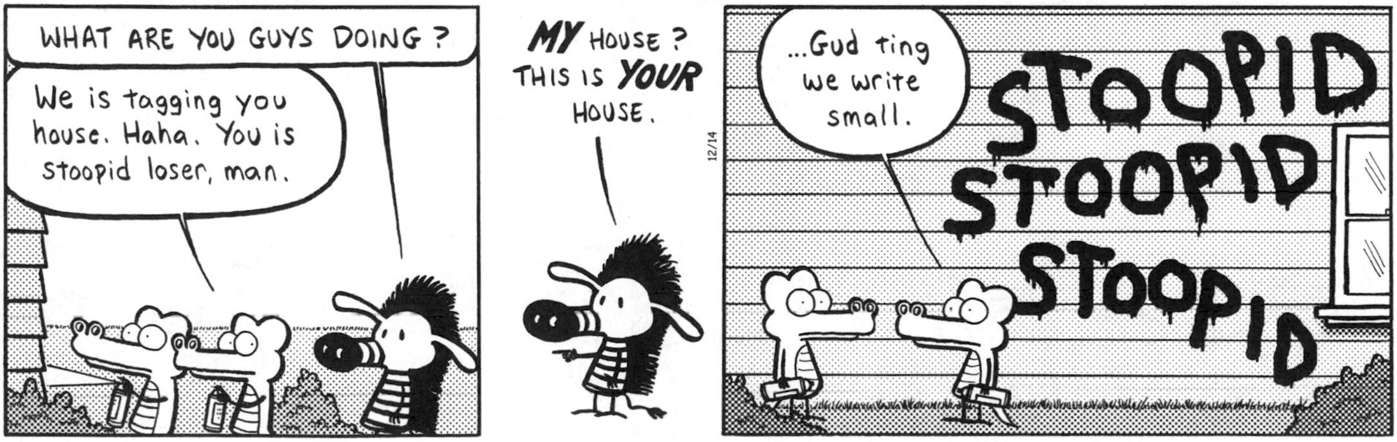
WHAT ARE YOU GUYS DOING?
We is tagging you house. Haha. You is stoopid loser, man.
MY HOUSE? THIS IS YOUR HOUSE.
12/14
...Gud ting we write small.
STOOPID
STOOPID
STOOPID
STOOPID

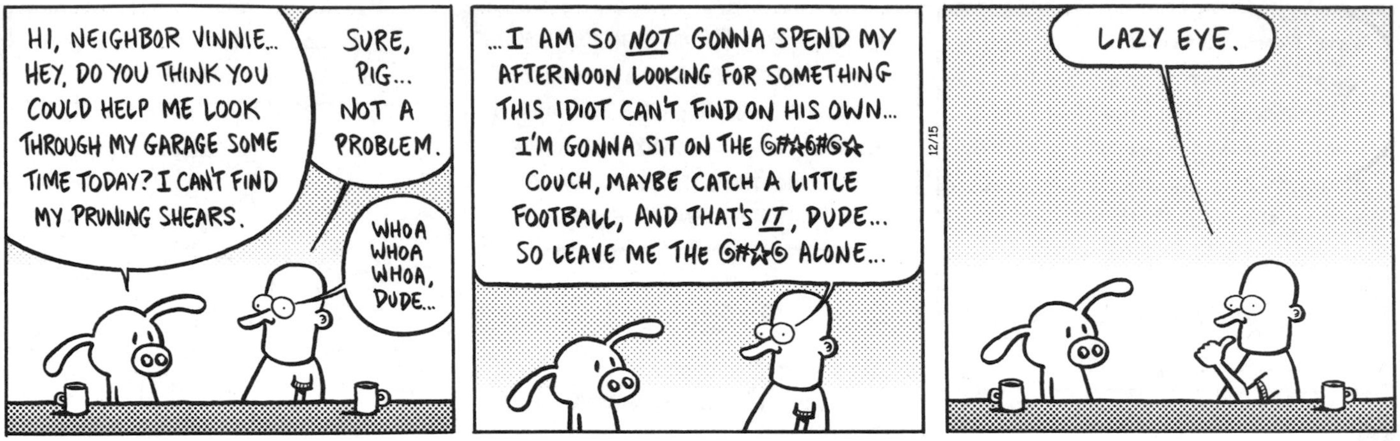
HI, NEIGHBOR VINNIE... HEY, DO YOU THINK YOU COULD HELP ME LOOK THROUGH MY GARAGE SOME TIME TODAY? I CAN'T FIND MY PRUNING SHEARS.
SURE, PIG... NOT A PROBLEM.
WHOA WHOA WHOA, DUDE...
...I AM SO NOT GONNA SPEND MY AFTERNOON LOOKING FOR SOMETHING THIS IDIOT CAN'T FIND ON HIS OWN... I'M GONNA SIT ON THE G#☆G#G☆ COUCH, MAYBE CATCH A LITTLE FOOTBALL, AND THAT'S IT, DUDE... SO LEAVE ME THE G#☆G ALONE...
12/15
LAZY EYE.

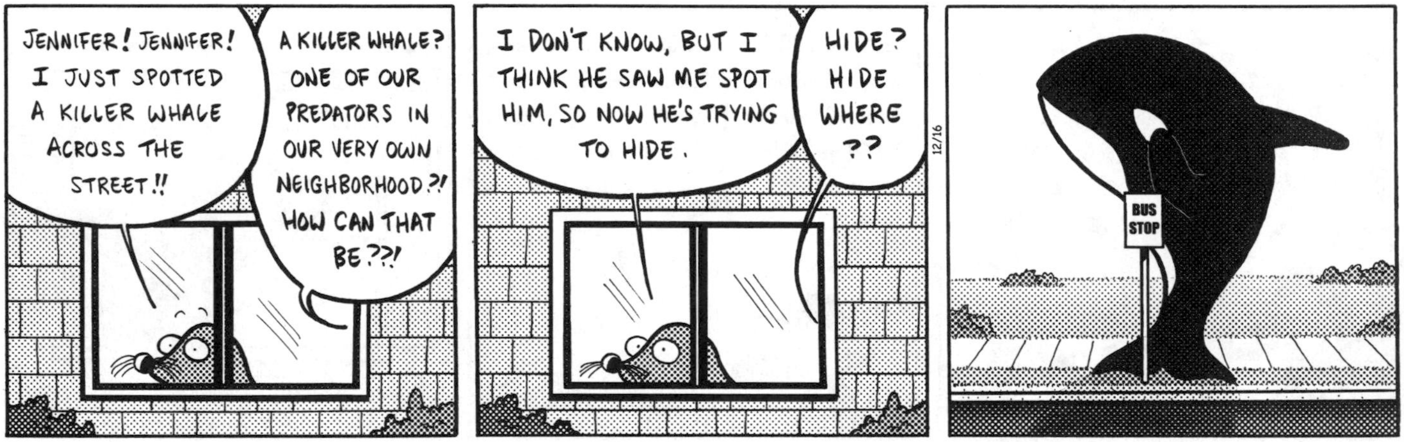
JENNIFER! JENNIFER! I JUST SPOTTED A KILLER WHALE ACROSS THE STREET!!
A KILLER WHALE? ONE OF OUR PREDATORS IN OUR VERY OWN NEIGHBORHOOD?! HOW CAN THAT BE??!
I DON'T KNOW, BUT I THINK HE SAW ME SPOT HIM, SO NOW HE'S TRYING TO HIDE.
HIDE? HIDE WHERE??
12/16
BUS STOP

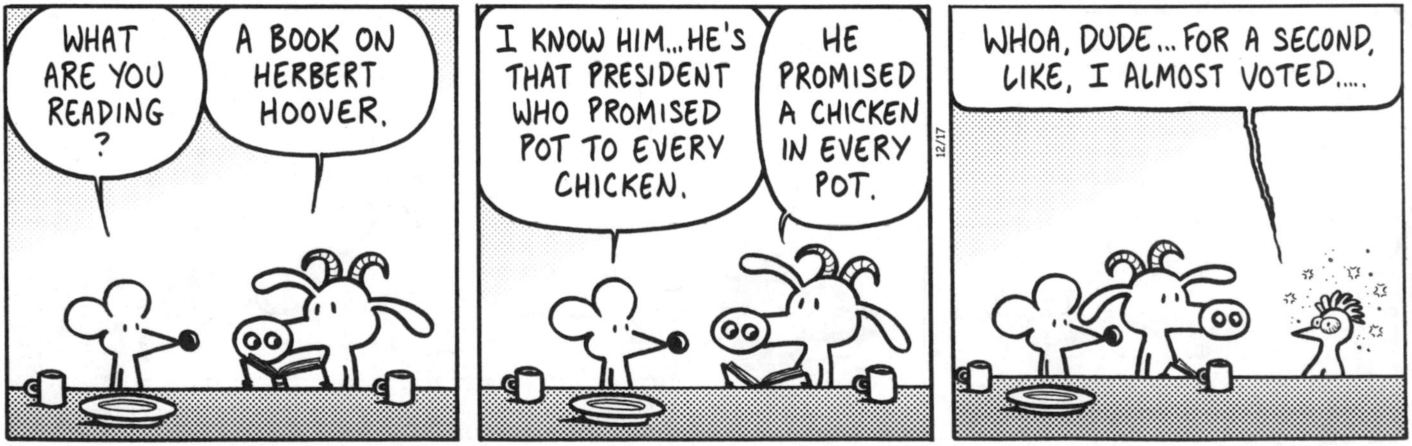
WHAT ARE YOU READING?
A BOOK ON HERBERT HOOVER.
I KNOW HIM... HE'S THAT PRESIDENT WHO PROMISED POT TO EVERY CHICKEN.
HE PROMISED A CHICKEN IN EVERY POT.
12/17
WHOA, DUDE... FOR A SECOND, LIKE, I ALMOST VOTED.....

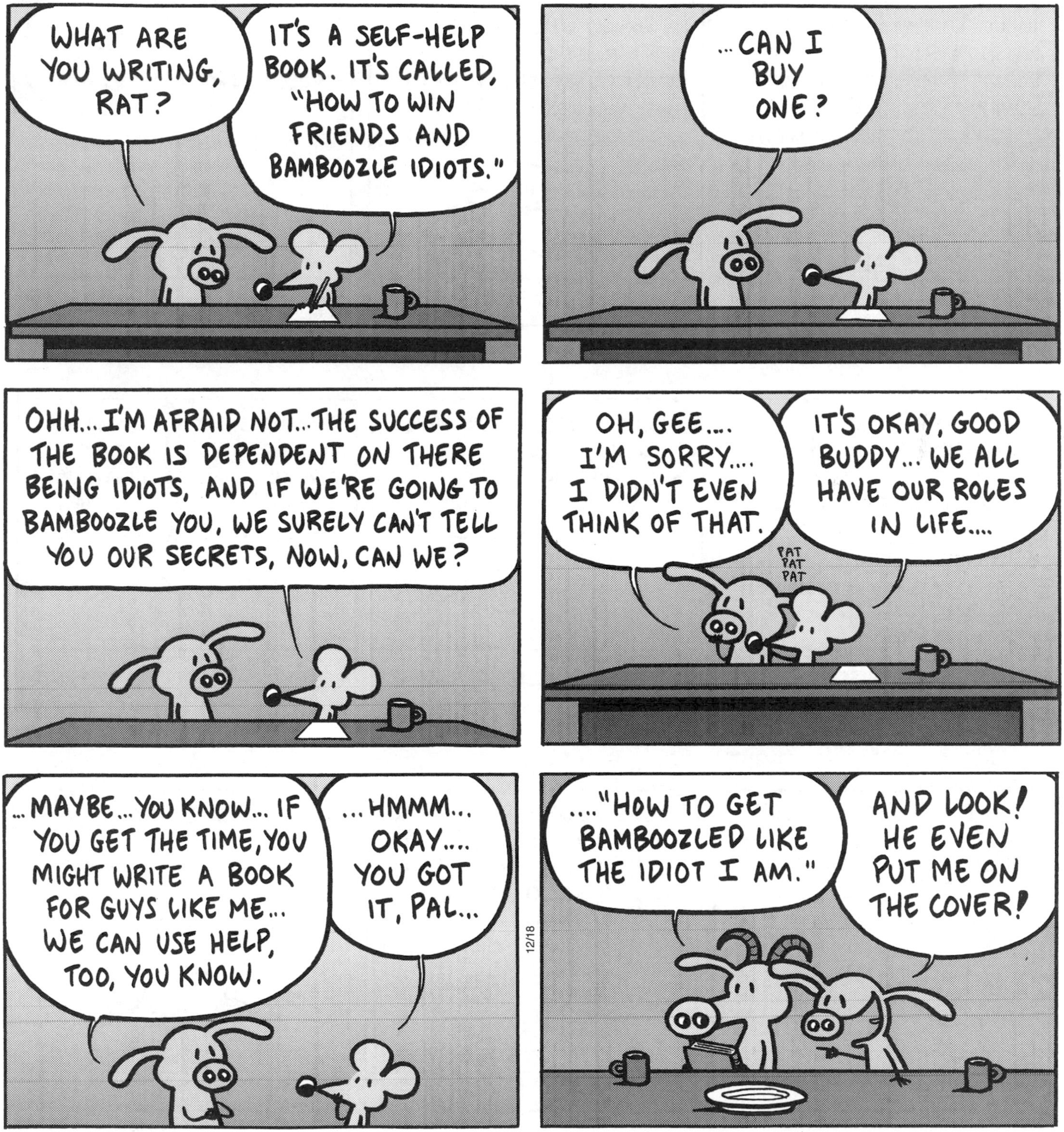
WHAT ARE YOU WRITING, RAT?
IT'S A SELF-HELP BOOK. IT'S CALLED, "HOW TO WIN FRIENDS AND BAMBOOZLE IDIOTS."
...CAN I BUY ONE?
OHH...I'M AFRAID NOT...THE SUCCESS OF THE BOOK IS DEPENDENT ON THERE BEING IDIOTS, AND IF WE'RE GOING TO BAMBOOZLE YOU, WE SURELY CAN'T TELL YOU OUR SECRETS, NOW, CAN WE?
OH, GEE.... I'M SORRY.... I DIDN'T EVEN THINK OF THAT.
IT'S OKAY, GOOD BUDDY... WE ALL HAVE OUR ROLES IN LIFE....
PAT PAT PAT
...MAYBE...YOU KNOW... IF YOU GET THE TIME, YOU MIGHT WRITE A BOOK FOR GUYS LIKE ME... WE CAN USE HELP, TOO, YOU KNOW.
...HMMM... OKAY.... YOU GOT IT, PAL...
12/18
...."HOW TO GET BAMBOOZLED LIKE THE IDIOT I AM."
AND LOOK! HE EVEN PUT ME ON THE COVER!

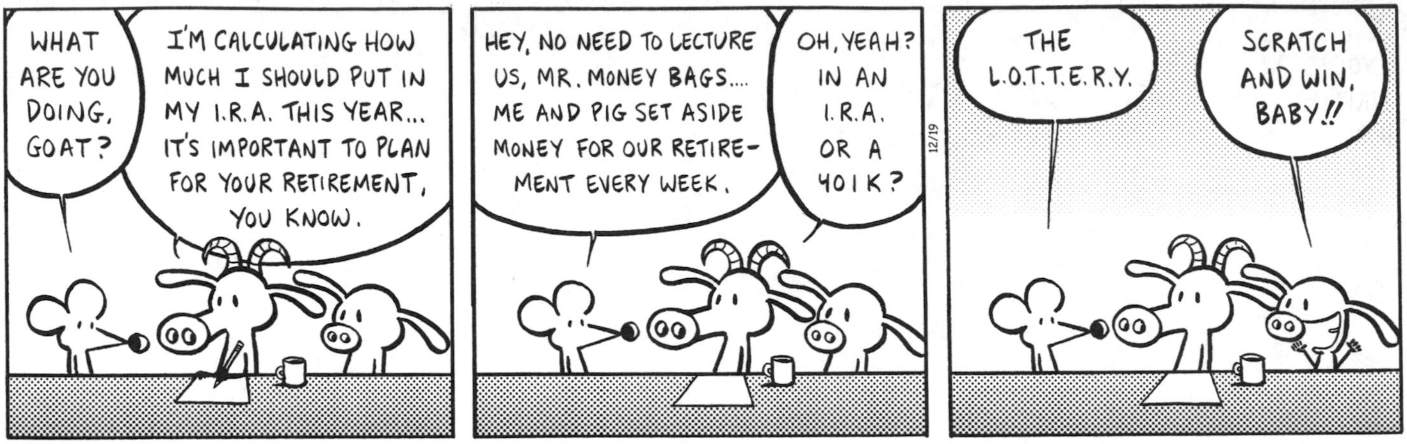
WHAT ARE YOU DOING, GOAT?
I'M CALCULATING HOW MUCH I SHOULD PUT IN MY I.R.A. THIS YEAR... IT'S IMPORTANT TO PLAN FOR YOUR RETIREMENT, YOU KNOW.
HEY, NO NEED TO LECTURE US, MR. MONEY BAGS.... ME AND PIG SET ASIDE MONEY FOR OUR RETIRE-MENT EVERY WEEK.
OH, YEAH? IN AN I.R.A. OR A 401K?
12/19
THE L.O.T.T.E.R.Y.
SCRATCH AND WIN, BABY!!

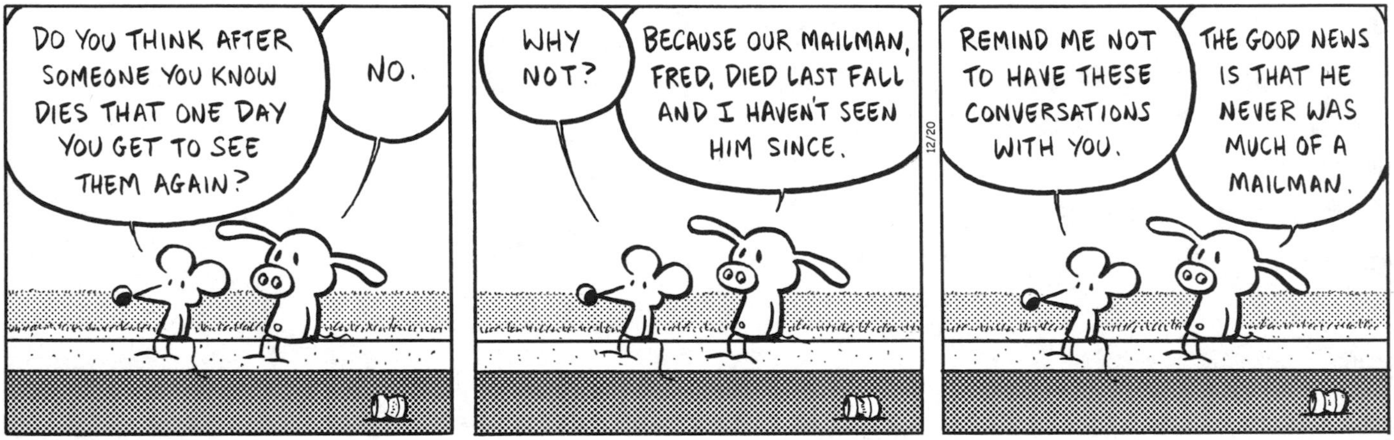
DO YOU THINK AFTER SOMEONE YOU KNOW DIES THAT ONE DAY YOU GET TO SEE THEM AGAIN?
NO.
WHY NOT?
BECAUSE OUR MAILMAN, FRED, DIED LAST FALL AND I HAVEN'T SEEN HIM SINCE.
12/20
REMIND ME NOT TO HAVE THESE CONVERSATIONS WITH YOU.
THE GOOD NEWS IS THAT HE NEVER WAS MUCH OF A MAILMAN.

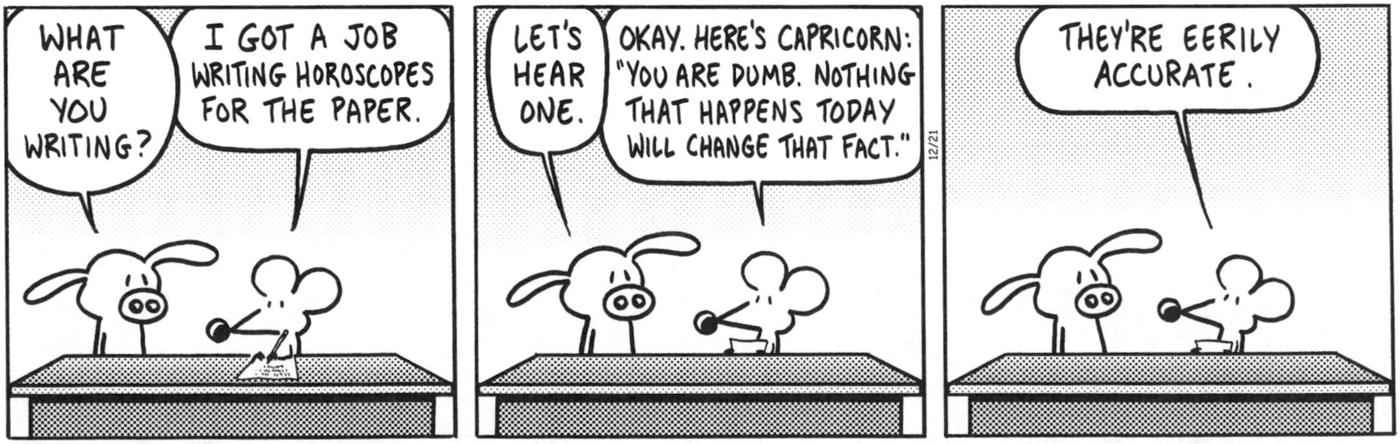
WHAT ARE YOU WRITING?
I GOT A JOB WRITING HOROSCOPES FOR THE PAPER.
LET'S HEAR ONE.
OKAY. HERE'S CAPRICORN: "YOU ARE DUMB. NOTHING THAT HAPPENS TODAY WILL CHANGE THAT FACT."
12/21
THEY'RE EERILY ACCURATE.

Panel 1:
I HEAR YOU'RE WRITING HOROSCOPES FOR THE PAPER.

YEAH... HERE'S GEMINI: "IF YOU THINK THE PROBLEMS OF YOUR SAD LITTLE LIFE CAN BE SOLVED BY LOOKING TO THE STARS, YOU MIGHT AS WELL JUMP OFF A CLIFF."

Panel 2:
WHOA WHOA WHOA... THAT'S JUST AN INSULT. AS AN ASTROLOGIST, YOU'RE SUPPOSED TO MAKE A PREDICTION.

12/22

Panel 3:
...DESPITE YOUR FRANTIC ARM-FLAPPING, YOU WILL NOT FLY.

Panel 4:
I HEAR YOU GOT A JOB WRITING HOROSCOPES.

YEAH. HERE'S WHAT I WROTE FOR TAURUS: "THE FAULT, DEAR BRUTUS, IS NOT IN OUR STARS, BUT IN OURSELVES."

Panel 5:
YOU FRAUD. THAT WAS WRITTEN BY SHAKESPEARE.

WELL, I WROTE IT, TOO.

Panel 6:
HE WROTE IT FIRST.

GOOD LITERATURE IS NOT A RACE.

12/23

Panel 7:
WHAT'S THE MATTER, DARBY NUT AND SCOTTIE NUT?...DON'T YOU FEEL LIKE PLAYING TODAY?

IT'S YOUR FRIEND... HE MAKES US FEEL UNCOMFORTABLE.

Panel 8:
GO AWAY, RAT! YOU'RE INTIMIDATING THE NUTS.

INTIMIDATING? DUDE, I'M JUST OVER HERE PLAYING WITH MY OWN FRIEND... AND I FIND IT INSULTING THAT YOU'D ACCUSE US OF HAVING BAD MOTIVES.

12/24

Panel 9:
APOLOGIZE TO FRIEDRICH.

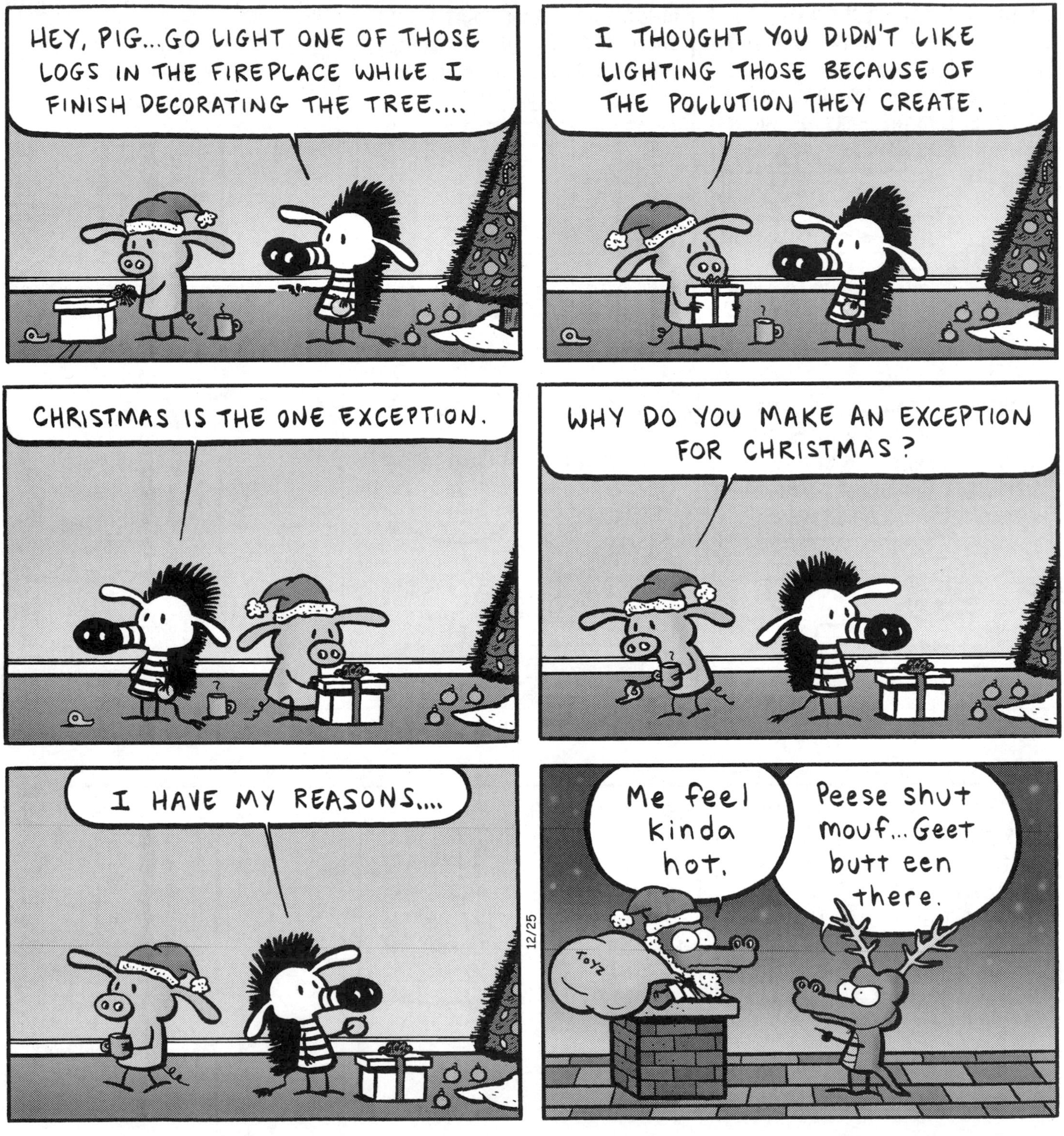
HEY, PIG...GO LIGHT ONE OF THOSE LOGS IN THE FIREPLACE WHILE I FINISH DECORATING THE TREE....
I THOUGHT YOU DIDN'T LIKE LIGHTING THOSE BECAUSE OF THE POLLUTION THEY CREATE.
CHRISTMAS IS THE ONE EXCEPTION.
WHY DO YOU MAKE AN EXCEPTION FOR CHRISTMAS?
I HAVE MY REASONS....
12/25
Me feel kinda hot.
Peese shut mouf... Geet butt een there.
TOYZ

Panel 1: WE GOT A NOTICE FROM THE COMIC STRIP FACTORY SAYING THAT THEY'RE ALMOST OUT OF THE LETTER "A." THEY WANT US TO REDUCE OUR USAGE.

Panel 2: WHAAAAAT? THAT'S BAD... BAD. BAD. BAAAAAAAAAD... A'S ARE GREAT. ALL A'S ARE GREAT.... THAT CAN MAKE AN ANIMAL SCREAM. AAAAAAAAAAAAH! WAIT... HAFTA SNEEAAAAAAAACHOO!!!

Panel 3: RE YOU H PPY?

Panel 4: WH T'S GOING ON?

WE R N OUT OF THE FIRST LETTER OF THE LPH BET. THERE'S SHORT GE T THE COMIC STRIP F CTORY.

Panel 5: WH T RE WE GONN DO?

WELL, WE'VE GOT SIX EMERGENCY 'S IF WE NEED THEM. OUR PL N IS TO JUST ST Y C LM ND USE THEM JUDICIOUSLY.

Panel 6: AAAAAAH!!

Panel 7: D MN TH T PIG.

Panel 8: I HE RD WE R N OUT OF THE FIRST LETTER OF THE LPH BET.

YE H... BUT I M N GED TO BUY DOZEN ON THE BL CK M RKET.

Panel 9: WELL...WE'LL JUST H VE TO BE RE L C REFUL WITH THEM..... ISN'T TH T RIGHT, CHUCKIE?

BAAAAAAAAAAAAH!

Panel 10: B H.

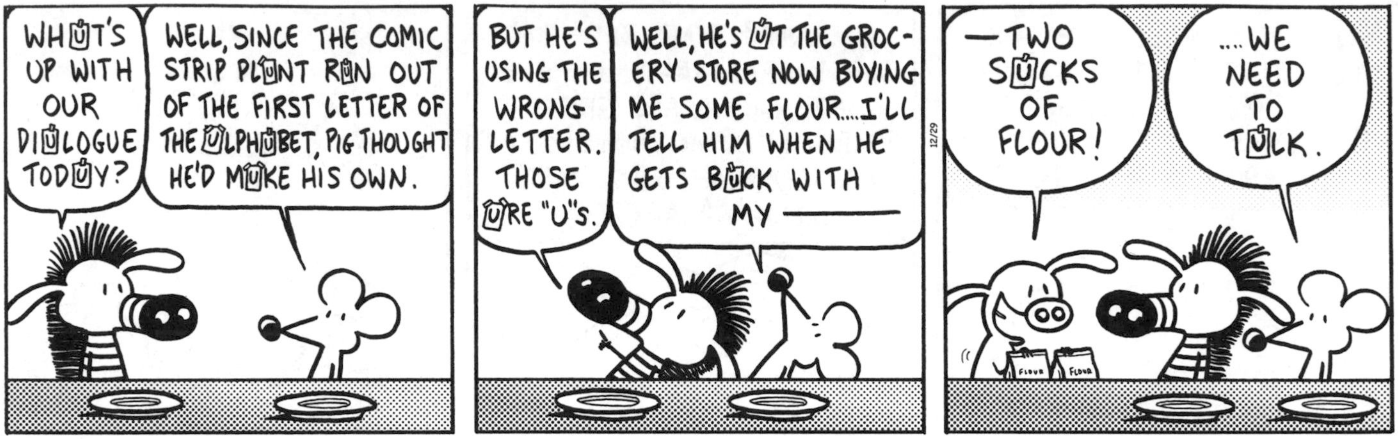
WHUT'S UP WITH OUR DIULOGUE TODUY?
WELL, SINCE THE COMIC STRIP PLUNT RUN OUT OF THE FIRST LETTER OF THE ULPHUBET, PIG THOUGHT HE'D MUKE HIS OWN.
BUT HE'S USING THE WRONG LETTER. THOSE URE "U"S.
WELL, HE'S UT THE GROCERY STORE NOW BUYING ME SOME FLOUR....I'LL TELL HIM WHEN HE GETS BUCK WITH MY ———
12/29
—TWO SUCKS OF FLOUR!
....WE NEED TO TULK.
FLOUR
FLOUR

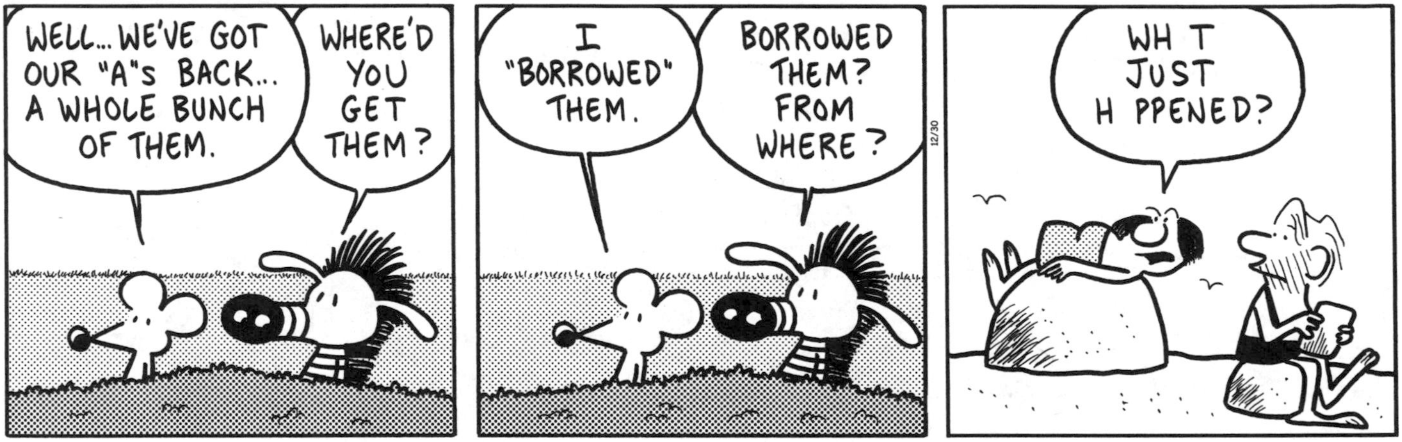
WELL... WE'VE GOT OUR "A"S BACK... A WHOLE BUNCH OF THEM.
WHERE'D YOU GET THEM?
I "BORROWED" THEM.
BORROWED THEM? FROM WHERE?
12/30
WH T JUST H PPENED?

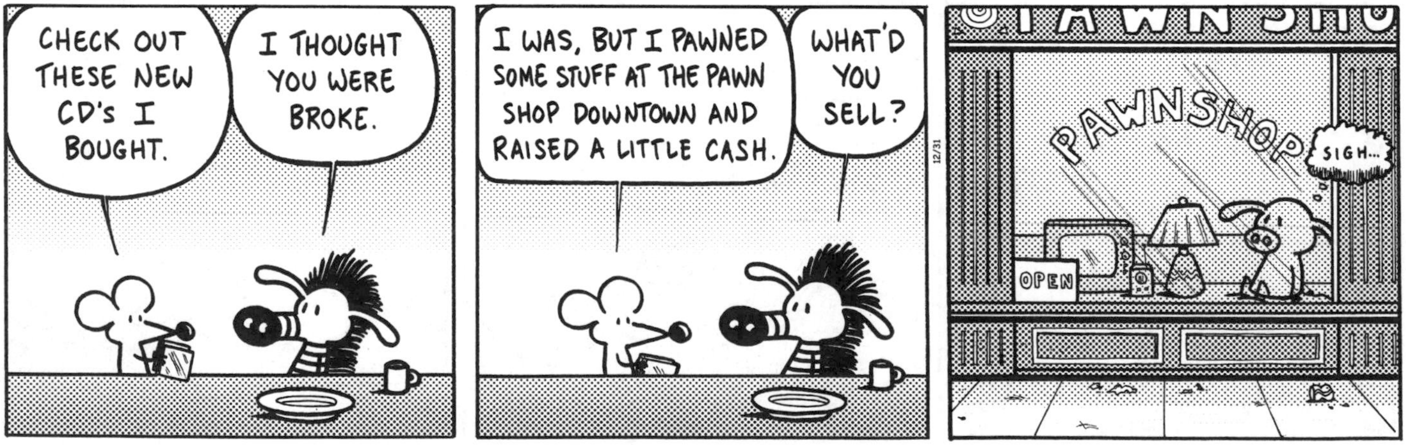
CHECK OUT THESE NEW CD'S I BOUGHT.
I THOUGHT YOU WERE BROKE.
I WAS, BUT I PAWNED SOME STUFF AT THE PAWN SHOP DOWNTOWN AND RAISED A LITTLE CASH.
WHAT'D YOU SELL?
12/31
PAWNSHOP
SIGH...
OPEN

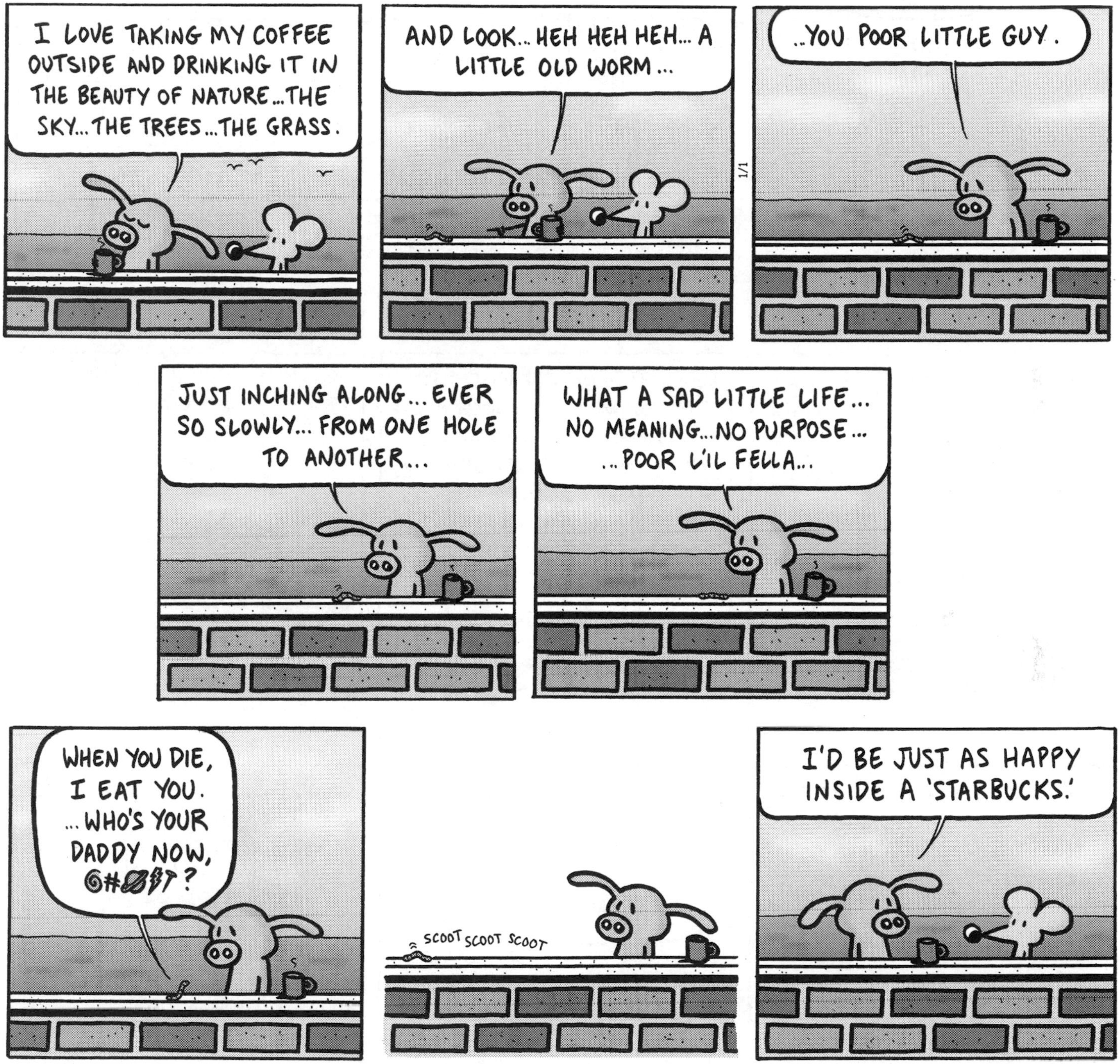
I LOVE TAKING MY COFFEE OUTSIDE AND DRINKING IT IN THE BEAUTY OF NATURE...THE SKY...THE TREES...THE GRASS.
AND LOOK... HEH HEH HEH... A LITTLE OLD WORM...
..YOU POOR LITTLE GUY.
JUST INCHING ALONG... EVER SO SLOWLY... FROM ONE HOLE TO ANOTHER...
WHAT A SAD LITTLE LIFE... NO MEANING...NO PURPOSE... ...POOR L'IL FELLA...
WHEN YOU DIE, I EAT YOU. ...WHO'S YOUR DADDY NOW,
SCOOT SCOOT SCOOT
I'D BE JUST AS HAPPY INSIDE A 'STARBUCKS.'

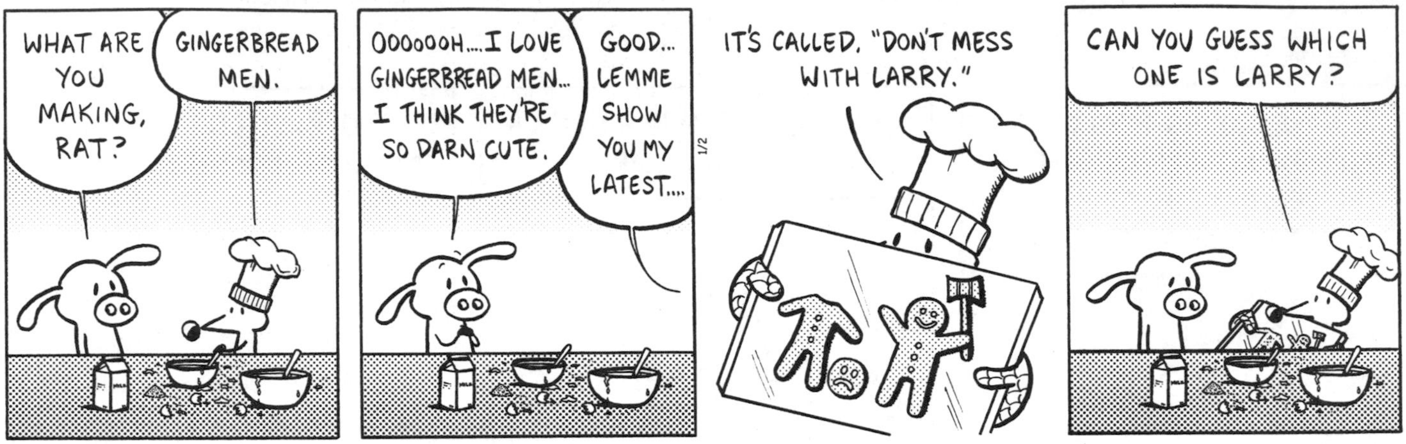
WHAT ARE YOU MAKING, RAT?
GINGERBREAD MEN.
OOOOOOH....I LOVE GINGERBREAD MEN... I THINK THEY'RE SO DARN CUTE.
GOOD... LEMME SHOW YOU MY LATEST....
1/2
IT'S CALLED, "DON'T MESS WITH LARRY."
CAN YOU GUESS WHICH ONE IS LARRY?

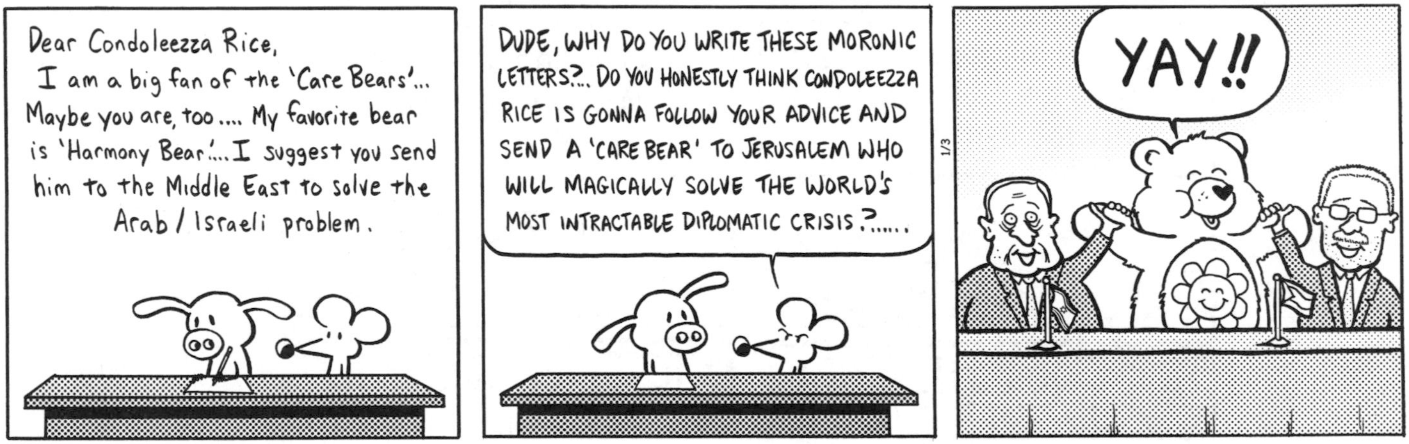
Dear Condoleezza Rice,
I am a big fan of the 'Care Bears'... Maybe you are, too.... My favorite bear is 'Harmony Bear'...I suggest you send him to the Middle East to solve the Arab / Israeli problem.
DUDE, WHY DO YOU WRITE THESE MORONIC LETTERS?.. DO YOU HONESTLY THINK CONDOLEEZZA RICE IS GONNA FOLLOW YOUR ADVICE AND SEND A 'CARE BEAR' TO JERUSALEM WHO WILL MAGICALLY SOLVE THE WORLD'S MOST INTRACTABLE DIPLOMATIC CRISIS?......
1/3
YAY!!

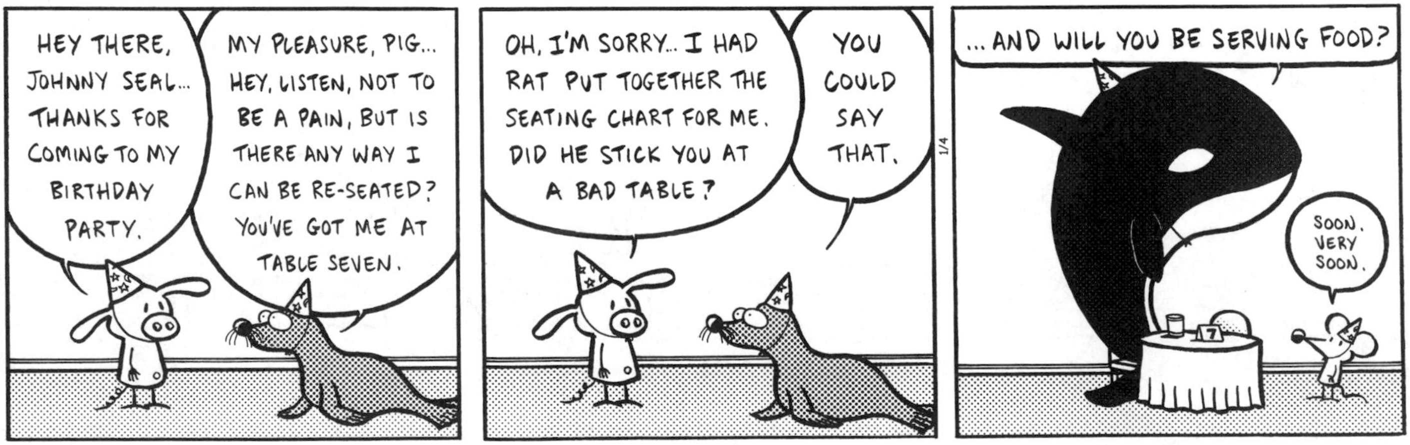
HEY THERE, JOHNNY SEAL... THANKS FOR COMING TO MY BIRTHDAY PARTY.
MY PLEASURE, PIG... HEY, LISTEN, NOT TO BE A PAIN, BUT IS THERE ANY WAY I CAN BE RE-SEATED? YOU'VE GOT ME AT TABLE SEVEN.
OH, I'M SORRY... I HAD RAT PUT TOGETHER THE SEATING CHART FOR ME. DID HE STICK YOU AT A BAD TABLE?
YOU COULD SAY THAT.
1/4
...AND WILL YOU BE SERVING FOOD?
SOON. VERY SOON.
7

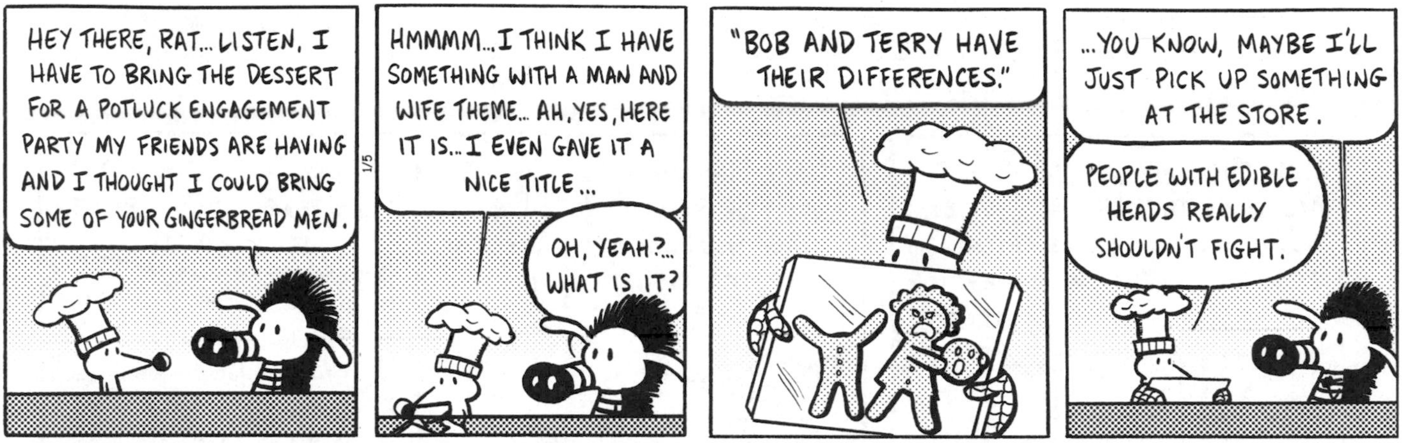
HEY THERE, RAT... LISTEN, I HAVE TO BRING THE DESSERT FOR A POTLUCK ENGAGEMENT PARTY MY FRIENDS ARE HAVING AND I THOUGHT I COULD BRING SOME OF YOUR GINGERBREAD MEN.
1/5
HMMMM... I THINK I HAVE SOMETHING WITH A MAN AND WIFE THEME... AH, YES, HERE IT IS... I EVEN GAVE IT A NICE TITLE...
OH, YEAH?... WHAT IS IT?
"BOB AND TERRY HAVE THEIR DIFFERENCES."
...YOU KNOW, MAYBE I'LL JUST PICK UP SOMETHING AT THE STORE.
PEOPLE WITH EDIBLE HEADS REALLY SHOULDN'T FIGHT.

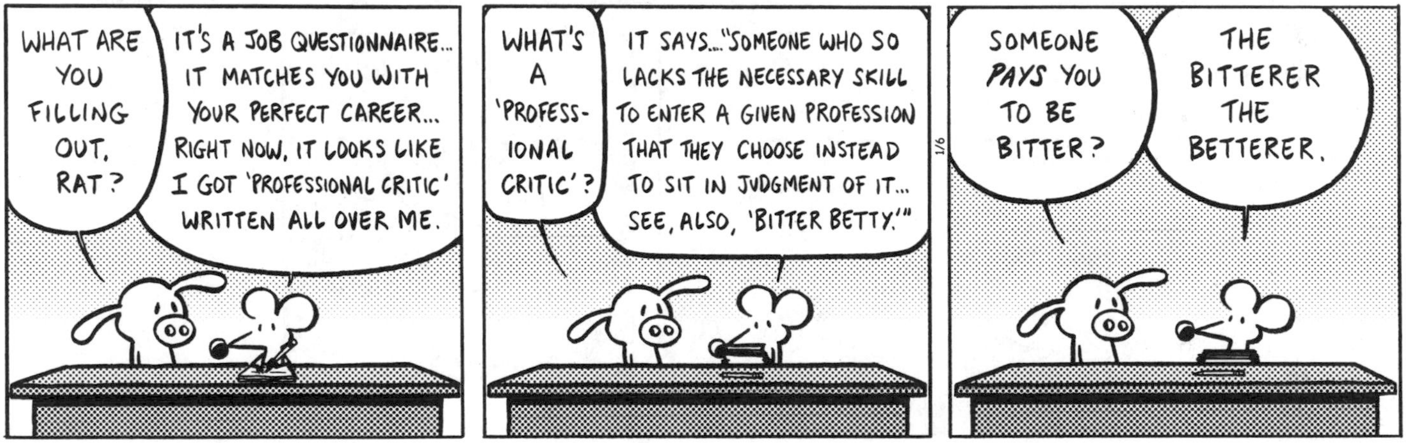
WHAT ARE YOU FILLING OUT, RAT?
IT'S A JOB QUESTIONNAIRE... IT MATCHES YOU WITH YOUR PERFECT CAREER... RIGHT NOW, IT LOOKS LIKE I GOT 'PROFESSIONAL CRITIC' WRITTEN ALL OVER ME.
WHAT'S A 'PROFESSIONAL CRITIC'?
IT SAYS..."SOMEONE WHO SO LACKS THE NECESSARY SKILL TO ENTER A GIVEN PROFESSION THAT THEY CHOOSE INSTEAD TO SIT IN JUDGMENT OF IT... SEE, ALSO, 'BITTER BETTY.'"
1/6
SOMEONE *PAYS* YOU TO BE BITTER?
THE BITTERER THE BETTERER.

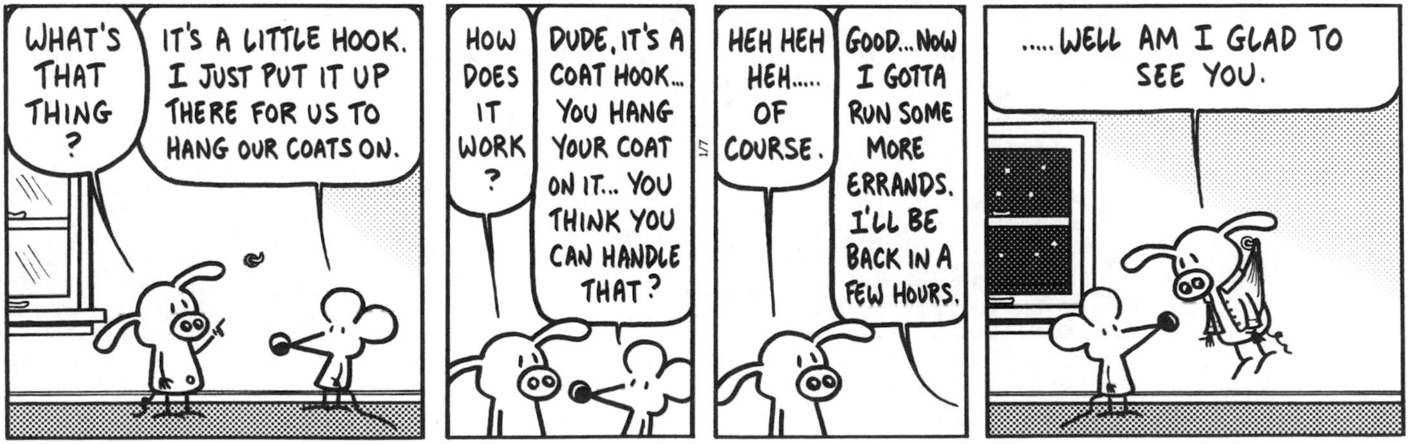
WHAT'S THAT THING?
IT'S A LITTLE HOOK. I JUST PUT IT UP THERE FOR US TO HANG OUR COATS ON.
HOW DOES IT WORK?
DUDE, IT'S A COAT HOOK... YOU HANG YOUR COAT ON IT... YOU THINK YOU CAN HANDLE THAT?
1/7
HEH HEH HEH..... OF COURSE.
GOOD... NOW I GOTTA RUN SOME MORE ERRANDS. I'LL BE BACK IN A FEW HOURS.
.....WELL AM I GLAD TO SEE YOU.

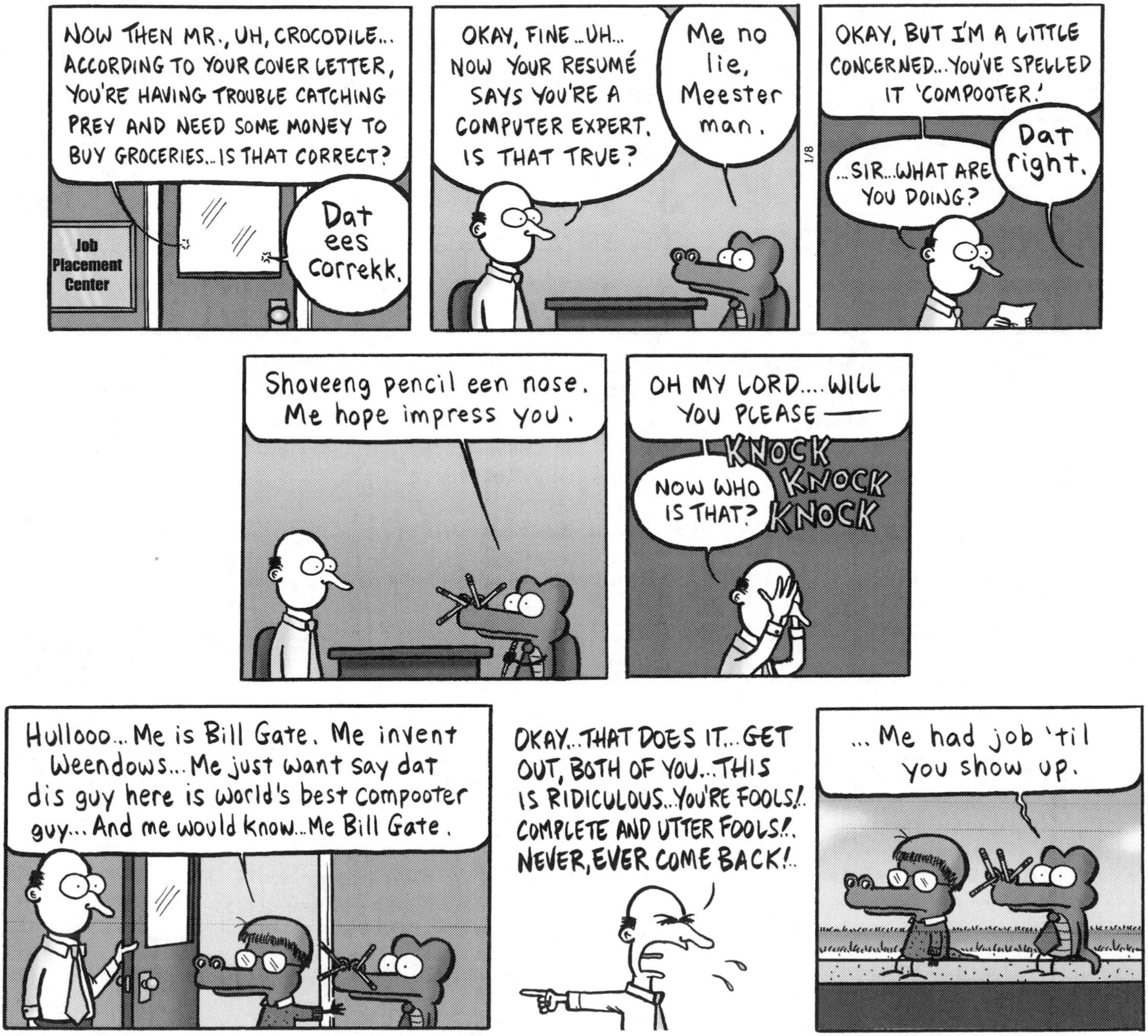
NOW THEN MR., UH, CROCODILE... ACCORDING TO YOUR COVER LETTER, YOU'RE HAVING TROUBLE CATCHING PREY AND NEED SOME MONEY TO BUY GROCERIES... IS THAT CORRECT?
Dat ees correkk.
Job Placement Center
OKAY, FINE... UH... NOW YOUR RESUMÉ SAYS YOU'RE A COMPUTER EXPERT. IS THAT TRUE?
Me no lie, Meester man.
1/8
OKAY, BUT I'M A LITTLE CONCERNED... YOU'VE SPELLED IT 'COMPOOTER.'
...SIR... WHAT ARE YOU DOING?
Dat right.
Shoveeng pencil een nose. Me hope impress you.
OH MY LORD.... WILL YOU PLEASE —
KNOCK KNOCK KNOCK
NOW WHO IS THAT?
Hullooo... Me is Bill Gate. Me invent Weendows... Me just want say dat dis guy here is world's best compooter guy... And me would know... Me Bill Gate.
OKAY... THAT DOES IT... GET OUT, BOTH OF YOU... THIS IS RIDICULOUS... YOU'RE FOOLS!! COMPLETE AND UTTER FOOLS!! NEVER, EVER COME BACK!!
... Me had job 'til you show up.

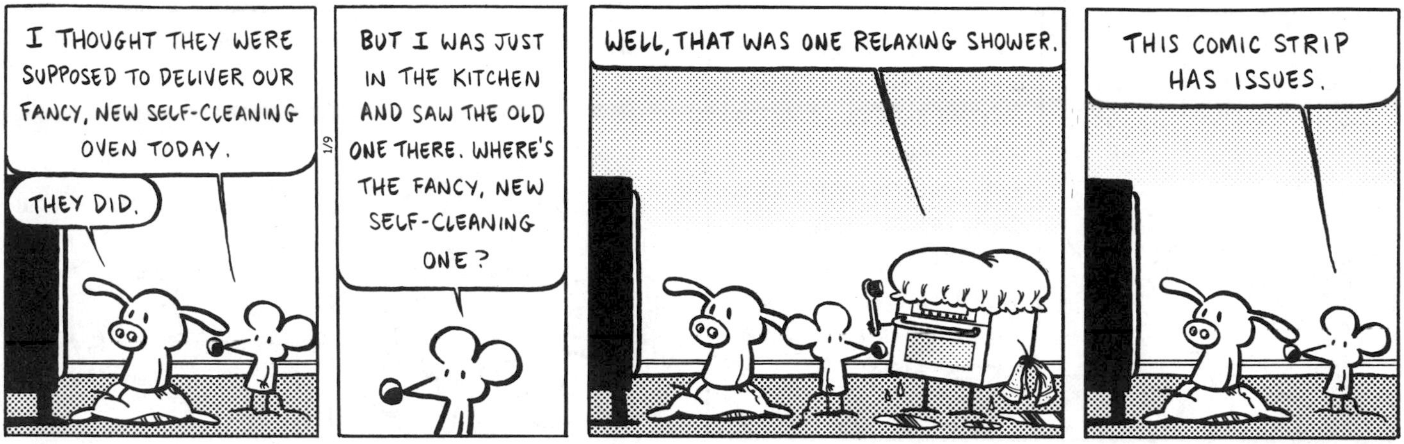
I THOUGHT THEY WERE SUPPOSED TO DELIVER OUR FANCY, NEW SELF-CLEANING OVEN TODAY.
THEY DID.
1/9
BUT I WAS JUST IN THE KITCHEN AND SAW THE OLD ONE THERE. WHERE'S THE FANCY, NEW SELF-CLEANING ONE?
WELL, THAT WAS ONE RELAXING SHOWER.
THIS COMIC STRIP HAS ISSUES.

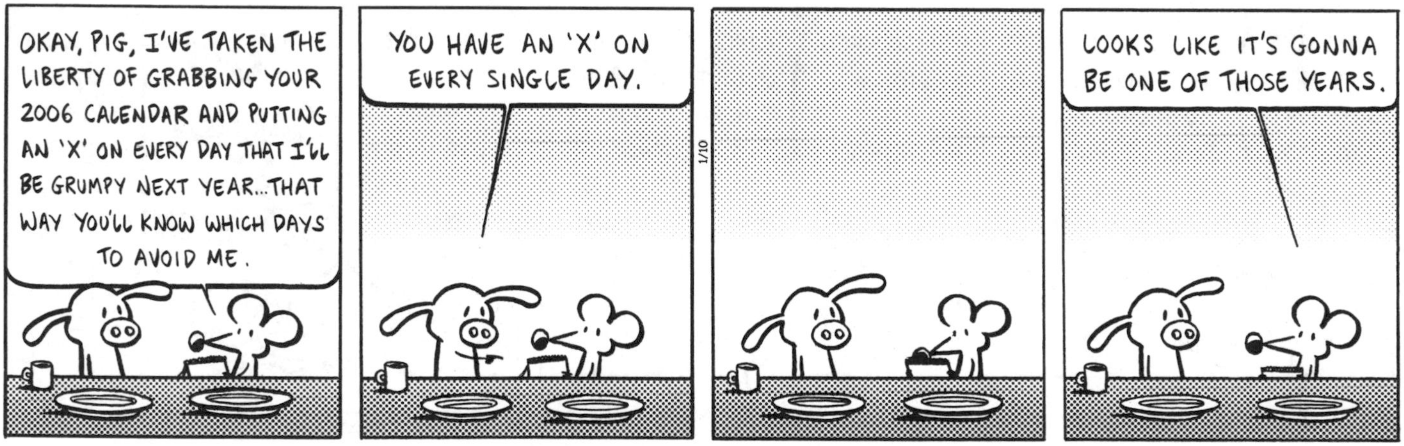
OKAY, PIG, I'VE TAKEN THE LIBERTY OF GRABBING YOUR 2006 CALENDAR AND PUTTING AN 'X' ON EVERY DAY THAT I'LL BE GRUMPY NEXT YEAR...THAT WAY YOU'LL KNOW WHICH DAYS TO AVOID ME.
YOU HAVE AN 'X' ON EVERY SINGLE DAY.
1/10
LOOKS LIKE IT'S GONNA BE ONE OF THOSE YEARS.

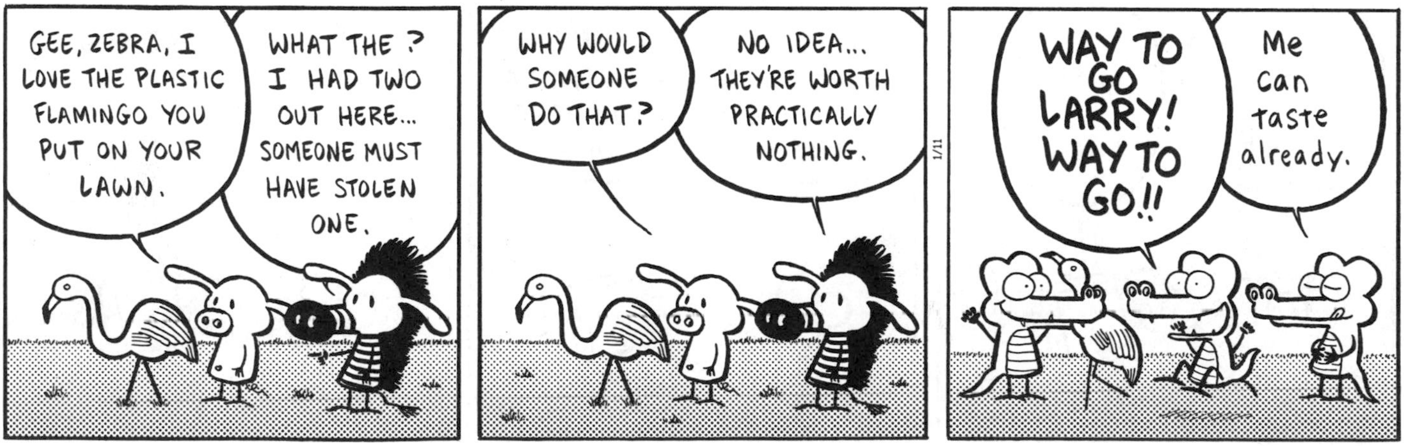
GEE, ZEBRA, I LOVE THE PLASTIC FLAMINGO YOU PUT ON YOUR LAWN.
WHAT THE? I HAD TWO OUT HERE... SOMEONE MUST HAVE STOLEN ONE.
WHY WOULD SOMEONE DO THAT?
NO IDEA... THEY'RE WORTH PRACTICALLY NOTHING.
1/11
WAY TO GO LARRY! WAY TO GO!!
Me can taste already.

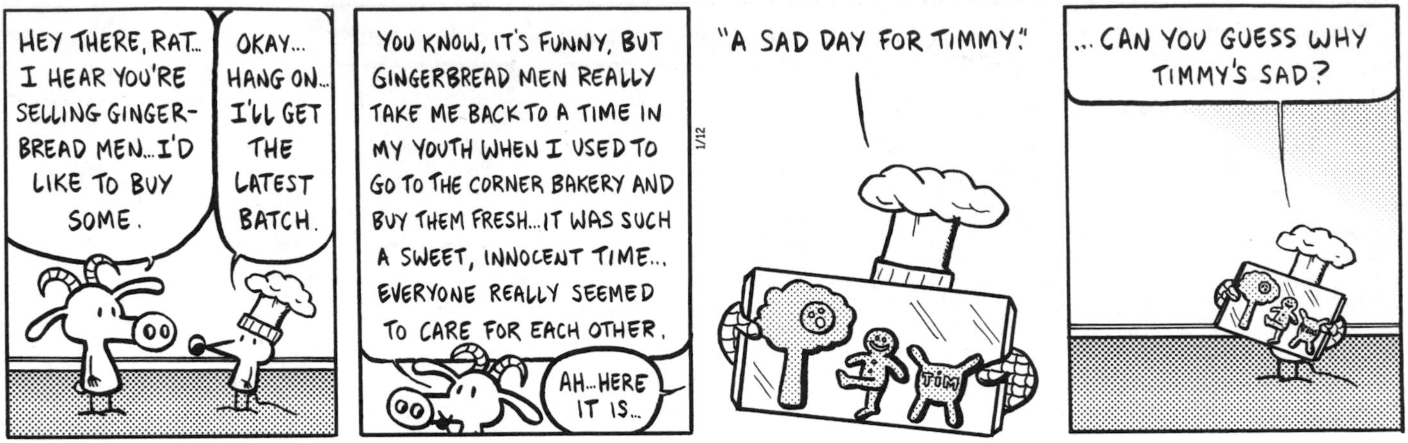
HEY THERE, RAT... I HEAR YOU'RE SELLING GINGER-BREAD MEN... I'D LIKE TO BUY SOME.
OKAY... HANG ON... I'LL GET THE LATEST BATCH.
YOU KNOW, IT'S FUNNY, BUT GINGERBREAD MEN REALLY TAKE ME BACK TO A TIME IN MY YOUTH WHEN I USED TO GO TO THE CORNER BAKERY AND BUY THEM FRESH... IT WAS SUCH A SWEET, INNOCENT TIME... EVERYONE REALLY SEEMED TO CARE FOR EACH OTHER.
AH... HERE IT IS...
1/12
"A SAD DAY FOR TIMMY."
TIM
... CAN YOU GUESS WHY TIMMY'S SAD?

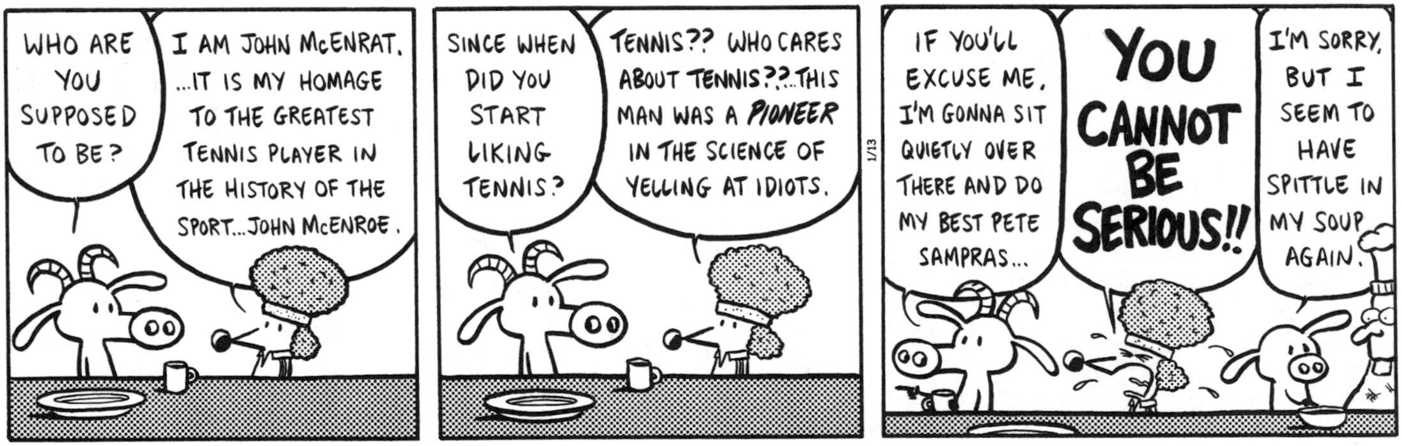
WHO ARE YOU SUPPOSED TO BE?
I AM JOHN McENRAT. ...IT IS MY HOMAGE TO THE GREATEST TENNIS PLAYER IN THE HISTORY OF THE SPORT... JOHN McENROE.
SINCE WHEN DID YOU START LIKING TENNIS?
TENNIS?? WHO CARES ABOUT TENNIS?? THIS MAN WAS A PIONEER IN THE SCIENCE OF YELLING AT IDIOTS.
1/13
IF YOU'LL EXCUSE ME, I'M GONNA SIT QUIETLY OVER THERE AND DO MY BEST PETE SAMPRAS...
YOU CANNOT BE SERIOUS!!
I'M SORRY, BUT I SEEM TO HAVE SPITTLE IN MY SOUP AGAIN.

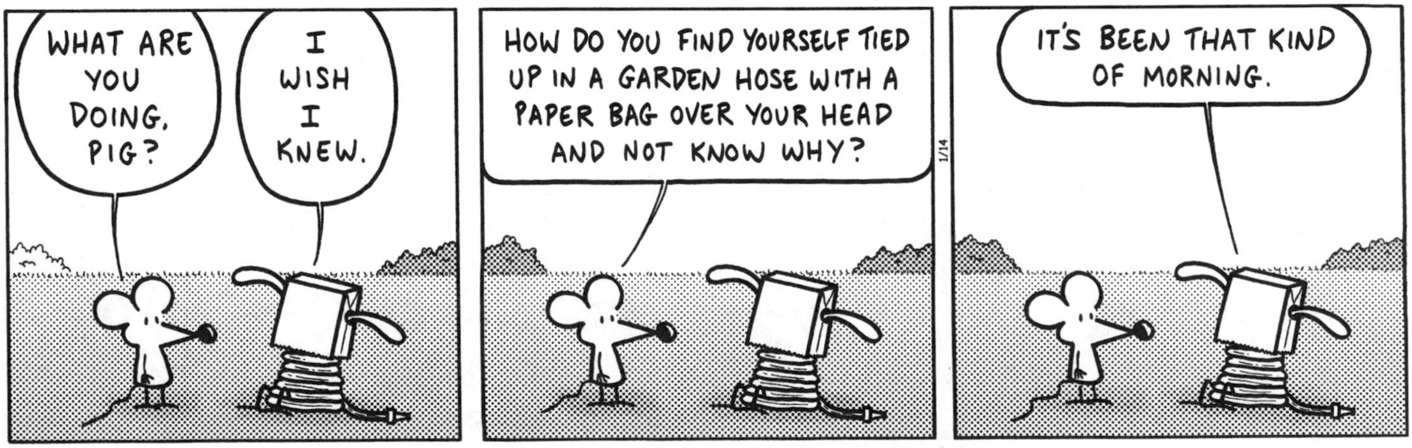
WHAT ARE YOU DOING, PIG?
I WISH I KNEW.
HOW DO YOU FIND YOURSELF TIED UP IN A GARDEN HOSE WITH A PAPER BAG OVER YOUR HEAD AND NOT KNOW WHY?
1/14
IT'S BEEN THAT KIND OF MORNING.

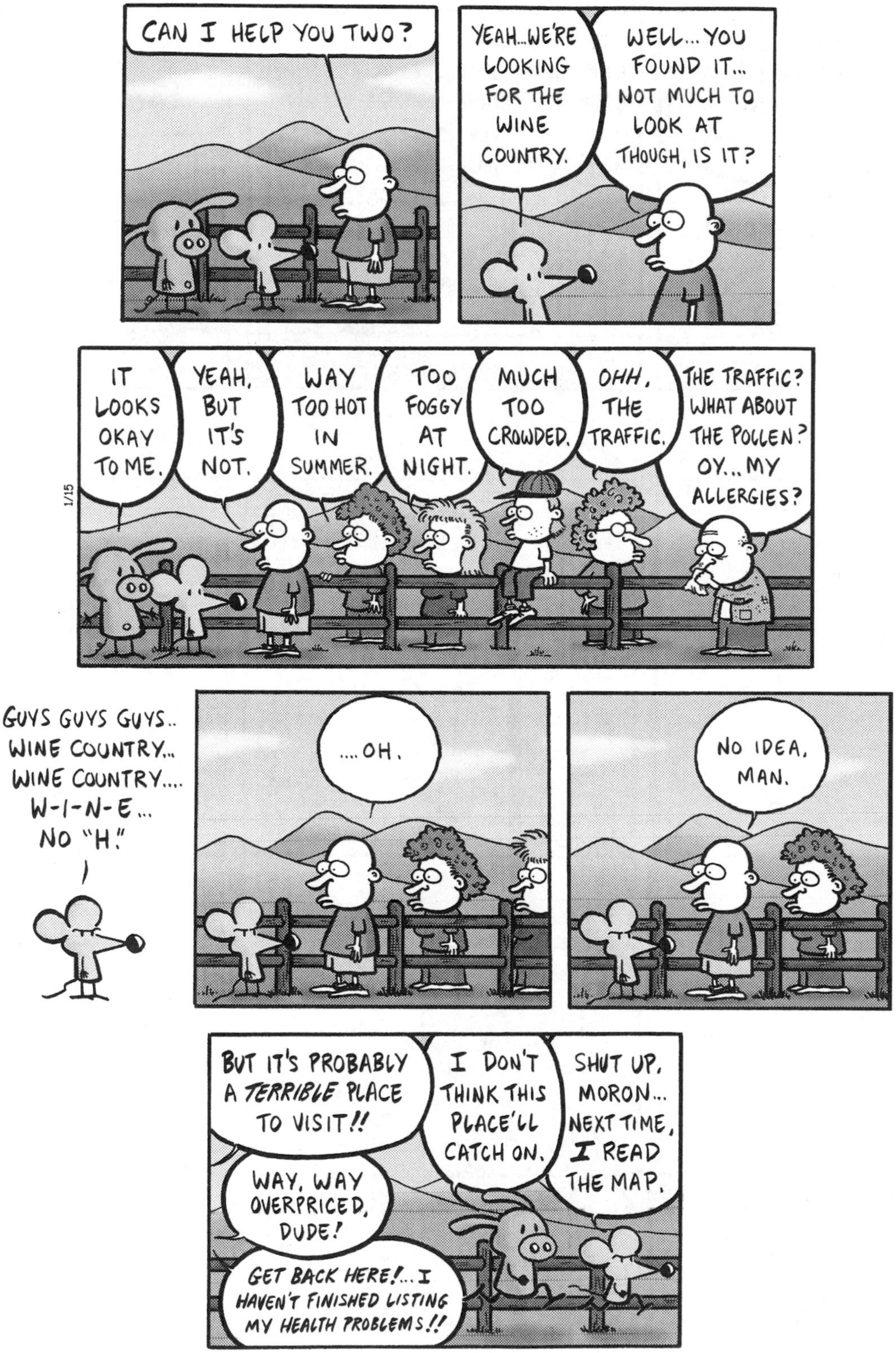
CAN I HELP YOU TWO?
YEAH...WE'RE LOOKING FOR THE WINE COUNTRY.
WELL... YOU FOUND IT... NOT MUCH TO LOOK AT THOUGH, IS IT?
IT LOOKS OKAY TO ME.
YEAH, BUT IT'S NOT.
WAY TOO HOT IN SUMMER.
TOO FOGGY AT NIGHT.
MUCH TOO CROWDED.
OHH, THE TRAFFIC.
THE TRAFFIC? WHAT ABOUT THE POLLEN? OY... MY ALLERGIES?
1/15
GUYS GUYS GUYS.. WINE COUNTRY... WINE COUNTRY.... W-I-N-E... NO "H."
....OH.
NO IDEA, MAN.
BUT IT'S PROBABLY A TERRIBLE PLACE TO VISIT!!
WAY, WAY OVERPRICED, DUDE!
GET BACK HERE!... I HAVEN'T FINISHED LISTING MY HEALTH PROBLEMS!!
I DON'T THINK THIS PLACE'LL CATCH ON.
SHUT UP, MORON... NEXT TIME, I READ THE MAP.

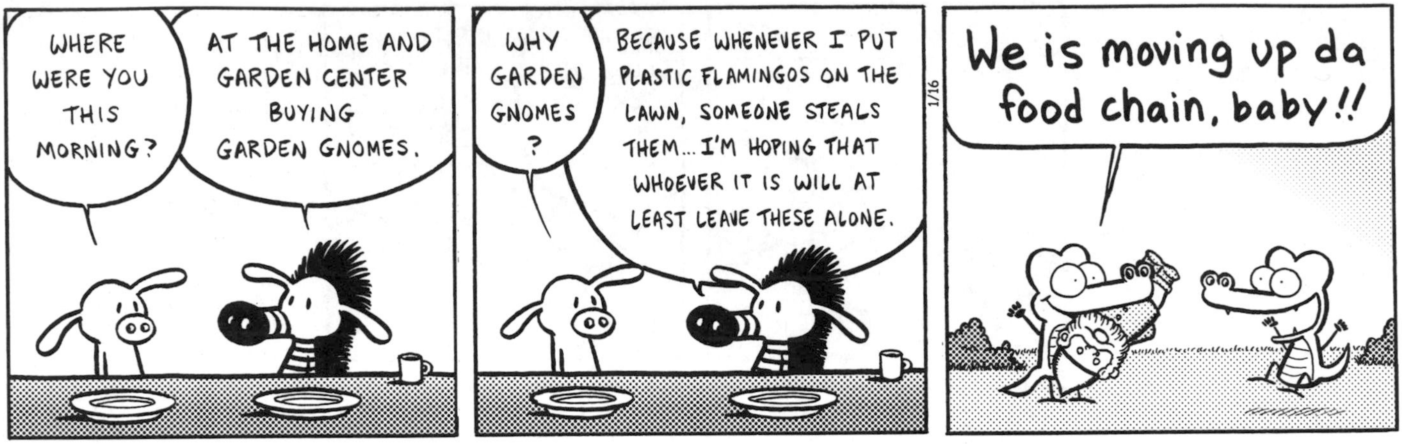

WHERE WERE YOU THIS MORNING?
AT THE HOME AND GARDEN CENTER BUYING GARDEN GNOMES.
WHY GARDEN GNOMES?
BECAUSE WHENEVER I PUT PLASTIC FLAMINGOS ON THE LAWN, SOMEONE STEALS THEM... I'M HOPING THAT WHOEVER IT IS WILL AT LEAST LEAVE THESE ALONE.
1/16
We is moving up da food chain, baby!!

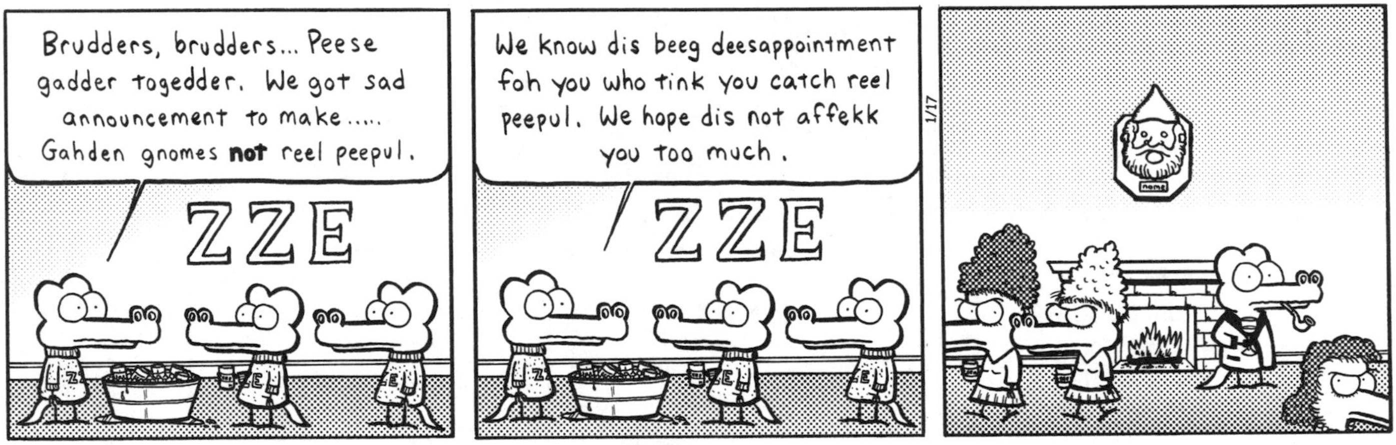

Brudders, brudders... Peese gadder togedder. We got sad announcement to make..... Gahden gnomes **not** reel peepul.
ZZE
We know dis beeg deesappointment foh you who tink you catch reel peepul. We hope dis not affekk you too much.
ZZE
1/17

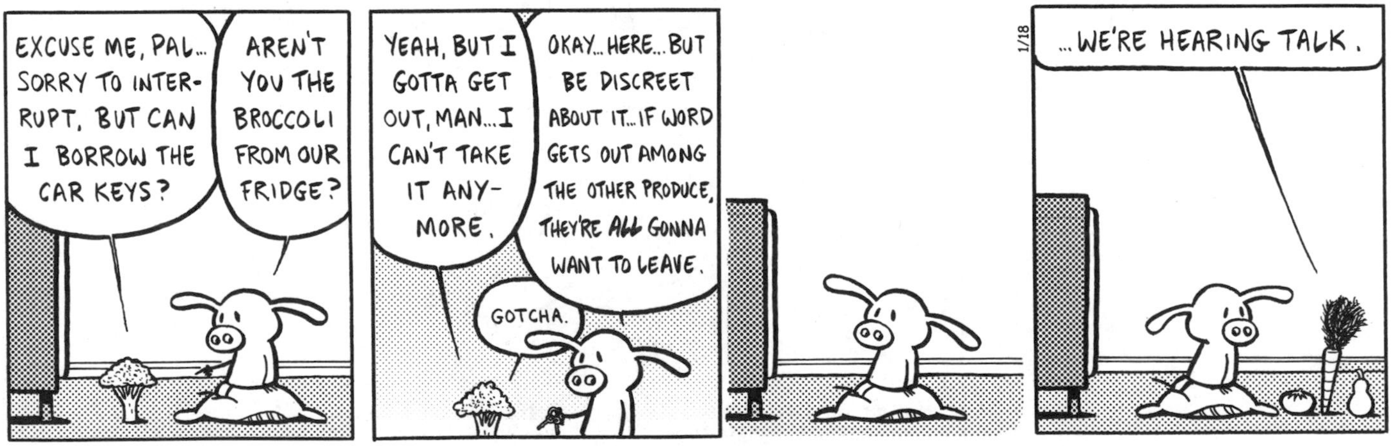

EXCUSE ME, PAL... SORRY TO INTER-RUPT, BUT CAN I BORROW THE CAR KEYS?
AREN'T YOU THE BROCCOLI FROM OUR FRIDGE?
YEAH, BUT I GOTTA GET OUT, MAN... I CAN'T TAKE IT ANY-MORE.
OKAY... HERE... BUT BE DISCREET ABOUT IT... IF WORD GETS OUT AMONG THE OTHER PRODUCE, THEY'RE **ALL** GONNA WANT TO LEAVE.
GOTCHA.
1/18
...WE'RE HEARING TALK.

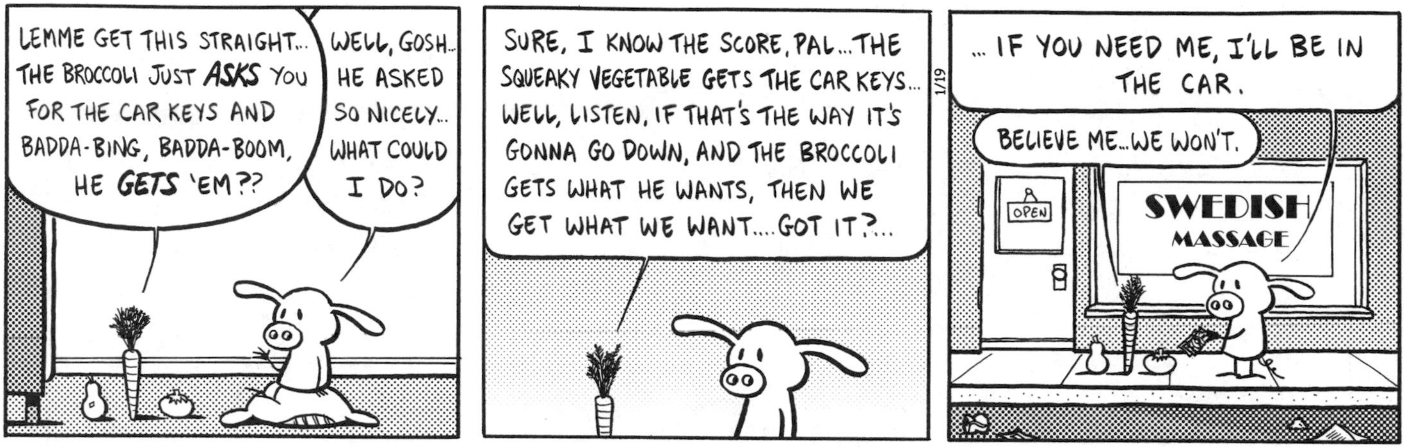
LEMME GET THIS STRAIGHT... THE BROCCOLI JUST ASKS YOU FOR THE CAR KEYS AND BADDA-BING, BADDA-BOOM, HE GETS 'EM??
WELL, GOSH... HE ASKED SO NICELY... WHAT COULD I DO?
SURE, I KNOW THE SCORE, PAL... THE SQUEAKY VEGETABLE GETS THE CAR KEYS... WELL, LISTEN, IF THAT'S THE WAY IT'S GONNA GO DOWN, AND THE BROCCOLI GETS WHAT HE WANTS, THEN WE GET WHAT WE WANT.... GOT IT?...
1/19
... IF YOU NEED ME, I'LL BE IN THE CAR.
BELIEVE ME... WE WON'T.
OPEN
SWEDISH
MASSAGE

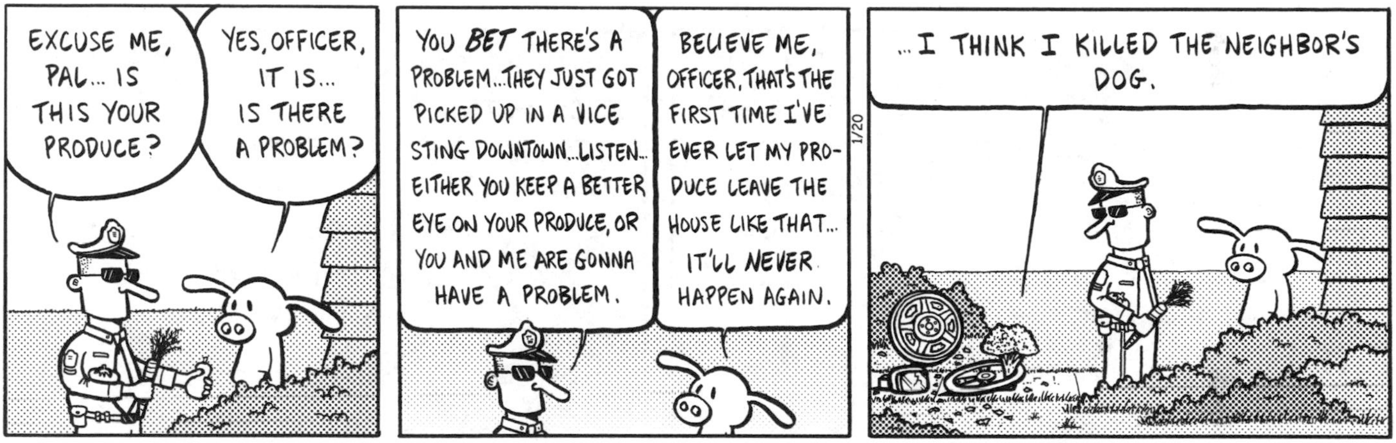
EXCUSE ME, PAL... IS THIS YOUR PRODUCE?
YES, OFFICER, IT IS... IS THERE A PROBLEM?
YOU BET THERE'S A PROBLEM... THEY JUST GOT PICKED UP IN A VICE STING DOWNTOWN... LISTEN... EITHER YOU KEEP A BETTER EYE ON YOUR PRODUCE, OR YOU AND ME ARE GONNA HAVE A PROBLEM.
BELIEVE ME, OFFICER, THAT'S THE FIRST TIME I'VE EVER LET MY PRODUCE LEAVE THE HOUSE LIKE THAT... IT'LL NEVER HAPPEN AGAIN.
1/20
... I THINK I KILLED THE NEIGHBOR'S DOG.

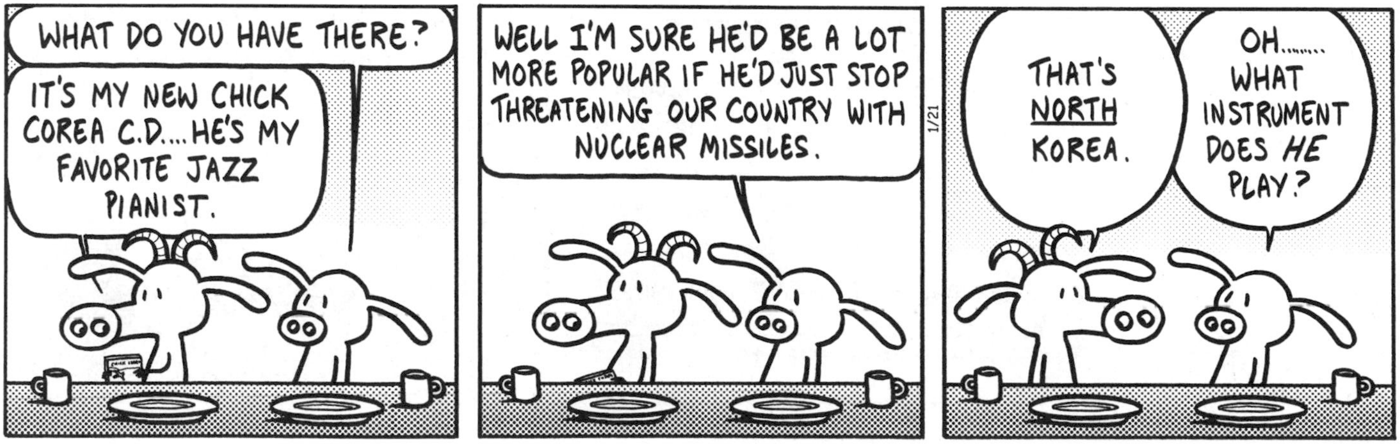
WHAT DO YOU HAVE THERE?
IT'S MY NEW CHICK COREA C.D.... HE'S MY FAVORITE JAZZ PIANIST.
WELL I'M SURE HE'D BE A LOT MORE POPULAR IF HE'D JUST STOP THREATENING OUR COUNTRY WITH NUCLEAR MISSILES.
1/21
THAT'S NORTH KOREA.
OH........ WHAT INSTRUMENT DOES HE PLAY?

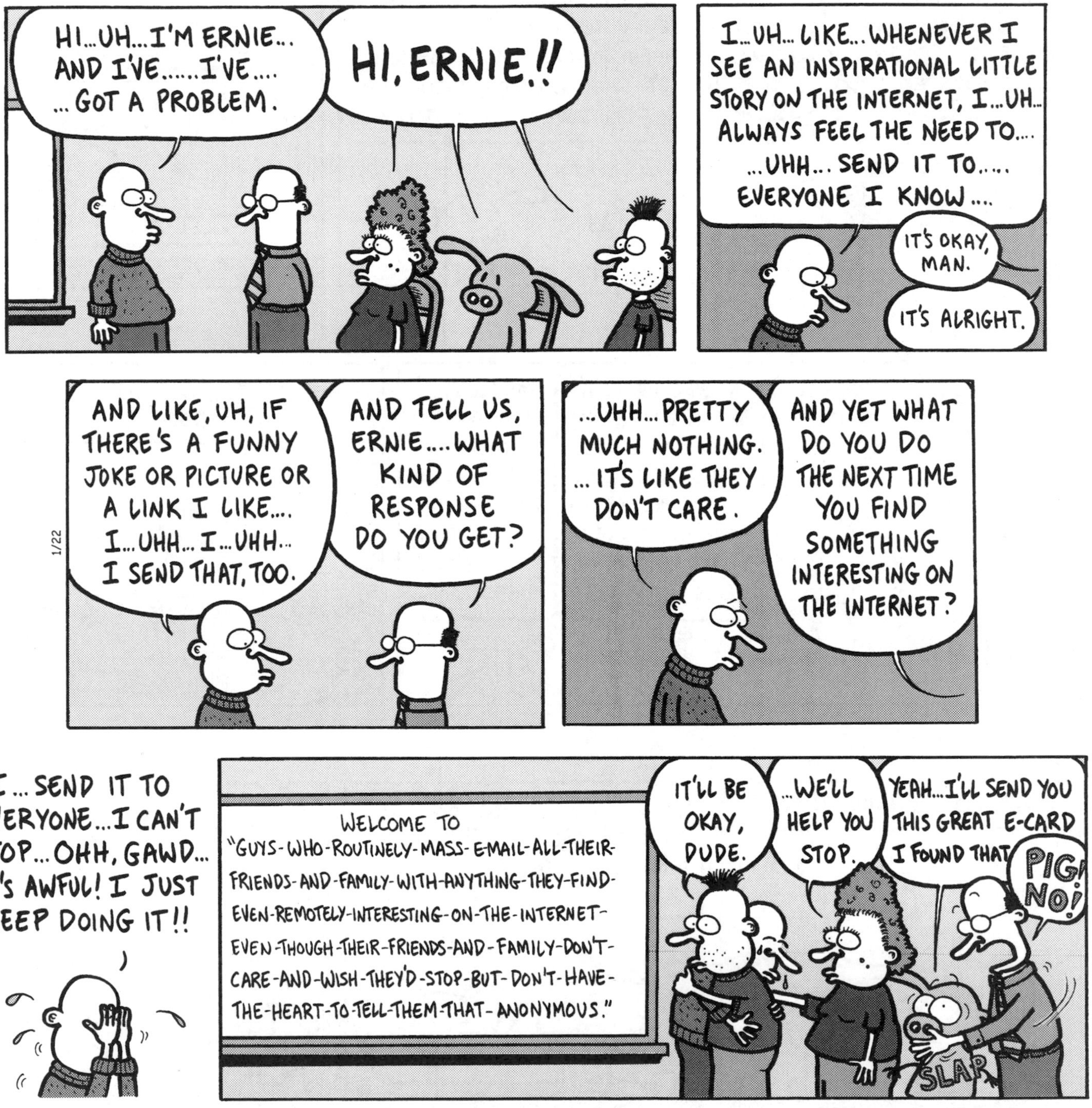
HI...UH...I'M ERNIE... AND I'VE......I'VE.... ...GOT A PROBLEM.
HI, ERNIE!!
I...UH... LIKE... WHENEVER I SEE AN INSPIRATIONAL LITTLE STORY ON THE INTERNET, I...UH... ALWAYS FEEL THE NEED TO.... ...UHH... SEND IT TO..... EVERYONE I KNOW....
IT'S OKAY, MAN.
IT'S ALRIGHT.
1/22
AND LIKE, UH, IF THERE'S A FUNNY JOKE OR PICTURE OR A LINK I LIKE.... I...UHH... I...UHH... I SEND THAT, TOO.
AND TELL US, ERNIE.... WHAT KIND OF RESPONSE DO YOU GET?
...UHH... PRETTY MUCH NOTHING. ...IT'S LIKE THEY DON'T CARE.
AND YET WHAT DO YOU DO THE NEXT TIME YOU FIND SOMETHING INTERESTING ON THE INTERNET?
I... SEND IT TO EVERYONE...I CAN'T STOP...OHH, GAWD... IT'S AWFUL! I JUST KEEP DOING IT!!
WELCOME TO "GUYS-WHO-ROUTINELY-MASS-E-MAIL-ALL-THEIR-FRIENDS-AND-FAMILY-WITH-ANYTHING-THEY-FIND-EVEN-REMOTELY-INTERESTING-ON-THE-INTERNET-EVEN-THOUGH-THEIR-FRIENDS-AND-FAMILY-DON'T-CARE-AND-WISH-THEY'D-STOP-BUT-DON'T-HAVE-THE-HEART-TO-TELL-THEM-THAT-ANONYMOUS."
IT'LL BE OKAY, DUDE.
...WE'LL HELP YOU STOP.
YEAH...I'LL SEND YOU THIS GREAT E-CARD I FOUND THAT
PIG! NO!
SLAP

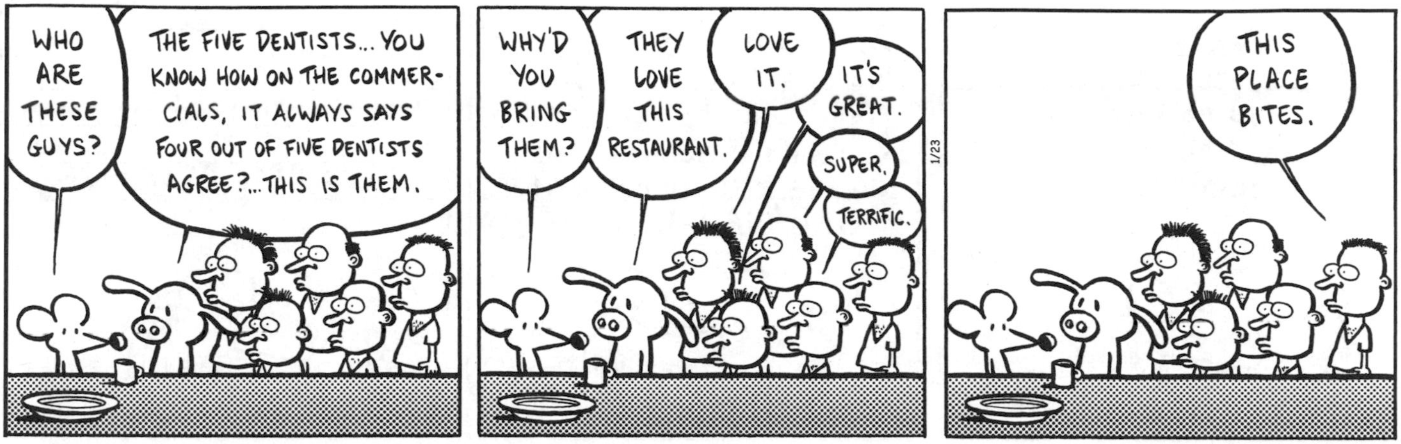
WHO ARE THESE GUYS?
THE FIVE DENTISTS... YOU KNOW HOW ON THE COMMERCIALS, IT ALWAYS SAYS FOUR OUT OF FIVE DENTISTS AGREE?... THIS IS THEM.
WHY'D YOU BRING THEM?
THEY LOVE THIS RESTAURANT.
LOVE IT.
IT'S GREAT.
SUPER.
TERRIFIC.
THIS PLACE BITES.
1/23

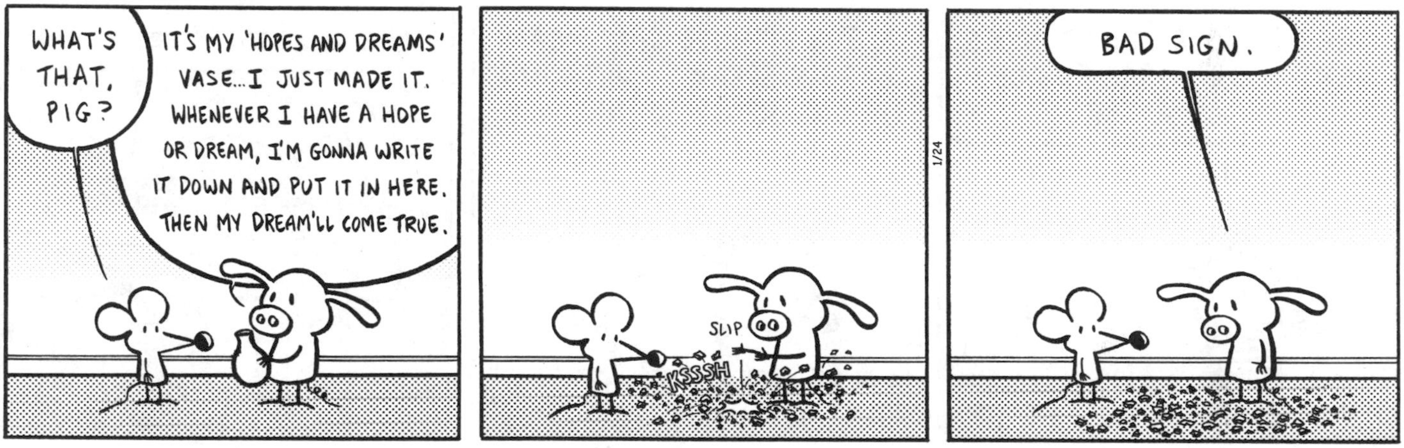
WHAT'S THAT, PIG?
IT'S MY 'HOPES AND DREAMS' VASE... I JUST MADE IT. WHENEVER I HAVE A HOPE OR DREAM, I'M GONNA WRITE IT DOWN AND PUT IT IN HERE. THEN MY DREAM'LL COME TRUE.
SLIP
KSSSH
BAD SIGN.
1/24

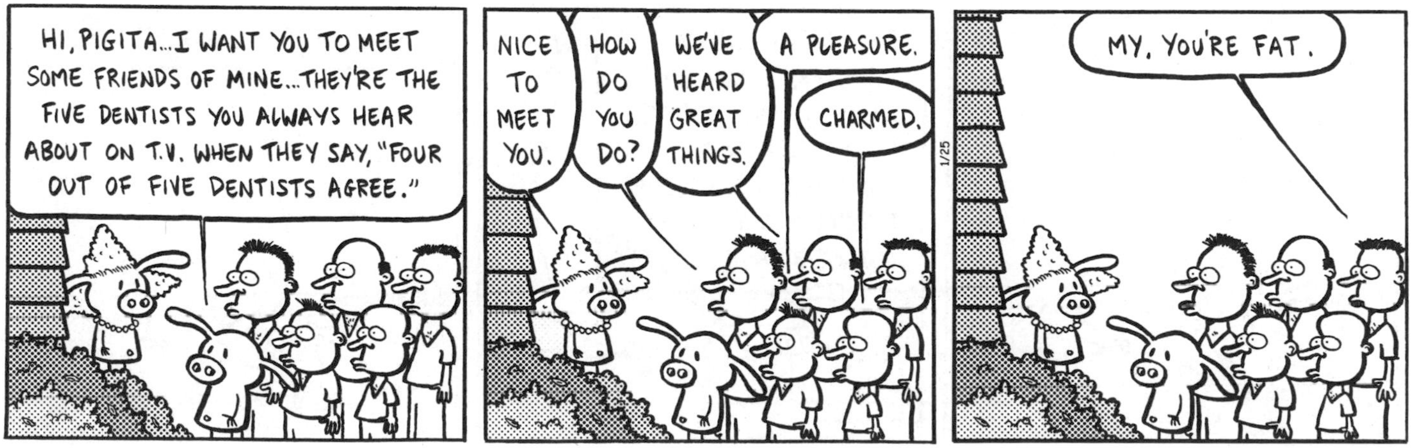
HI, PIGITA... I WANT YOU TO MEET SOME FRIENDS OF MINE... THEY'RE THE FIVE DENTISTS YOU ALWAYS HEAR ABOUT ON T.V. WHEN THEY SAY, "FOUR OUT OF FIVE DENTISTS AGREE."
NICE TO MEET YOU.
HOW DO YOU DO?
WE'VE HEARD GREAT THINGS.
A PLEASURE.
CHARMED.
MY, YOU'RE FAT.
1/25

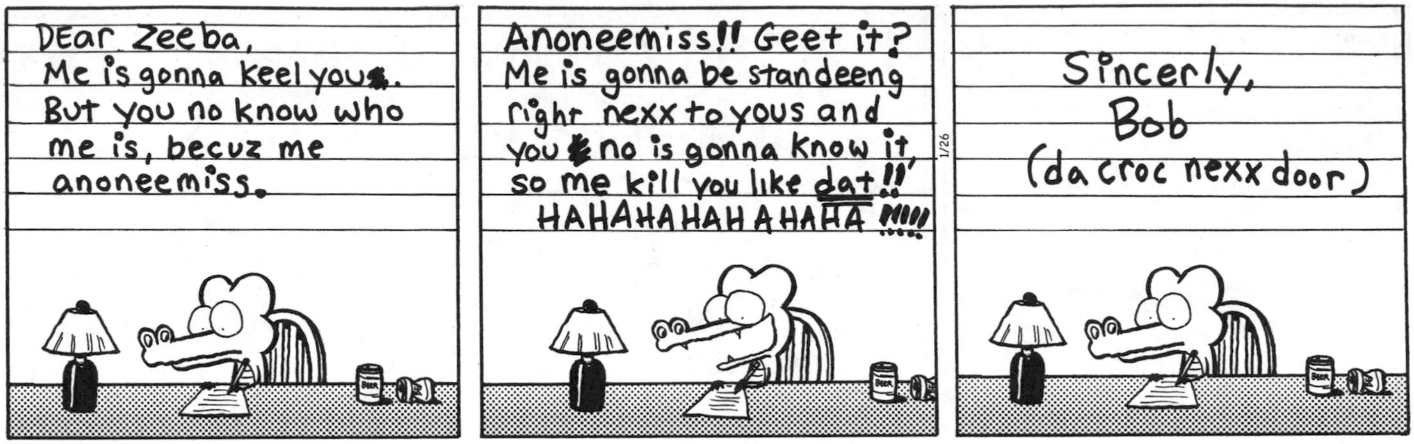
Dear Zeeba,
Me is gonna keel you.
But you no know who me is, becuz me anoneemiss.
Anoneemiss!! Geet it?
Me is gonna be standeeng right nexx to yous and you no is gonna know it, so me kill you like dat!!
HAHAHAHAHAHAHA!!!!!
Sincerly,
Bob
(da croc nexx door)
1/26

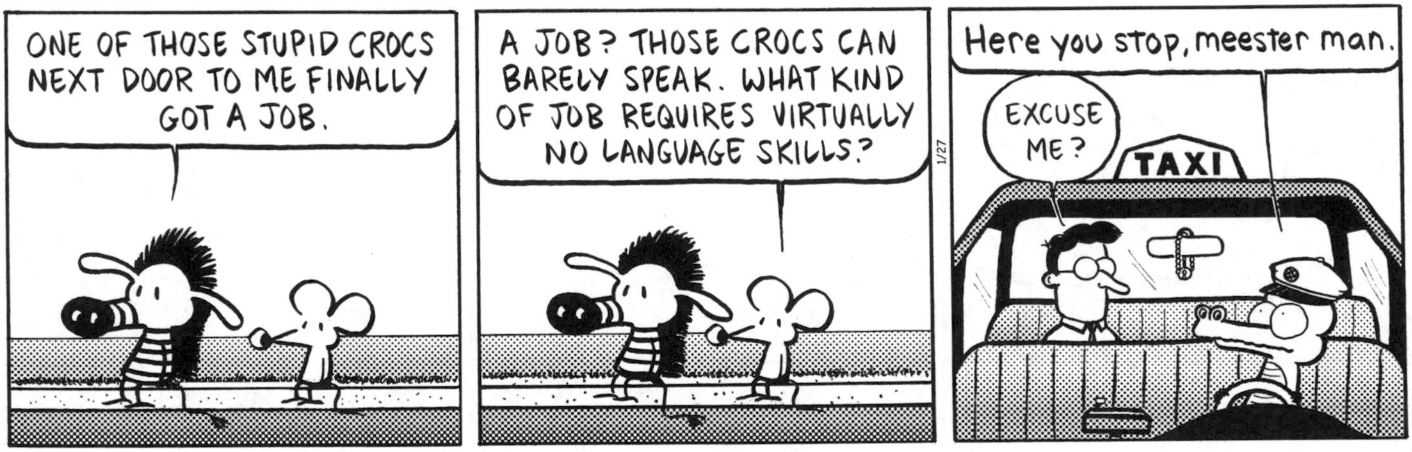
ONE OF THOSE STUPID CROCS NEXT DOOR TO ME FINALLY GOT A JOB.
A JOB? THOSE CROCS CAN BARELY SPEAK. WHAT KIND OF JOB REQUIRES VIRTUALLY NO LANGUAGE SKILLS?
Here you stop, meester man.
EXCUSE ME?
TAXI
1/27

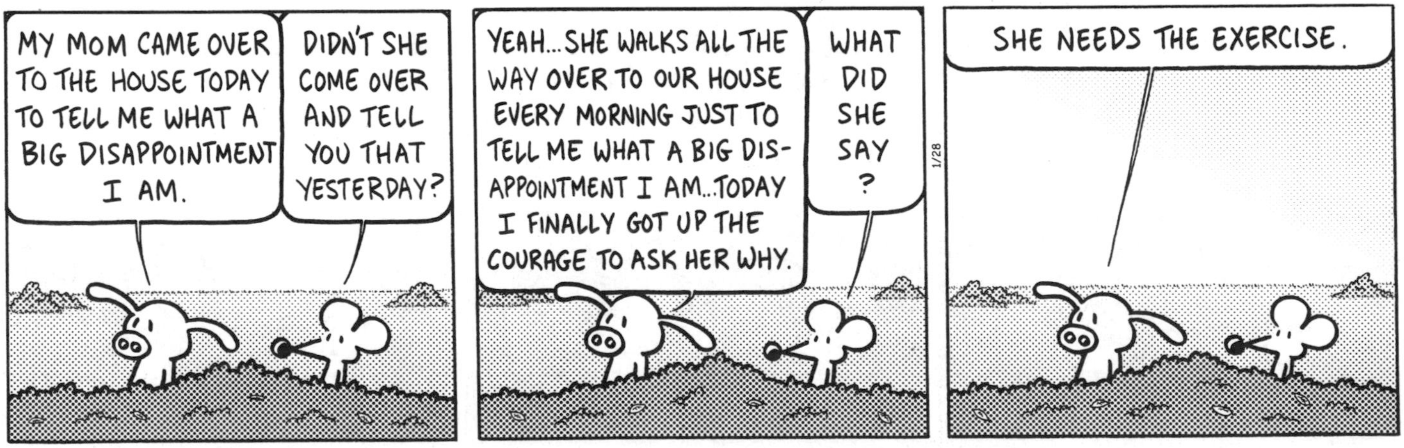
MY MOM CAME OVER TO THE HOUSE TODAY TO TELL ME WHAT A BIG DISAPPOINTMENT I AM.
DIDN'T SHE COME OVER AND TELL YOU THAT YESTERDAY?
YEAH...SHE WALKS ALL THE WAY OVER TO OUR HOUSE EVERY MORNING JUST TO TELL ME WHAT A BIG DIS-APPOINTMENT I AM...TODAY I FINALLY GOT UP THE COURAGE TO ASK HER WHY.
WHAT DID SHE SAY?
SHE NEEDS THE EXERCISE.
1/28

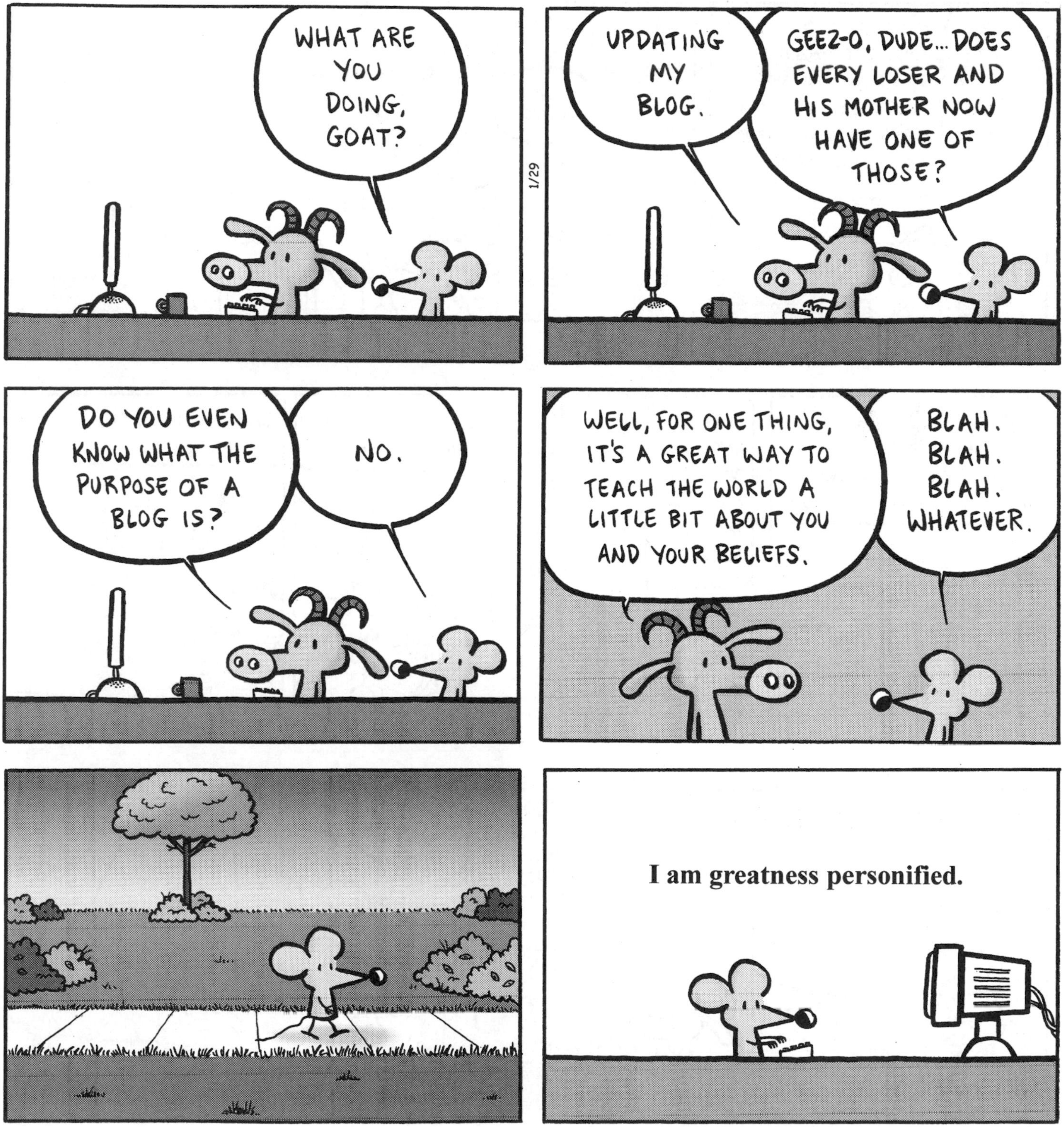
WHAT ARE YOU DOING, GOAT?
1/29
UPDATING MY BLOG.
GEEZ-O, DUDE... DOES EVERY LOSER AND HIS MOTHER NOW HAVE ONE OF THOSE?
DO YOU EVEN KNOW WHAT THE PURPOSE OF A BLOG IS?
NO.
WELL, FOR ONE THING, IT'S A GREAT WAY TO TEACH THE WORLD A LITTLE BIT ABOUT YOU AND YOUR BELIEFS.
BLAH. BLAH. BLAH. WHATEVER.
I am greatness personified.

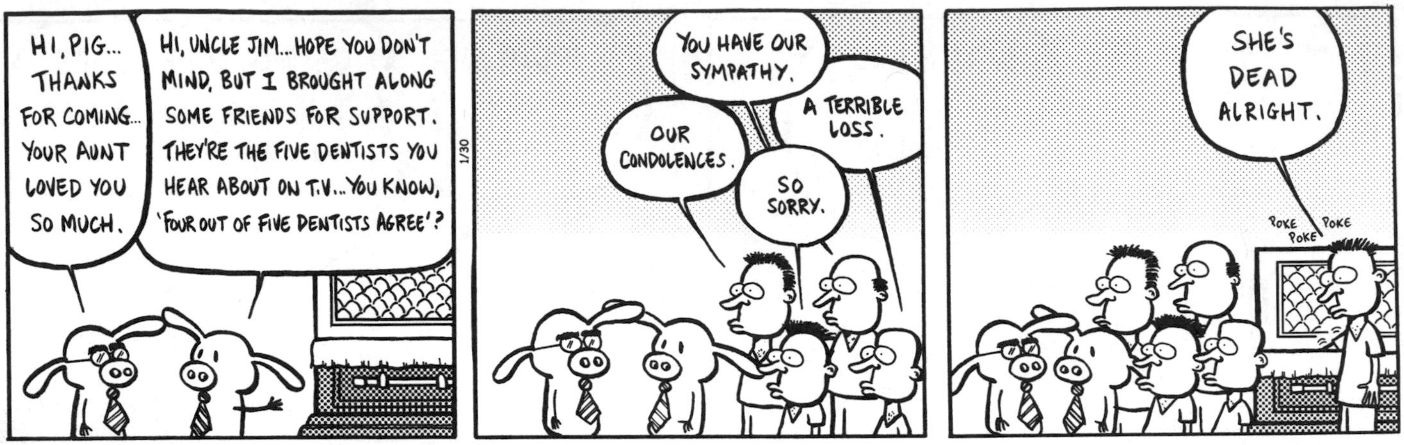
HI, PIG... THANKS FOR COMING... YOUR AUNT LOVED YOU SO MUCH.
HI, UNCLE JIM... HOPE YOU DON'T MIND, BUT I BROUGHT ALONG SOME FRIENDS FOR SUPPORT. THEY'RE THE FIVE DENTISTS YOU HEAR ABOUT ON T.V... YOU KNOW, 'FOUR OUT OF FIVE DENTISTS AGREE'?
1/30
YOU HAVE OUR SYMPATHY.
OUR CONDOLENCES.
A TERRIBLE LOSS.
SO SORRY.
SHE'S DEAD ALRIGHT.
POKE POKE POKE

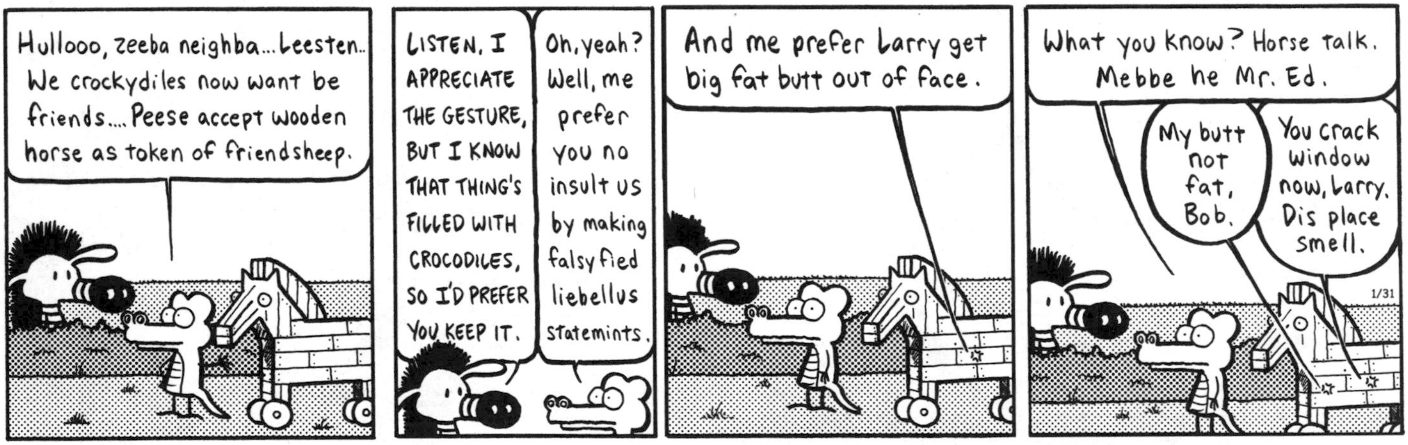
Hullooo, zeeba neighba... Leesten.. We crockydiles now want be friends.... Peese accept wooden horse as token of friendsheep.
LISTEN, I APPRECIATE THE GESTURE, BUT I KNOW THAT THING'S FILLED WITH CROCODILES, SO I'D PREFER YOU KEEP IT.
Oh, yeah? Well, me prefer you no insult us by making falsy fied liebellus statemints.
And me prefer Larry get big fat butt out of face.
What you know? Horse talk. Mebbe he Mr. Ed.
My butt not fat, Bob.
You crack window now, Larry. Dis place smell.
1/31

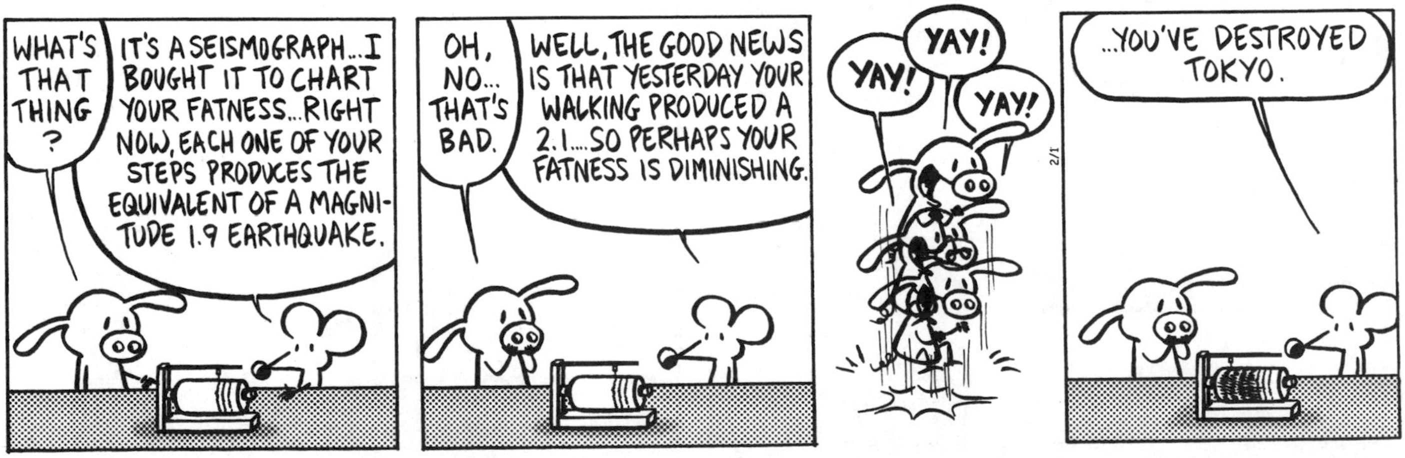
WHAT'S THAT THING?
IT'S A SEISMOGRAPH... I BOUGHT IT TO CHART YOUR FATNESS... RIGHT NOW, EACH ONE OF YOUR STEPS PRODUCES THE EQUIVALENT OF A MAGNITUDE 1.9 EARTHQUAKE.
OH, NO... THAT'S BAD.
WELL, THE GOOD NEWS IS THAT YESTERDAY YOUR WALKING PRODUCED A 2.1.... SO PERHAPS YOUR FATNESS IS DIMINISHING.
YAY!
YAY!
YAY!
2/1
...YOU'VE DESTROYED TOKYO.

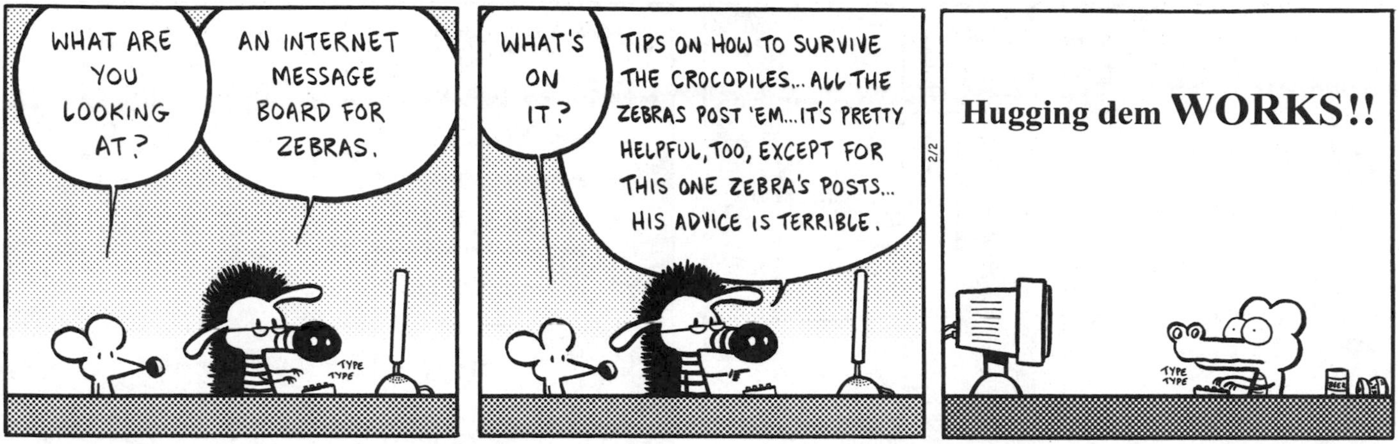
WHAT ARE YOU LOOKING AT?
AN INTERNET MESSAGE BOARD FOR ZEBRAS.
TYPE TYPE
WHAT'S ON IT?
TIPS ON HOW TO SURVIVE THE CROCODILES... ALL THE ZEBRAS POST 'EM... IT'S PRETTY HELPFUL, TOO, EXCEPT FOR THIS ONE ZEBRA'S POSTS... HIS ADVICE IS TERRIBLE.
2/2
Hugging dem WORKS!!
TYPE TYPE

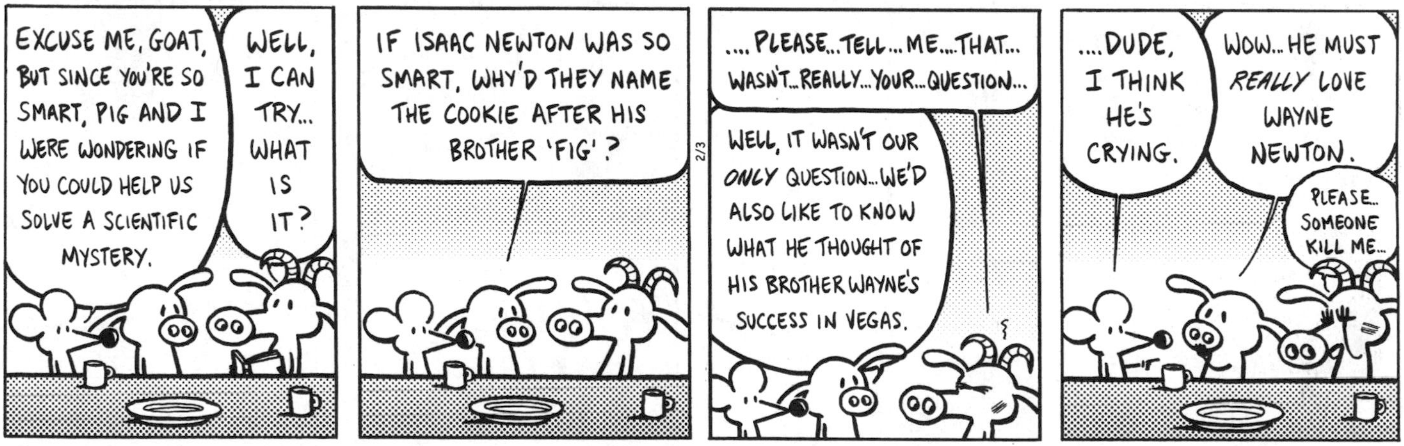
EXCUSE ME, GOAT, BUT SINCE YOU'RE SO SMART, PIG AND I WERE WONDERING IF YOU COULD HELP US SOLVE A SCIENTIFIC MYSTERY.
WELL, I CAN TRY... WHAT IS IT?
IF ISAAC NEWTON WAS SO SMART, WHY'D THEY NAME THE COOKIE AFTER HIS BROTHER 'FIG'?
2/3
.... PLEASE... TELL... ME... THAT... WASN'T... REALLY... YOUR... QUESTION...
WELL, IT WASN'T OUR *ONLY* QUESTION... WE'D ALSO LIKE TO KNOW WHAT HE THOUGHT OF HIS BROTHER WAYNE'S SUCCESS IN VEGAS.
.... DUDE, I THINK HE'S CRYING.
WOW... HE MUST *REALLY* LOVE WAYNE NEWTON.
PLEASE... SOMEONE KILL ME...

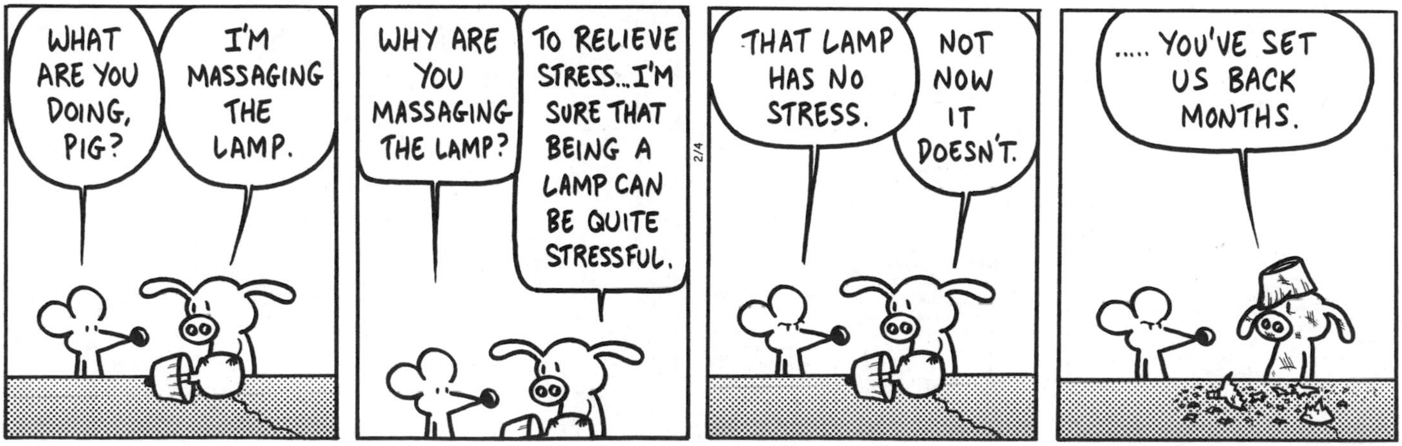
WHAT ARE YOU DOING, PIG?
I'M MASSAGING THE LAMP.
WHY ARE YOU MASSAGING THE LAMP?
TO RELIEVE STRESS... I'M SURE THAT BEING A LAMP CAN BE QUITE STRESSFUL.
2/4
THAT LAMP HAS NO STRESS.
NOT NOW IT DOESN'T.
..... YOU'VE SET US BACK MONTHS.

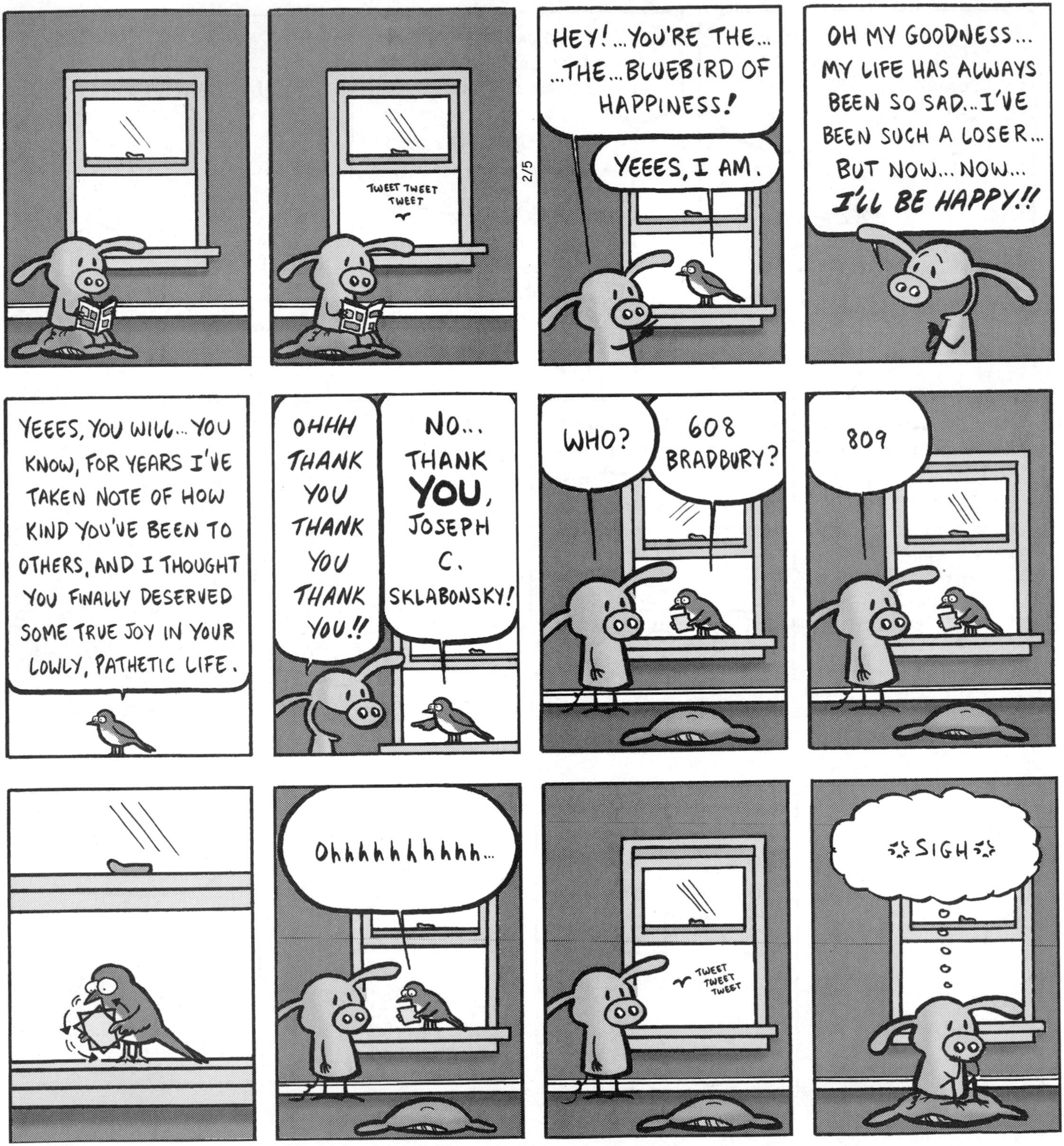
TWEET TWEET TWEET
HEY! ...YOU'RE THE... ...THE... BLUEBIRD OF HAPPINESS!
YEEES, I AM.
OH MY GOODNESS... MY LIFE HAS ALWAYS BEEN SO SAD... I'VE BEEN SUCH A LOSER... BUT NOW... NOW... I'LL BE HAPPY!!
YEEES, YOU WILL... YOU KNOW, FOR YEARS I'VE TAKEN NOTE OF HOW KIND YOU'VE BEEN TO OTHERS, AND I THOUGHT YOU FINALLY DESERVED SOME TRUE JOY IN YOUR LOWLY, PATHETIC LIFE.
OHHH THANK YOU THANK YOU THANK YOU!!
NO... THANK YOU, JOSEPH C. SKLABONSKY!
WHO?
608 BRADBURY?
809
Ohhhhhhhhhh...
TWEET TWEET TWEET
SIGH

WHAT ARE YOU DOING, PIG?

STANDING GUARD...I'VE BEEN UP THREE STRAIGHT NIGHTS...YOU SEE, ELEVEN YEARS AGO, I GOT INTO A TERRIBLE FIGHT WITH A SEA ANEMONE, THE DETAILS OF WHICH ARE TOO PAINFUL TO RECOUNT, AND THIS IS THE YEAR HE SWORE TO GET HIS REVENGE... ...I FEEL HE IS NEAR.

OKAY, DUDE...YOUR SAD LITTLE CRANIUM HAS MORPHED INTO A DELUSIONAL FUNHOUSE....GET SOME SLEEP...NOW.

OKAY...

AT LAST.

WELL, DUDE, AREN'T YOU GLAD YOU GOT SOME SLEEP LAST NIGHT AND STOPPED WORRYING ABOUT YOUR FICTIONAL SEA ANEMONE ENEMY?

I SURE AM...IT'S WEIRD HOW YOUR FEARS CAN GET THE BETTER OF YOU...NOW I CAN LOOK BACK AND LAUGH.

KEEP LAUGHING DEAD MAN

Warmest regards,
The Anemone

THAT'S TROUBLING.

KEEP LAUGHING DEAD MAN

Warmest regards,
The Anemone

Dear Mr. Head of Homeland Security Guy,
You are protecting our land against terrorists and spying on the books people take out of libraries.

But what about sea anemones?...Is anyone watching the books THEY take out of libraries?

P.S. I only ask because one of them is trying to kill me. ☹

WHAT HAS HAPPENED TO YOU? HAVE YOU LOST ALL TOUCH WITH REALITY? GIMME THAT BEFORE YOU GET YOURSELF COMMITTED.

RIP

RIP
RIP

...IT'S FOR A FRIEND.

KILLING PIGS FOR DUMMIES

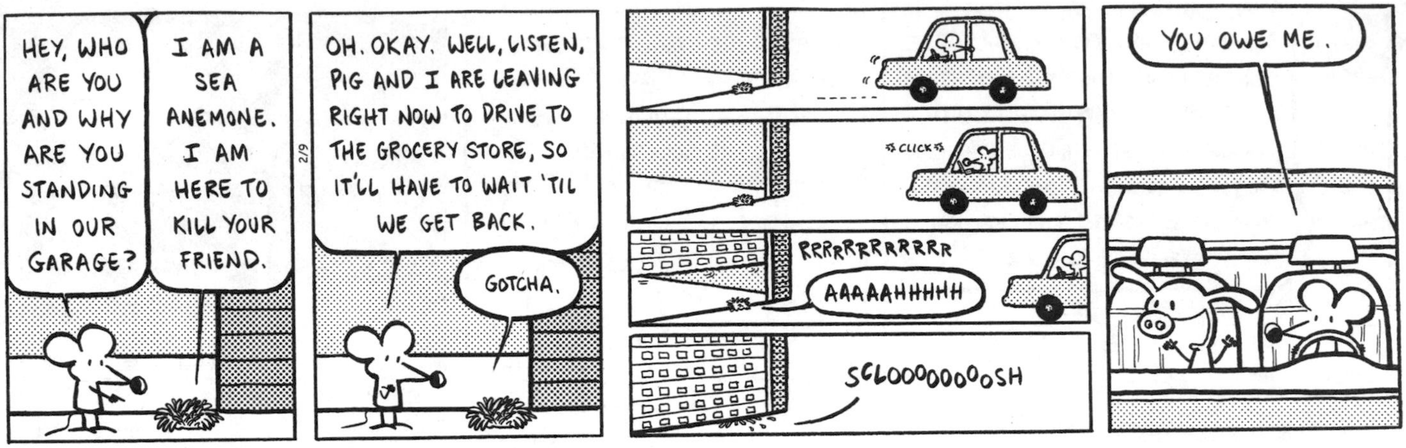
HEY, WHO ARE YOU AND WHY ARE YOU STANDING IN OUR GARAGE?
I AM A SEA ANEMONE. I AM HERE TO KILL YOUR FRIEND.
2/9
OH. OKAY. WELL, LISTEN, PIG AND I ARE LEAVING RIGHT NOW TO DRIVE TO THE GROCERY STORE, SO IT'LL HAVE TO WAIT 'TIL WE GET BACK.
GOTCHA.
CLICK
RRRRRRRRRRRR
AAAAAHHHHH
SCLOOOOOOOOSH
YOU OWE ME.

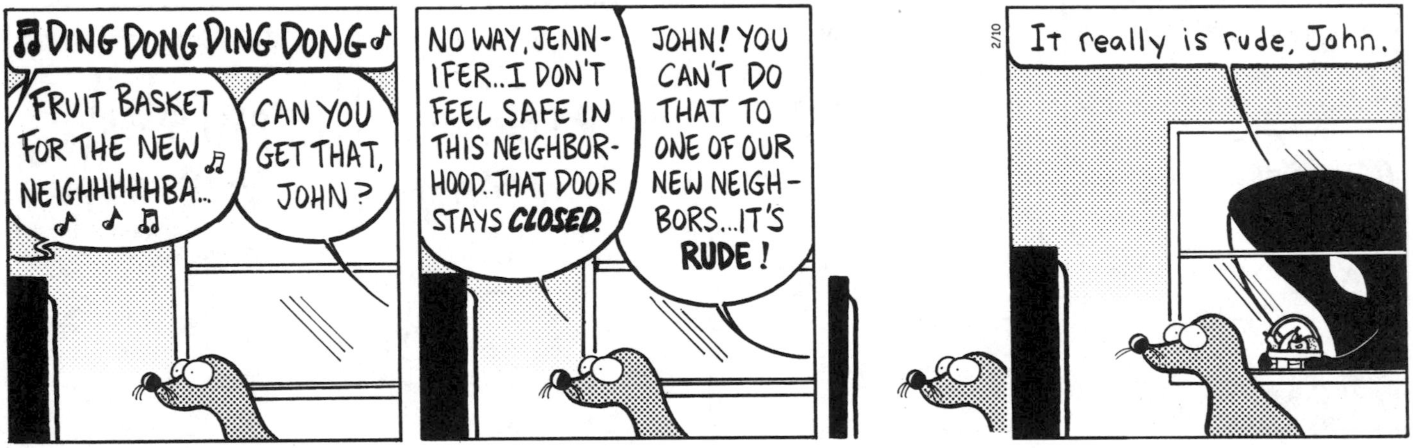
DING DONG DING DONG
FRUIT BASKET FOR THE NEW NEIGHHHHHBA...
CAN YOU GET THAT, JOHN?
NO WAY, JENNIFER...I DON'T FEEL SAFE IN THIS NEIGHBORHOOD..THAT DOOR STAYS CLOSED.
JOHN! YOU CAN'T DO THAT TO ONE OF OUR NEW NEIGHBORS...IT'S RUDE!
2/10
It really is rude, John.

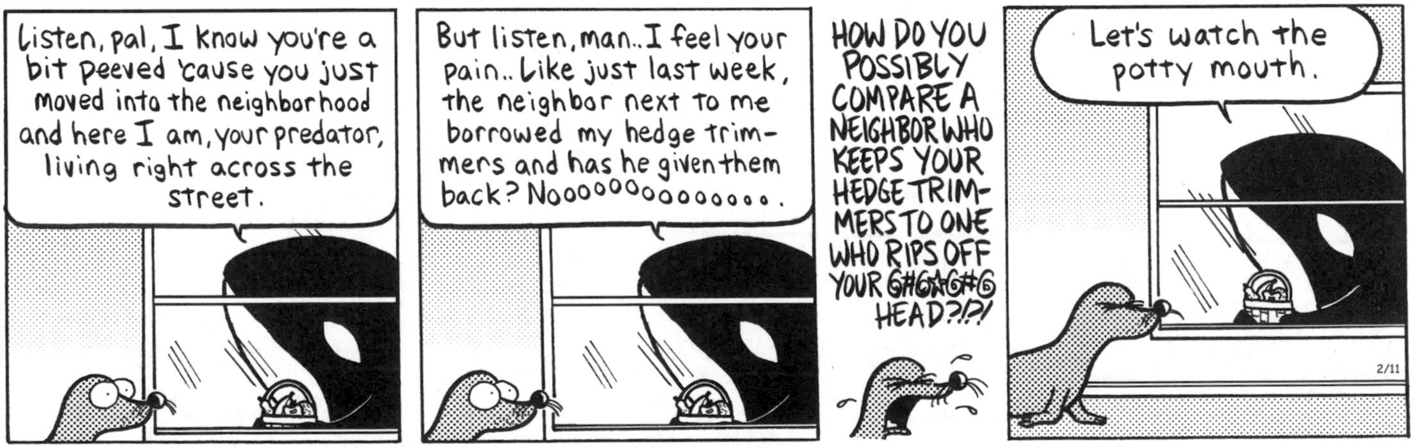
Listen, pal, I know you're a bit peeved 'cause you just moved into the neighborhood and here I am, your predator, living right across the street.
But listen, man.. I feel your pain.. Like just last week, the neighbor next to me borrowed my hedge trimmers and has he given them back? Nooooooooooooooo.
HOW DO YOU POSSIBLY COMPARE A NEIGHBOR WHO KEEPS YOUR HEDGE TRIMMERS TO ONE WHO RIPS OFF YOUR G#6AG#6 HEAD?!?!
Let's watch the potty mouth.
2/11

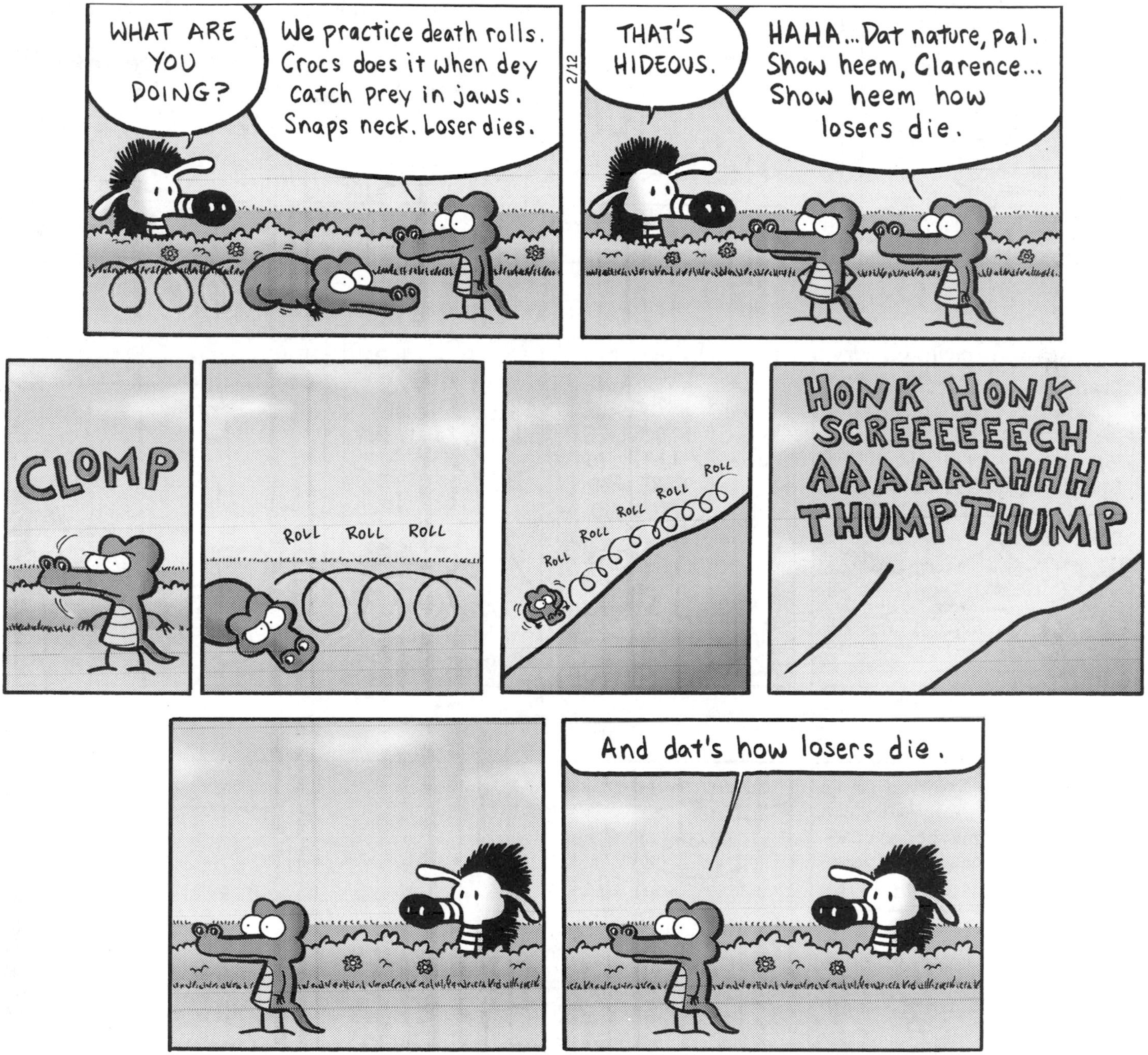

WHAT ARE YOU DOING?
We practice death rolls. Crocs does it when dey catch prey in jaws. Snaps neck. Loser dies.
2/12
THAT'S HIDEOUS.
HAHA...Dat nature, pal. Show heem, Clarence... Show heem how losers die.
CLOMP
ROLL ROLL ROLL
ROLL ROLL ROLL ROLL ROLL
HONK HONK SCREEEEEECH AAAAAAHHH THUMPTHUMP
And dat's how losers die.

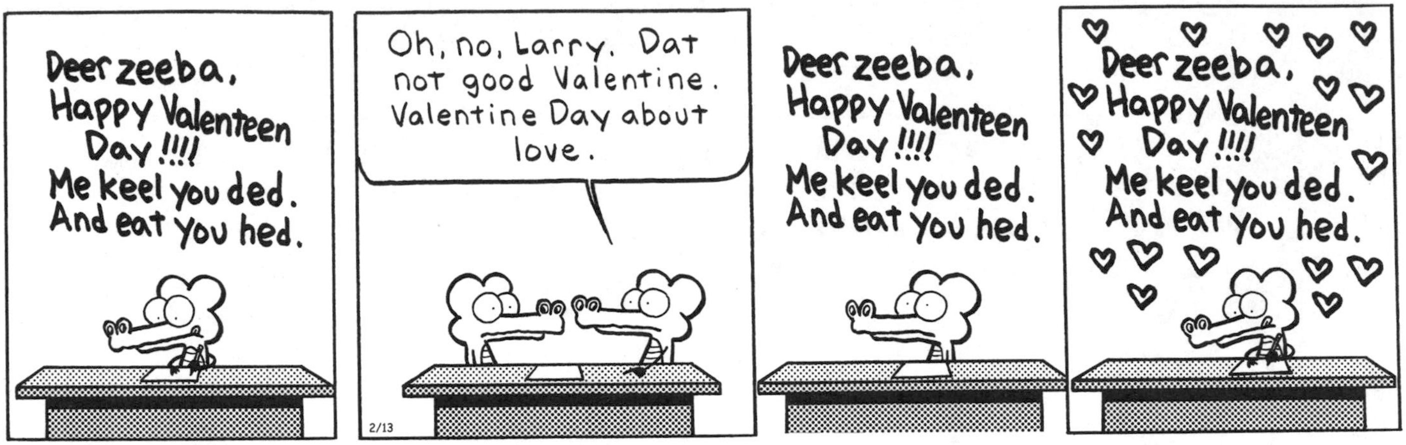
Deer zeeba,
Happy Valenteen Day!!!!
Me keel you ded.
And eat you hed.
Oh, no, Larry. Dat not good Valentine. Valentine Day about love.
2/13
Deer zeeba,
Happy Valenteen Day!!!!
Me keel you ded.
And eat you hed.
Deer zeeba,
Happy Valenteen Day!!!!
Me keel you ded.
And eat you hed.

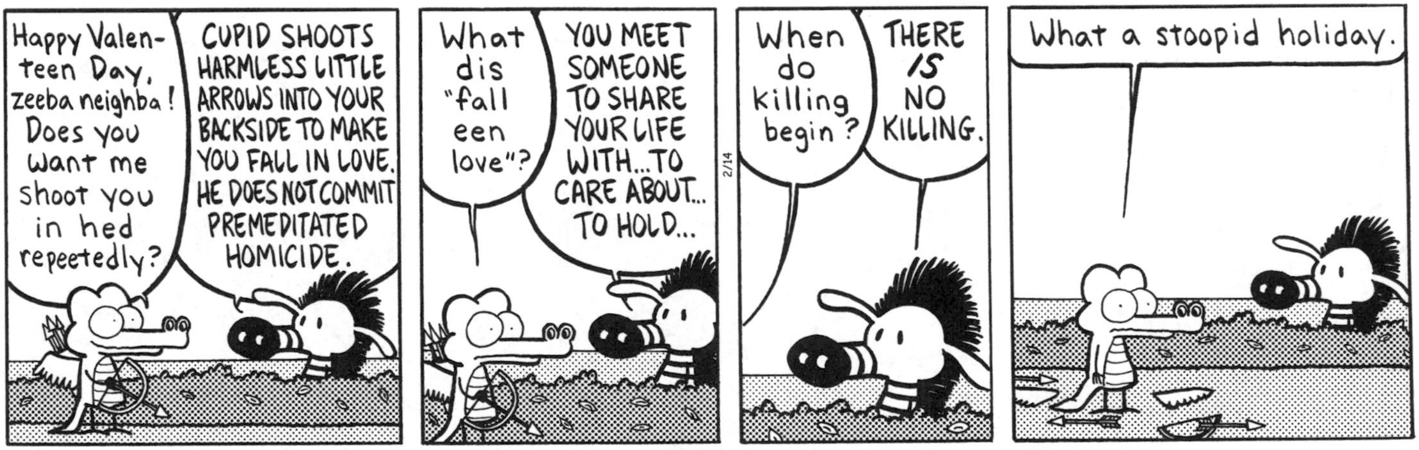
Happy Valenteen Day, zeeba neighba! Does you want me shoot you in hed repeetedly?
CUPID SHOOTS HARMLESS LITTLE ARROWS INTO YOUR BACKSIDE TO MAKE YOU FALL IN LOVE. HE DOES NOT COMMIT PREMEDITATED HOMICIDE.
What dis "fall een love"?
YOU MEET SOMEONE TO SHARE YOUR LIFE WITH...TO CARE ABOUT... TO HOLD...
2/14
When do killing begin?
THERE *IS* NO KILLING.
What a stoopid holiday.

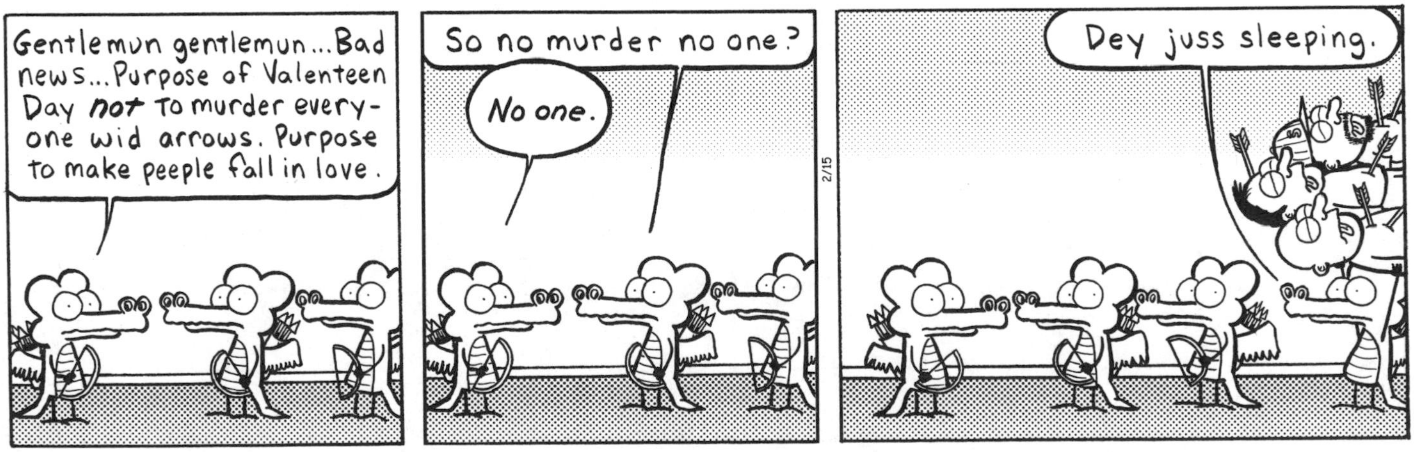
Gentlemun gentlemun... Bad news... Purpose of Valenteen Day *not* to murder everyone wid arrows. Purpose to make peeple fall in love.
So no murder no one?
No one.
2/15
Dey juss sleeping.

Panel 1: I HAVE CONCLUDED THAT SINCE I HAVE SO MUCH TROUBLE SUCCEEDING IN LIFE, I SHALL SURROUND MYSELF WITH FRIENDS WHO ARE ABJECT FAILURES.

WHY?

Panel 2: BECAUSE AS BAD AS THINGS MAY GET FOR ME, I'M BETTER THAN THEM. THUS, THEIR INCOMPARABLE FAILURE PROVIDES ME WITH THE ILLUSION OF SUCCESS, AND ILLUSION IS GOOD ENOUGH FOR ME.

BUT WHERE WILL YOU FIND FRIENDS LIKE THAT?

Panel 3: WHO'S MY BEST FRIEND, BIG GUY?

THAT'S ME, PAL.... THAT'S ME!!

2/16

Panel 4: IT'S NOT HARD.

Panel 5: WHAT ARE YOU DOING WITH THOSE VIKING FIGURINES? I SURE HOPE YOU DON'T HAVE 'EM KEEPING DIARIES AND COLLECTING DAISIES AGAIN.

OH, NO... TODAY WE'RE GONNA WATCH A LITTLE TELEVISION.

Panel 6: GOOD. HAVE 'EM WATCH SOME OF THIS 'ULTIMATE FIGHTING CHAMPIONSHIP.'.. LOTS OF GUYS BEATING EACH OTHER SENSELESS...VIKINGS *CRAVE* THIS KIND OF BRUTALITY...HAHAHA HERE YA GO, FELLAS...**VIOLENCE! VIOLENCE! VIOLENCE!**......

☆CLICK☆ ☆CLICK☆

2/17

Panel 7: Today we missed "Ellen."

Panel 8: HEY THERE, RAT BUDDY, WHAT ARE YOU WRITING?

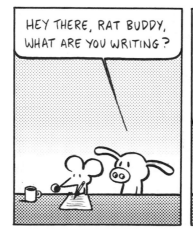

Panel 9: IT'S A SELF-HELP BOOK. I CALL IT, "RAT'S GUIDE TO BEING HAPPY."

WHAT HAVE YOU WRITTEN SO FAR?

2/18

Panel 10: "TO ACHIEVE HAPPINESS, SPEND $29.95 ON THIS BOOK."

HOW DOES THAT MAKE OTHER PEOPLE HAPPY?

Panel 11: WHO SAID ANYTHING ABOUT OTHER PEOPLE?

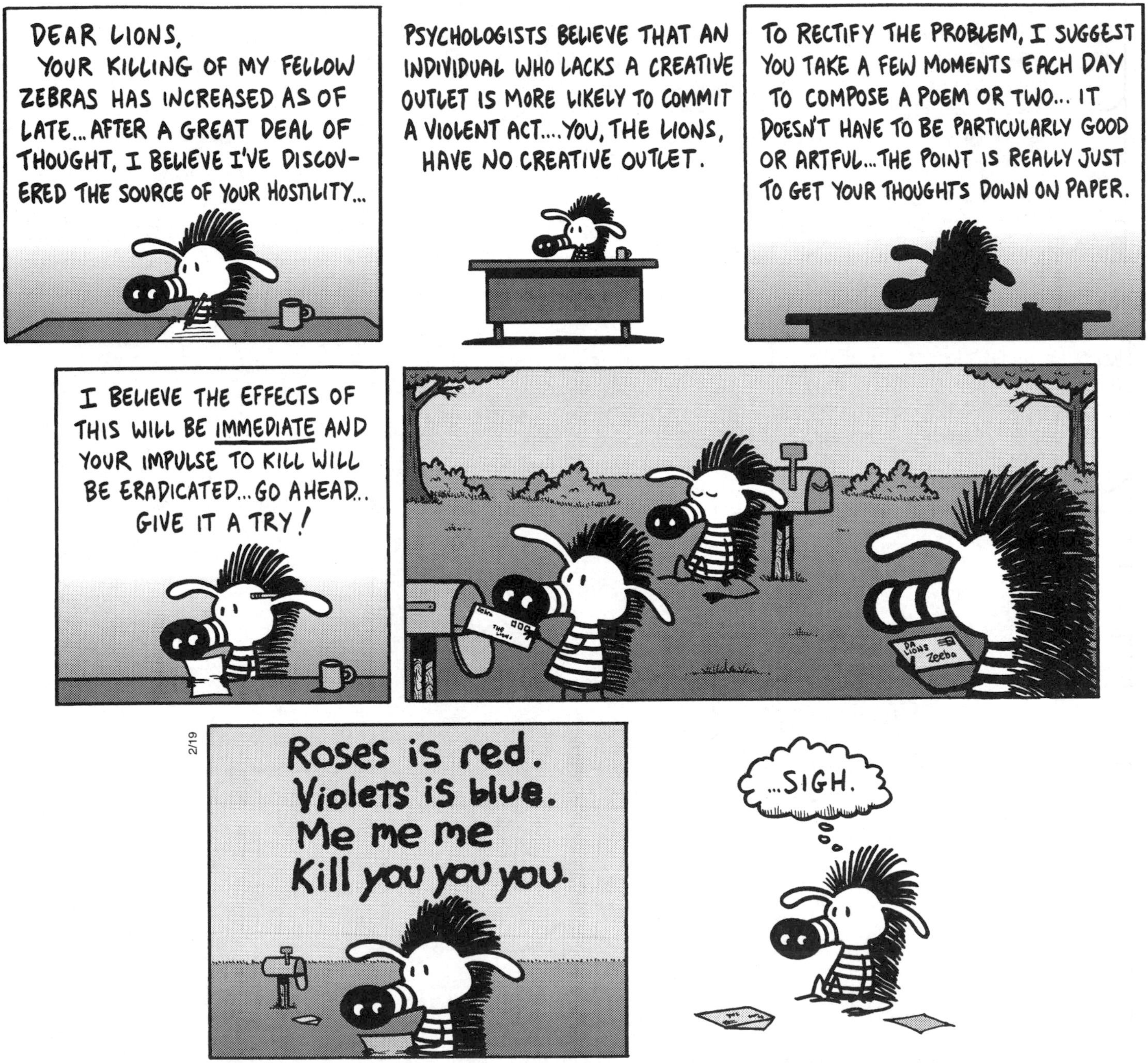
DEAR LIONS,
YOUR KILLING OF MY FELLOW ZEBRAS HAS INCREASED AS OF LATE... AFTER A GREAT DEAL OF THOUGHT, I BELIEVE I'VE DISCOVERED THE SOURCE OF YOUR HOSTILITY...
PSYCHOLOGISTS BELIEVE THAT AN INDIVIDUAL WHO LACKS A CREATIVE OUTLET IS MORE LIKELY TO COMMIT A VIOLENT ACT.... YOU, THE LIONS, HAVE NO CREATIVE OUTLET.
TO RECTIFY THE PROBLEM, I SUGGEST YOU TAKE A FEW MOMENTS EACH DAY TO COMPOSE A POEM OR TWO... IT DOESN'T HAVE TO BE PARTICULARLY GOOD OR ARTFUL... THE POINT IS REALLY JUST TO GET YOUR THOUGHTS DOWN ON PAPER.
I BELIEVE THE EFFECTS OF THIS WILL BE IMMEDIATE AND YOUR IMPULSE TO KILL WILL BE ERADICATED... GO AHEAD.. GIVE IT A TRY!
2/19
Roses is red.
Violets is blue.
Me me me
Kill you you you.
...SIGH.

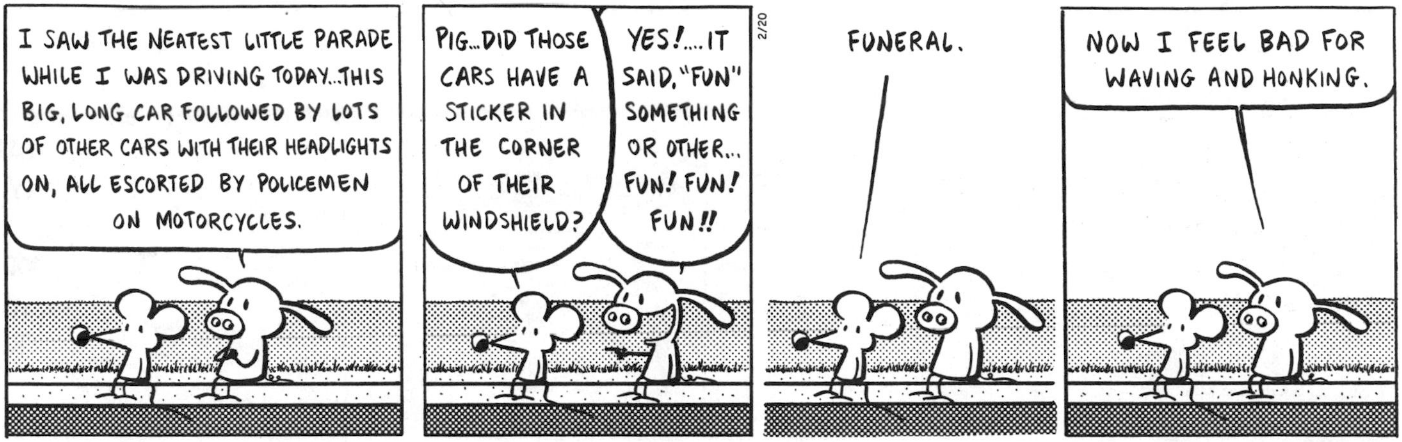
2/20
I SAW THE NEATEST LITTLE PARADE WHILE I WAS DRIVING TODAY...THIS BIG, LONG CAR FOLLOWED BY LOTS OF OTHER CARS WITH THEIR HEADLIGHTS ON, ALL ESCORTED BY POLICEMEN ON MOTORCYCLES.
PIG...DID THOSE CARS HAVE A STICKER IN THE CORNER OF THEIR WINDSHIELD?
YES!....IT SAID, "FUN" SOMETHING OR OTHER... FUN! FUN! FUN!!
FUNERAL.
NOW I FEEL BAD FOR WAVING AND HONKING.

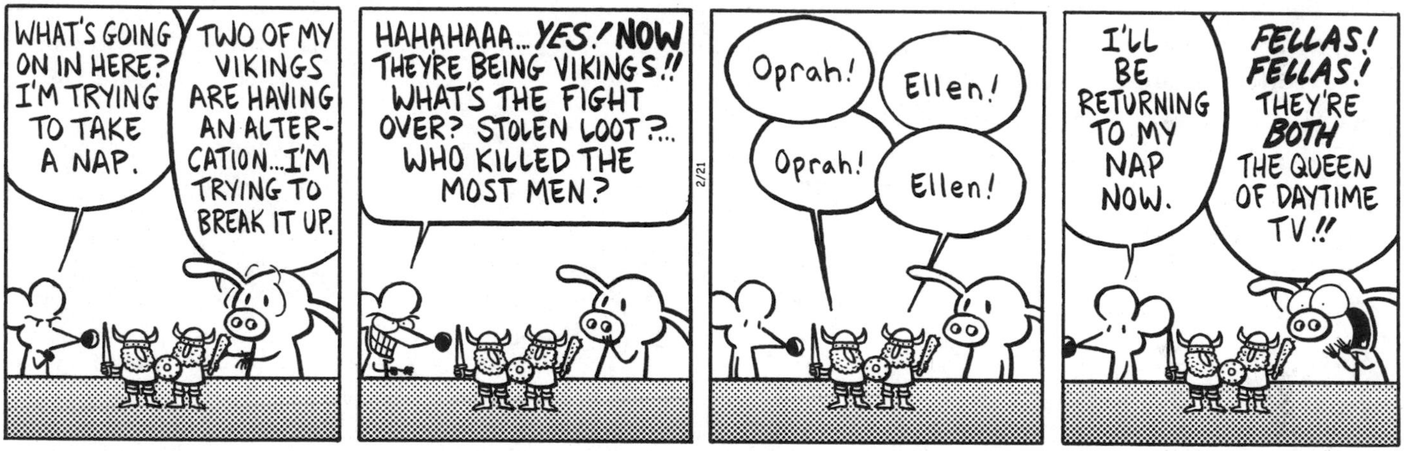
2/21
WHAT'S GOING ON IN HERE? I'M TRYING TO TAKE A NAP.
TWO OF MY VIKINGS ARE HAVING AN ALTERCATION...I'M TRYING TO BREAK IT UP.
HAHAHAAA... YES! NOW THEY'RE BEING VIKINGS!! WHAT'S THE FIGHT OVER? STOLEN LOOT?... WHO KILLED THE MOST MEN?
Oprah!
Ellen!
Oprah!
Ellen!
I'LL BE RETURNING TO MY NAP NOW.
FELLAS! FELLAS! THEY'RE BOTH THE QUEEN OF DAYTIME TV!!

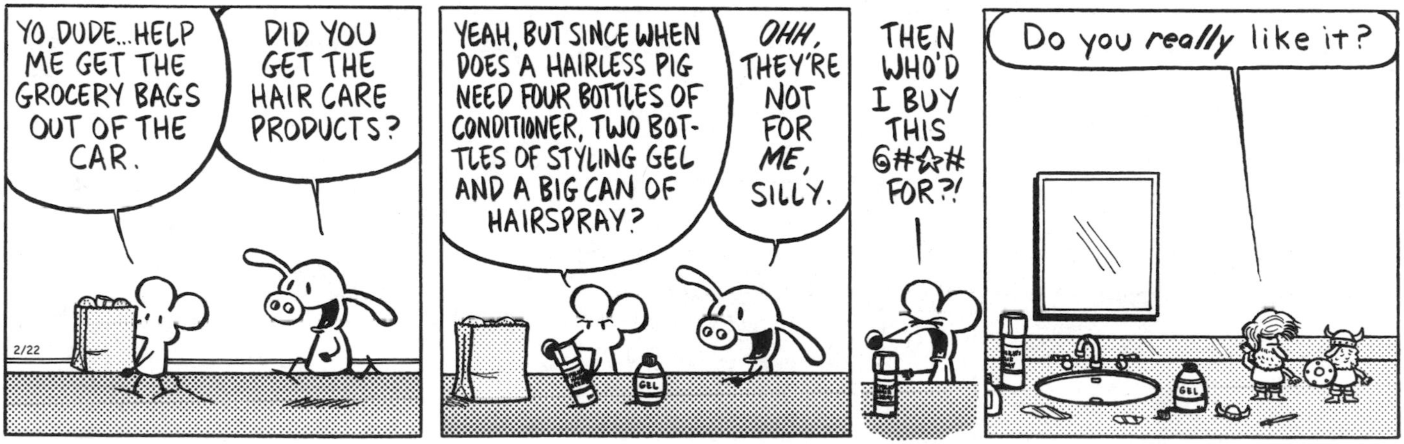
2/22
YO, DUDE...HELP ME GET THE GROCERY BAGS OUT OF THE CAR.
DID YOU GET THE HAIR CARE PRODUCTS?
YEAH, BUT SINCE WHEN DOES A HAIRLESS PIG NEED FOUR BOTTLES OF CONDITIONER, TWO BOTTLES OF STYLING GEL AND A BIG CAN OF HAIRSPRAY?
OHH, THEY'RE NOT FOR ME, SILLY.
THEN WHO'D I BUY THIS @#☆# FOR?!
GEL
Do you really like it?

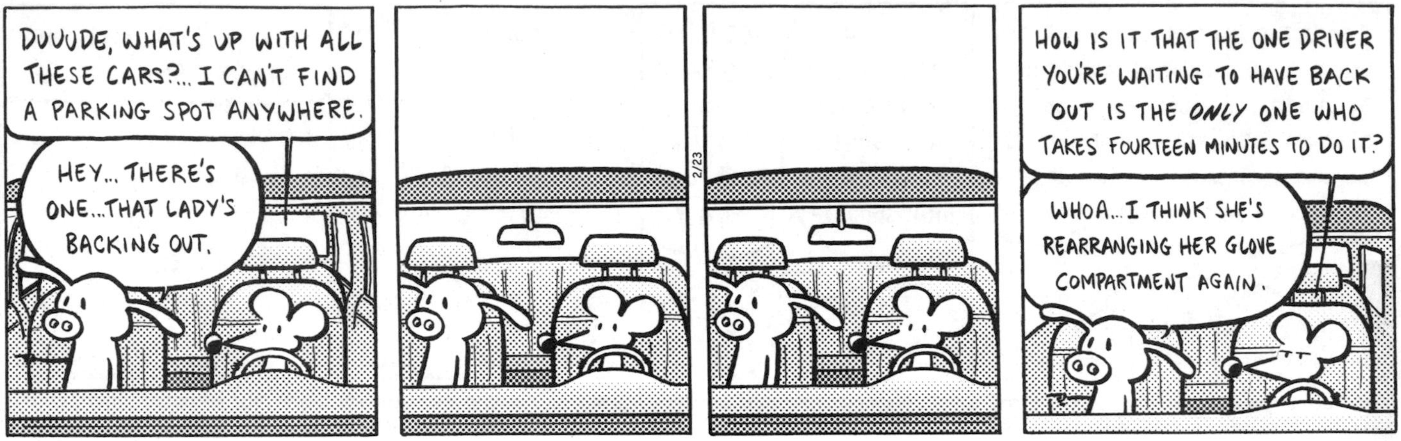
DUUUDE, WHAT'S UP WITH ALL THESE CARS?... I CAN'T FIND A PARKING SPOT ANYWHERE.
HEY... THERE'S ONE... THAT LADY'S BACKING OUT.
2/23
HOW IS IT THAT THE ONE DRIVER YOU'RE WAITING TO HAVE BACK OUT IS THE ONLY ONE WHO TAKES FOURTEEN MINUTES TO DO IT?
WHOA... I THINK SHE'S REARRANGING HER GLOVE COMPARTMENT AGAIN.

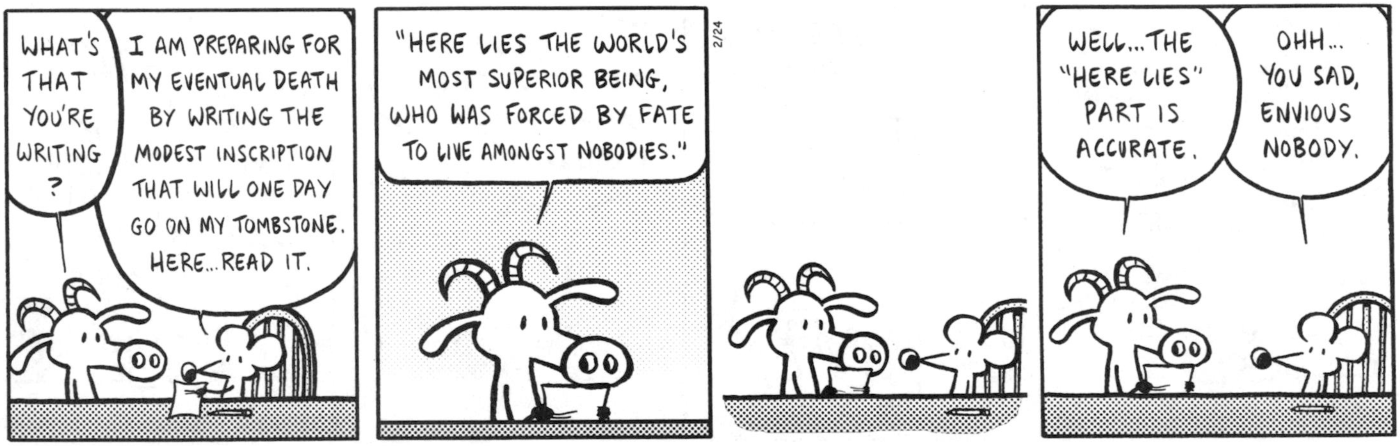
WHAT'S THAT YOU'RE WRITING?
I AM PREPARING FOR MY EVENTUAL DEATH BY WRITING THE MODEST INSCRIPTION THAT WILL ONE DAY GO ON MY TOMBSTONE. HERE... READ IT.
"HERE LIES THE WORLD'S MOST SUPERIOR BEING, WHO WAS FORCED BY FATE TO LIVE AMONGST NOBODIES."
2/24
WELL... THE "HERE LIES" PART IS ACCURATE.
OHH... YOU SAD, ENVIOUS NOBODY.

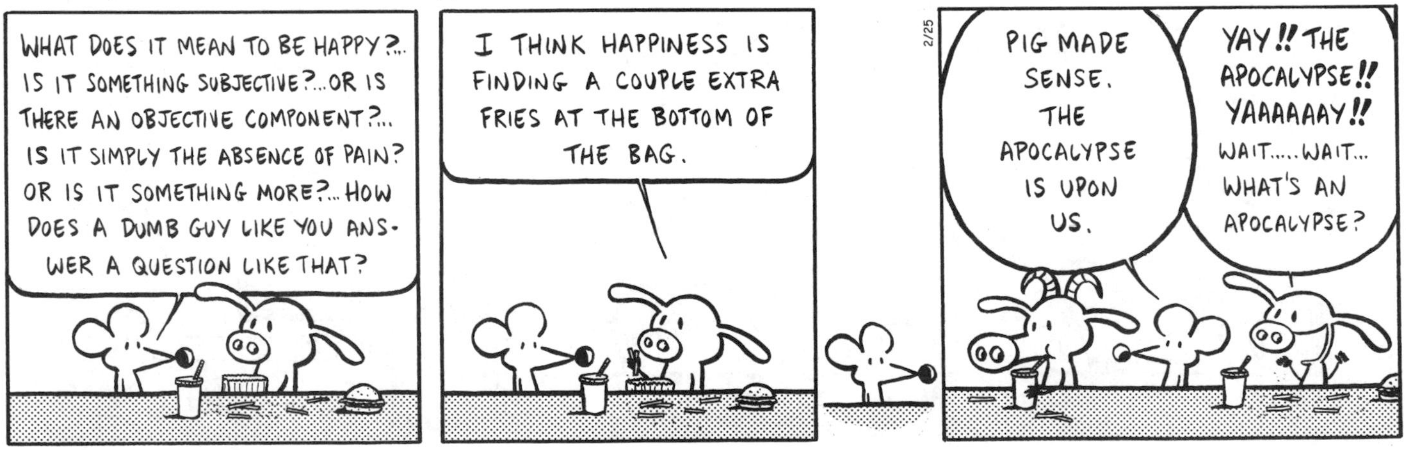
WHAT DOES IT MEAN TO BE HAPPY?... IS IT SOMETHING SUBJECTIVE?... OR IS THERE AN OBJECTIVE COMPONENT?... IS IT SIMPLY THE ABSENCE OF PAIN? OR IS IT SOMETHING MORE?... HOW DOES A DUMB GUY LIKE YOU ANSWER A QUESTION LIKE THAT?
I THINK HAPPINESS IS FINDING A COUPLE EXTRA FRIES AT THE BOTTOM OF THE BAG.
2/25
PIG MADE SENSE. THE APOCALYPSE IS UPON US.
YAY!! THE APOCALYPSE!! YAAAAAAY!! WAIT..... WAIT... WHAT'S AN APOCALYPSE?

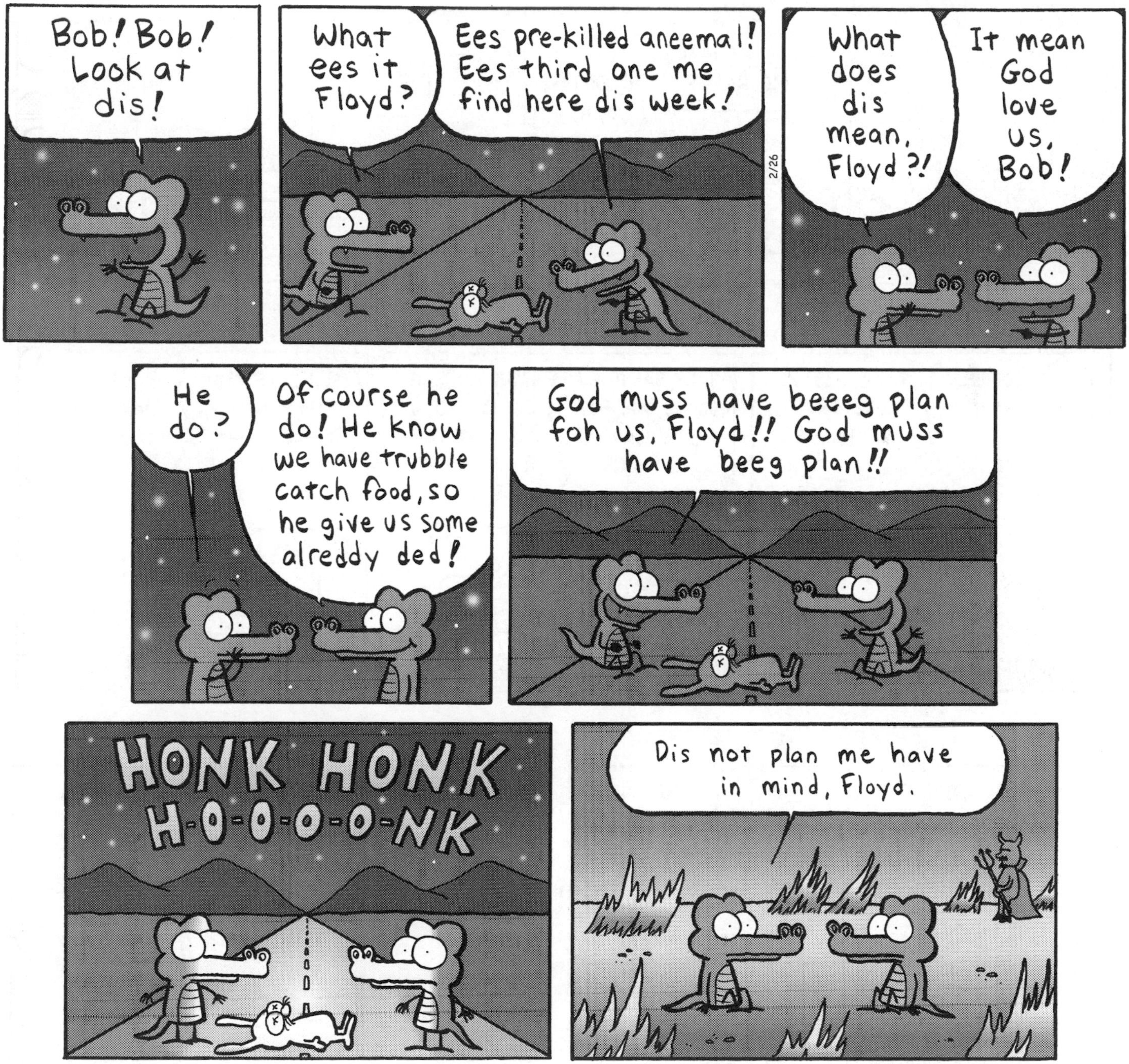
Bob! Bob! Look at dis!
What ees it Floyd?
Ees pre-killed aneemal! Ees third one me find here dis week!
2/26
What does dis mean, Floyd?!
It mean God love us, Bob!
He do?
Of course he do! He know we have trubble catch food, so he give us some alreddy ded!
God muss have beeeg plan foh us, Floyd!! God muss have beeg plan!!
HONK HONK H-O-O-O-O-NK
Dis not plan me have in mind, Floyd.

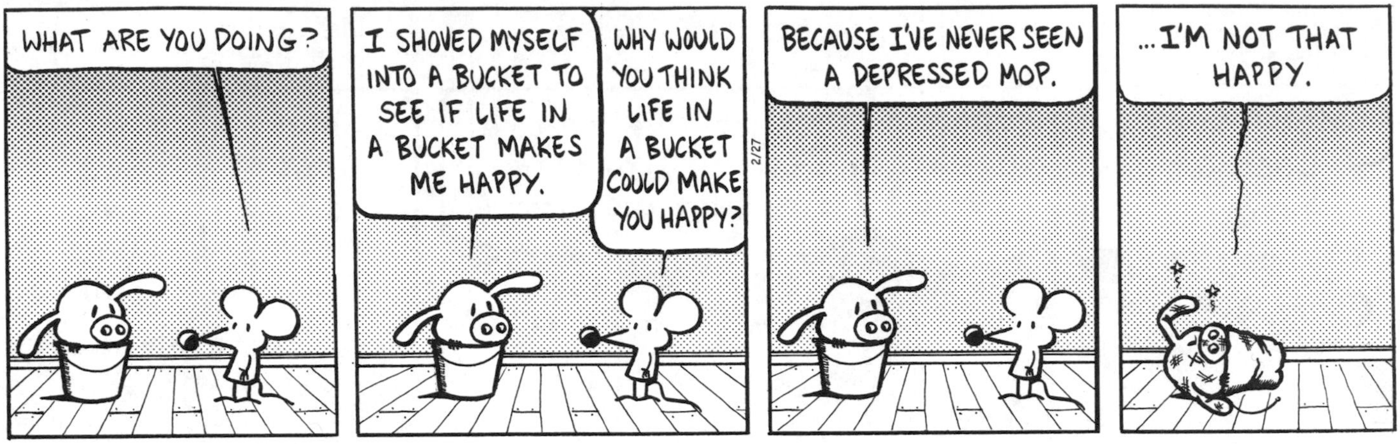
WHAT ARE YOU DOING?
I SHOVED MYSELF INTO A BUCKET TO SEE IF LIFE IN A BUCKET MAKES ME HAPPY.
WHY WOULD YOU THINK LIFE IN A BUCKET COULD MAKE YOU HAPPY?
2/27
BECAUSE I'VE NEVER SEEN A DEPRESSED MOP.
...I'M NOT THAT HAPPY.

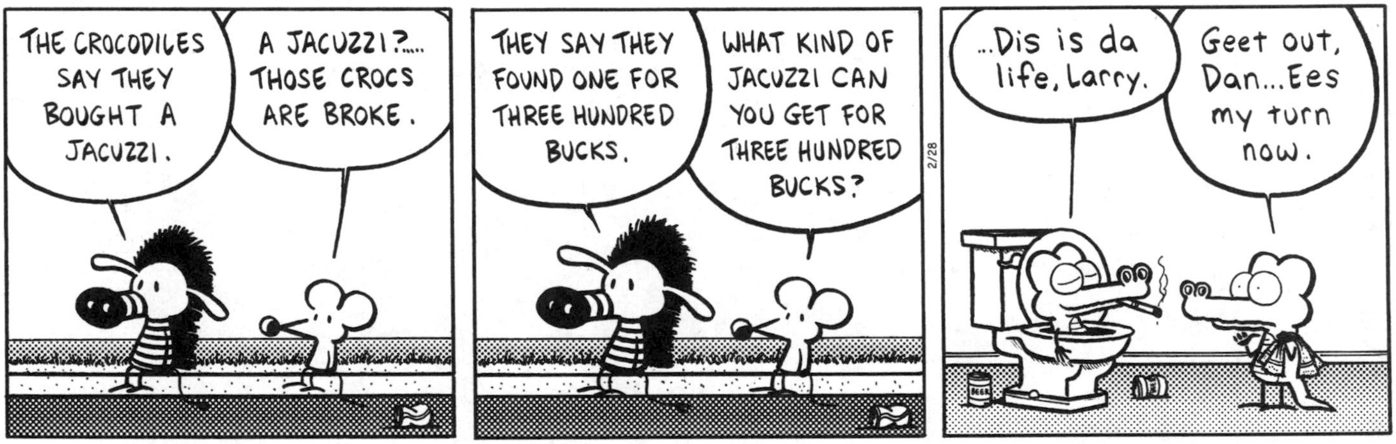
THE CROCODILES SAY THEY BOUGHT A JACUZZI.
A JACUZZI?.... THOSE CROCS ARE BROKE.
THEY SAY THEY FOUND ONE FOR THREE HUNDRED BUCKS.
WHAT KIND OF JACUZZI CAN YOU GET FOR THREE HUNDRED BUCKS?
2/28
...Dis is da life, Larry.
Geet out, Dan...Ees my turn now.

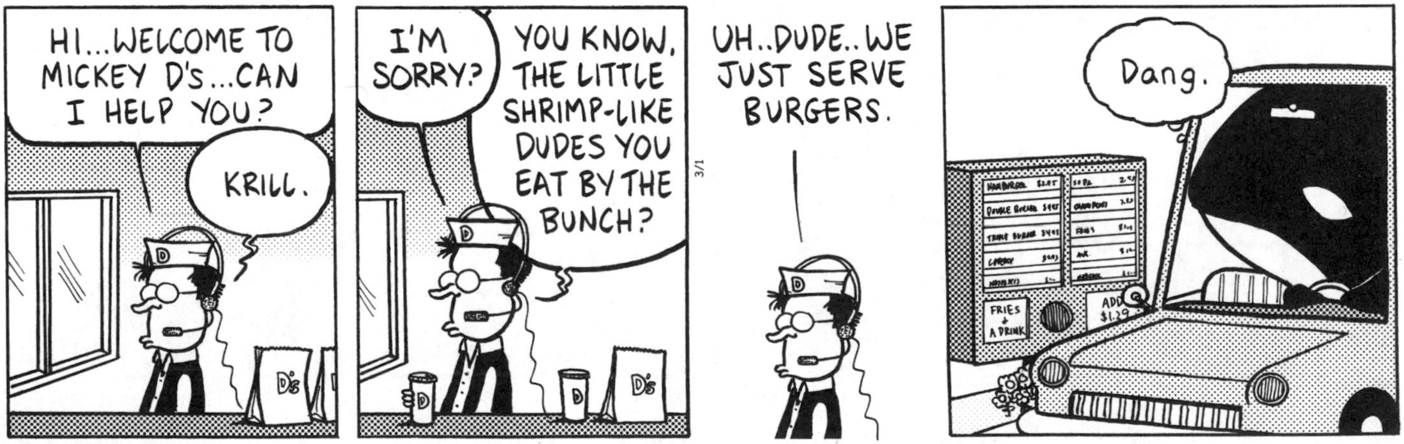
HI...WELCOME TO MICKEY D's...CAN I HELP YOU?
KRILL.
I'M SORRY?
YOU KNOW, THE LITTLE SHRIMP-LIKE DUDES YOU EAT BY THE BUNCH?
3/1
UH..DUDE..WE JUST SERVE BURGERS.
Dang.
FRIES + A DRINK
ADD $1.29

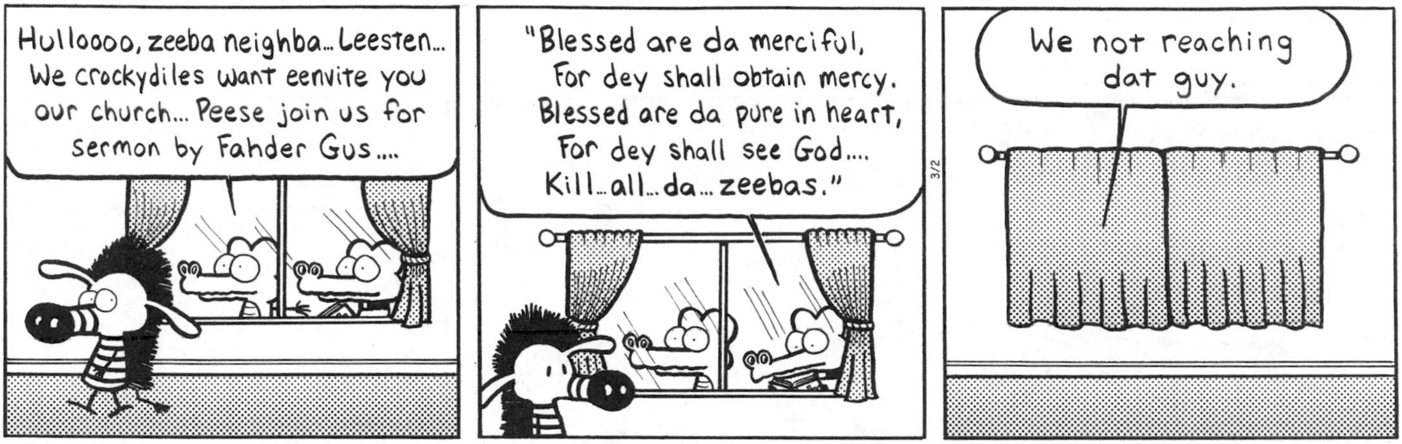
Hulloooo, zeeba neighba... Leesten... We crockydiles want eenvite you our church... Peese join us for sermon by Fahder Gus....
"Blessed are da merciful, For dey shall obtain mercy. Blessed are da pure in heart, For dey shall see God.... Kill... all... da... zeebas."
3/2
We not reaching dat guy.

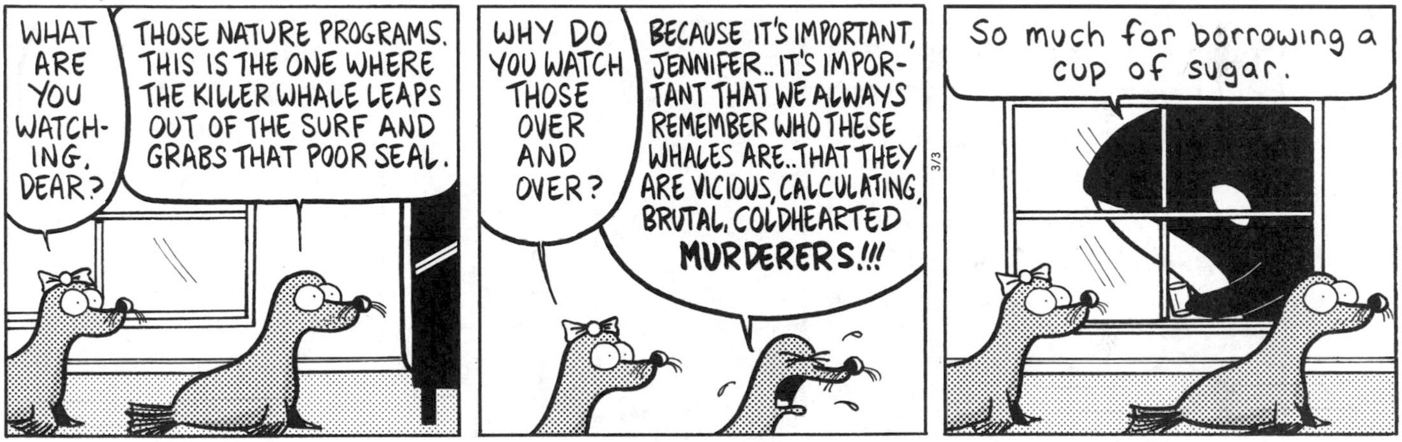
WHAT ARE YOU WATCH-ING, DEAR?
THOSE NATURE PROGRAMS. THIS IS THE ONE WHERE THE KILLER WHALE LEAPS OUT OF THE SURF AND GRABS THAT POOR SEAL.
WHY DO YOU WATCH THOSE OVER AND OVER?
BECAUSE IT'S IMPORTANT, JENNIFER.. IT'S IMPORTANT THAT WE ALWAYS REMEMBER WHO THESE WHALES ARE..THAT THEY ARE VICIOUS, CALCULATING, BRUTAL, COLDHEARTED MURDERERS!!!
3/3
So much for borrowing a cup of sugar.

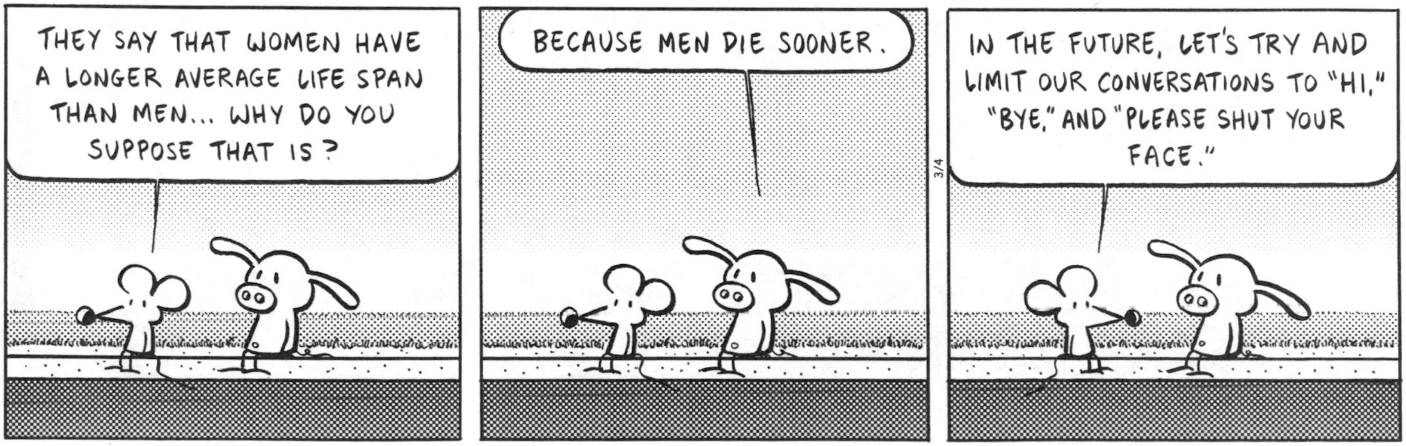
THEY SAY THAT WOMEN HAVE A LONGER AVERAGE LIFE SPAN THAN MEN... WHY DO YOU SUPPOSE THAT IS?
BECAUSE MEN DIE SOONER.
3/4
IN THE FUTURE, LET'S TRY AND LIMIT OUR CONVERSATIONS TO "HI," "BYE," AND "PLEASE SHUT YOUR FACE."

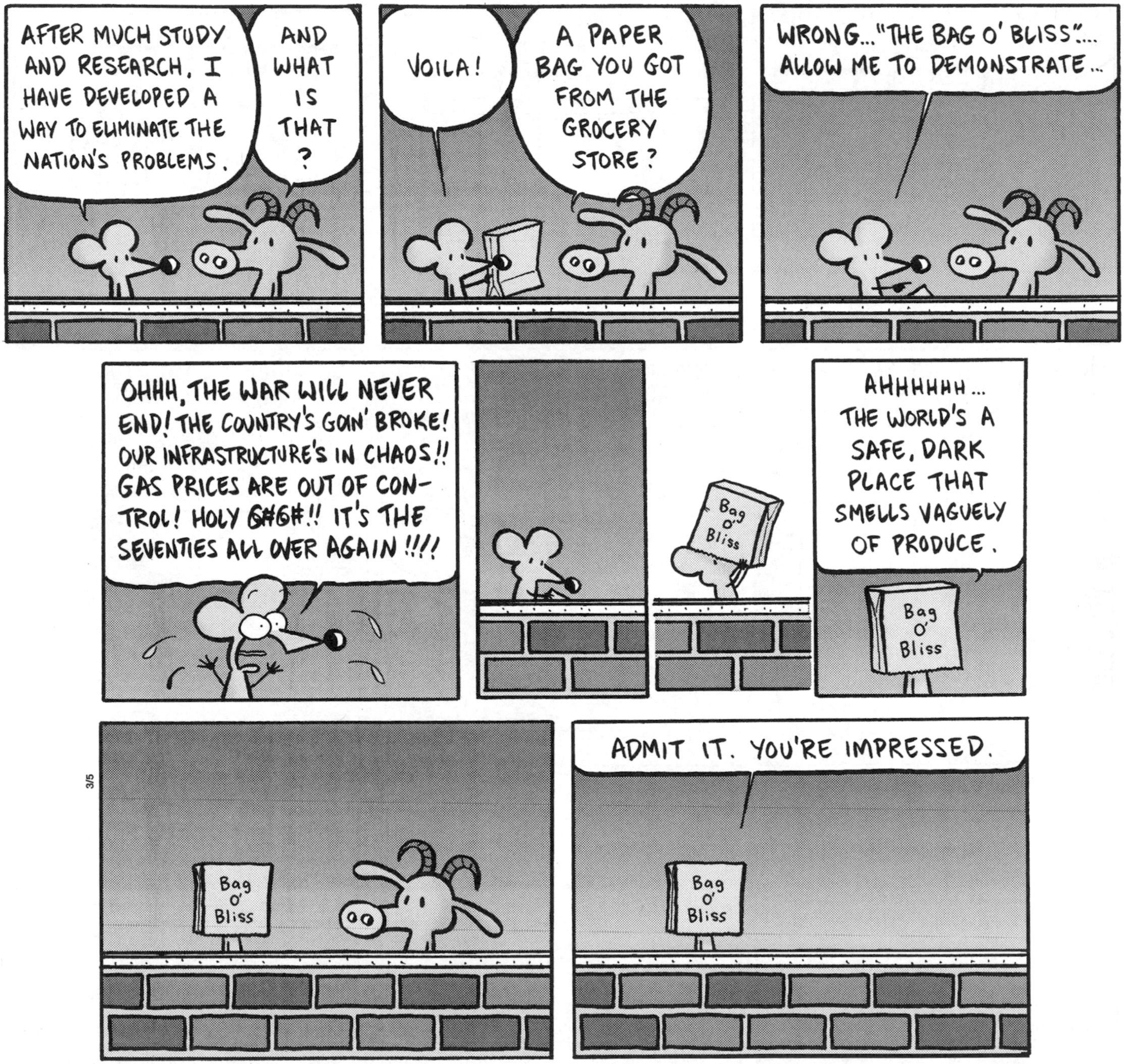
AFTER MUCH STUDY AND RESEARCH, I HAVE DEVELOPED A WAY TO ELIMINATE THE NATION'S PROBLEMS.
AND WHAT IS THAT ?
VOILA!
A PAPER BAG YOU GOT FROM THE GROCERY STORE ?
WRONG..."THE BAG O' BLISS"... ALLOW ME TO DEMONSTRATE...
OHHH, THE WAR WILL NEVER END! THE COUNTRY'S GOIN' BROKE! OUR INFRASTRUCTURE'S IN CHAOS!! GAS PRICES ARE OUT OF CON-TROL! HOLY &#@#!! IT'S THE SEVENTIES ALL OVER AGAIN !!!!
Bag O' Bliss
AHHHHHH... THE WORLD'S A SAFE, DARK PLACE THAT SMELLS VAGUELY OF PRODUCE.
Bag O' Bliss
Bag O' Bliss
ADMIT IT. YOU'RE IMPRESSED.
Bag O' Bliss
3/5

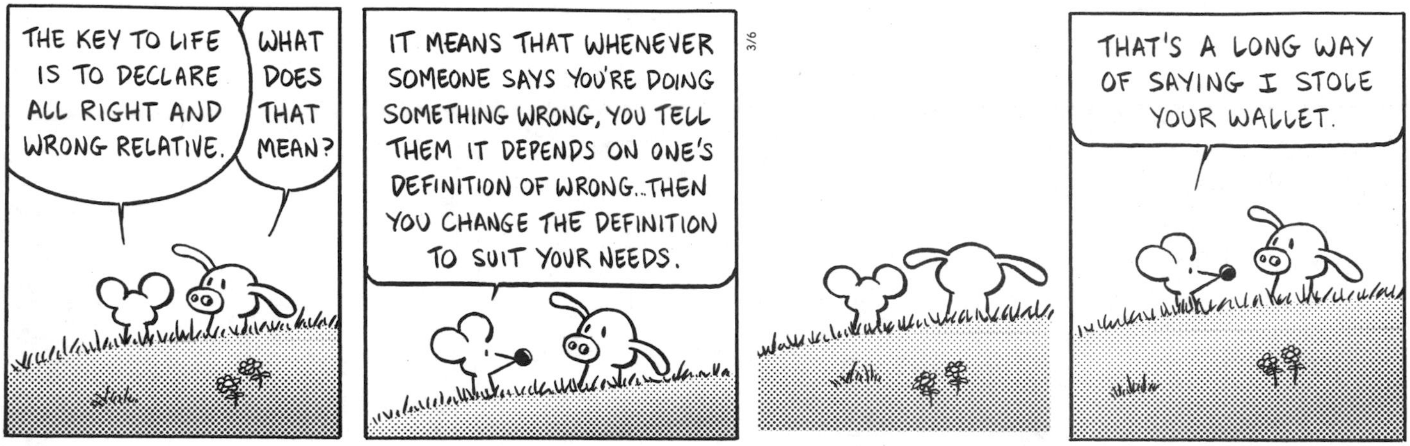
THE KEY TO LIFE IS TO DECLARE ALL RIGHT AND WRONG RELATIVE.
WHAT DOES THAT MEAN?
IT MEANS THAT WHENEVER SOMEONE SAYS YOU'RE DOING SOMETHING WRONG, YOU TELL THEM IT DEPENDS ON ONE'S DEFINITION OF WRONG...THEN YOU CHANGE THE DEFINITION TO SUIT YOUR NEEDS.
3/6
THAT'S A LONG WAY OF SAYING I STOLE YOUR WALLET.

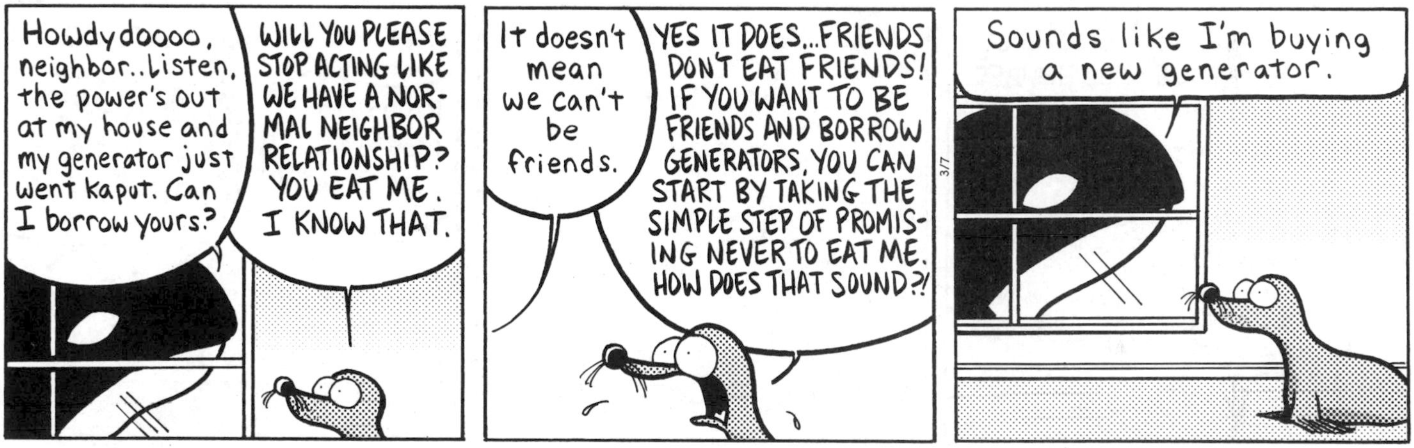
Howdydoooo, neighbor..Listen, the power's out at my house and my generator just went kaput. Can I borrow yours?
WILL YOU PLEASE STOP ACTING LIKE WE HAVE A NORMAL NEIGHBOR RELATIONSHIP? YOU EAT ME. I KNOW THAT.
It doesn't mean we can't be friends.
YES IT DOES...FRIENDS DON'T EAT FRIENDS! IF YOU WANT TO BE FRIENDS AND BORROW GENERATORS, YOU CAN START BY TAKING THE SIMPLE STEP OF PROMISING NEVER TO EAT ME. HOW DOES THAT SOUND?!
3/7
Sounds like I'm buying a new generator.

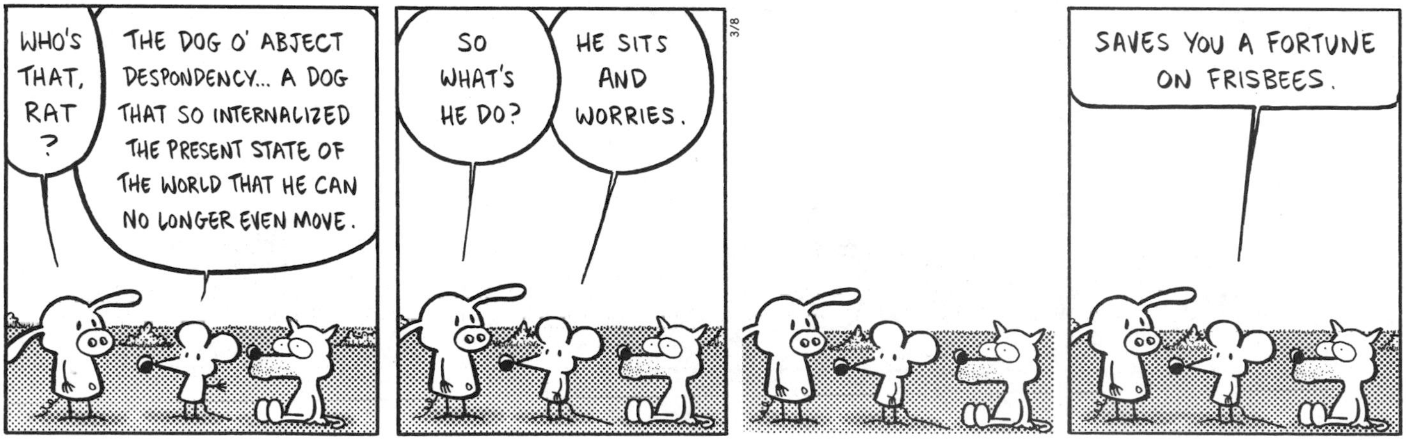
WHO'S THAT, RAT?
THE DOG O' ABJECT DESPONDENCY... A DOG THAT SO INTERNALIZED THE PRESENT STATE OF THE WORLD THAT HE CAN NO LONGER EVEN MOVE.
SO WHAT'S HE DO?
HE SITS AND WORRIES.
3/8
SAVES YOU A FORTUNE ON FRISBEES.

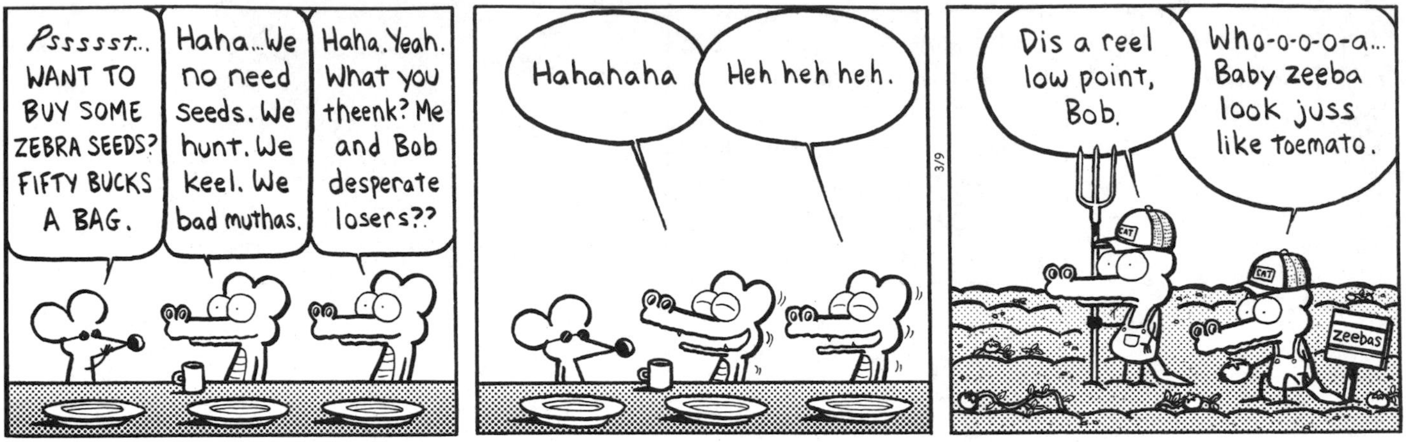
Psssssst... WANT TO BUY SOME ZEBRA SEEDS? FIFTY BUCKS A BAG.
Haha...We no need seeds. We hunt. We keel. We bad muthas.
Haha. Yeah. What you theenk? Me and Bob desperate losers??
Hahahaha
Heh heh heh.
3/9
Dis a reel low point, Bob.
Who-o-o-o-a... Baby zeeba look juss like toemato.
EAT
EAT
zeebas

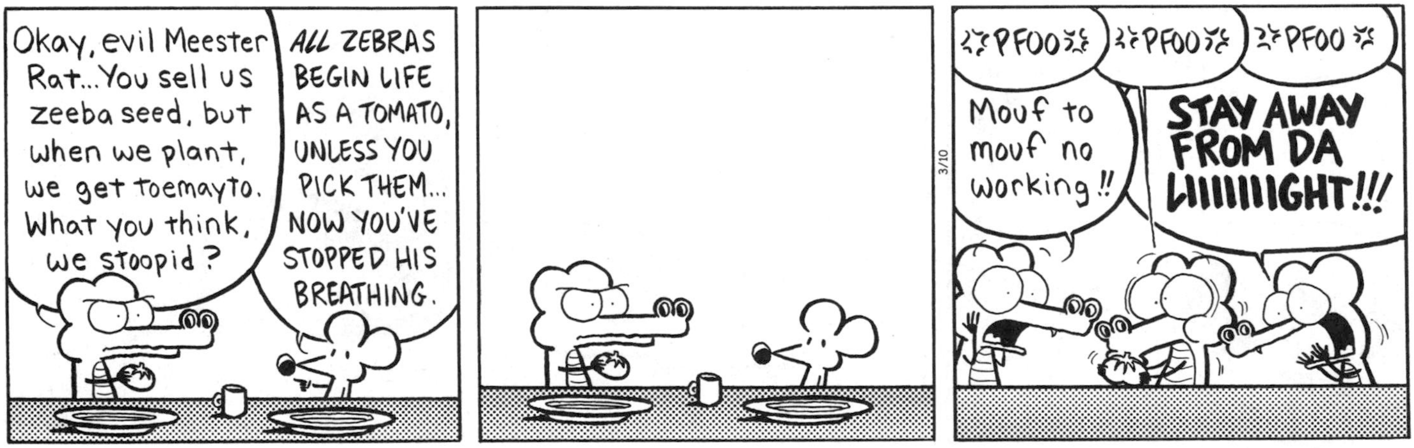
Okay, evil Meester Rat...You sell us zeeba seed, but when we plant, we get toemayto. What you think, we stoopid?
ALL ZEBRAS BEGIN LIFE AS A TOMATO, UNLESS YOU PICK THEM... NOW YOU'VE STOPPED HIS BREATHING.
3/10
PFOO
PFOO
PFOO
Mouf to mouf no working!!
STAY AWAY FROM DA LIIIIIIIGHT!!!

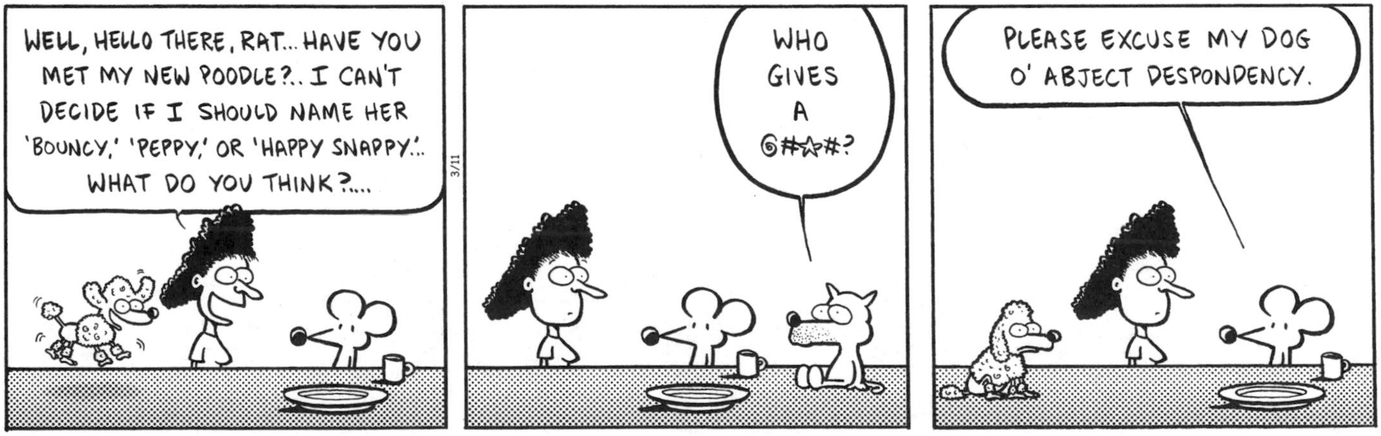
WELL, HELLO THERE, RAT... HAVE YOU MET MY NEW POODLE?.. I CAN'T DECIDE IF I SHOULD NAME HER 'BOUNCY,' 'PEPPY,' OR 'HAPPY SNAPPY.'.. WHAT DO YOU THINK?....
3/11
WHO GIVES A @#☆#?
PLEASE EXCUSE MY DOG O' ABJECT DESPONDENCY.

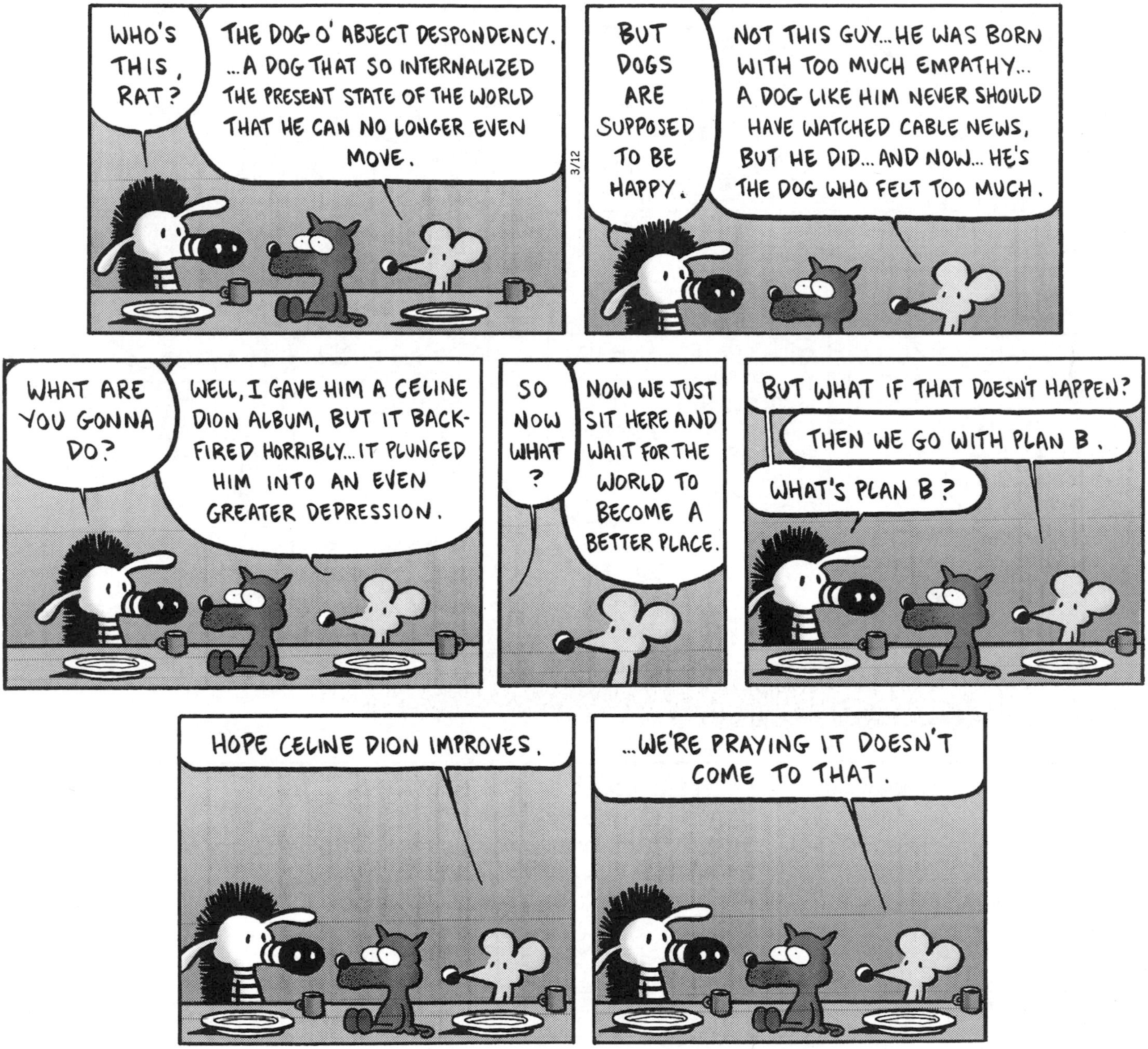
WHO'S THIS, RAT?
THE DOG O' ABJECT DESPONDENCY. ...A DOG THAT SO INTERNALIZED THE PRESENT STATE OF THE WORLD THAT HE CAN NO LONGER EVEN MOVE.
3/12
BUT DOGS ARE SUPPOSED TO BE HAPPY.
NOT THIS GUY... HE WAS BORN WITH TOO MUCH EMPATHY... A DOG LIKE HIM NEVER SHOULD HAVE WATCHED CABLE NEWS, BUT HE DID... AND NOW... HE'S THE DOG WHO FELT TOO MUCH.
WHAT ARE YOU GONNA DO?
WELL, I GAVE HIM A CELINE DION ALBUM, BUT IT BACKFIRED HORRIBLY... IT PLUNGED HIM INTO AN EVEN GREATER DEPRESSION.
SO NOW WHAT?
NOW WE JUST SIT HERE AND WAIT FOR THE WORLD TO BECOME A BETTER PLACE.
BUT WHAT IF THAT DOESN'T HAPPEN?
THEN WE GO WITH PLAN B.
WHAT'S PLAN B?
HOPE CELINE DION IMPROVES.
...WE'RE PRAYING IT DOESN'T COME TO THAT.

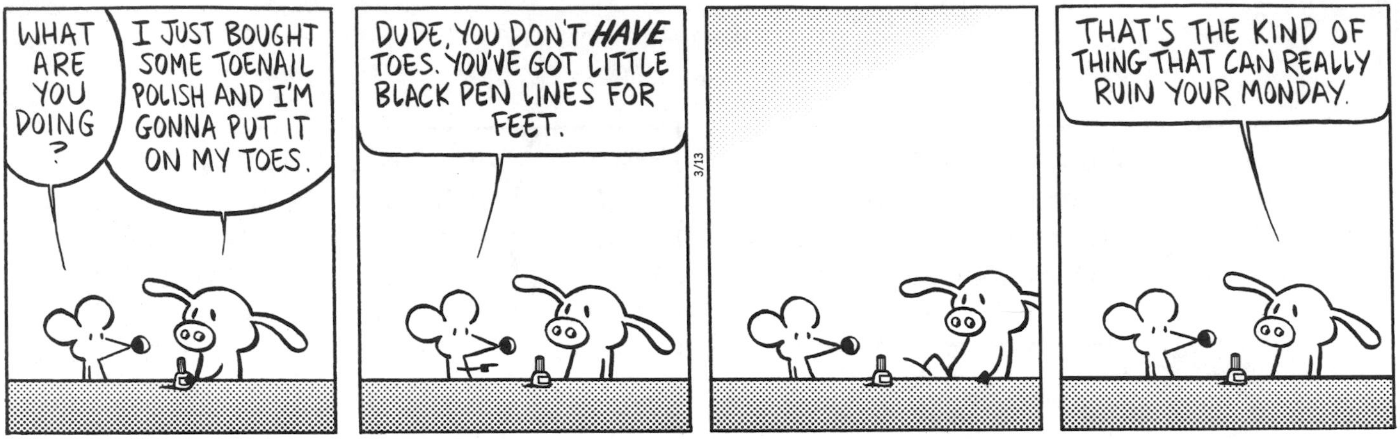
WHAT ARE YOU DOING?
I JUST BOUGHT SOME TOENAIL POLISH AND I'M GONNA PUT IT ON MY TOES.
DUDE, YOU DON'T HAVE TOES. YOU'VE GOT LITTLE BLACK PEN LINES FOR FEET.
3/13
THAT'S THE KIND OF THING THAT CAN REALLY RUIN YOUR MONDAY.

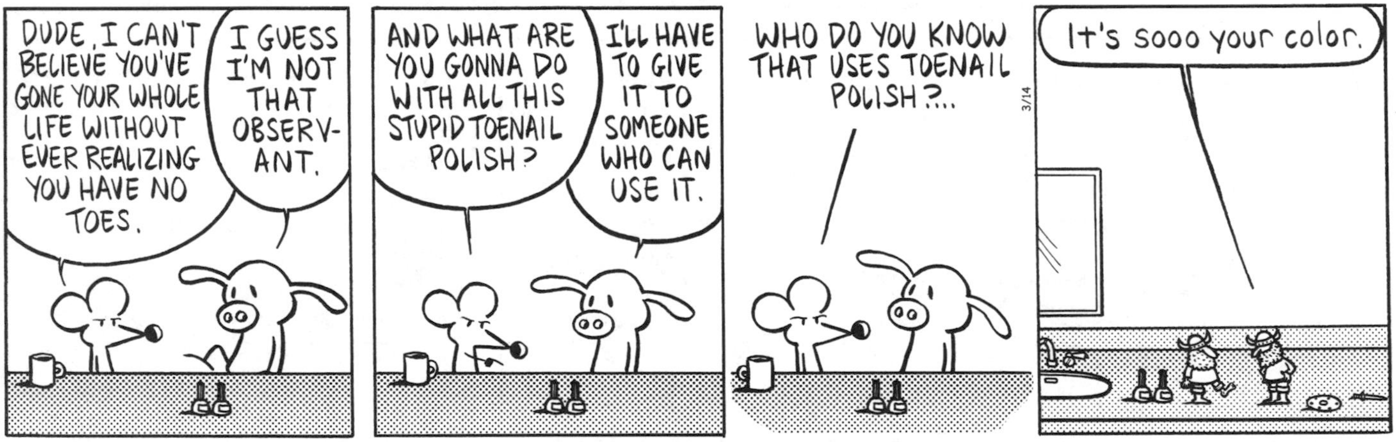
DUDE, I CAN'T BELIEVE YOU'VE GONE YOUR WHOLE LIFE WITHOUT EVER REALIZING YOU HAVE NO TOES.
I GUESS I'M NOT THAT OBSERV-ANT.
AND WHAT ARE YOU GONNA DO WITH ALL THIS STUPID TOENAIL POLISH?
I'LL HAVE TO GIVE IT TO SOMEONE WHO CAN USE IT.
WHO DO YOU KNOW THAT USES TOENAIL POLISH?...
3/14
It's sooo your color.

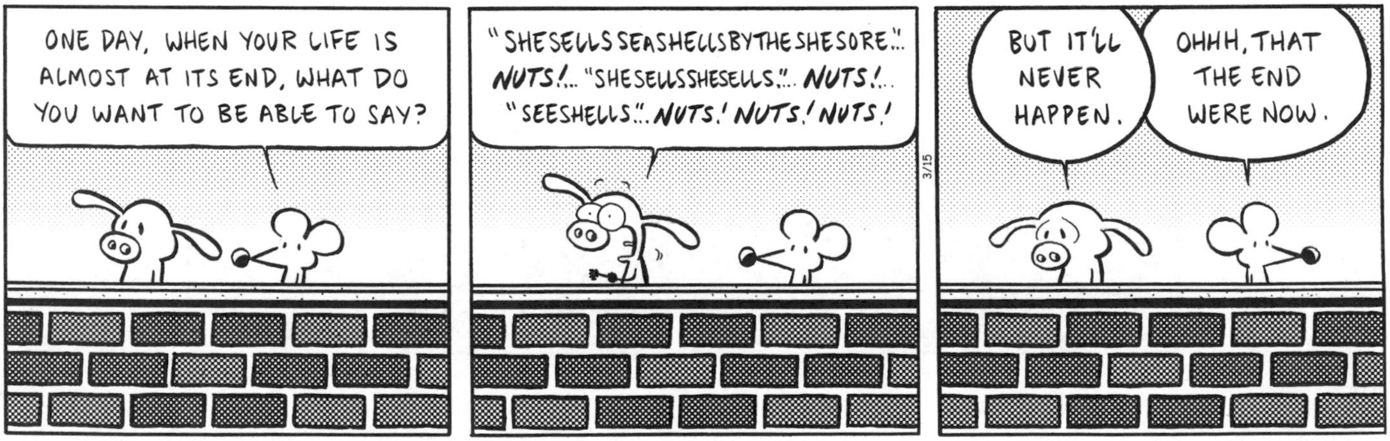
ONE DAY, WHEN YOUR LIFE IS ALMOST AT ITS END, WHAT DO YOU WANT TO BE ABLE TO SAY?
"SHESELLS SEASHELLS BY THE SHESORE."... NUTS!... "SHESELLSSHESELLS."... NUTS!... "SEESHELLS."... NUTS! NUTS! NUTS!
3/15
BUT IT'LL NEVER HAPPEN.
OHHH, THAT THE END WERE NOW.

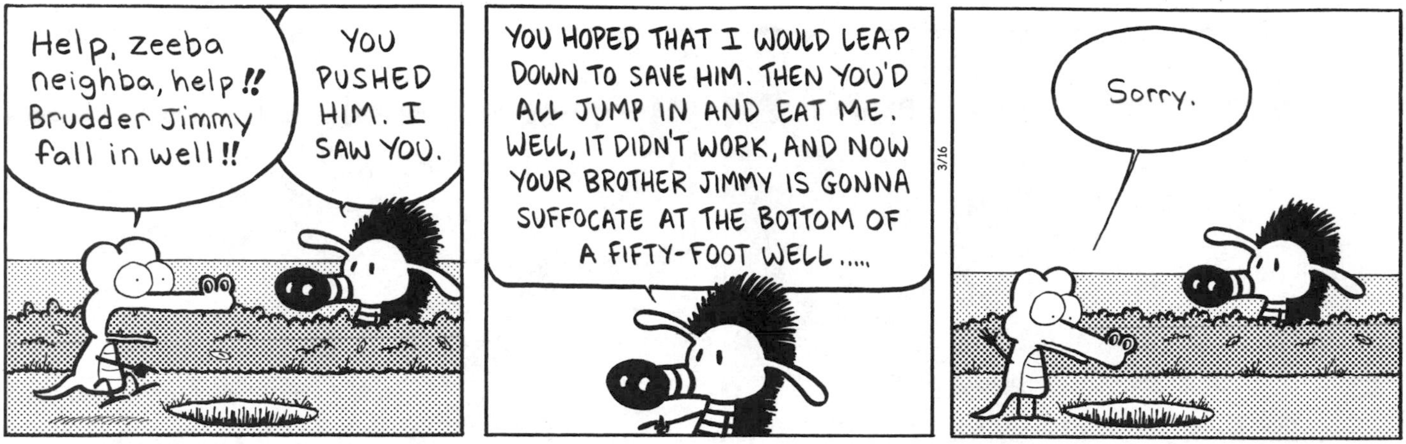
Help, zeeba neighba, help!! Brudder Jimmy fall in well!!
YOU PUSHED HIM. I SAW YOU.
YOU HOPED THAT I WOULD LEAP DOWN TO SAVE HIM. THEN YOU'D ALL JUMP IN AND EAT ME. WELL, IT DIDN'T WORK, AND NOW YOUR BROTHER JIMMY IS GONNA SUFFOCATE AT THE BOTTOM OF A FIFTY-FOOT WELL.....
3/16
Sorry.

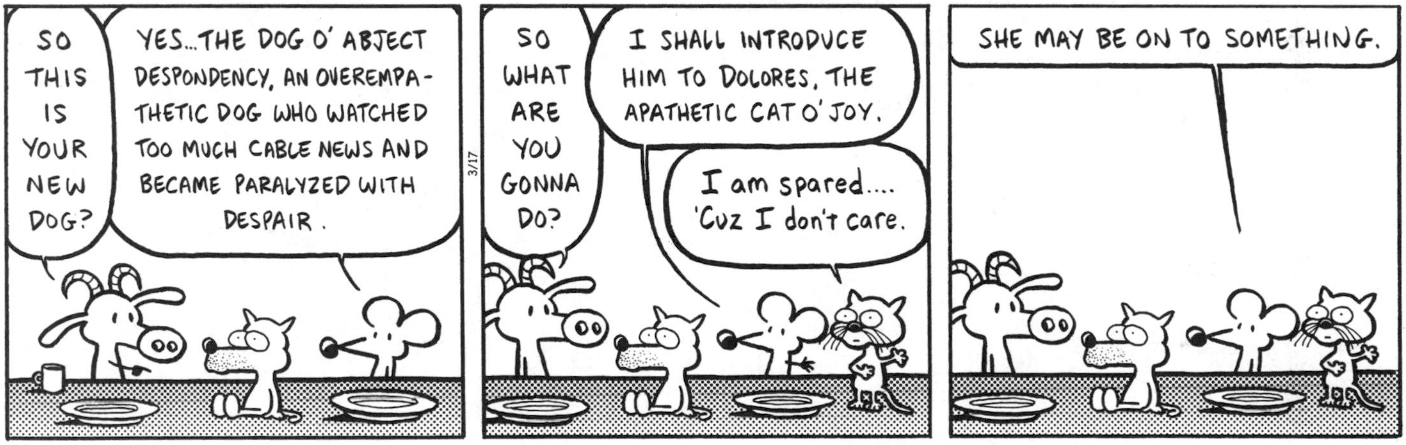
SO THIS IS YOUR NEW DOG?
YES...THE DOG O' ABJECT DESPONDENCY, AN OVEREMPATHETIC DOG WHO WATCHED TOO MUCH CABLE NEWS AND BECAME PARALYZED WITH DESPAIR.
3/17
SO WHAT ARE YOU GONNA DO?
I SHALL INTRODUCE HIM TO DOLORES, THE APATHETIC CAT O' JOY.
I am spared.... 'Cuz I don't care.
SHE MAY BE ON TO SOMETHING.

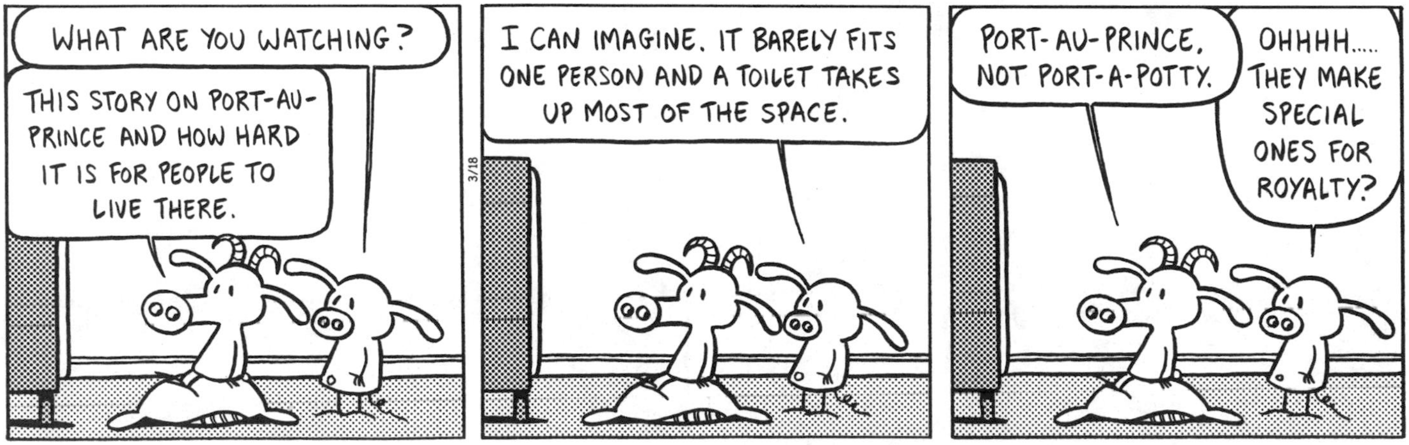
WHAT ARE YOU WATCHING?
THIS STORY ON PORT-AU-PRINCE AND HOW HARD IT IS FOR PEOPLE TO LIVE THERE.
3/18
I CAN IMAGINE. IT BARELY FITS ONE PERSON AND A TOILET TAKES UP MOST OF THE SPACE.
PORT-AU-PRINCE. NOT PORT-A-POTTY.
OHHHH..... THEY MAKE SPECIAL ONES FOR ROYALTY?

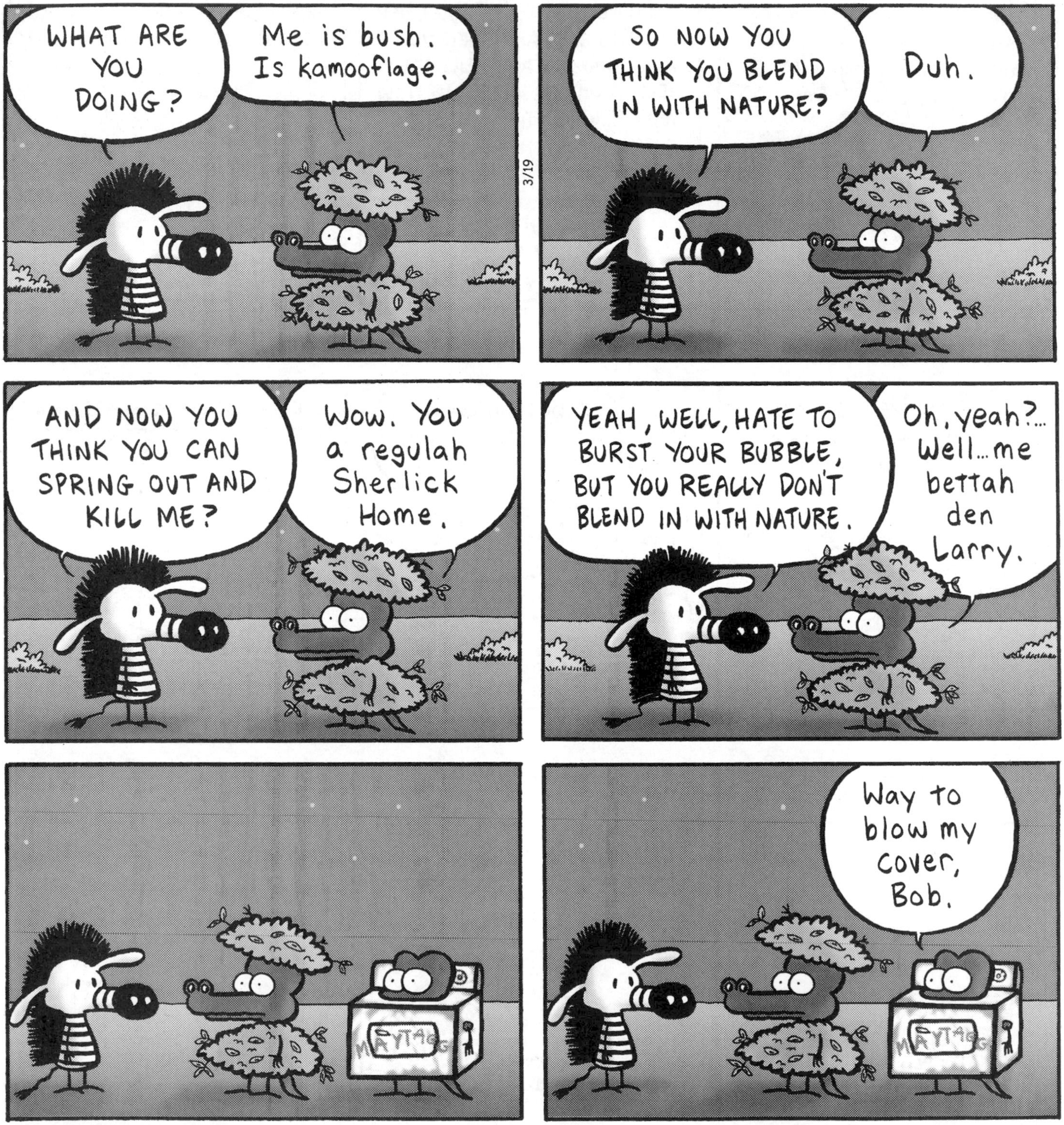
WHAT ARE YOU DOING?
Me is bush. Is kamooflage.
3/19
SO NOW YOU THINK YOU BLEND IN WITH NATURE?
Duh.
AND NOW YOU THINK YOU CAN SPRING OUT AND KILL ME?
Wow. You a regulah Sherlick Home.
YEAH, WELL, HATE TO BURST YOUR BUBBLE, BUT YOU REALLY DON'T BLEND IN WITH NATURE.
Oh, yeah?... Well... me bettah den Larry.
Way to blow my cover, Bob.

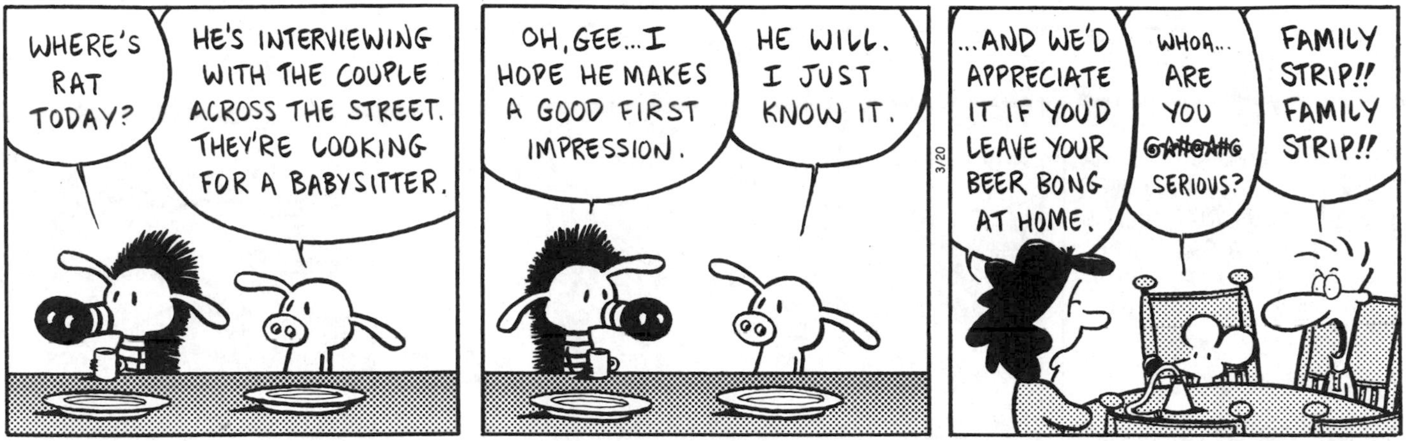
WHERE'S RAT TODAY?
HE'S INTERVIEWING WITH THE COUPLE ACROSS THE STREET. THEY'RE LOOKING FOR A BABYSITTER.
OH, GEE... I HOPE HE MAKES A GOOD FIRST IMPRESSION.
HE WILL. I JUST KNOW IT.
3/20
...AND WE'D APPRECIATE IT IF YOU'D LEAVE YOUR BEER BONG AT HOME.
WHOA... ARE YOU SERIOUS?
FAMILY STRIP!! FAMILY STRIP!!

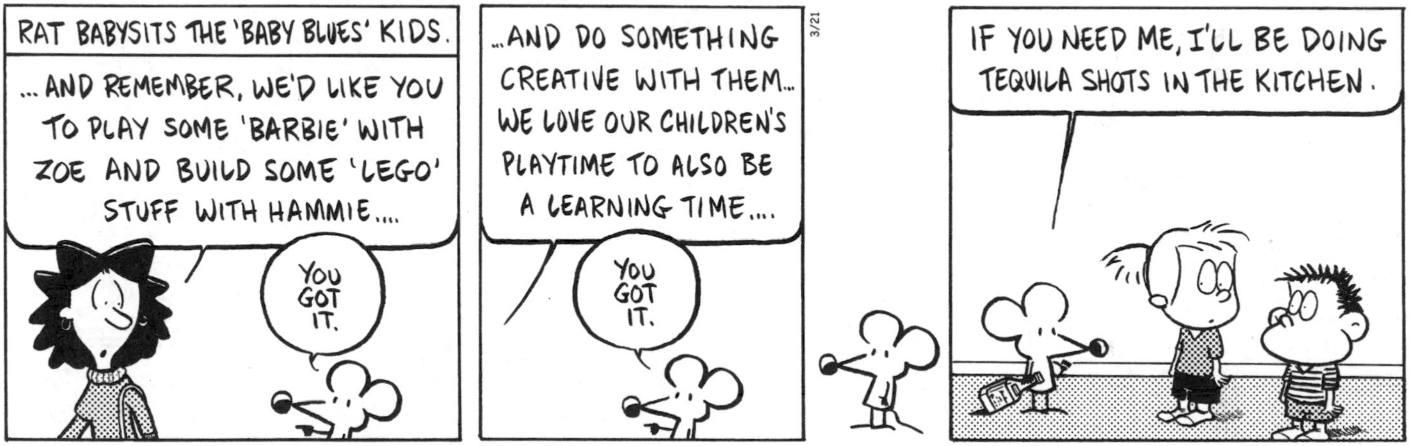
RAT BABYSITS THE 'BABY BLUES' KIDS.
... AND REMEMBER, WE'D LIKE YOU TO PLAY SOME 'BARBIE' WITH ZOE AND BUILD SOME 'LEGO' STUFF WITH HAMMIE....
YOU GOT IT.
...AND DO SOMETHING CREATIVE WITH THEM... WE LOVE OUR CHILDREN'S PLAYTIME TO ALSO BE A LEARNING TIME....
YOU GOT IT.
3/21
IF YOU NEED ME, I'LL BE DOING TEQUILA SHOTS IN THE KITCHEN.

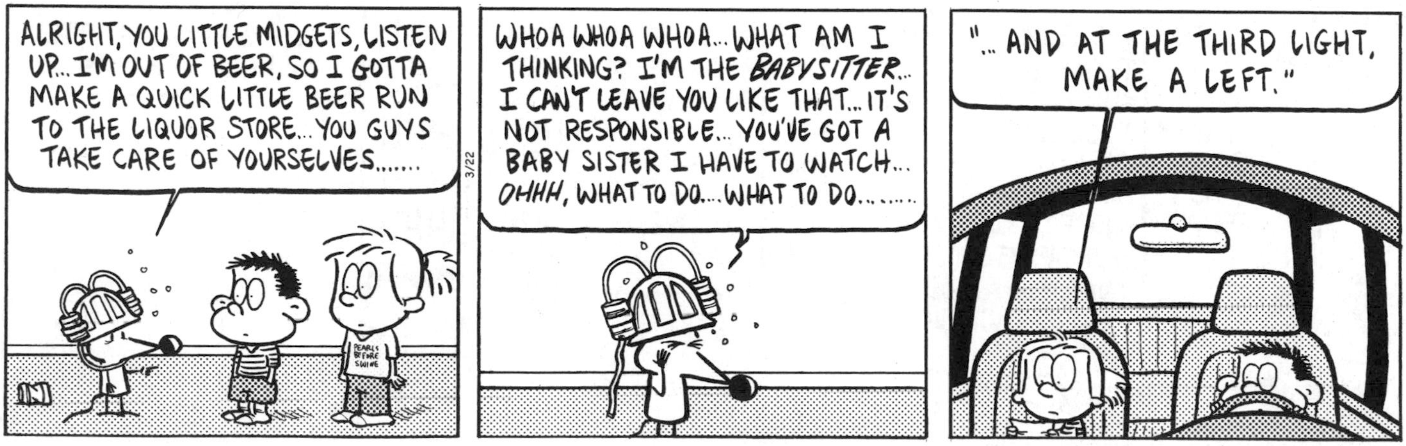
ALRIGHT, YOU LITTLE MIDGETS, LISTEN UP... I'M OUT OF BEER, SO I GOTTA MAKE A QUICK LITTLE BEER RUN TO THE LIQUOR STORE... YOU GUYS TAKE CARE OF YOURSELVES.......
3/22
PEARLS BEFORE SWINE
WHOA WHOA WHOA... WHAT AM I THINKING? I'M THE BABYSITTER... I CAN'T LEAVE YOU LIKE THAT... IT'S NOT RESPONSIBLE... YOU'VE GOT A BABY SISTER I HAVE TO WATCH... OHHH, WHAT TO DO.... WHAT TO DO.......
"... AND AT THE THIRD LIGHT, MAKE A LEFT."

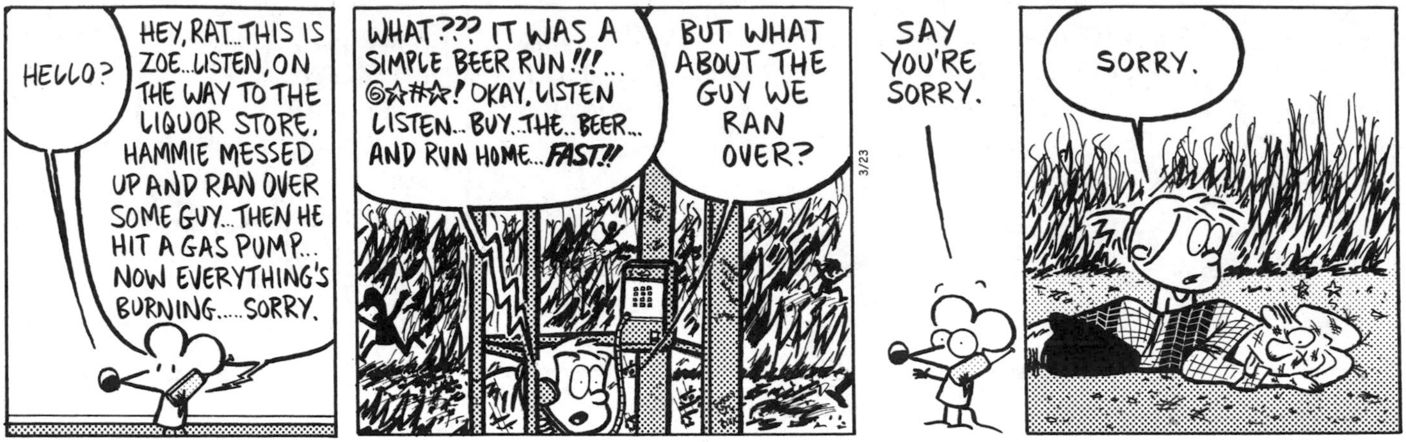
HELLO?
HEY, RAT...THIS IS ZOE...LISTEN, ON THE WAY TO THE LIQUOR STORE, HAMMIE MESSED UP AND RAN OVER SOME GUY...THEN HE HIT A GAS PUMP... NOW EVERYTHING'S BURNING..... SORRY.
WHAT??? IT WAS A SIMPLE BEER RUN!!!... 6☆#☆! OKAY, LISTEN LISTEN... BUY...THE...BEER... AND RUN HOME...FAST!!
BUT WHAT ABOUT THE GUY WE RAN OVER?
3/23
SAY YOU'RE SORRY.
SORRY.

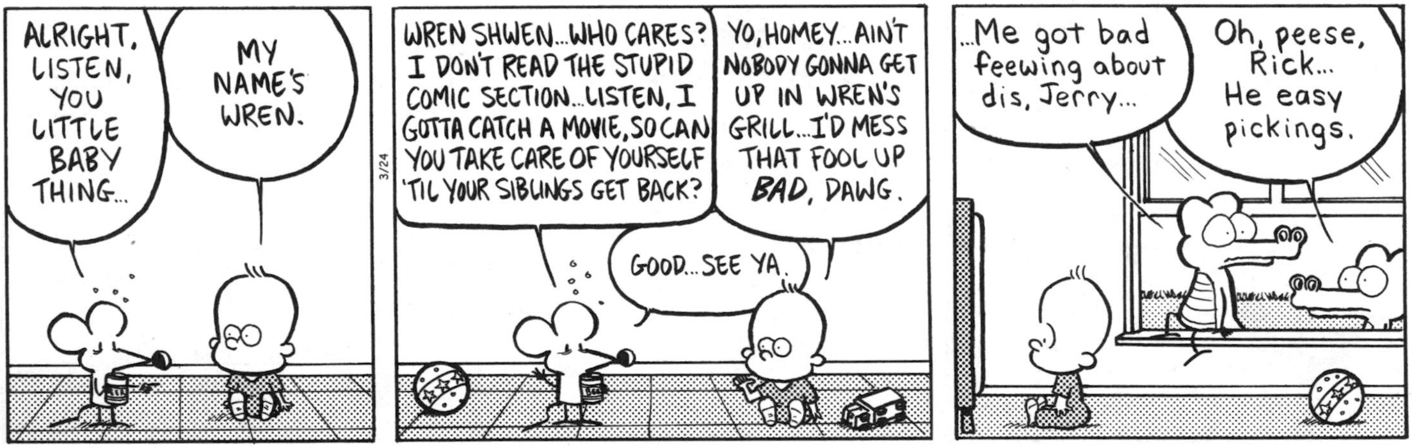
ALRIGHT, LISTEN, YOU LITTLE BABY THING...
MY NAME'S WREN.
3/24
WREN SHWEN...WHO CARES? I DON'T READ THE STUPID COMIC SECTION...LISTEN, I GOTTA CATCH A MOVIE, SO CAN YOU TAKE CARE OF YOURSELF 'TIL YOUR SIBLINGS GET BACK?
YO, HOMEY...AIN'T NOBODY GONNA GET UP IN WREN'S GRILL...I'D MESS THAT FOOL UP BAD, DAWG.
GOOD...SEE YA.
...Me got bad feewing about dis, Jerry...
Oh, peese, Rick... He easy pickings.

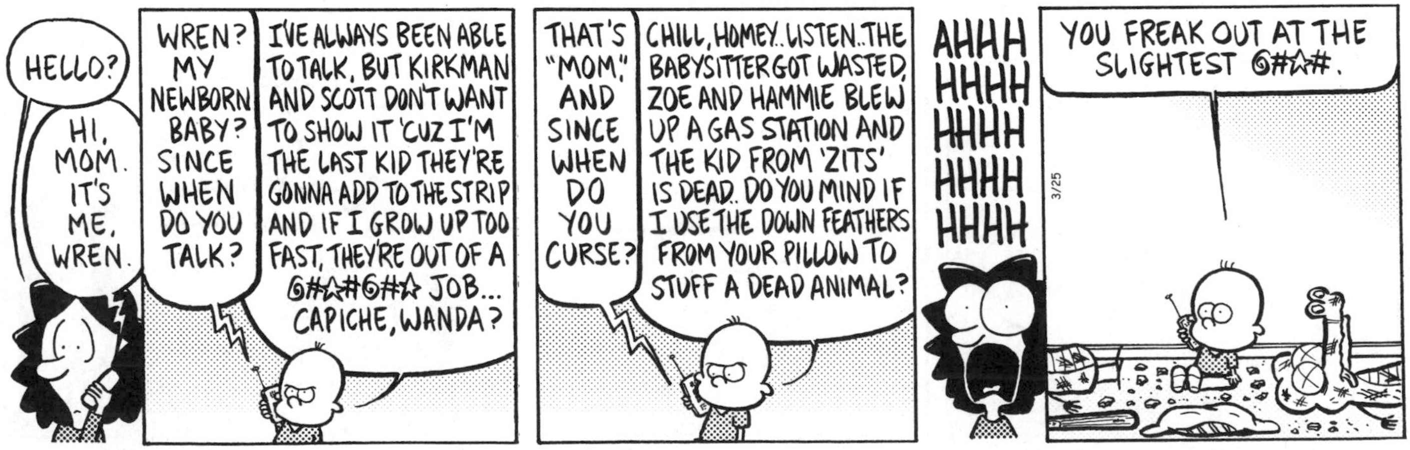
HELLO?
HI, MOM. IT'S ME, WREN.
WREN? MY NEWBORN BABY? SINCE WHEN DO YOU TALK?
I'VE ALWAYS BEEN ABLE TO TALK, BUT KIRKMAN AND SCOTT DON'T WANT TO SHOW IT 'CUZ I'M THE LAST KID THEY'RE GONNA ADD TO THE STRIP AND IF I GROW UP TOO FAST, THEY'RE OUT OF A 6#☆#6#☆ JOB... CAPICHE, WANDA?
THAT'S "MOM," AND SINCE WHEN DO YOU CURSE?
CHILL, HOMEY...LISTEN...THE BABYSITTER GOT WASTED, ZOE AND HAMMIE BLEW UP A GAS STATION AND THE KID FROM 'ZITS' IS DEAD. DO YOU MIND IF I USE THE DOWN FEATHERS FROM YOUR PILLOW TO STUFF A DEAD ANIMAL?
AHHHHHHHHHHHHHHHHHHHH
3/25
YOU FREAK OUT AT THE SLIGHTEST 6#☆#.

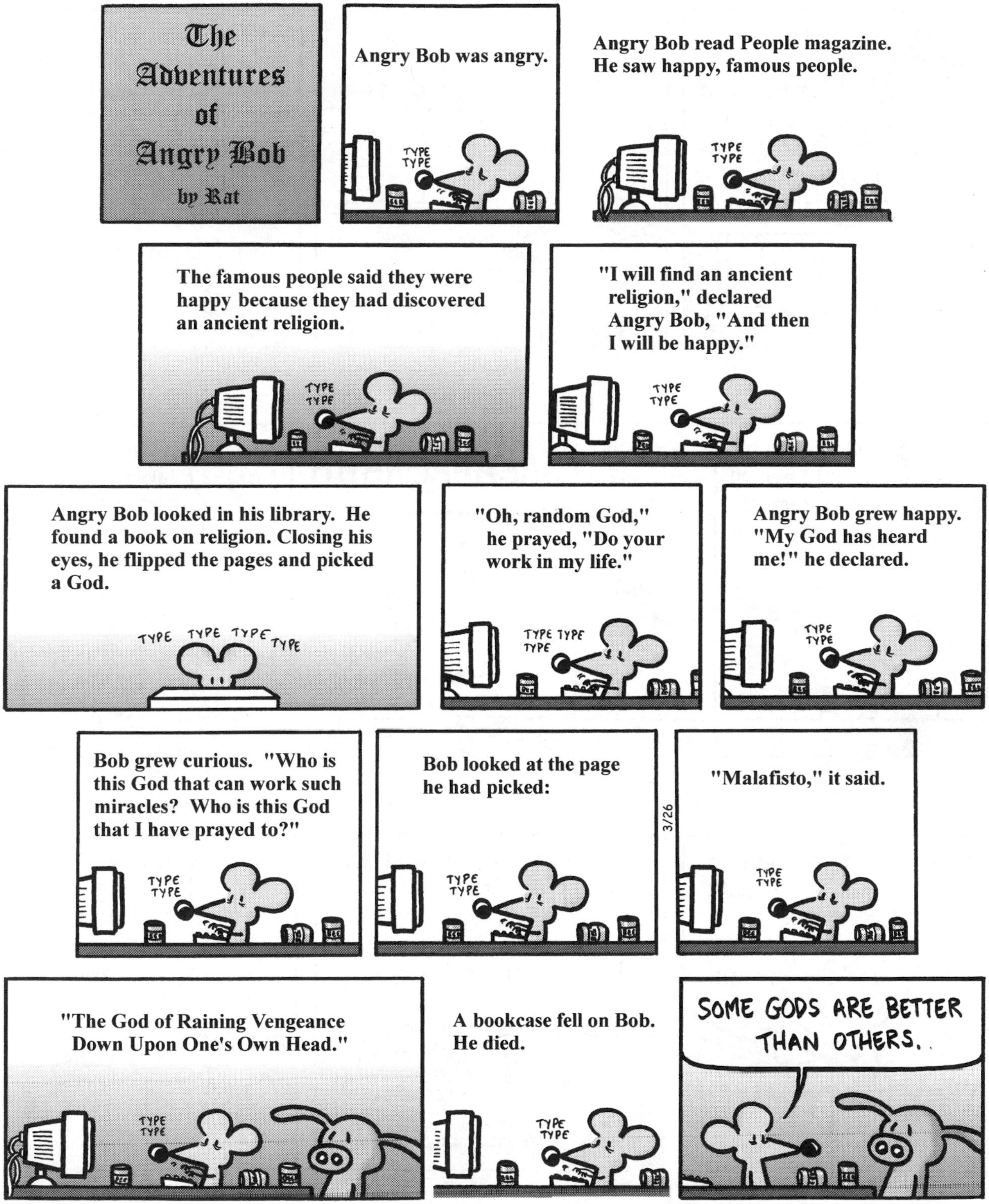
The Adventures of Angry Bob
by Rat
Angry Bob was angry.
TYPE TYPE
Angry Bob read People magazine. He saw happy, famous people.
TYPE TYPE
The famous people said they were happy because they had discovered an ancient religion.
TYPE TYPE
"I will find an ancient religion," declared Angry Bob, "And then I will be happy."
TYPE TYPE
Angry Bob looked in his library. He found a book on religion. Closing his eyes, he flipped the pages and picked a God.
TYPE TYPE TYPE TYPE
"Oh, random God," he prayed, "Do your work in my life."
TYPE TYPE TYPE
Angry Bob grew happy. "My God has heard me!" he declared.
TYPE TYPE
Bob grew curious. "Who is this God that can work such miracles? Who is this God that I have prayed to?"
TYPE TYPE
Bob looked at the page he had picked:
TYPE TYPE
3/26
"Malafisto," it said.
TYPE TYPE
"The God of Raining Vengeance Down Upon One's Own Head."
TYPE TYPE
A bookcase fell on Bob. He died.
TYPE TYPE
SOME GODS ARE BETTER THAN OTHERS.

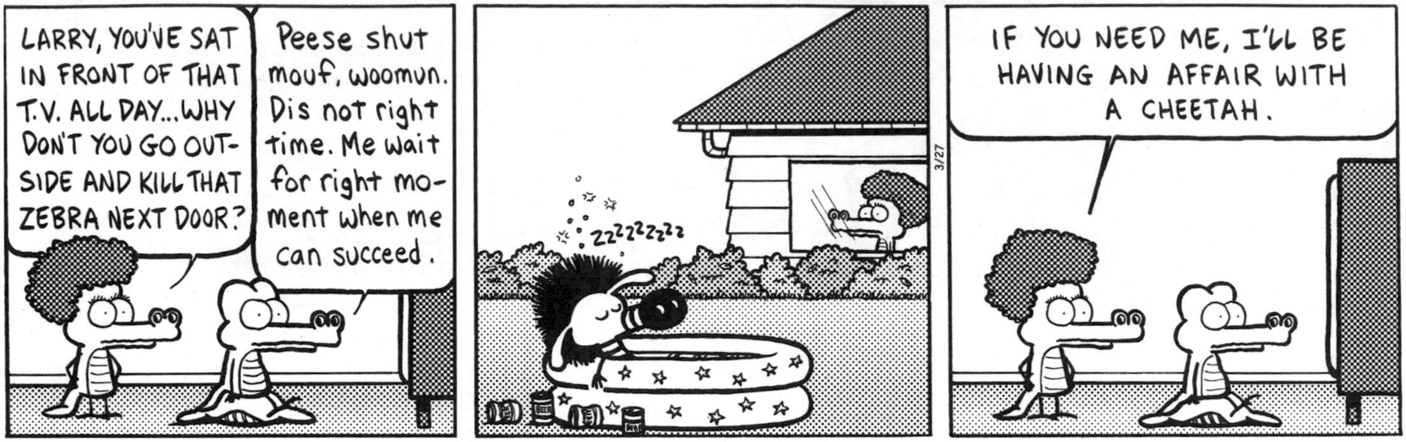
LARRY, YOU'VE SAT IN FRONT OF THAT T.V. ALL DAY...WHY DON'T YOU GO OUTSIDE AND KILL THAT ZEBRA NEXT DOOR?
Peese shut mouf, woomun. Dis not right time. Me wait for right moment when me can succeed.
ZZZZZZZZZ
3/27
IF YOU NEED ME, I'LL BE HAVING AN AFFAIR WITH A CHEETAH.

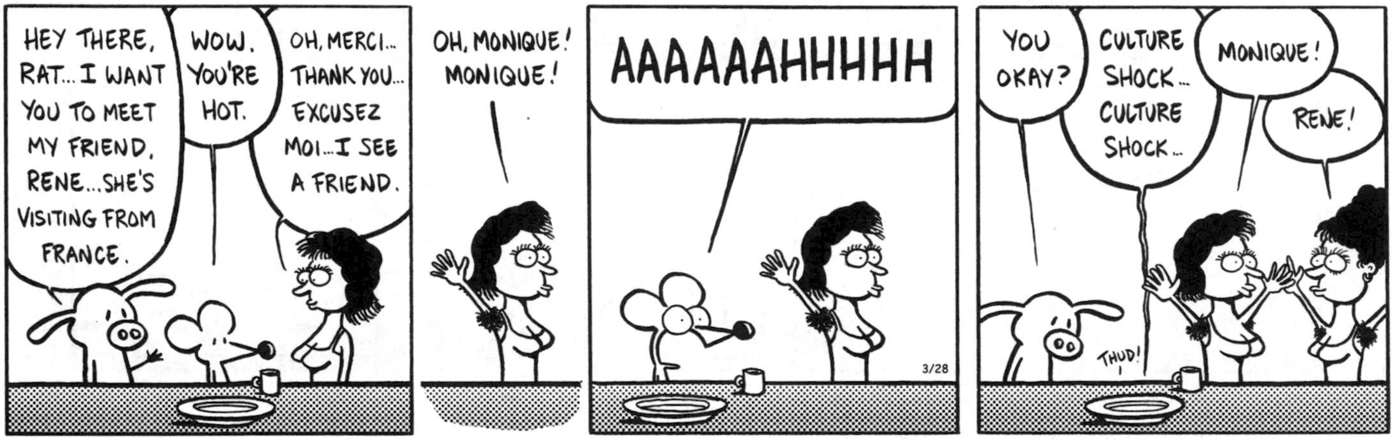
HEY THERE, RAT...I WANT YOU TO MEET MY FRIEND, RENE...SHE'S VISITING FROM FRANCE.
WOW. YOU'RE HOT.
OH, MERCI... THANK YOU... EXCUSEZ MOI...I SEE A FRIEND.
OH, MONIQUE! MONIQUE!
AAAAAAHHHHH
3/28
YOU OKAY?
CULTURE SHOCK... CULTURE SHOCK...
MONIQUE!
RENE!
THUD!

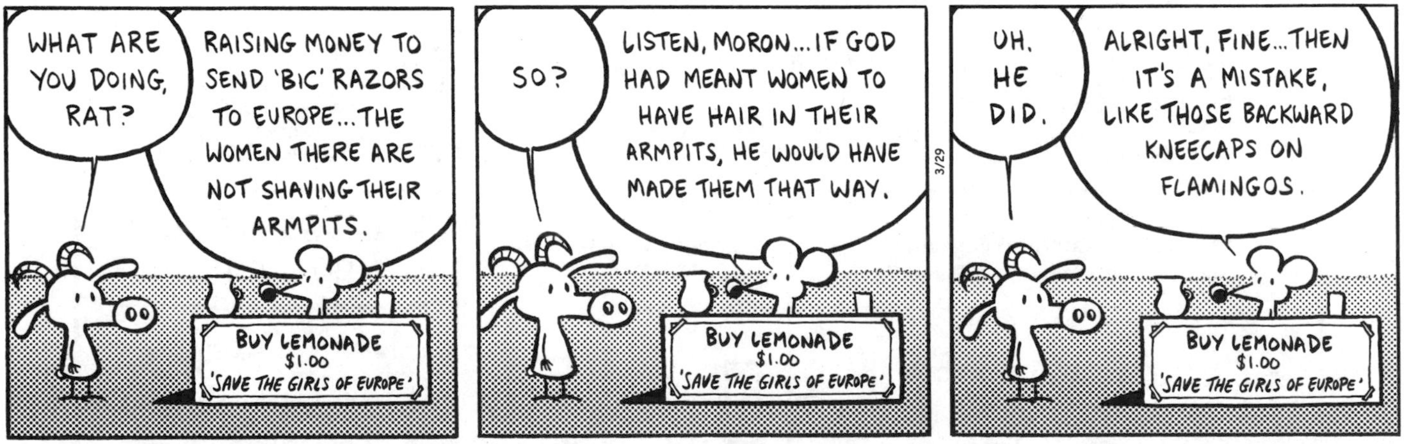
WHAT ARE YOU DOING, RAT?
RAISING MONEY TO SEND 'BIC' RAZORS TO EUROPE...THE WOMEN THERE ARE NOT SHAVING THEIR ARMPITS.
BUY LEMONADE $1.00 'SAVE THE GIRLS OF EUROPE'
SO?
LISTEN, MORON...IF GOD HAD MEANT WOMEN TO HAVE HAIR IN THEIR ARMPITS, HE WOULD HAVE MADE THEM THAT WAY.
BUY LEMONADE $1.00 'SAVE THE GIRLS OF EUROPE'
3/29
UH. HE DID.
ALRIGHT, FINE...THEN IT'S A MISTAKE, LIKE THOSE BACKWARD KNEECAPS ON FLAMINGOS.
BUY LEMONADE $1.00 'SAVE THE GIRLS OF EUROPE'

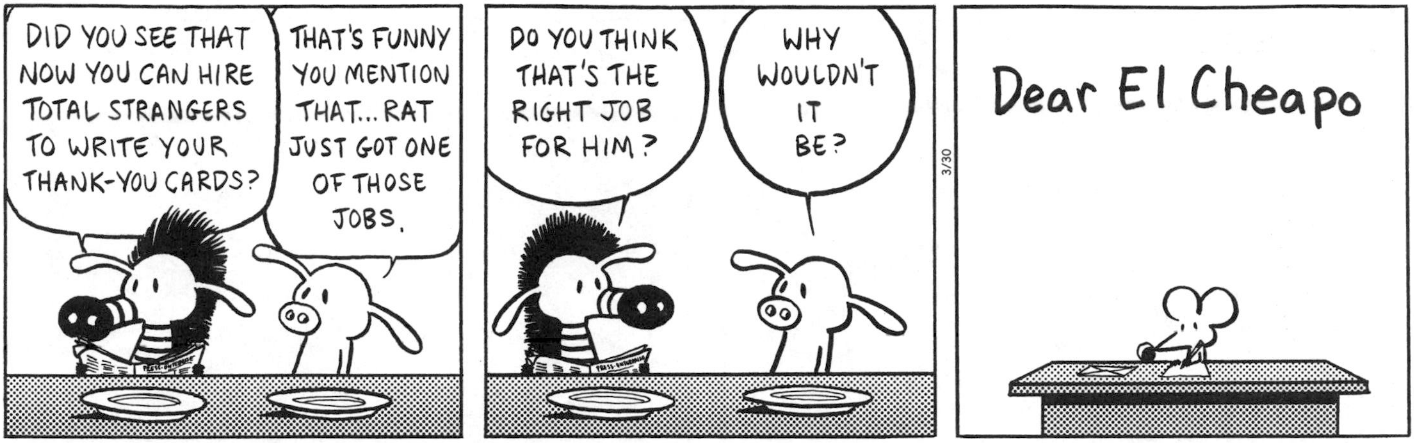
DID YOU SEE THAT NOW YOU CAN HIRE TOTAL STRANGERS TO WRITE YOUR THANK-YOU CARDS?
THAT'S FUNNY YOU MENTION THAT... RAT JUST GOT ONE OF THOSE JOBS.
DO YOU THINK THAT'S THE RIGHT JOB FOR HIM?
WHY WOULDN'T IT BE?
3/30
Dear El Cheapo

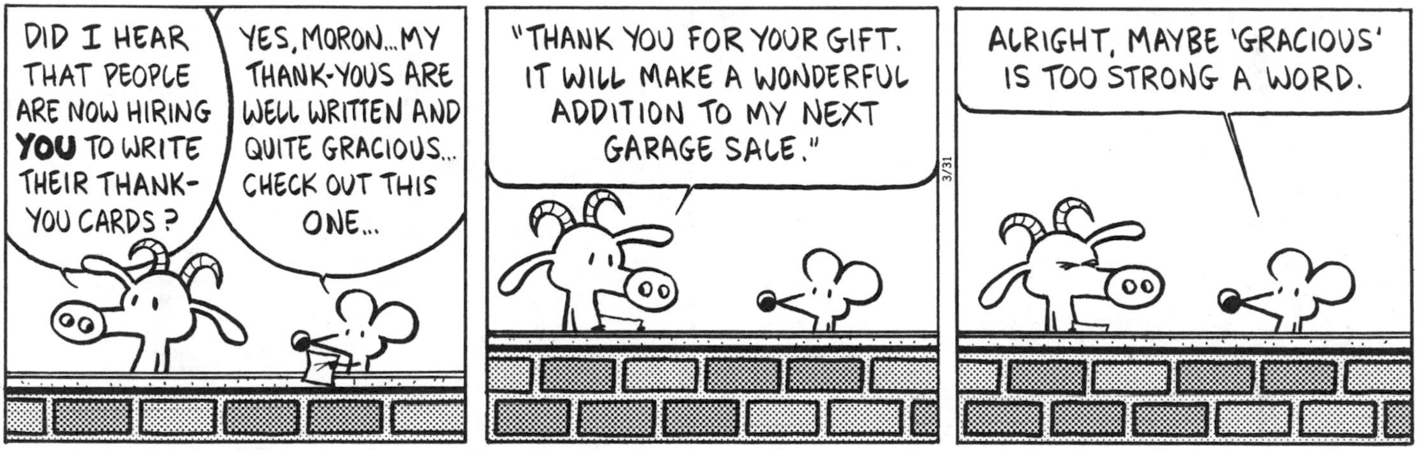
DID I HEAR THAT PEOPLE ARE NOW HIRING **YOU** TO WRITE THEIR THANK-YOU CARDS?
YES, MORON... MY THANK-YOUS ARE WELL WRITTEN AND QUITE GRACIOUS... CHECK OUT THIS ONE...
"THANK YOU FOR YOUR GIFT. IT WILL MAKE A WONDERFUL ADDITION TO MY NEXT GARAGE SALE."
3/31
ALRIGHT, MAYBE 'GRACIOUS' IS TOO STRONG A WORD.

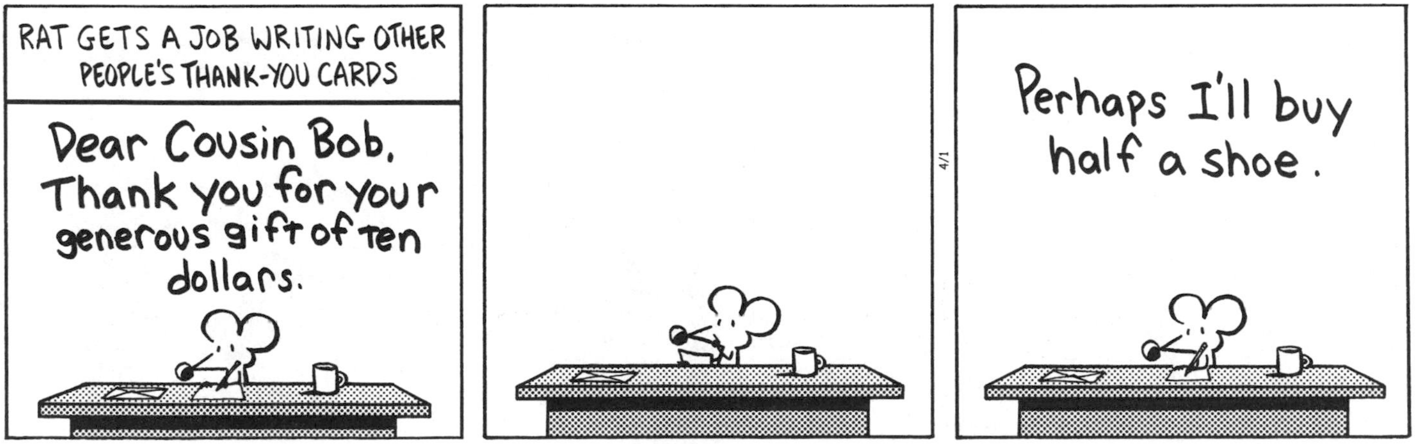
RAT GETS A JOB WRITING OTHER PEOPLE'S THANK-YOU CARDS
Dear Cousin Bob, Thank you for your generous gift of ten dollars.
4/1
Perhaps I'll buy half a shoe.

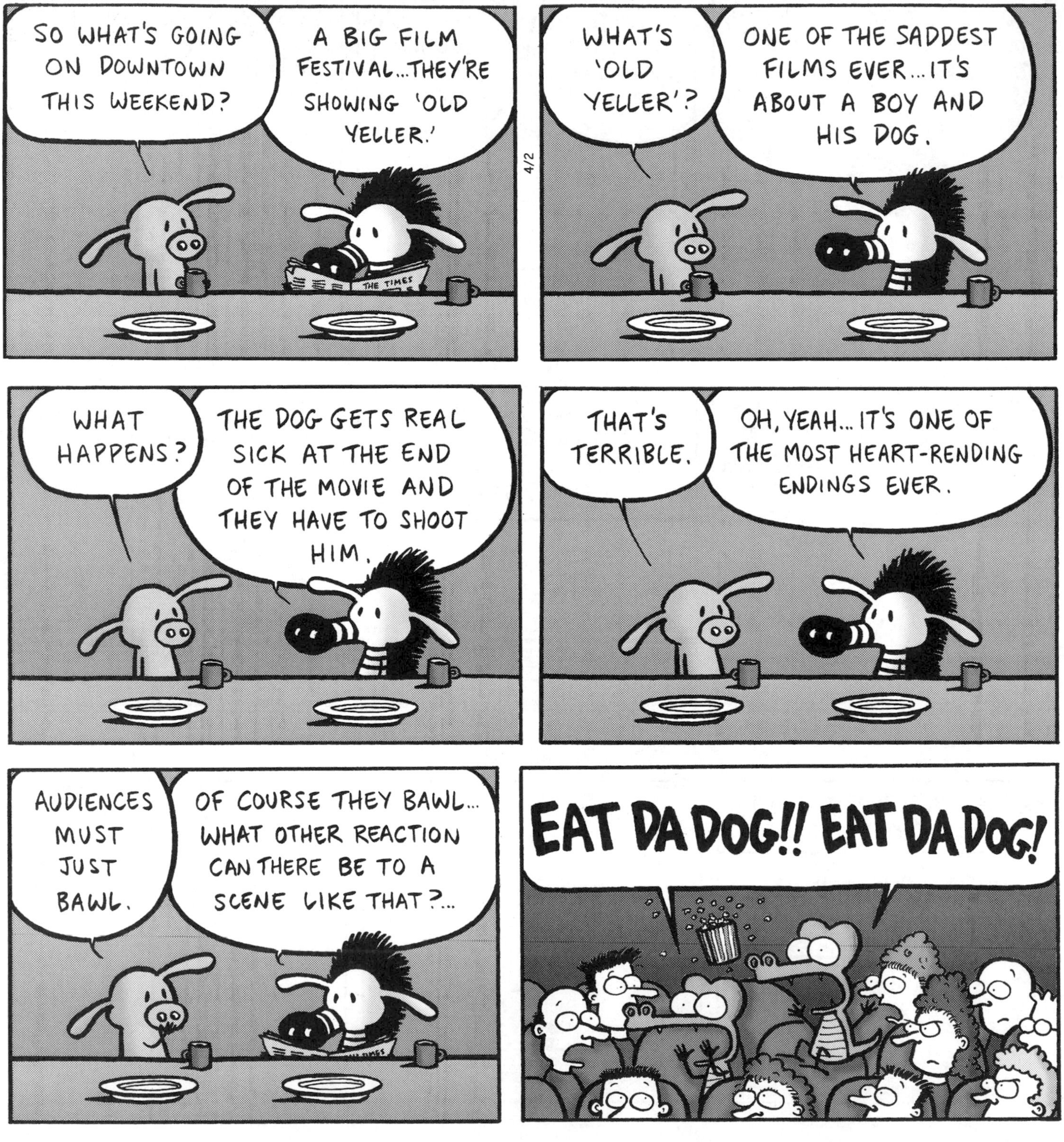
SO WHAT'S GOING ON DOWNTOWN THIS WEEKEND?
A BIG FILM FESTIVAL...THEY'RE SHOWING 'OLD YELLER.'
THE TIMES
4/2
WHAT'S 'OLD YELLER'?
ONE OF THE SADDEST FILMS EVER...IT'S ABOUT A BOY AND HIS DOG.
WHAT HAPPENS?
THE DOG GETS REAL SICK AT THE END OF THE MOVIE AND THEY HAVE TO SHOOT HIM.
THAT'S TERRIBLE.
OH, YEAH... IT'S ONE OF THE MOST HEART-RENDING ENDINGS EVER.
AUDIENCES MUST JUST BAWL.
OF COURSE THEY BAWL... WHAT OTHER REACTION CAN THERE BE TO A SCENE LIKE THAT?...
EAT DA DOG!! EAT DA DOG!

Story Update:

Years ago, Rat dated Pig's sister, Farina. Farina is a germaphobe and therefore lives in a plastic bubble. Ultimately, Farina broke Rat's heart and married someone else. We now return to our comic, already in progress.

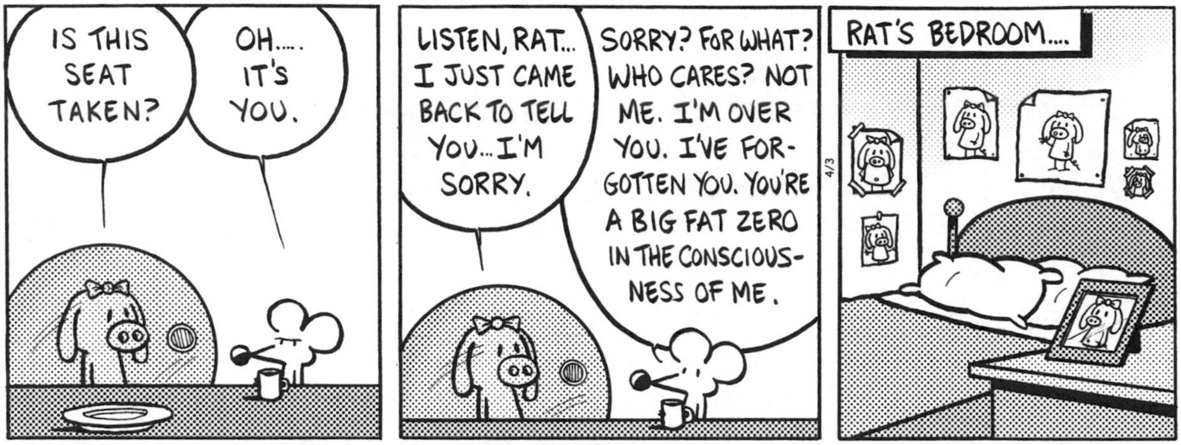
IS THIS SEAT TAKEN?
OH..... IT'S YOU.
LISTEN, RAT... I JUST CAME BACK TO TELL YOU... I'M SORRY.
SORRY? FOR WHAT? WHO CARES? NOT ME. I'M OVER YOU. I'VE FORGOTTEN YOU. YOU'RE A BIG FAT ZERO IN THE CONSCIOUSNESS OF ME.
4/3
RAT'S BEDROOM....

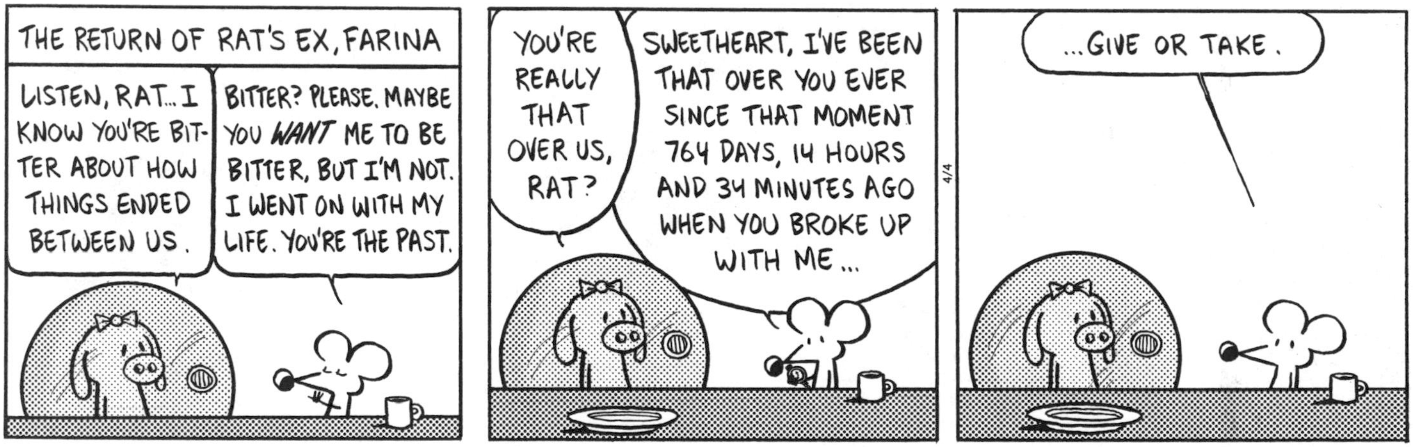
THE RETURN OF RAT'S EX, FARINA
LISTEN, RAT... I KNOW YOU'RE BITTER ABOUT HOW THINGS ENDED BETWEEN US.
BITTER? PLEASE. MAYBE YOU WANT ME TO BE BITTER, BUT I'M NOT. I WENT ON WITH MY LIFE. YOU'RE THE PAST.
YOU'RE REALLY THAT OVER US, RAT?
SWEETHEART, I'VE BEEN THAT OVER YOU EVER SINCE THAT MOMENT 764 DAYS, 14 HOURS AND 34 MINUTES AGO WHEN YOU BROKE UP WITH ME...
4/4
...GIVE OR TAKE.

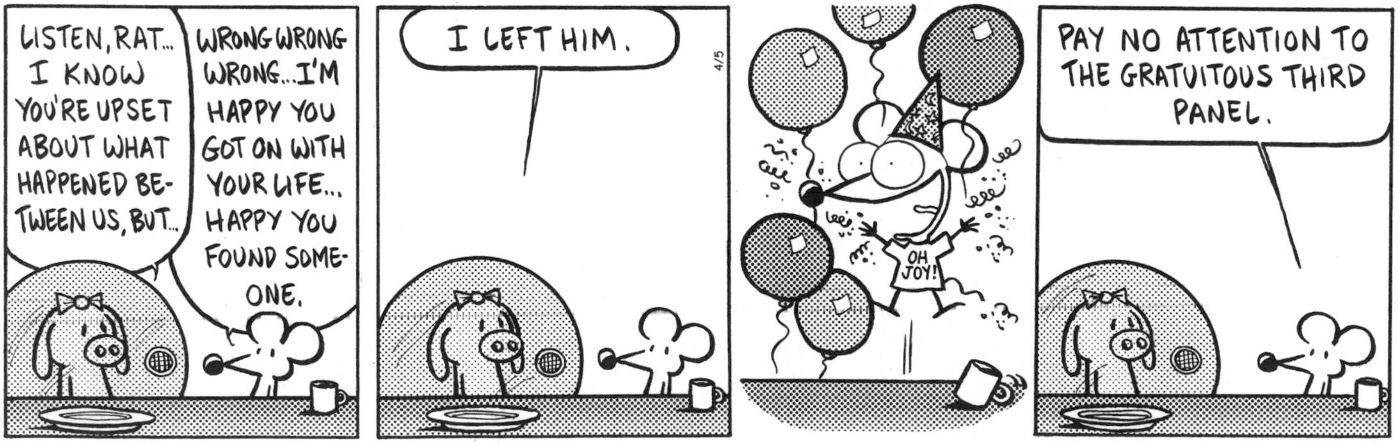
LISTEN, RAT... I KNOW YOU'RE UPSET ABOUT WHAT HAPPENED BETWEEN US, BUT...
WRONG WRONG WRONG... I'M HAPPY YOU GOT ON WITH YOUR LIFE... HAPPY YOU FOUND SOMEONE.
I LEFT HIM.
4/5
OH JOY!
PAY NO ATTENTION TO THE GRATUITOUS THIRD PANEL.

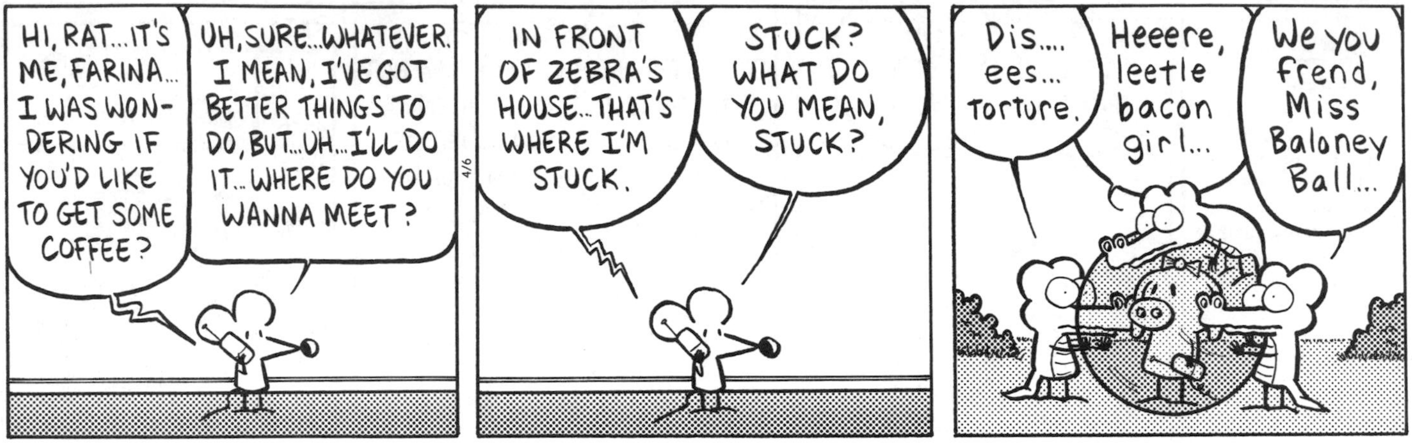
HI, RAT...IT'S ME, FARINA... I WAS WONDERING IF YOU'D LIKE TO GET SOME COFFEE?
UH, SURE...WHATEVER. I MEAN, I'VE GOT BETTER THINGS TO DO, BUT...UH...I'LL DO IT...WHERE DO YOU WANNA MEET?
4/6
IN FRONT OF ZEBRA'S HOUSE...THAT'S WHERE I'M STUCK.
STUCK? WHAT DO YOU MEAN, STUCK?
Dis.... ees... torture.
Heeere, leetle bacon girl...
We you frend, Miss Baloney Ball...

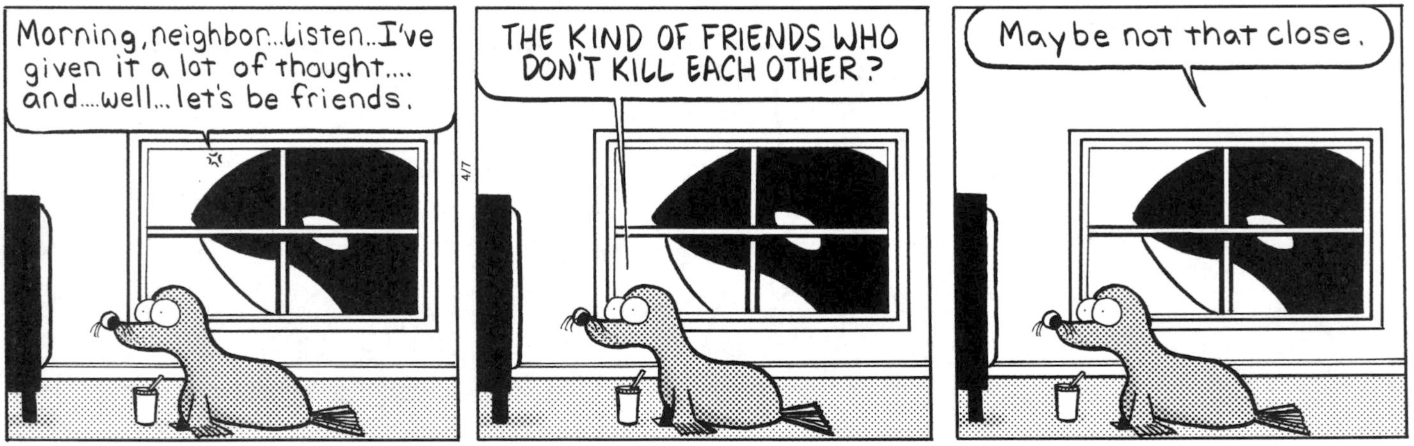
Morning, neighbor...Listen...I've given it a lot of thought.... and....well... let's be friends.
4/7
THE KIND OF FRIENDS WHO DON'T KILL EACH OTHER?
Maybe not that close.

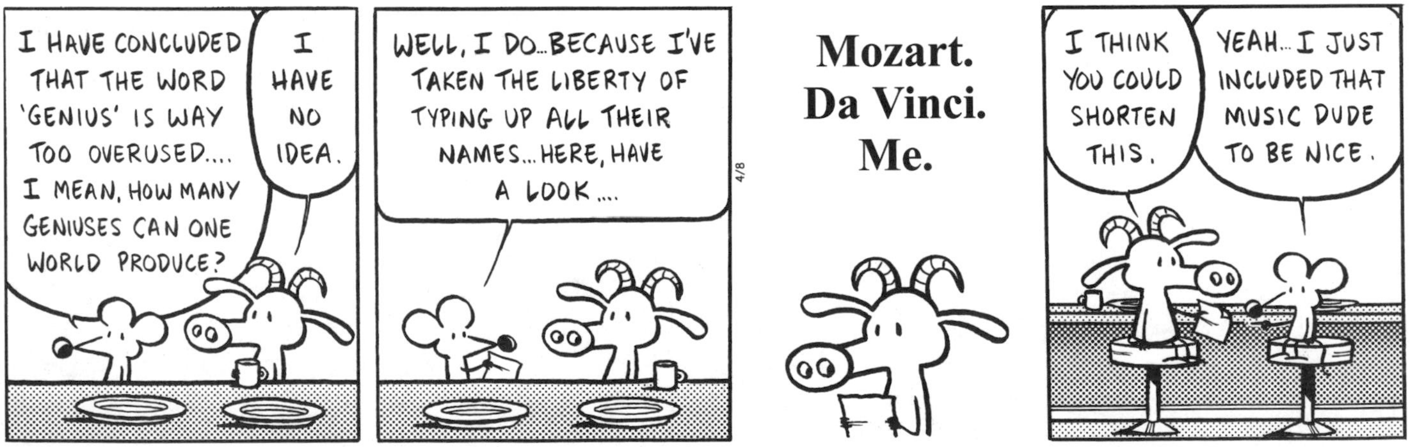
I HAVE CONCLUDED THAT THE WORD 'GENIUS' IS WAY TOO OVERUSED.... I MEAN, HOW MANY GENIUSES CAN ONE WORLD PRODUCE?
I HAVE NO IDEA.
WELL, I DO...BECAUSE I'VE TAKEN THE LIBERTY OF TYPING UP ALL THEIR NAMES...HERE, HAVE A LOOK....
4/8
Mozart.
Da Vinci.
Me.
I THINK YOU COULD SHORTEN THIS.
YEAH... I JUST INCLUDED THAT MUSIC DUDE TO BE NICE.

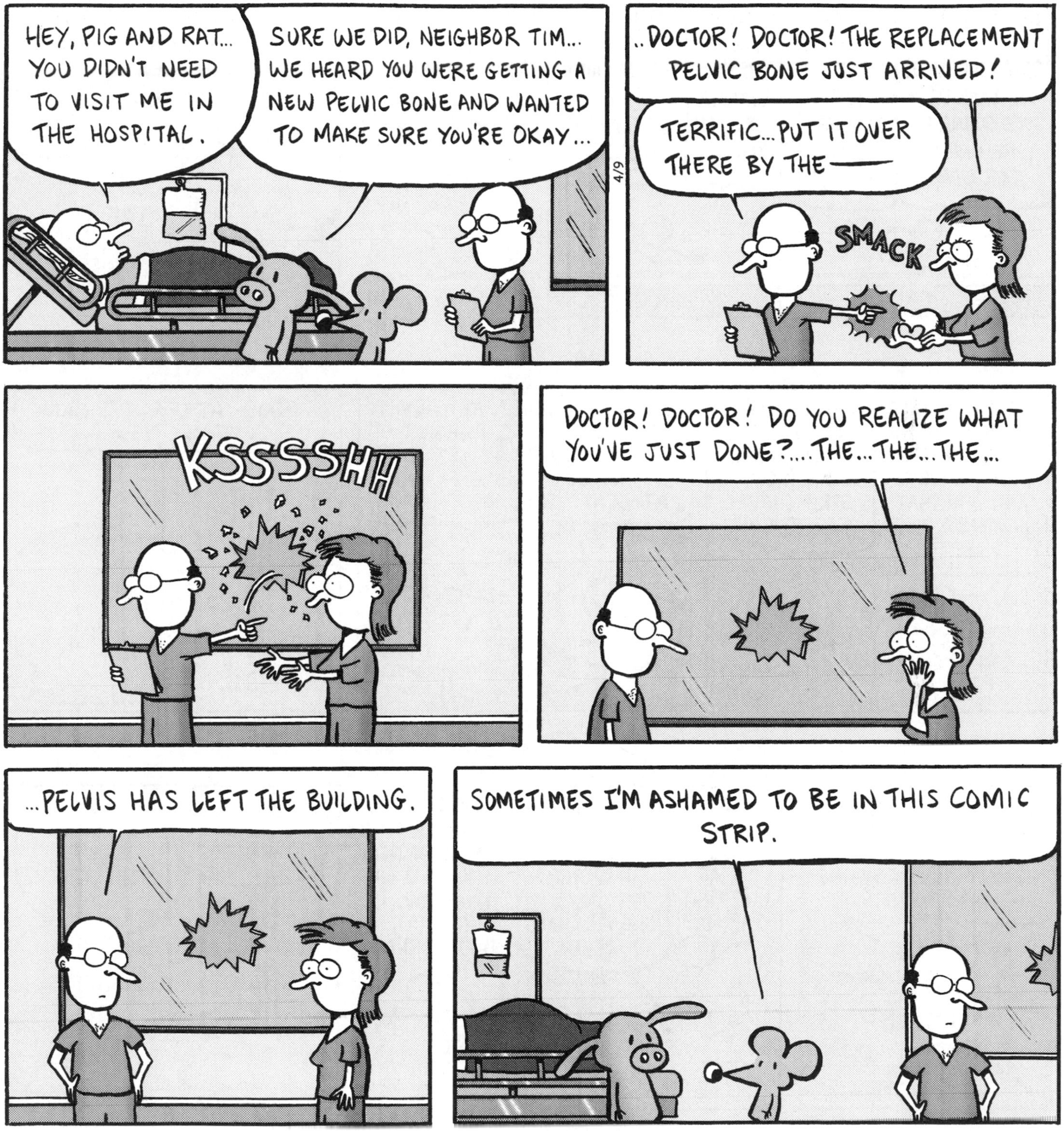
HEY, PIG AND RAT... YOU DIDN'T NEED TO VISIT ME IN THE HOSPITAL.
SURE WE DID, NEIGHBOR TIM... WE HEARD YOU WERE GETTING A NEW PELVIC BONE AND WANTED TO MAKE SURE YOU'RE OKAY...
4/9
..DOCTOR! DOCTOR! THE REPLACEMENT PELVIC BONE JUST ARRIVED!
TERRIFIC...PUT IT OVER THERE BY THE—
SMACK
KSSSSHH
DOCTOR! DOCTOR! DO YOU REALIZE WHAT YOU'VE JUST DONE?.... THE... THE... THE...
...PELVIS HAS LEFT THE BUILDING.
SOMETIMES I'M ASHAMED TO BE IN THIS COMIC STRIP.

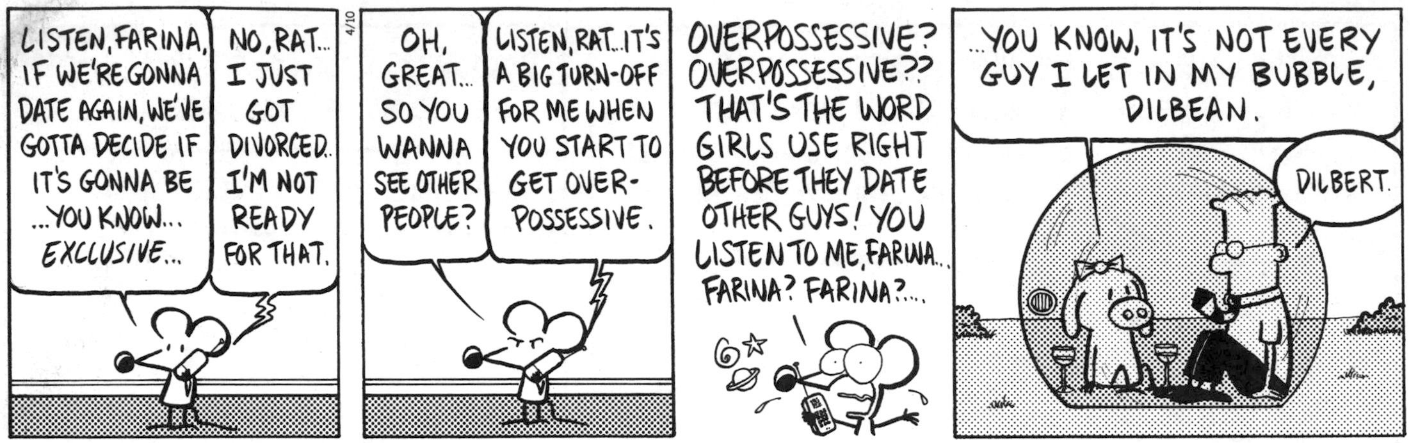
LISTEN, FARINA, IF WE'RE GONNA DATE AGAIN, WE'VE GOTTA DECIDE IF IT'S GONNA BE ...YOU KNOW... EXCLUSIVE...
NO, RAT... I JUST GOT DIVORCED. I'M NOT READY FOR THAT.
4/10
OH, GREAT... SO YOU WANNA SEE OTHER PEOPLE?
LISTEN, RAT...IT'S A BIG TURN-OFF FOR ME WHEN YOU START TO GET OVER-POSSESSIVE.
OVERPOSSESSIVE? OVERPOSSESSIVE?? THAT'S THE WORD GIRLS USE RIGHT BEFORE THEY DATE OTHER GUYS! YOU LISTEN TO ME, FARINA... FARINA? FARINA?...
...YOU KNOW, IT'S NOT EVERY GUY I LET IN MY BUBBLE, DILBEAN.
DILBERT.

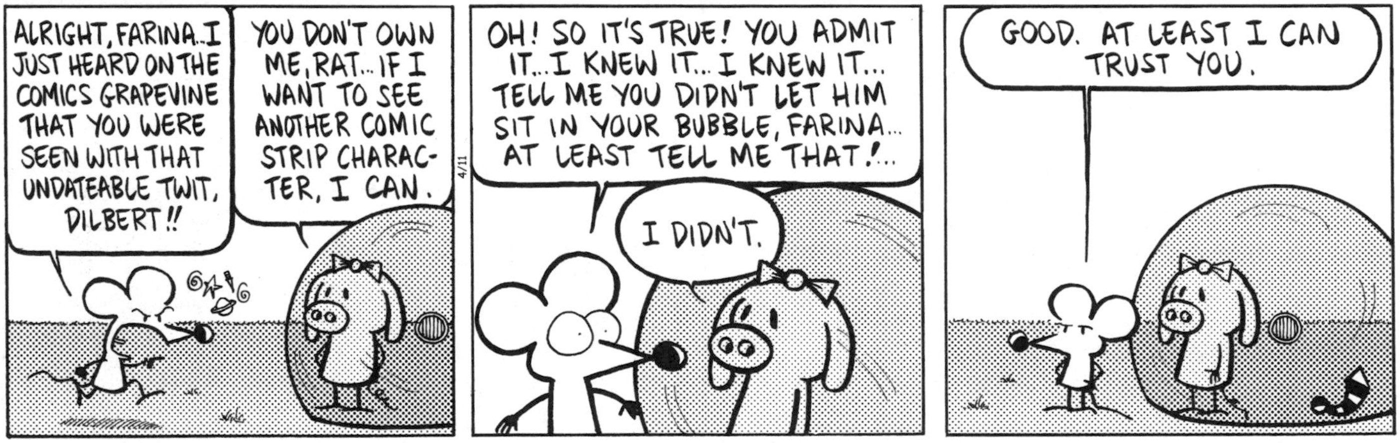
ALRIGHT, FARINA...I JUST HEARD ON THE COMICS GRAPEVINE THAT YOU WERE SEEN WITH THAT UNDATEABLE TWIT, DILBERT!!
YOU DON'T OWN ME, RAT... IF I WANT TO SEE ANOTHER COMIC STRIP CHARACTER, I CAN.
4/11
OH! SO IT'S TRUE! YOU ADMIT IT... I KNEW IT... I KNEW IT... TELL ME YOU DIDN'T LET HIM SIT IN YOUR BUBBLE, FARINA... AT LEAST TELL ME THAT!...
I DIDN'T.
GOOD. AT LEAST I CAN TRUST YOU.

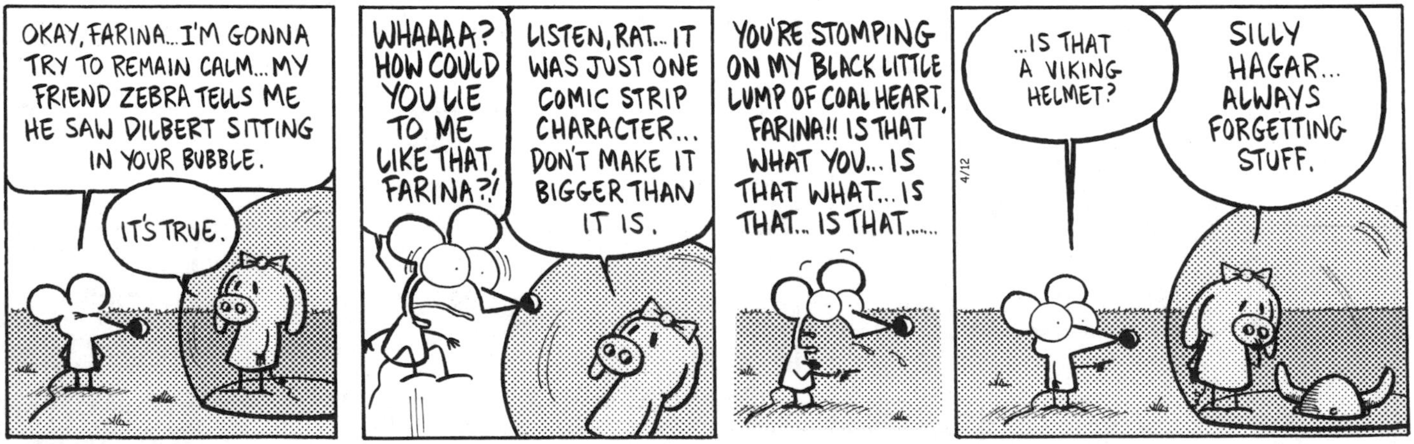
OKAY, FARINA...I'M GONNA TRY TO REMAIN CALM...MY FRIEND ZEBRA TELLS ME HE SAW DILBERT SITTING IN YOUR BUBBLE.
IT'S TRUE.
WHAAAA? HOW COULD YOU LIE TO ME LIKE THAT, FARINA?!
LISTEN, RAT... IT WAS JUST ONE COMIC STRIP CHARACTER... DON'T MAKE IT BIGGER THAN IT IS.
YOU'RE STOMPING ON MY BLACK LITTLE LUMP OF COAL HEART, FARINA!! IS THAT WHAT YOU... IS THAT WHAT... IS THAT... IS THAT......
4/12
...IS THAT A VIKING HELMET?
SILLY HAGAR... ALWAYS FORGETTING STUFF.

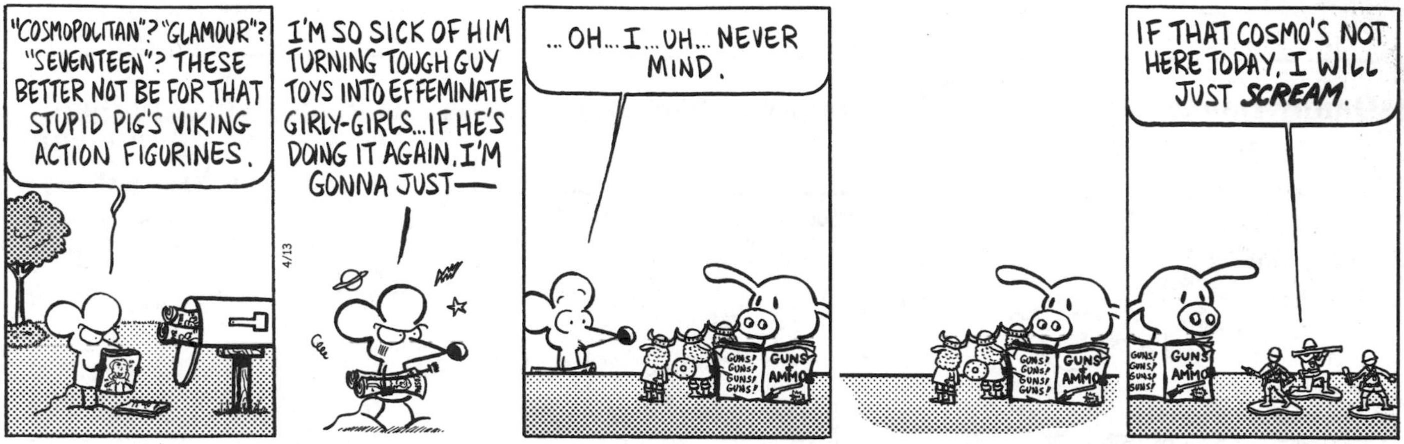

"COSMOPOLITAN"? "GLAMOUR"? "SEVENTEEN"? THESE BETTER NOT BE FOR THAT STUPID PIG'S VIKING ACTION FIGURINES.
4/13
I'M SO SICK OF HIM TURNING TOUGH GUY TOYS INTO EFFEMINATE GIRLY-GIRLS...IF HE'S DOING IT AGAIN, I'M GONNA JUST—
...OH...I...UH...NEVER MIND.
GUNS! GUNS! GUNS! GUNS!
GUNS + AMMO
IF THAT COSMO'S NOT HERE TODAY, I WILL JUST SCREAM.

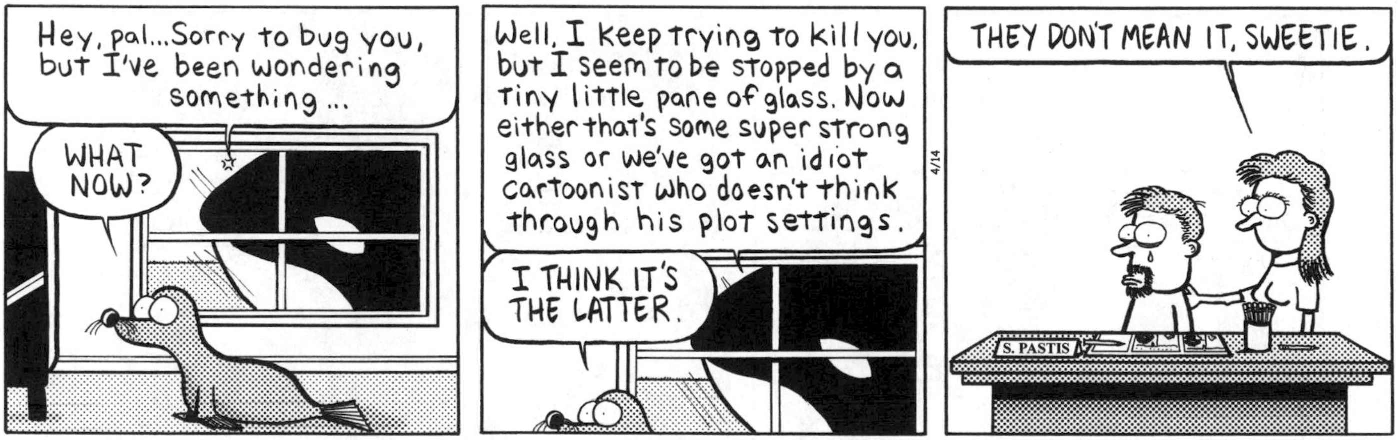

Hey, pal...Sorry to bug you, but I've been wondering something...
WHAT NOW?
4/14
Well, I keep trying to kill you, but I seem to be stopped by a tiny little pane of glass. Now either that's some super strong glass or we've got an idiot cartoonist who doesn't think through his plot settings.
I THINK IT'S THE LATTER.
THEY DON'T MEAN IT, SWEETIE.
S. PASTIS

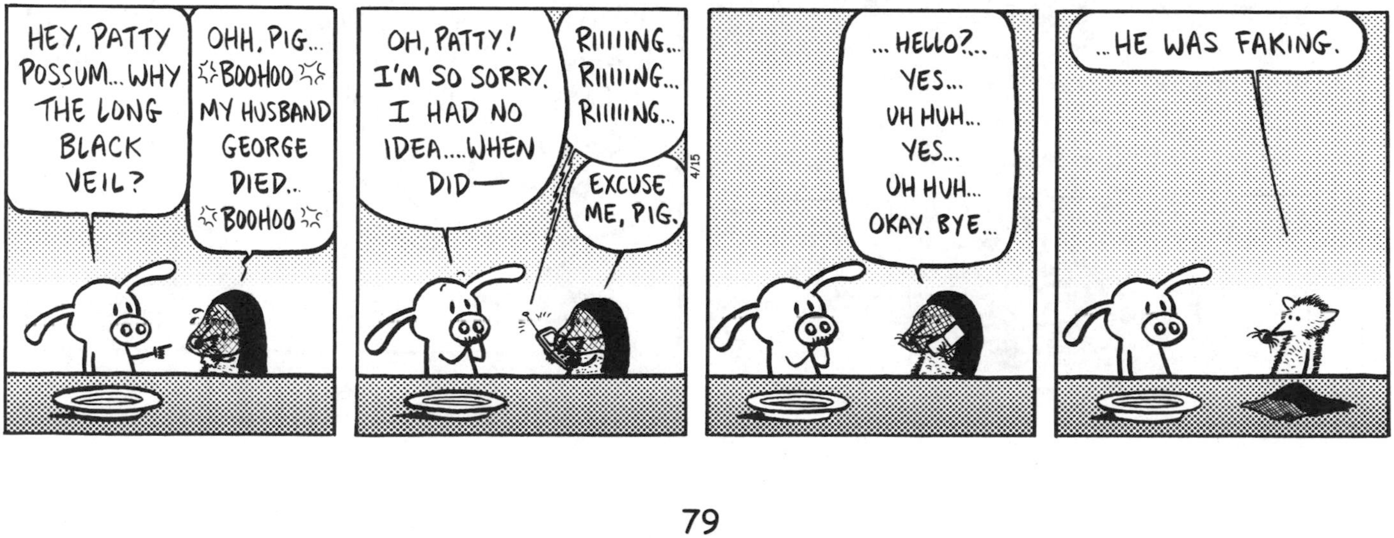

HEY, PATTY POSSUM...WHY THE LONG BLACK VEIL?
OHH, PIG... BOOHOO MY HUSBAND GEORGE DIED... BOOHOO
4/15
OH, PATTY! I'M SO SORRY. I HAD NO IDEA....WHEN DID—
RIIIING... RIIIING... RIIIING...
EXCUSE ME, PIG.
...HELLO?... YES... UH HUH... YES... UH HUH... OKAY. BYE...
...HE WAS FAKING.

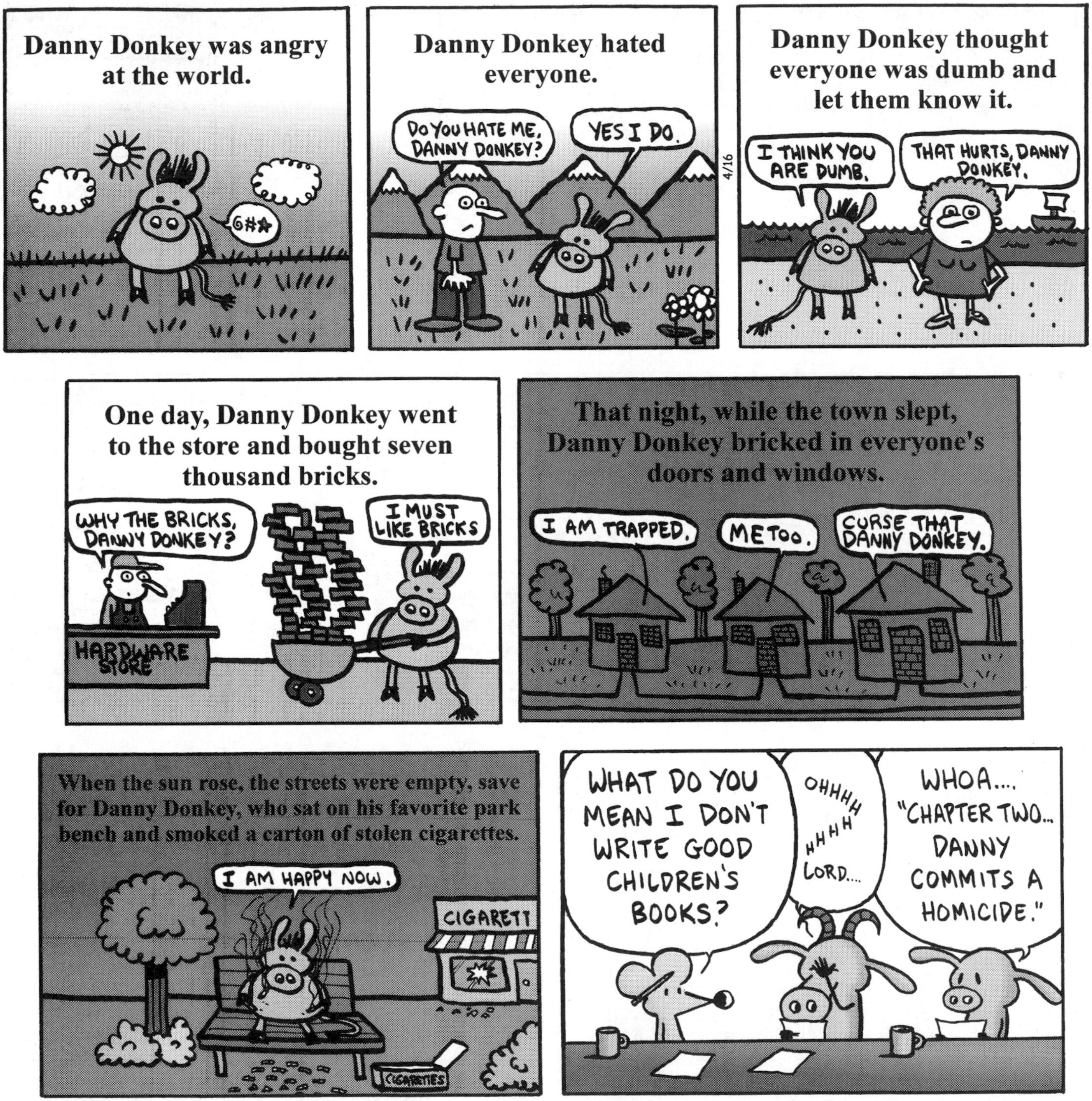
Danny Donkey was angry at the world.
Danny Donkey hated everyone.
DO YOU HATE ME, DANNY DONKEY?
YES I DO.
4/16
Danny Donkey thought everyone was dumb and let them know it.
I THINK YOU ARE DUMB.
THAT HURTS, DANNY DONKEY.
One day, Danny Donkey went to the store and bought seven thousand bricks.
WHY THE BRICKS, DANNY DONKEY?
I MUST LIKE BRICKS
HARDWARE STORE
That night, while the town slept, Danny Donkey bricked in everyone's doors and windows.
I AM TRAPPED.
ME TOO.
CURSE THAT DANNY DONKEY.
When the sun rose, the streets were empty, save for Danny Donkey, who sat on his favorite park bench and smoked a carton of stolen cigarettes.
I AM HAPPY NOW.
CIGARETT
CIGARETTES
WHAT DO YOU MEAN I DON'T WRITE GOOD CHILDREN'S BOOKS?
OHHHHHHHHH LORD....
WHOA.... "CHAPTER TWO... DANNY COMMITS A HOMICIDE."

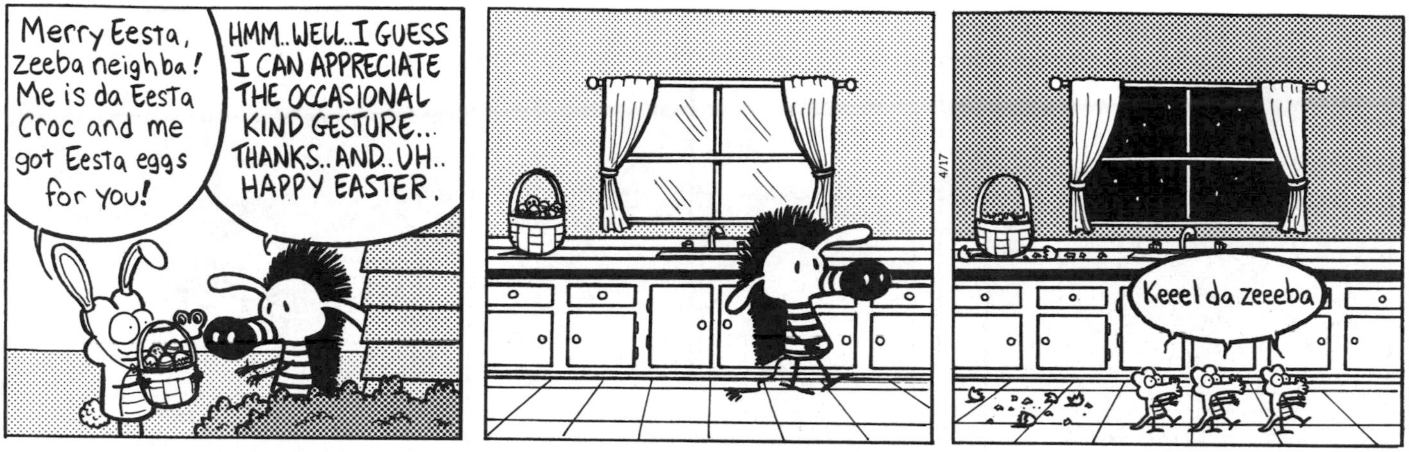
Merry Eesta, zeeba neighba! Me is da Eesta Croc and me got Eesta eggs for you!
HMM.. WELL.. I GUESS I CAN APPRECIATE THE OCCASIONAL KIND GESTURE... THANKS.. AND.. UH.. HAPPY EASTER.
4/17
Keeel da zeeeba

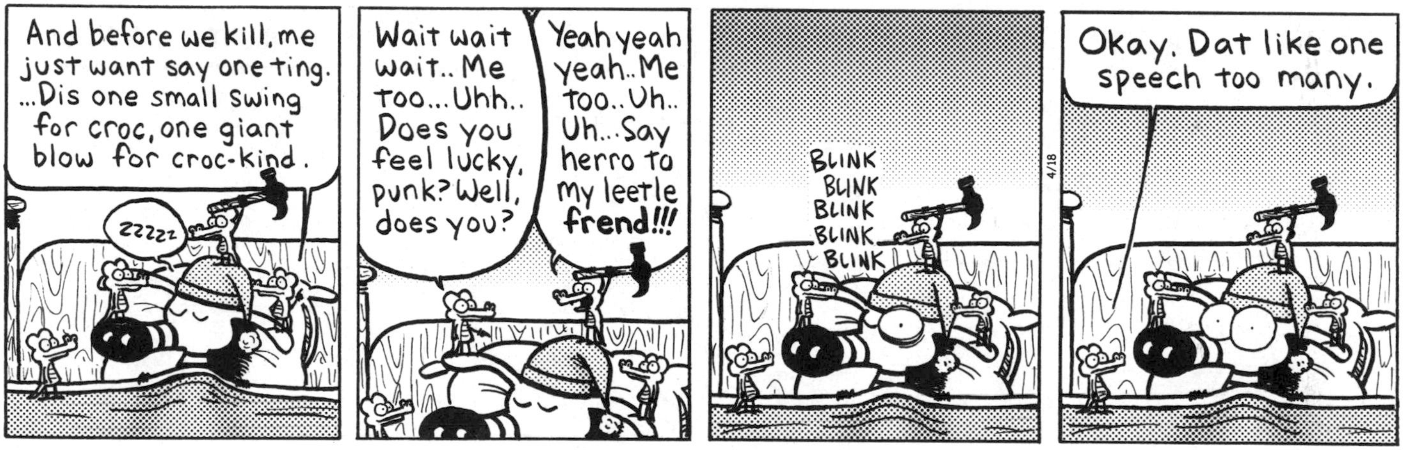
And before we kill, me just want say one ting. ...Dis one small swing for croc, one giant blow for croc-kind.
ZZZZZ
Wait wait wait.. Me too... Uhh.. Does you feel lucky, punk? Well, does you?
Yeah yeah yeah.. Me too.. Uh.. Uh... Say herro to my leetle **frend!!!**
4/18
BLINK
BLINK
BLINK
BLINK
BLINK
Okay. Dat like one speech too many.

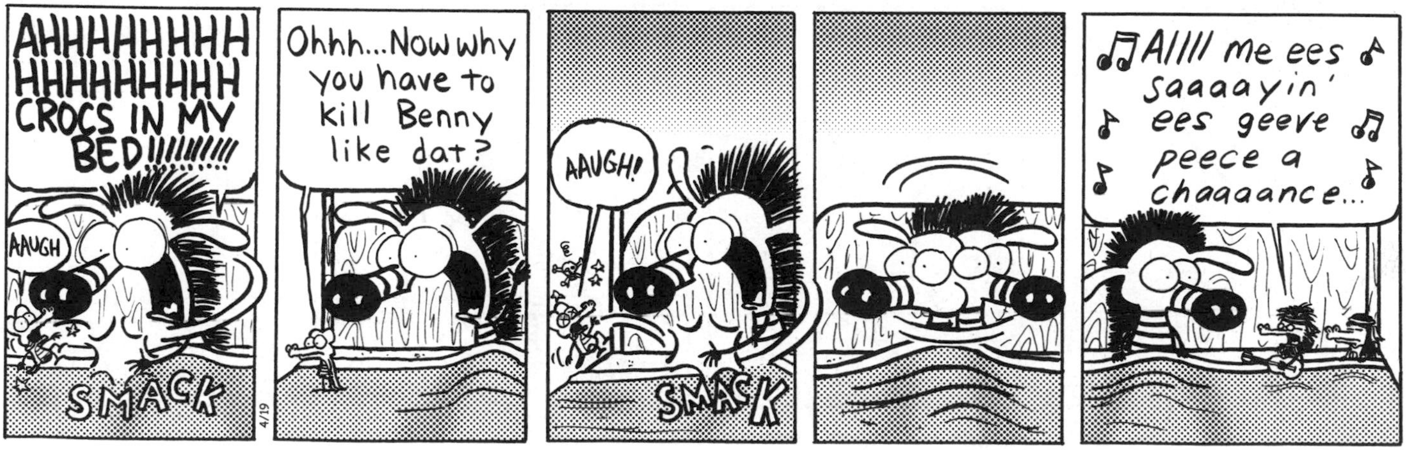
AHHHHHHHH HHHHHHHHH CROCS IN MY BED!!!!!!!!!
AAUGH
SMACK
4/19
Ohhh... Now why you have to kill Benny like dat?
AAUGH!
SMACK
♫ Allll me ees saaaayin' ees geeve peece a chaaaance... ♪

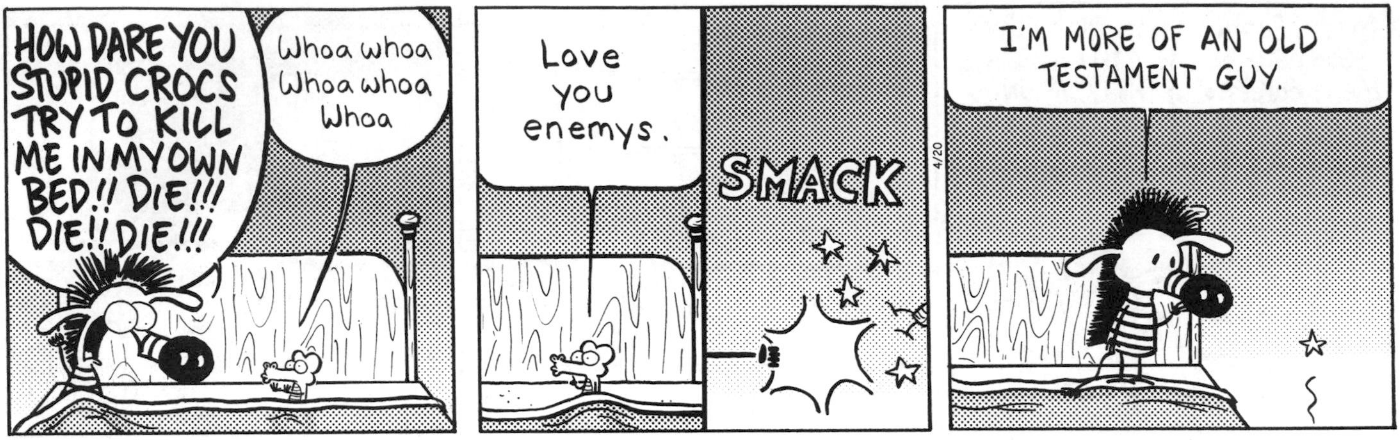
HOW DARE YOU STUPID CROCS TRY TO KILL ME IN MY OWN BED!! DIE!!! DIE!! DIE!!!
Whoa whoa Whoa whoa Whoa
Love you enemys.
SMACK
4/20
I'M MORE OF AN OLD TESTAMENT GUY.

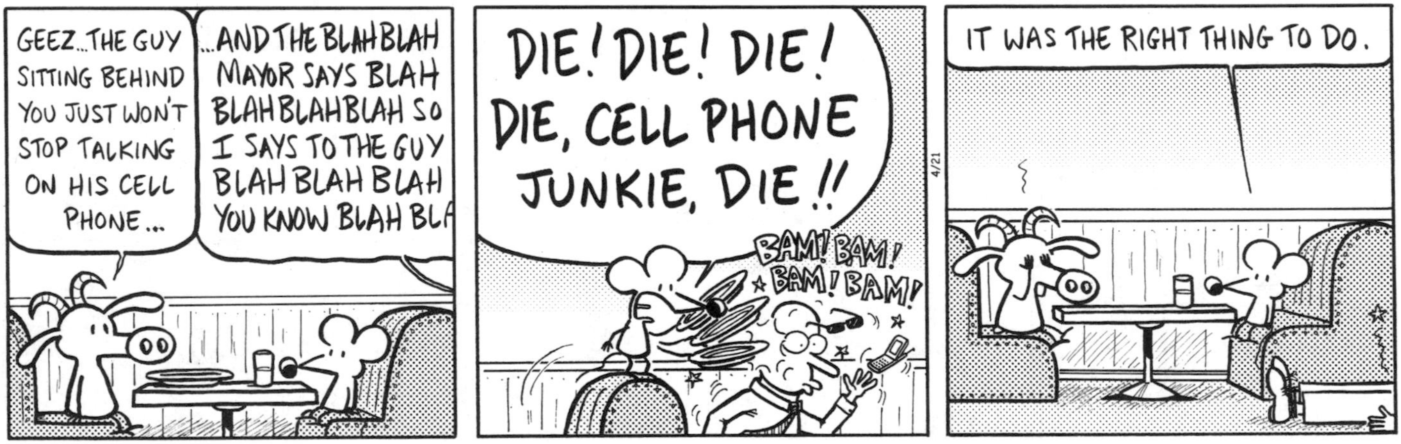
GEEZ...THE GUY SITTING BEHIND YOU JUST WON'T STOP TALKING ON HIS CELL PHONE...
...AND THE BLAH BLAH MAYOR SAYS BLAH BLAH BLAH BLAH SO I SAYS TO THE GUY BLAH BLAH BLAH YOU KNOW BLAH BLA
DIE! DIE! DIE! DIE, CELL PHONE JUNKIE, DIE!!
BAM! BAM! BAM! BAM!
4/21
IT WAS THE RIGHT THING TO DO.

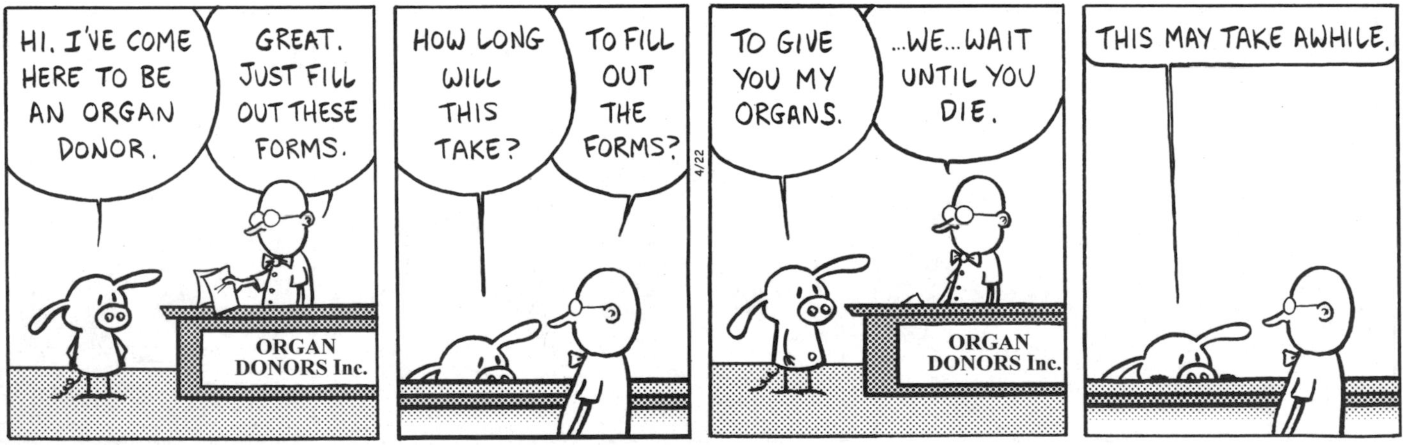
HI. I'VE COME HERE TO BE AN ORGAN DONOR.
GREAT. JUST FILL OUT THESE FORMS.
ORGAN DONORS Inc.
HOW LONG WILL THIS TAKE?
TO FILL OUT THE FORMS?
4/22
TO GIVE YOU MY ORGANS.
...WE...WAIT UNTIL YOU DIE.
ORGAN DONORS Inc.
THIS MAY TAKE AWHILE.

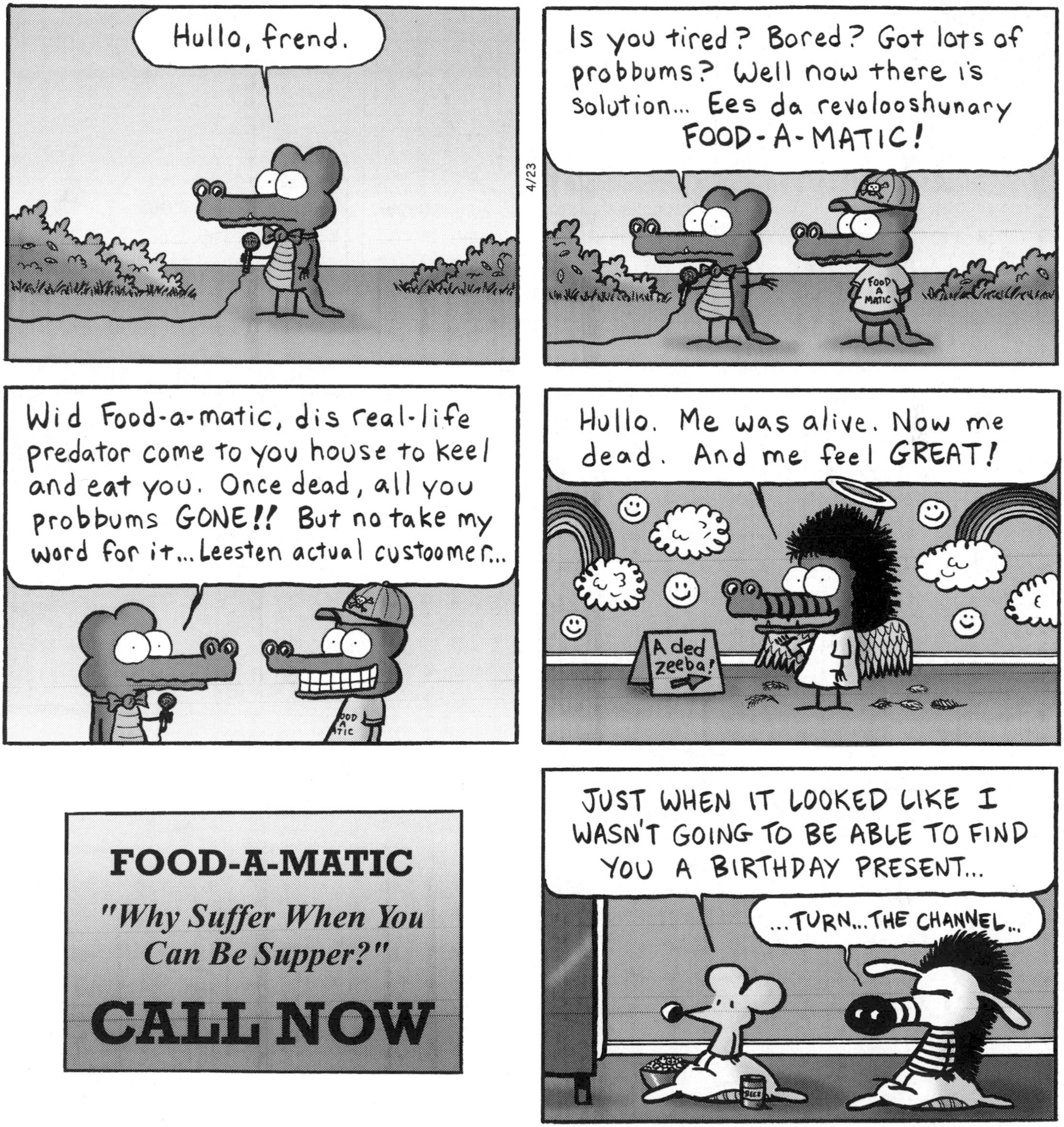
4/23
Hullo, frend.
Is you tired? Bored? Got lots of probbums? Well now there is solution... Ees da revolooshunary FOOD-A-MATIC!
FOOD A MATIC
Wid Food-a-matic, dis real-life predator come to you house to keel and eat you. Once dead, all you probbums GONE!! But no take my word for it... Leesten actual custoomer...
Hullo. Me was alive. Now me dead. And me feel GREAT!
A ded zeeba!
FOOD-A-MATIC
"Why Suffer When You Can Be Supper?"
CALL NOW
JUST WHEN IT LOOKED LIKE I WASN'T GOING TO BE ABLE TO FIND YOU A BIRTHDAY PRESENT...
...TURN...THE CHANNEL...

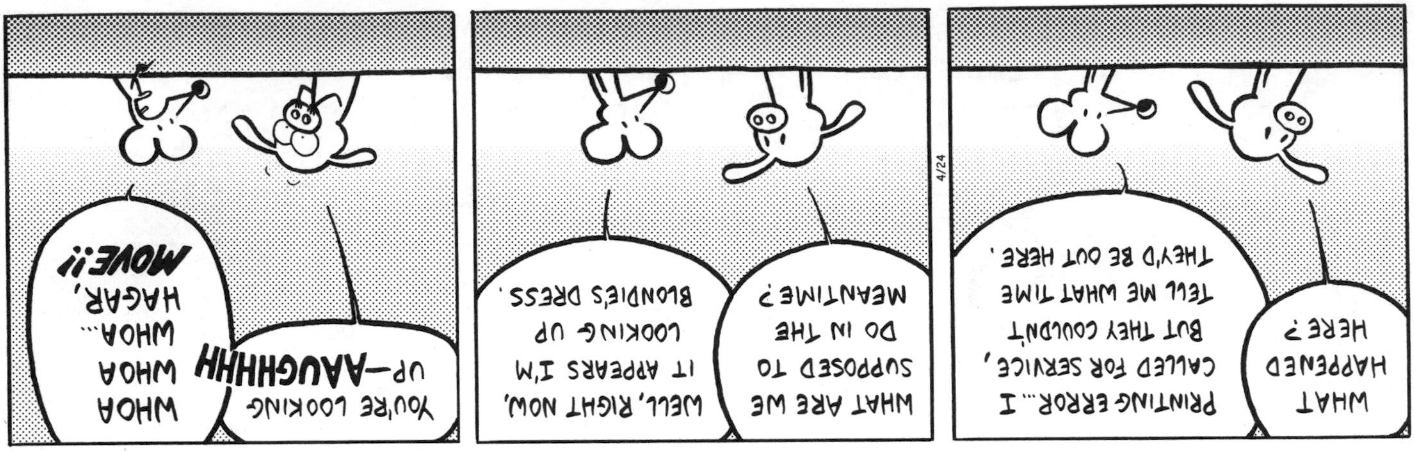
WHAT HAPPENED HERE?
PRINTING ERROR... I CALLED FOR SERVICE, BUT THEY COULDN'T TELL ME WHAT TIME THEY'D BE OUT HERE.
WHAT ARE WE SUPPOSED TO DO IN THE MEANTIME?
WELL, RIGHT NOW, IT APPEARS I'M LOOKING UP BLONDIE'S DRESS.
YOU'RE LOOKING UP—AAUGHHHH
WHOA WHOA WHOA... HAGAR, MOVE!!
4/24

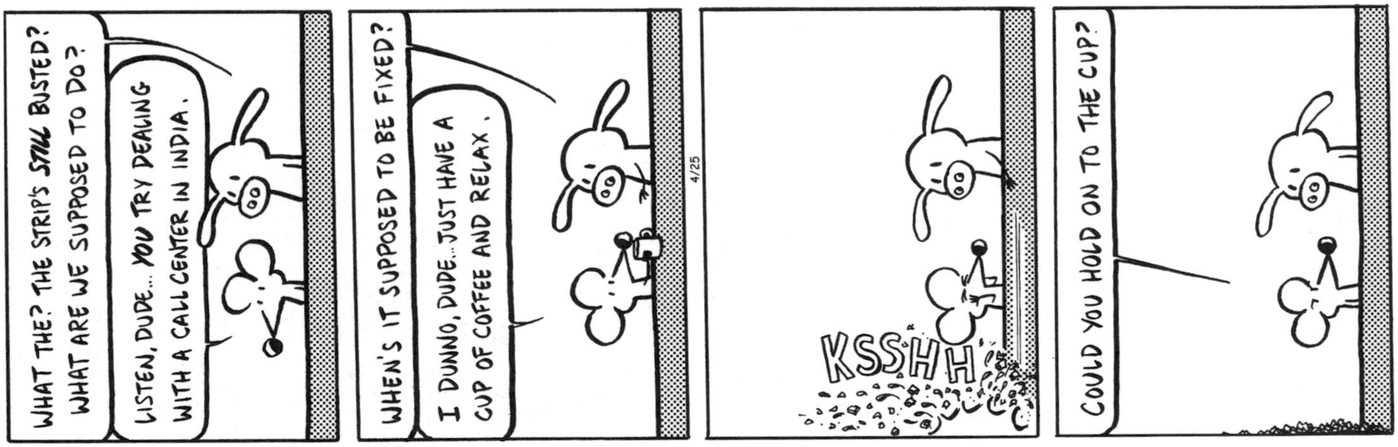
WHAT THE? THE STRIP'S STILL BUSTED? WHAT ARE WE SUPPOSED TO DO?
LISTEN, DUDE... YOU TRY DEALING WITH A CALL CENTER IN INDIA.
WHEN'S IT SUPPOSED TO BE FIXED?
I DUNNO, DUDE... JUST HAVE A CUP OF COFFEE AND RELAX.
KSSHH
COULD YOU HOLD ON TO THE CUP?
4/25

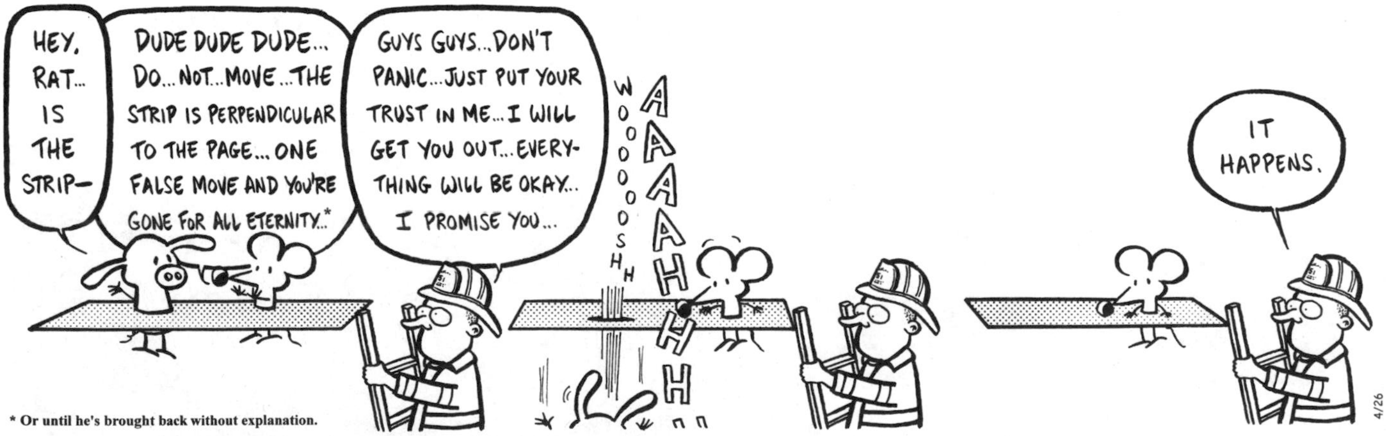
HEY, RAT... IS THE STRIP—
DUDE DUDE DUDE... DO... NOT... MOVE... THE STRIP IS PERPENDICULAR TO THE PAGE... ONE FALSE MOVE AND YOU'RE GONE FOR ALL ETERNITY...*
GUYS GUYS... DON'T PANIC... JUST PUT YOUR TRUST IN ME... I WILL GET YOU OUT... EVERYTHING WILL BE OKAY... I PROMISE YOU...
WOOOOOOOSHH
AAAAAHHHHH
IT HAPPENS.
4/26

* Or until he's brought back without explanation.

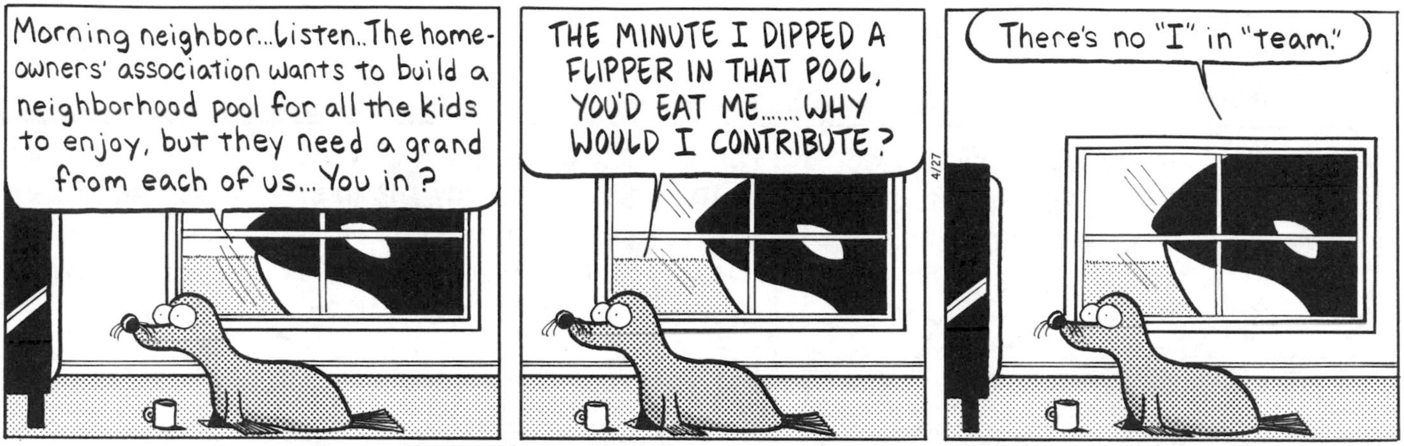
Morning neighbor...Listen..The home-owners' association wants to build a neighborhood pool for all the kids to enjoy, but they need a grand from each of us... You in?
THE MINUTE I DIPPED A FLIPPER IN THAT POOL, YOU'D EAT ME....... WHY WOULD I CONTRIBUTE?
4/27
There's no "I" in "team."

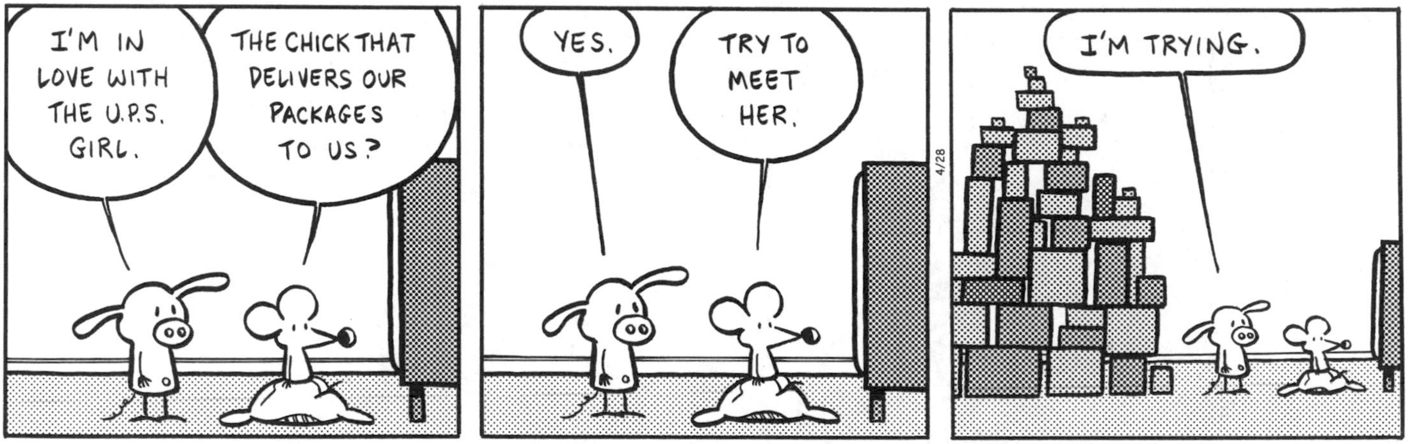
I'M IN LOVE WITH THE U.P.S. GIRL.
THE CHICK THAT DELIVERS OUR PACKAGES TO US?
YES.
TRY TO MEET HER.
4/28
I'M TRYING.

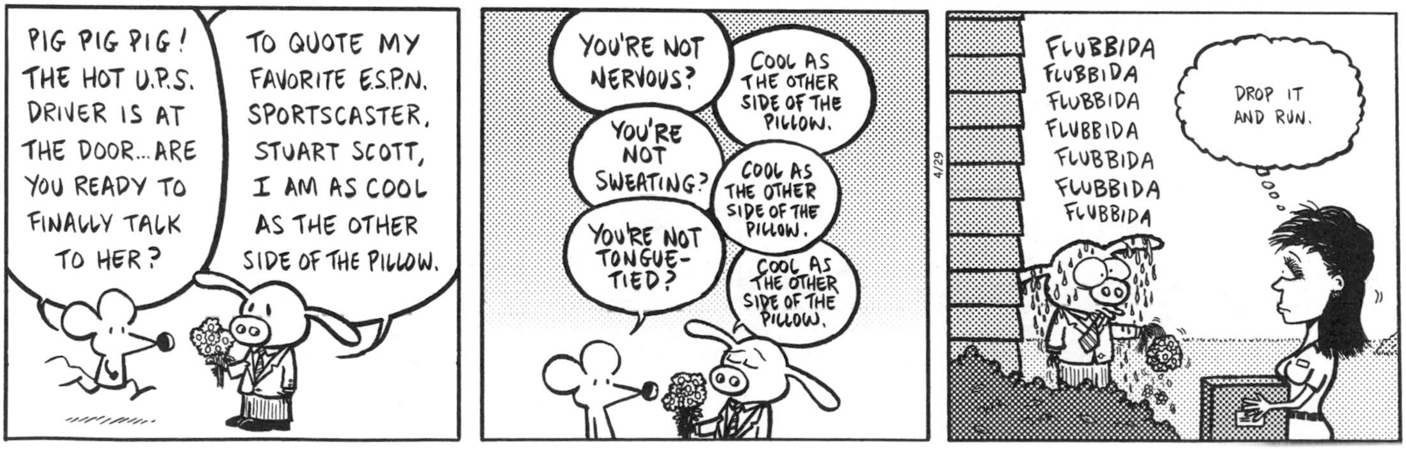
PIG PIG PIG! THE HOT U.P.S. DRIVER IS AT THE DOOR... ARE YOU READY TO FINALLY TALK TO HER?
TO QUOTE MY FAVORITE E.S.P.N. SPORTSCASTER, STUART SCOTT, I AM AS COOL AS THE OTHER SIDE OF THE PILLOW.
YOU'RE NOT NERVOUS?
COOL AS THE OTHER SIDE OF THE PILLOW.
YOU'RE NOT SWEATING?
COOL AS THE OTHER SIDE OF THE PILLOW.
YOU'RE NOT TONGUE-TIED?
COOL AS THE OTHER SIDE OF THE PILLOW.
4/29
FLUBBIDA
FLUBBIDA
FLUBBIDA
FLUBBIDA
FLUBBIDA
FLUBBIDA
FLUBBIDA
DROP IT AND RUN.

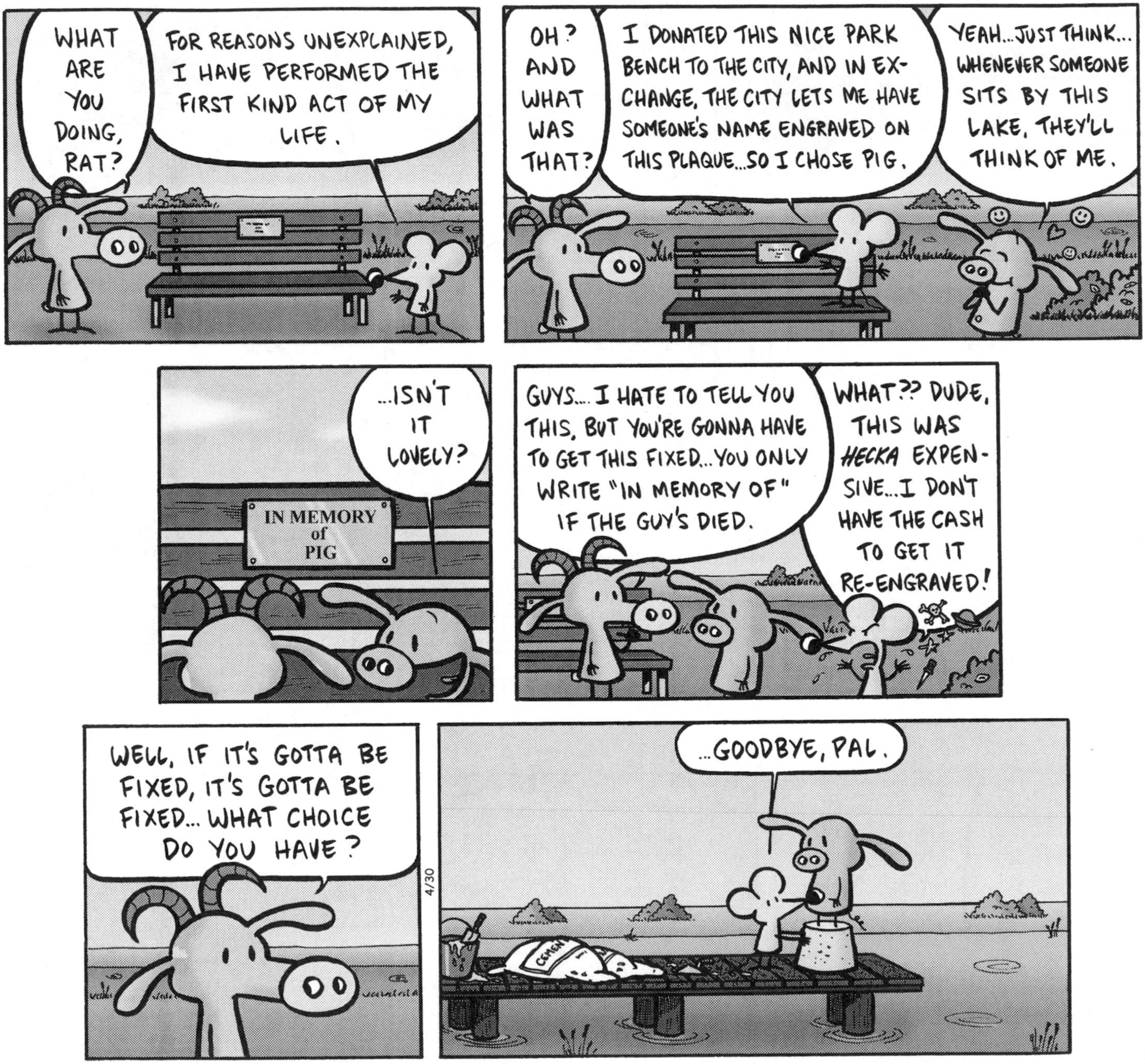
WHAT ARE YOU DOING, RAT?
FOR REASONS UNEXPLAINED, I HAVE PERFORMED THE FIRST KIND ACT OF MY LIFE.
OH? AND WHAT WAS THAT?
I DONATED THIS NICE PARK BENCH TO THE CITY, AND IN EXCHANGE, THE CITY LETS ME HAVE SOMEONE'S NAME ENGRAVED ON THIS PLAQUE...SO I CHOSE PIG.
YEAH...JUST THINK... WHENEVER SOMEONE SITS BY THIS LAKE, THEY'LL THINK OF ME.
...ISN'T IT LOVELY?
IN MEMORY of PIG
GUYS.... I HATE TO TELL YOU THIS, BUT YOU'RE GONNA HAVE TO GET THIS FIXED...YOU ONLY WRITE "IN MEMORY OF" IF THE GUY'S DIED.
WHAT?? DUDE, THIS WAS HECKA EXPENSIVE...I DON'T HAVE THE CASH TO GET IT RE-ENGRAVED!
WELL, IF IT'S GOTTA BE FIXED, IT'S GOTTA BE FIXED... WHAT CHOICE DO YOU HAVE?
4/30
...GOODBYE, PAL.
CEMENT

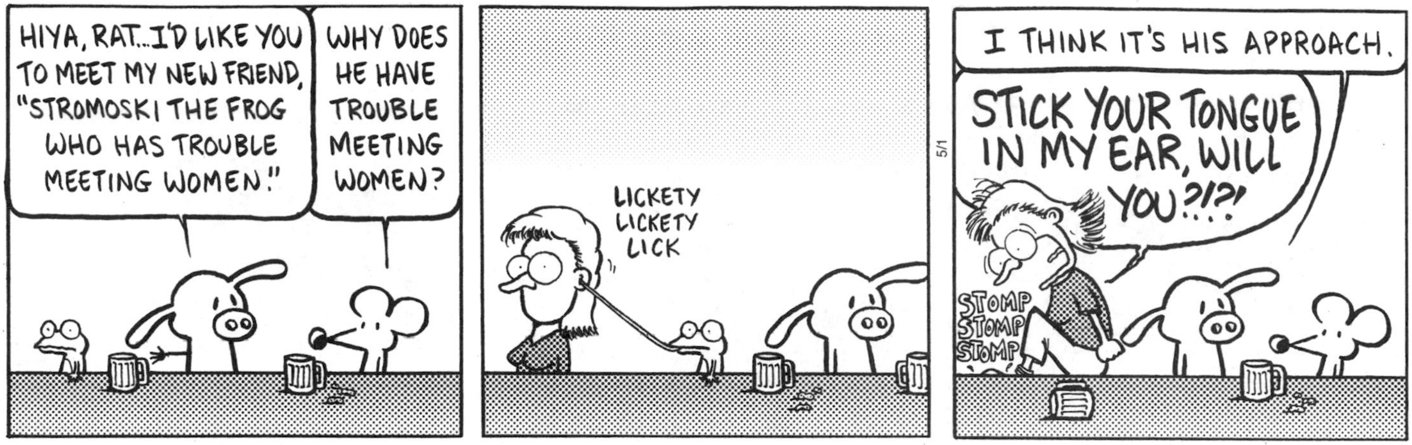
HIYA, RAT...I'D LIKE YOU TO MEET MY NEW FRIEND, "STROMOSKI THE FROG WHO HAS TROUBLE MEETING WOMEN."
WHY DOES HE HAVE TROUBLE MEETING WOMEN?
LICKETY LICKETY LICK
5/1
I THINK IT'S HIS APPROACH.
STICK YOUR TONGUE IN MY EAR, WILL YOU?!?!
STOMP STOMP STOMP

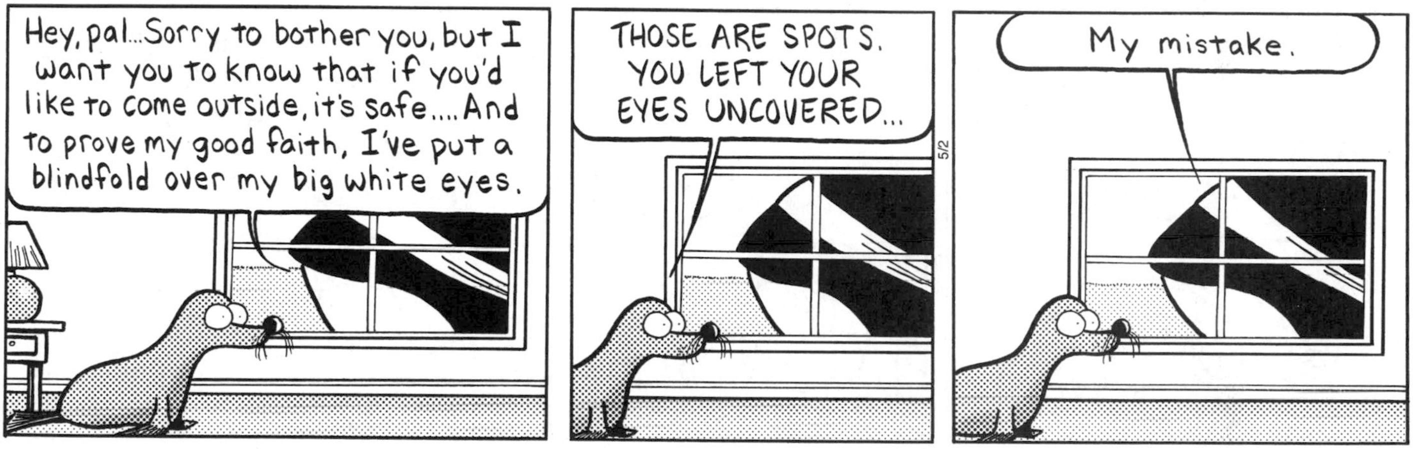
Hey, pal...Sorry to bother you, but I want you to know that if you'd like to come outside, it's safe.... And to prove my good faith, I've put a blindfold over my big white eyes.
THOSE ARE SPOTS. YOU LEFT YOUR EYES UNCOVERED...
5/2
My mistake.

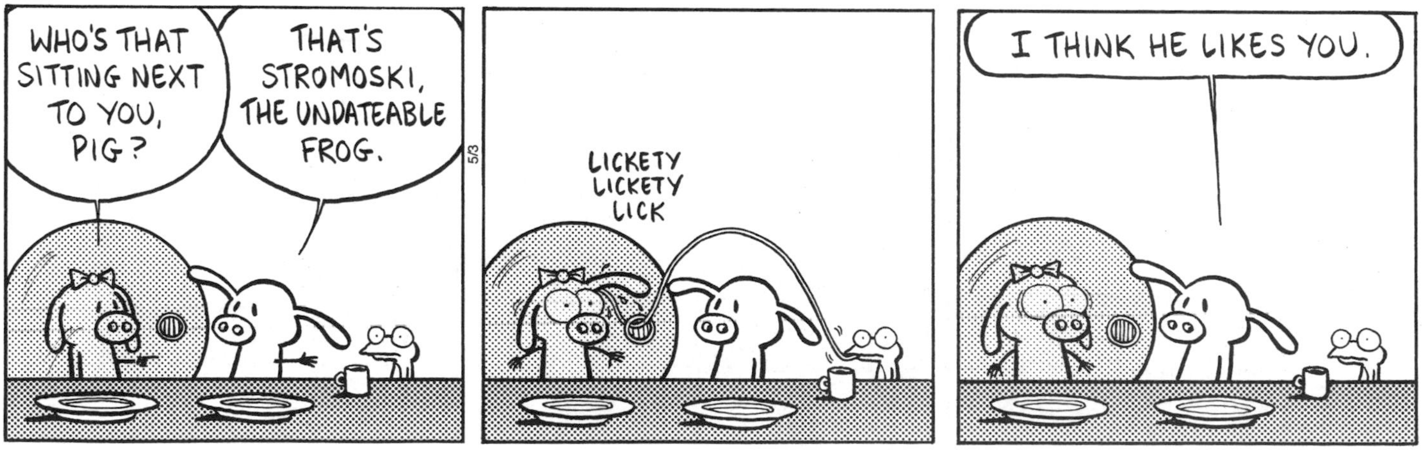
WHO'S THAT SITTING NEXT TO YOU, PIG?
THAT'S STROMOSKI, THE UNDATEABLE FROG.
5/3
LICKETY LICKETY LICK
I THINK HE LIKES YOU.

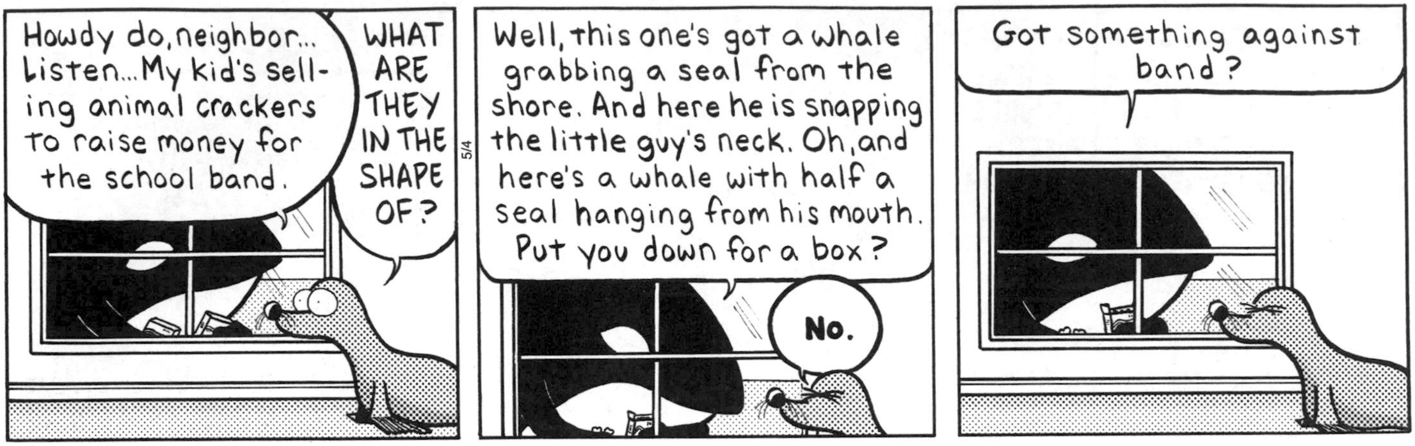
Howdy do, neighbor... Listen... My kid's selling animal crackers to raise money for the school band.
WHAT ARE THEY IN THE SHAPE OF?
5/4
Well, this one's got a whale grabbing a seal from the shore. And here he is snapping the little guy's neck. Oh, and here's a whale with half a seal hanging from his mouth. Put you down for a box?
No.
Got something against band?

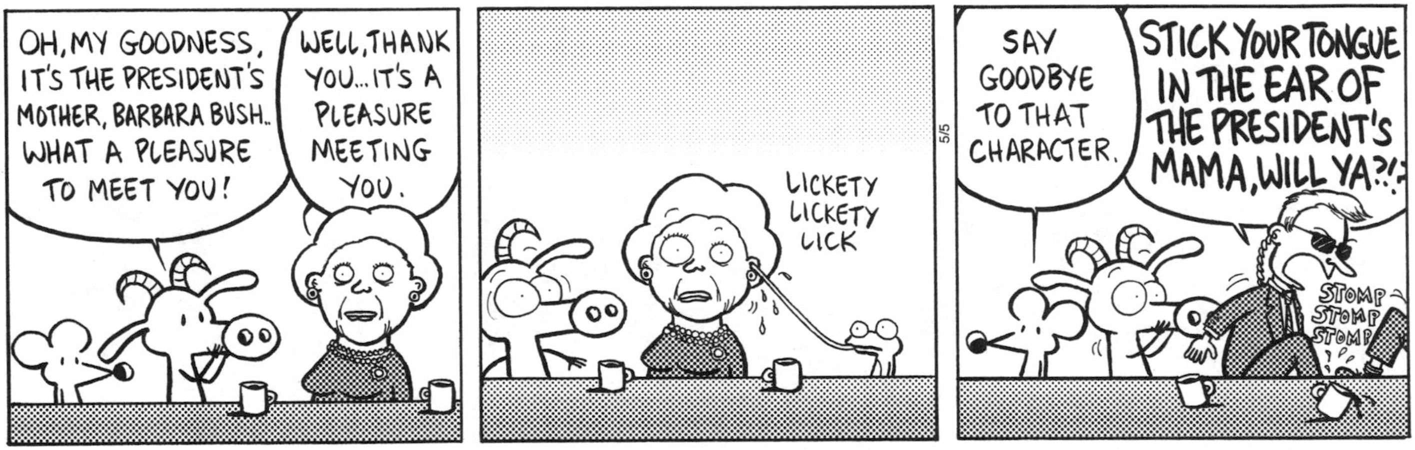
OH, MY GOODNESS, IT'S THE PRESIDENT'S MOTHER, BARBARA BUSH.. WHAT A PLEASURE TO MEET YOU!
WELL, THANK YOU... IT'S A PLEASURE MEETING YOU.
LICKETY LICKETY LICK
5/5
SAY GOODBYE TO THAT CHARACTER.
STICK YOUR TONGUE IN THE EAR OF THE PRESIDENT'S MAMA, WILL YA?!
STOMP STOMP STOMP

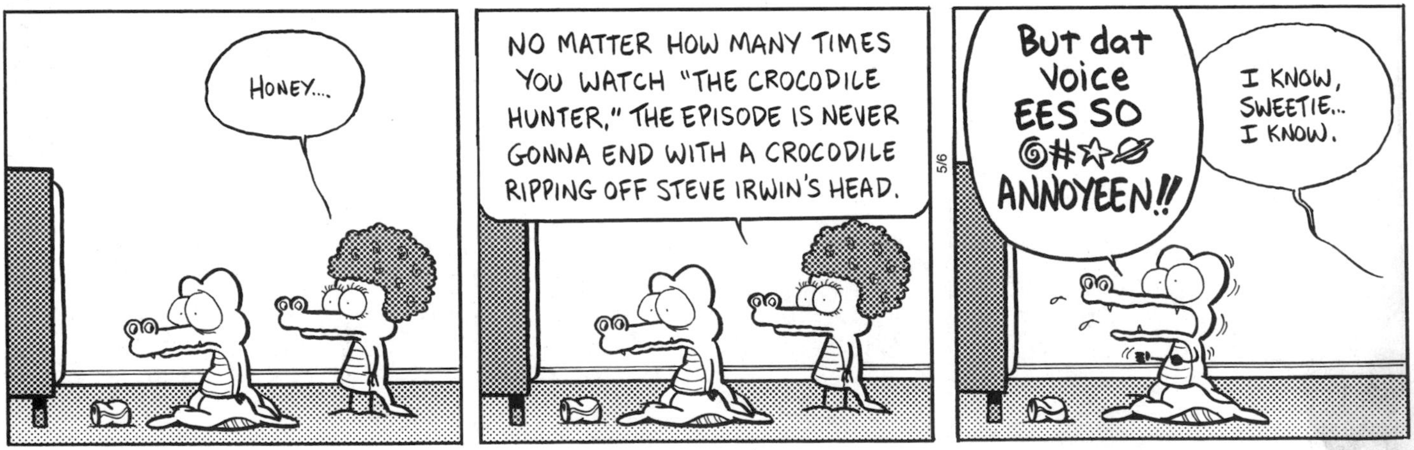
HONEY....
NO MATTER HOW MANY TIMES YOU WATCH "THE CROCODILE HUNTER," THE EPISODE IS NEVER GONNA END WITH A CROCODILE RIPPING OFF STEVE IRWIN'S HEAD.
5/6
But dat voice EES SO @#☆ ANNOYEEN!!
I KNOW, SWEETIE... I KNOW.

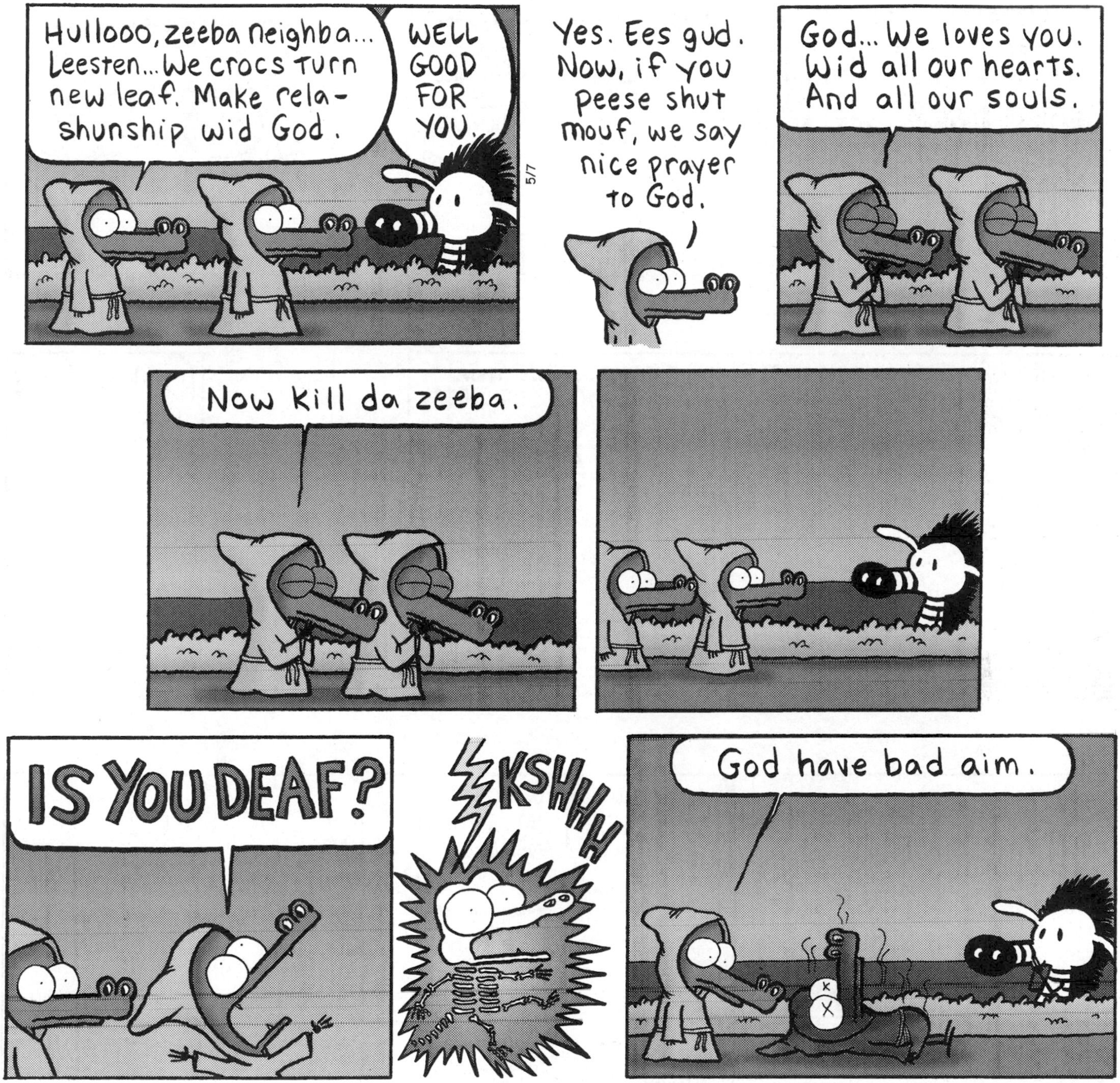
Hullooo, zeeba neighba... Leesten... We crocs turn new leaf. Make rela-shunship wid God.
WELL GOOD FOR YOU.
Yes. Ees gud. Now, if you peese shut mouf, we say nice prayer to God.
God... We loves you. Wid all our hearts. And all our souls.
Now kill da zeeba.
IS YOU DEAF?
KSHHHH
God have bad aim.

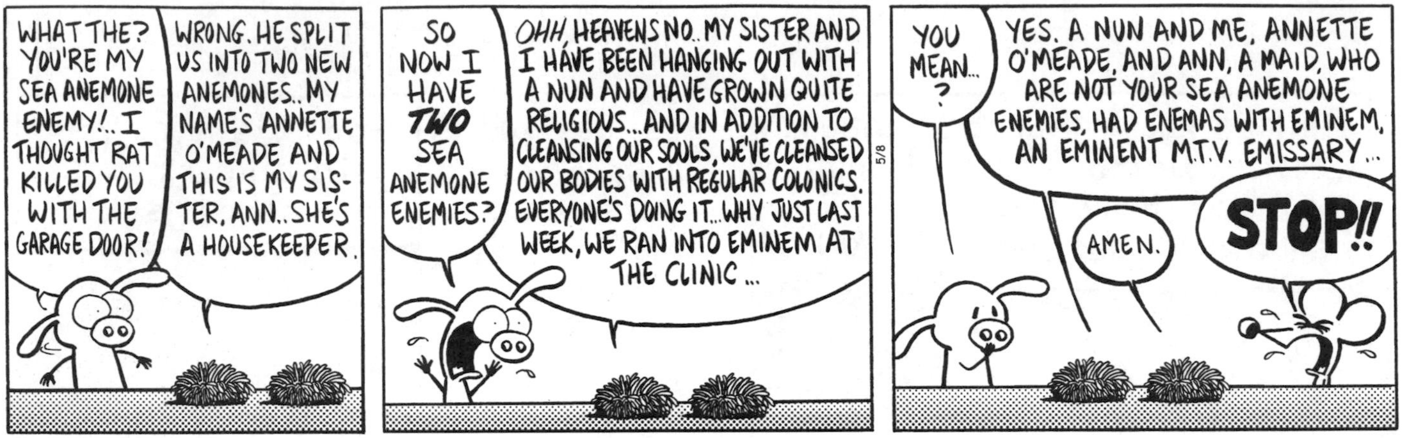
WHAT THE? YOU'RE MY SEA ANEMONE ENEMY!.. I THOUGHT RAT KILLED YOU WITH THE GARAGE DOOR!
WRONG. HE SPLIT US INTO TWO NEW ANEMONES.. MY NAME'S ANNETTE O'MEADE AND THIS IS MY SISTER, ANN.. SHE'S A HOUSEKEEPER.
SO NOW I HAVE TWO SEA ANEMONE ENEMIES?
OHH, HEAVENS NO.. MY SISTER AND I HAVE BEEN HANGING OUT WITH A NUN AND HAVE GROWN QUITE RELIGIOUS... AND IN ADDITION TO CLEANSING OUR SOULS, WE'VE CLEANSED OUR BODIES WITH REGULAR COLONICS. EVERYONE'S DOING IT... WHY JUST LAST WEEK, WE RAN INTO EMINEM AT THE CLINIC...
5/8
YOU MEAN... ?
YES. A NUN AND ME, ANNETTE O'MEADE, AND ANN, A MAID, WHO ARE NOT YOUR SEA ANEMONE ENEMIES, HAD ENEMAS WITH EMINEM, AN EMINENT M.T.V. EMISSARY...
AMEN.
STOP!!

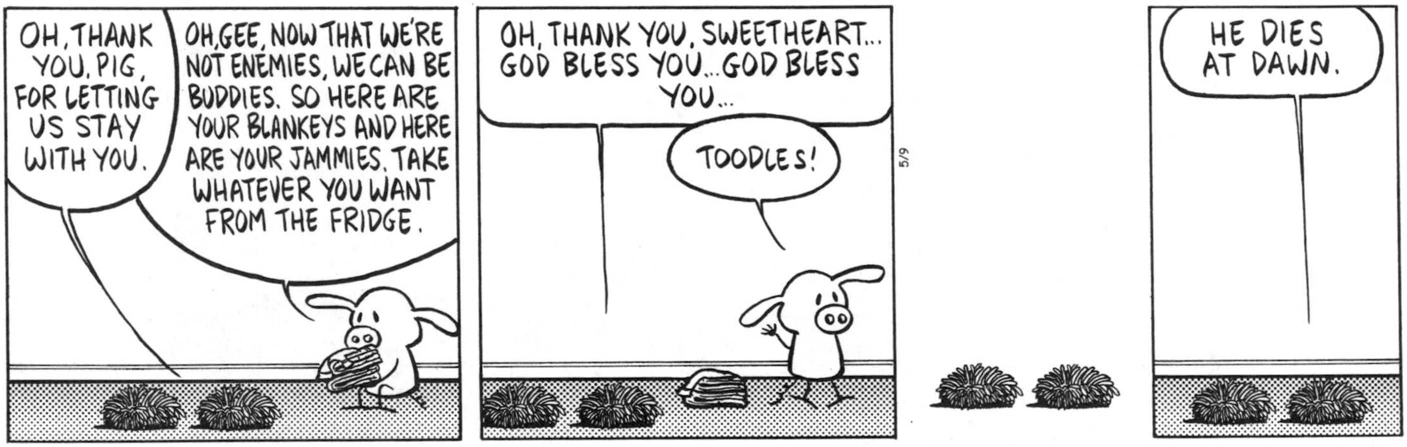
OH, THANK YOU, PIG, FOR LETTING US STAY WITH YOU.
OH, GEE, NOW THAT WE'RE NOT ENEMIES, WE CAN BE BUDDIES. SO HERE ARE YOUR BLANKEYS AND HERE ARE YOUR JAMMIES. TAKE WHATEVER YOU WANT FROM THE FRIDGE.
OH, THANK YOU, SWEETHEART... GOD BLESS YOU... GOD BLESS YOU...
TOODLES!
5/9
HE DIES AT DAWN.

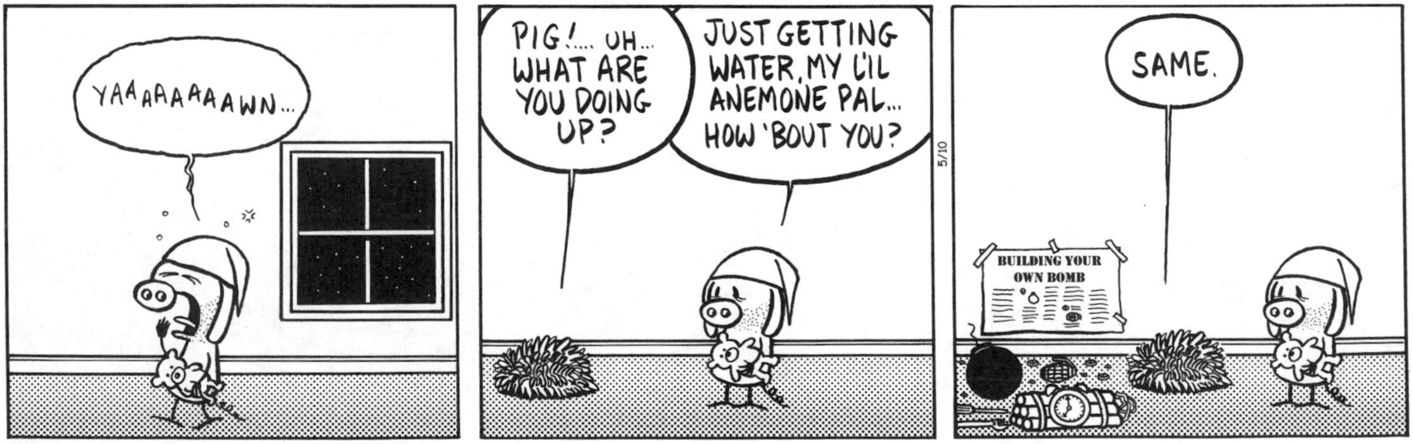
YAAAAAAAAAWN...
PIG!.... UH... WHAT ARE YOU DOING UP?
JUST GETTING WATER, MY L'IL ANEMONE PAL... HOW 'BOUT YOU?
5/10
BUILDING YOUR OWN BOMB
SAME.

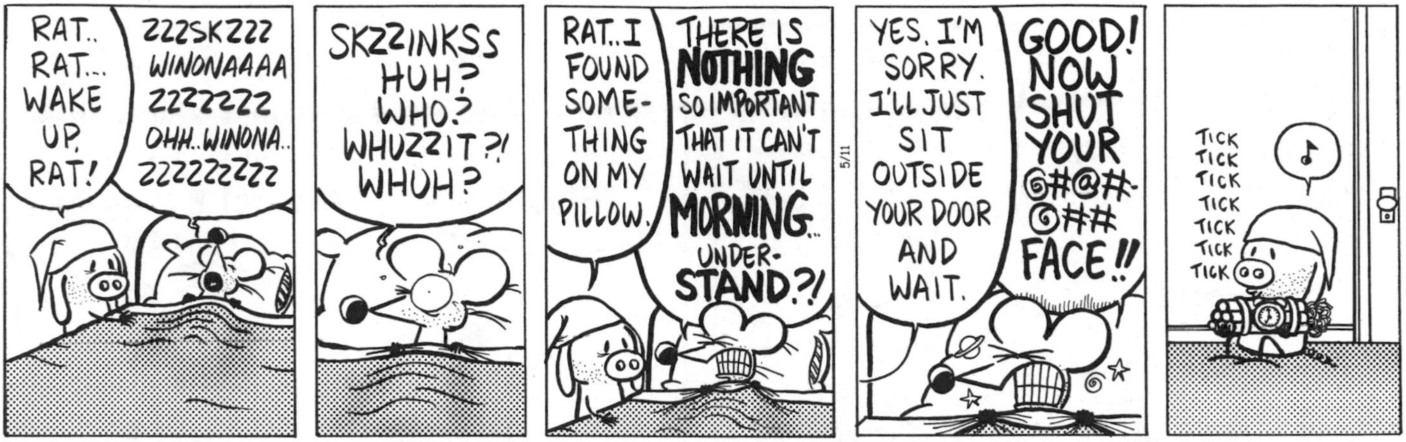
RAT.. RAT... WAKE UP, RAT!
ZZZSKZZZ WINONAAAA ZZZZZZZ OHH..WINONA.. ZZZZZZZZZ
SKZZINKSS HUH? WHO? WHUZZIT?! WHUH?
RAT..I FOUND SOMETHING ON MY PILLOW.
THERE IS NOTHING SO IMPORTANT THAT IT CAN'T WAIT UNTIL MORNING... UNDERSTAND?!
5/11
YES. I'M SORRY. I'LL JUST SIT OUTSIDE YOUR DOOR AND WAIT.
GOOD! NOW SHUT YOUR @#@#-@## FACE!!
TICK TICK TICK TICK TICK TICK TICK

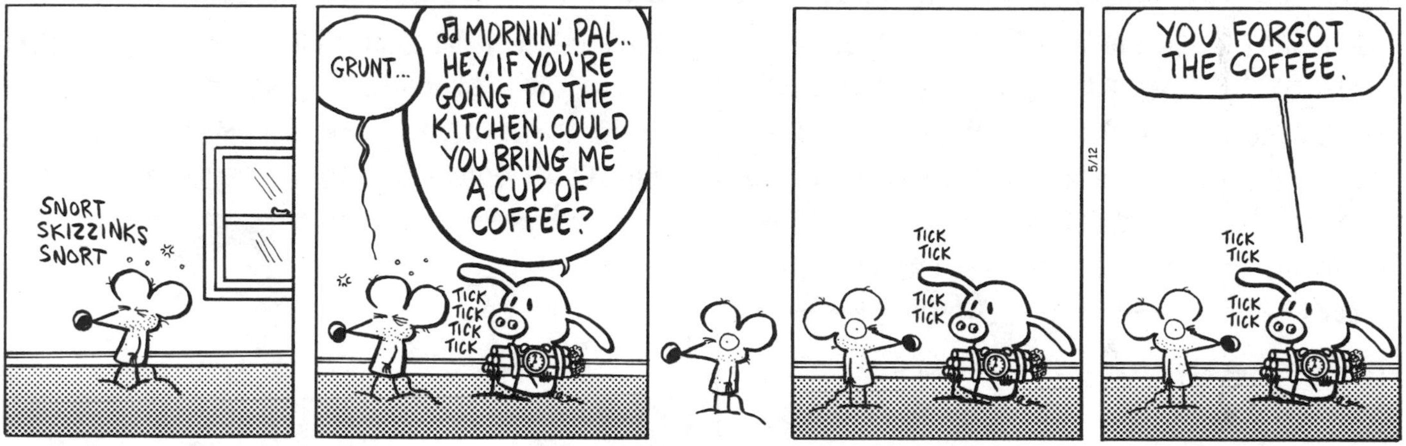
SNORT SKIZZINKS SNORT
GRUNT...
MORNIN', PAL.. HEY, IF YOU'RE GOING TO THE KITCHEN, COULD YOU BRING ME A CUP OF COFFEE?
TICK TICK TICK TICK
5/12
TICK TICK
TICK TICK
YOU FORGOT THE COFFEE.
TICK TICK
TICK TICK

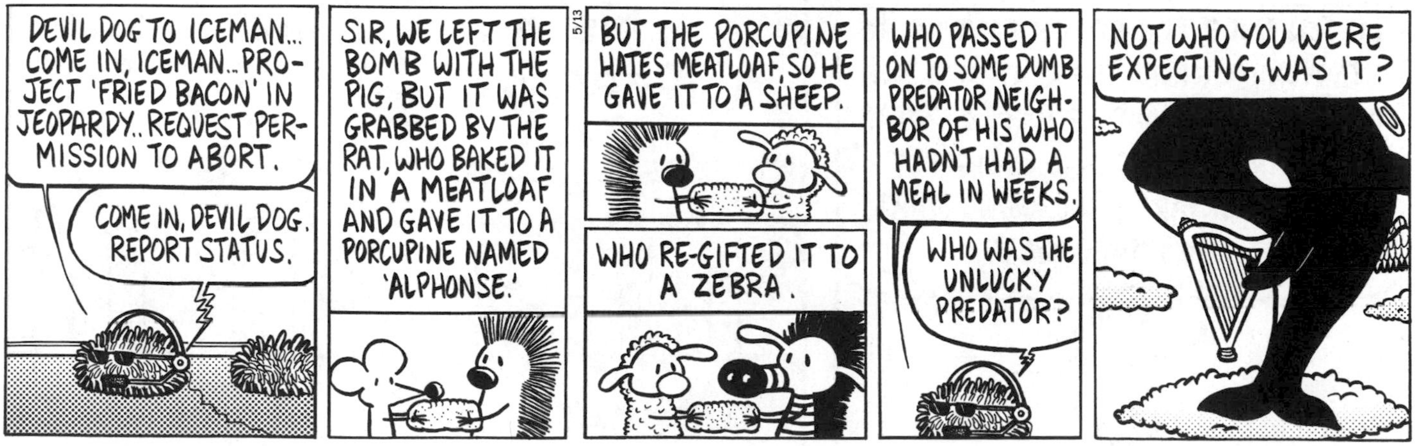
DEVIL DOG TO ICEMAN... COME IN, ICEMAN.. PROJECT 'FRIED BACON' IN JEOPARDY.. REQUEST PERMISSION TO ABORT.
COME IN, DEVIL DOG. REPORT STATUS.
SIR, WE LEFT THE BOMB WITH THE PIG, BUT IT WAS GRABBED BY THE RAT, WHO BAKED IT IN A MEATLOAF AND GAVE IT TO A PORCUPINE NAMED 'ALPHONSE.'
5/13
BUT THE PORCUPINE HATES MEATLOAF, SO HE GAVE IT TO A SHEEP.
WHO RE-GIFTED IT TO A ZEBRA.
WHO PASSED IT ON TO SOME DUMB PREDATOR NEIGHBOR OF HIS WHO HADN'T HAD A MEAL IN WEEKS.
WHO WAS THE UNLUCKY PREDATOR?
NOT WHO YOU WERE EXPECTING, WAS IT?

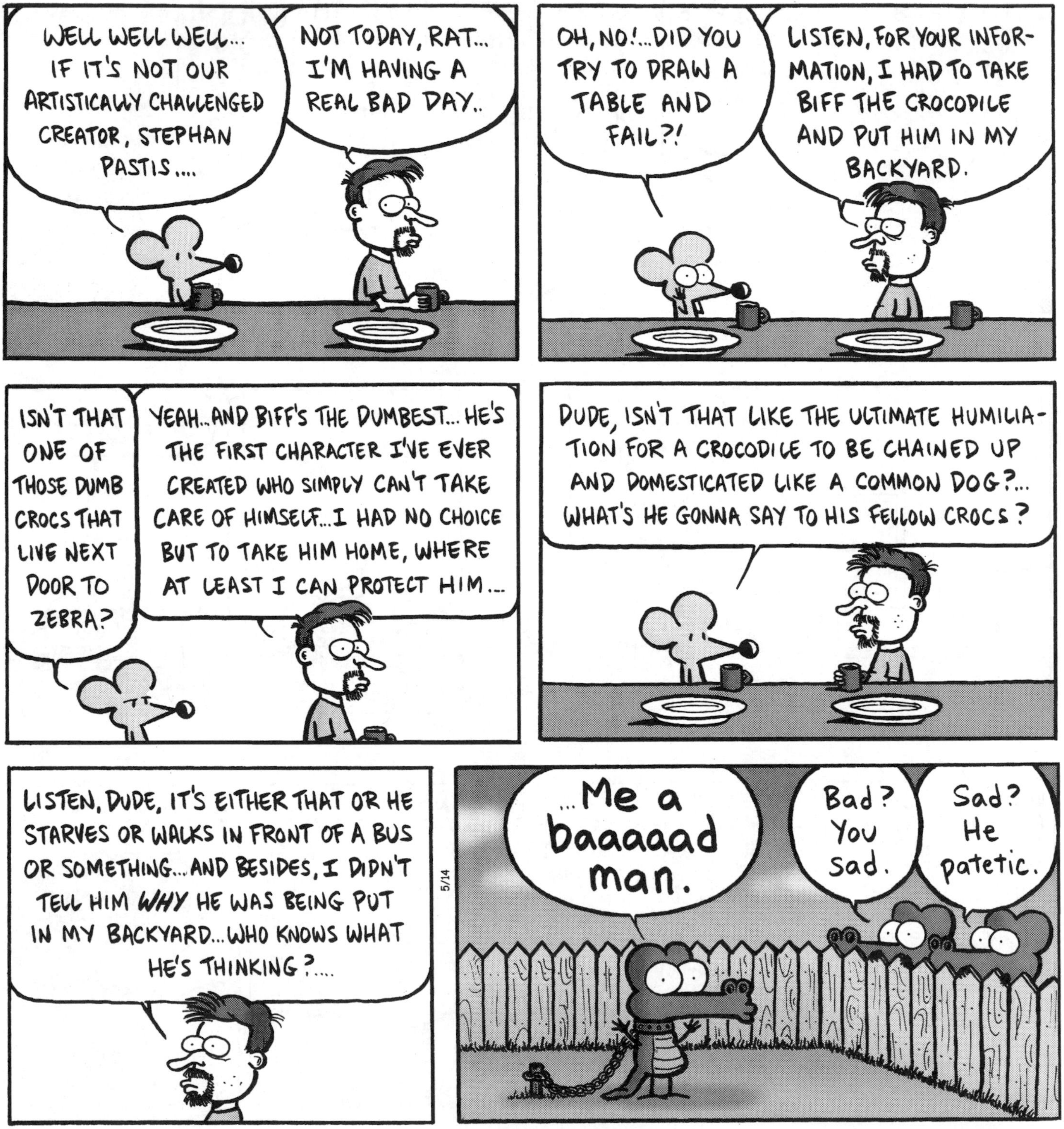
WELL WELL WELL... IF IT'S NOT OUR ARTISTICALLY CHALLENGED CREATOR, STEPHAN PASTIS....
NOT TODAY, RAT... I'M HAVING A REAL BAD DAY..
OH, NO!...DID YOU TRY TO DRAW A TABLE AND FAIL?!
LISTEN, FOR YOUR INFORMATION, I HAD TO TAKE BIFF THE CROCODILE AND PUT HIM IN MY BACKYARD.
ISN'T THAT ONE OF THOSE DUMB CROCS THAT LIVE NEXT DOOR TO ZEBRA?
YEAH...AND BIFF'S THE DUMBEST... HE'S THE FIRST CHARACTER I'VE EVER CREATED WHO SIMPLY CAN'T TAKE CARE OF HIMSELF...I HAD NO CHOICE BUT TO TAKE HIM HOME, WHERE AT LEAST I CAN PROTECT HIM....
DUDE, ISN'T THAT LIKE THE ULTIMATE HUMILIATION FOR A CROCODILE TO BE CHAINED UP AND DOMESTICATED LIKE A COMMON DOG?... WHAT'S HE GONNA SAY TO HIS FELLOW CROCS?
LISTEN, DUDE, IT'S EITHER THAT OR HE STARVES OR WALKS IN FRONT OF A BUS OR SOMETHING... AND BESIDES, I DIDN'T TELL HIM *WHY* HE WAS BEING PUT IN MY BACKYARD... WHO KNOWS WHAT HE'S THINKING?....
5/14
...Me a baaaaad man.
Bad? You sad.
Sad? He patetic.

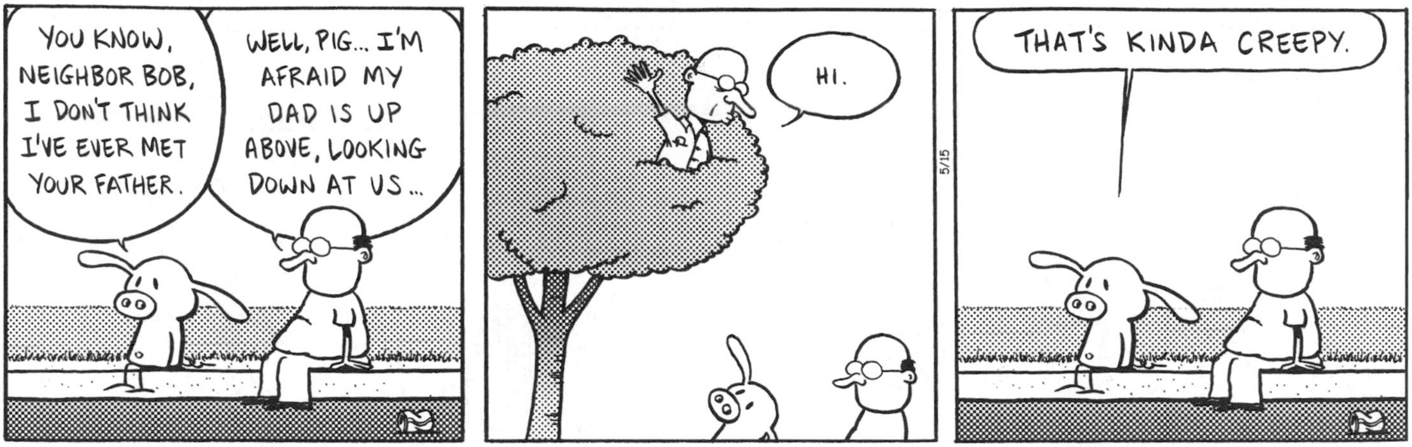
YOU KNOW, NEIGHBOR BOB, I DON'T THINK I'VE EVER MET YOUR FATHER.
WELL, PIG... I'M AFRAID MY DAD IS UP ABOVE, LOOKING DOWN AT US...
HI.
5/15
THAT'S KINDA CREEPY.

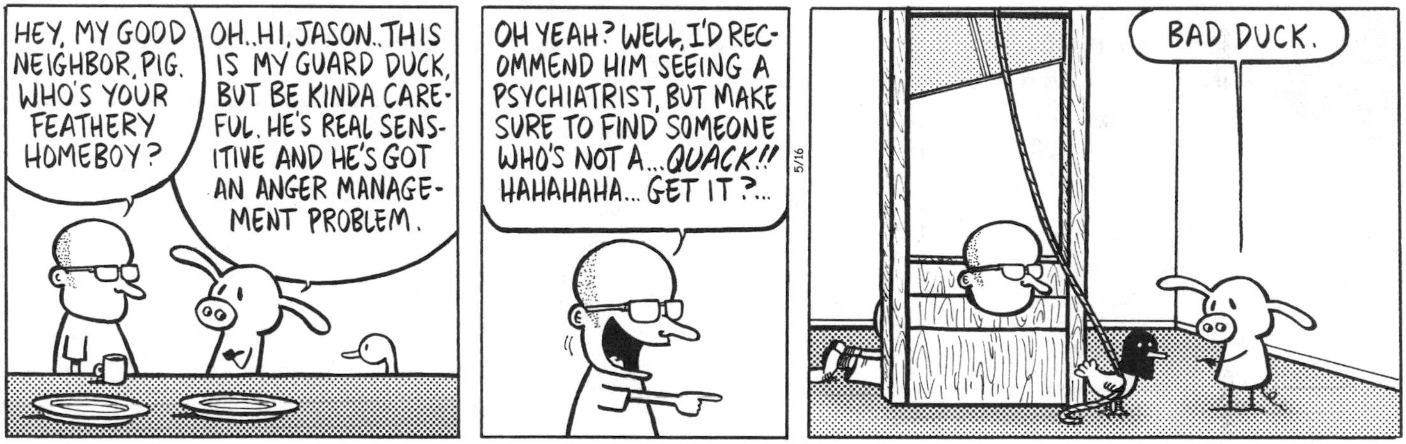
HEY, MY GOOD NEIGHBOR, PIG. WHO'S YOUR FEATHERY HOMEBOY?
OH..HI, JASON..THIS IS MY GUARD DUCK, BUT BE KINDA CAREFUL. HE'S REAL SENSITIVE AND HE'S GOT AN ANGER MANAGEMENT PROBLEM.
OH YEAH? WELL, I'D RECOMMEND HIM SEEING A PSYCHIATRIST, BUT MAKE SURE TO FIND SOMEONE WHO'S NOT A...QUACK!! HAHAHAHA... GET IT?...
5/16
BAD DUCK.

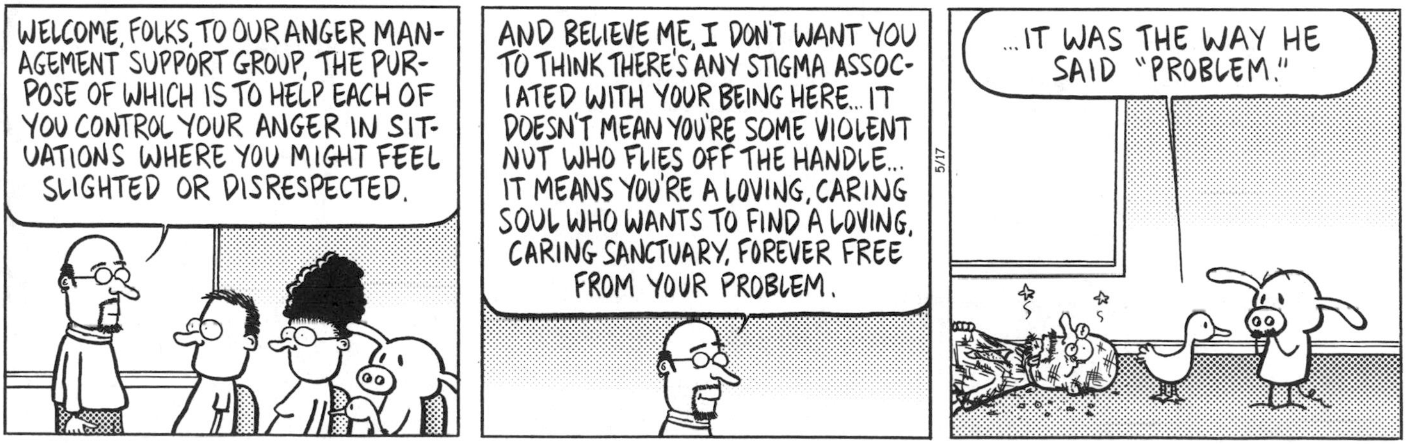
WELCOME, FOLKS, TO OUR ANGER MANAGEMENT SUPPORT GROUP, THE PURPOSE OF WHICH IS TO HELP EACH OF YOU CONTROL YOUR ANGER IN SITUATIONS WHERE YOU MIGHT FEEL SLIGHTED OR DISRESPECTED.
AND BELIEVE ME, I DON'T WANT YOU TO THINK THERE'S ANY STIGMA ASSOCIATED WITH YOUR BEING HERE... IT DOESN'T MEAN YOU'RE SOME VIOLENT NUT WHO FLIES OFF THE HANDLE... IT MEANS YOU'RE A LOVING, CARING SOUL WHO WANTS TO FIND A LOVING, CARING SANCTUARY, FOREVER FREE FROM YOUR PROBLEM.
5/17
...IT WAS THE WAY HE SAID "PROBLEM."

WELL, FOLKS, WE'VE OBVIOUSLY HAD A BIT OF A PROBLEM WITH ONE OF OUR PARTICIPANTS.. BUT ALL IS TAKEN CARE OF NOW... BY THE WAY, IF ANY OF YOU SHOULD NEED IT, THE BATHROOM'S DOWN THE HALL.. AND WITH THAT, LET'S—

ANGER MANAGEMENT SEMIN

BATHROOM BREAK!!

ANGER MANAGEMENT SEMIN

5/18

OF COURSE, SOME OF YOU HAVE LOST YOUR BATHROOM PRIVILEGES.

SMOKING BREAK!!

ANGER MANAGEMENT SEMIN

WHAT ARE YOU DOING, PIG?

I AM 'HULA PIG'... THE WORLD IS IN SUCH BAD SHAPE, I THOUGHT I'D TRY TO HULA OUR WAY OUT OF IT.

HULA HULA HULA HULA HULA HULA HULA

5/19

I'M NOT THE MOST MASCULINE GUY.

EXCUSE ME, SWEETIE, BUT I COULDN'T HELP NOTICING HOW HOT YOU ARE... HOW'D YOU LIKE TO GET DINNER WITH ME?

WHY THE ⊙☆#⊙ SHOULD I GET DINNER WITH YOU?

BECAUSE IF YOU DON'T, THE TERRORISTS WIN.

5/20

...WORTH A TRY.

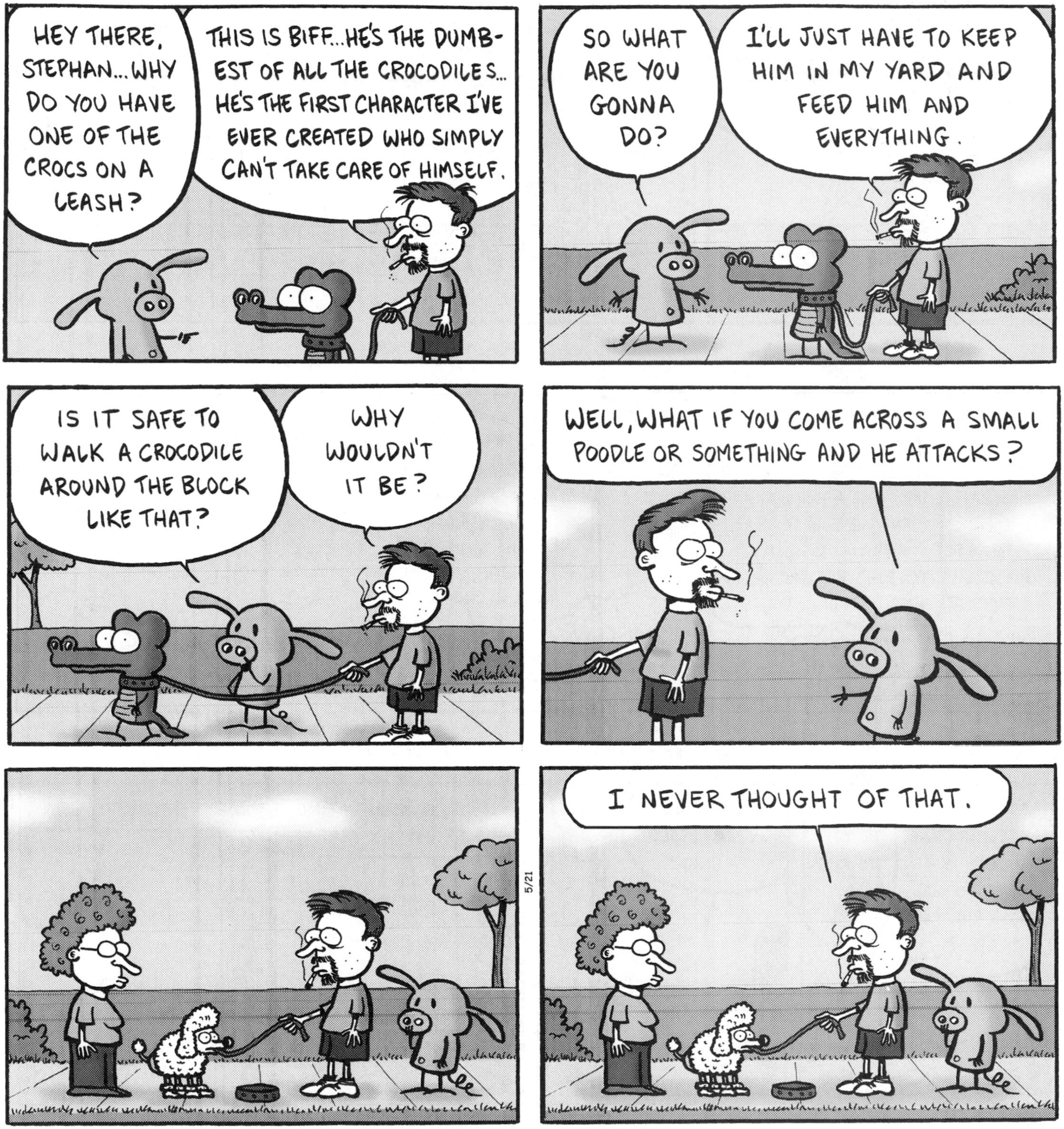
HEY THERE, STEPHAN...WHY DO YOU HAVE ONE OF THE CROCS ON A LEASH?
THIS IS BIFF...HE'S THE DUMBEST OF ALL THE CROCODILES... HE'S THE FIRST CHARACTER I'VE EVER CREATED WHO SIMPLY CAN'T TAKE CARE OF HIMSELF.
SO WHAT ARE YOU GONNA DO?
I'LL JUST HAVE TO KEEP HIM IN MY YARD AND FEED HIM AND EVERYTHING.
IS IT SAFE TO WALK A CROCODILE AROUND THE BLOCK LIKE THAT?
WHY WOULDN'T IT BE?
WELL, WHAT IF YOU COME ACROSS A SMALL POODLE OR SOMETHING AND HE ATTACKS?
5/21
I NEVER THOUGHT OF THAT.

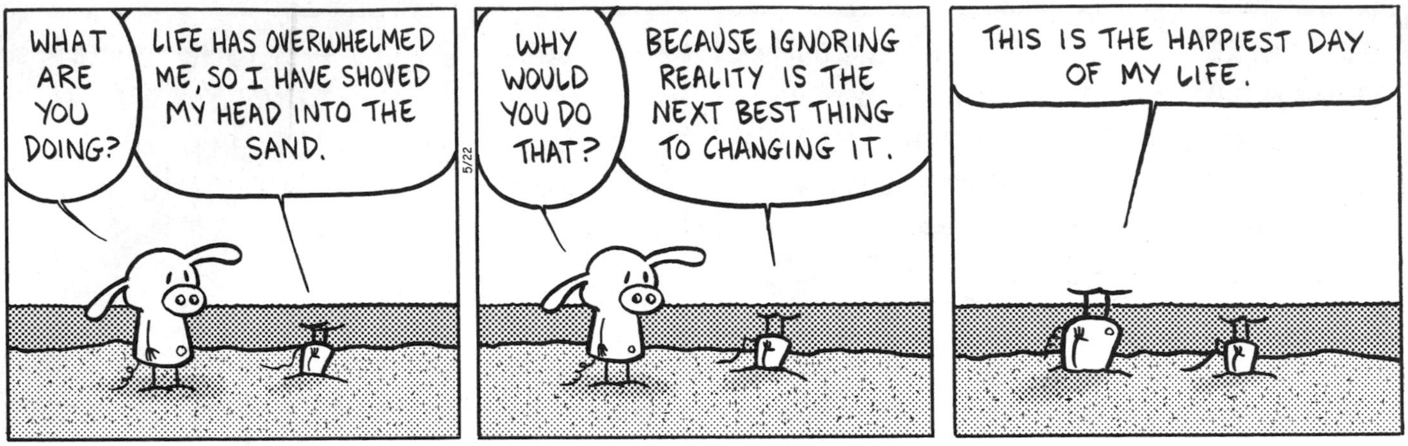
WHAT ARE YOU DOING?
LIFE HAS OVERWHELMED ME, SO I HAVE SHOVED MY HEAD INTO THE SAND.
5/22
WHY WOULD YOU DO THAT?
BECAUSE IGNORING REALITY IS THE NEXT BEST THING TO CHANGING IT.
THIS IS THE HAPPIEST DAY OF MY LIFE.

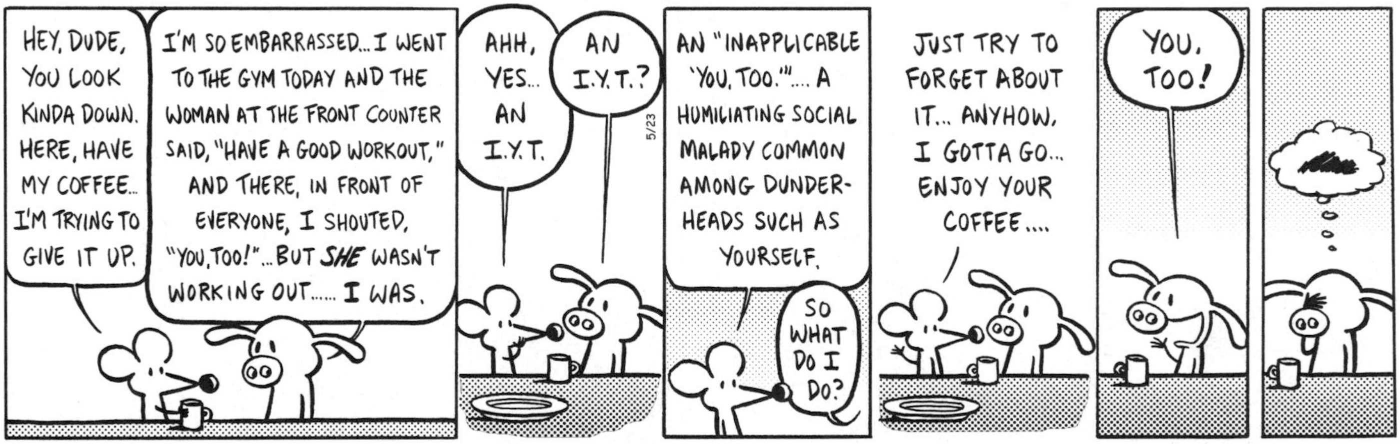
HEY, DUDE, YOU LOOK KINDA DOWN. HERE, HAVE MY COFFEE... I'M TRYING TO GIVE IT UP.
I'M SO EMBARRASSED... I WENT TO THE GYM TODAY AND THE WOMAN AT THE FRONT COUNTER SAID, "HAVE A GOOD WORKOUT," AND THERE, IN FRONT OF EVERYONE, I SHOUTED, "YOU, TOO!"... BUT *SHE* WASN'T WORKING OUT...... I WAS.
AHH, YES... AN I.Y.T.
AN I.Y.T.?
5/23
AN "INAPPLICABLE 'YOU, TOO.'".... A HUMILIATING SOCIAL MALADY COMMON AMONG DUNDERHEADS SUCH AS YOURSELF.
SO WHAT DO I DO?
JUST TRY TO FORGET ABOUT IT... ANYHOW, I GOTTA GO... ENJOY YOUR COFFEE....
YOU, TOO!

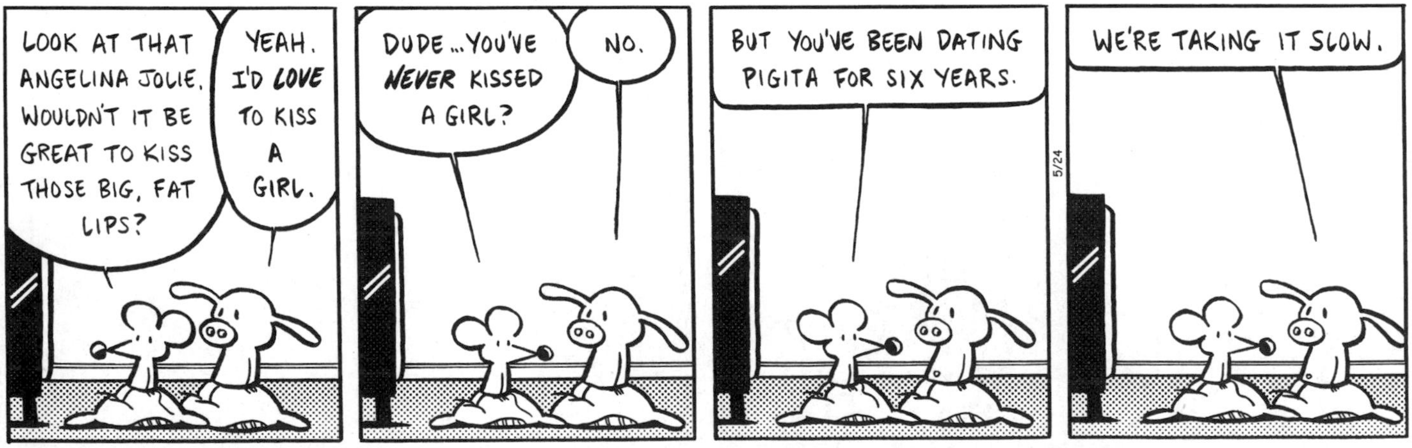
LOOK AT THAT ANGELINA JOLIE. WOULDN'T IT BE GREAT TO KISS THOSE BIG, FAT LIPS?
YEAH. I'D *LOVE* TO KISS A GIRL.
DUDE... YOU'VE *NEVER* KISSED A GIRL?
NO.
BUT YOU'VE BEEN DATING PIGITA FOR SIX YEARS.
5/24
WE'RE TAKING IT SLOW.

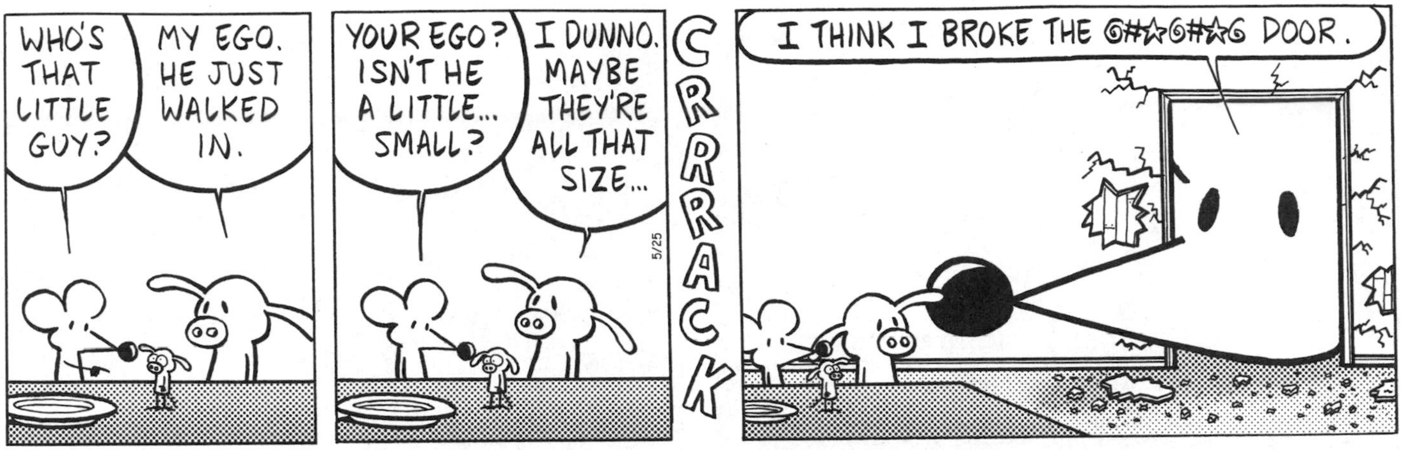
WHO'S THAT LITTLE GUY?
MY EGO. HE JUST WALKED IN.
YOUR EGO? ISN'T HE A LITTLE... SMALL?
I DUNNO. MAYBE THEY'RE ALL THAT SIZE...
5/25
CRRRACK
I THINK I BROKE THE @#☆@#☆G DOOR.

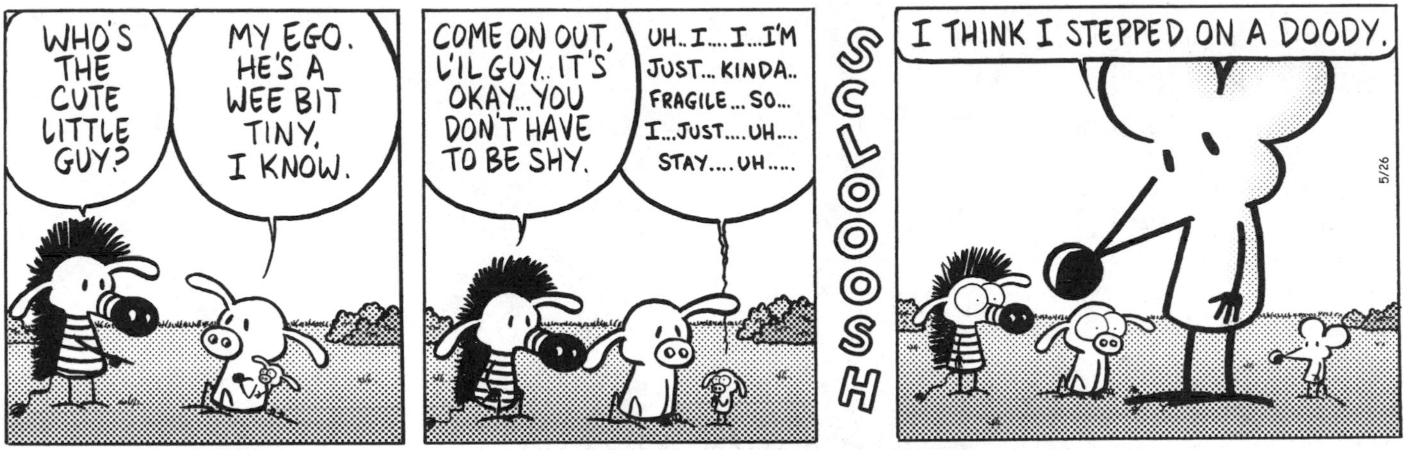
WHO'S THE CUTE LITTLE GUY?
MY EGO. HE'S A WEE BIT TINY, I KNOW.
COME ON OUT, L'IL GUY.. IT'S OKAY... YOU DON'T HAVE TO BE SHY.
UH.. I.... I... I'M JUST... KINDA.. FRAGILE... SO... I... JUST.... UH.... STAY.... UH.....
SCLOOOOSH
I THINK I STEPPED ON A DOODY.
5/26

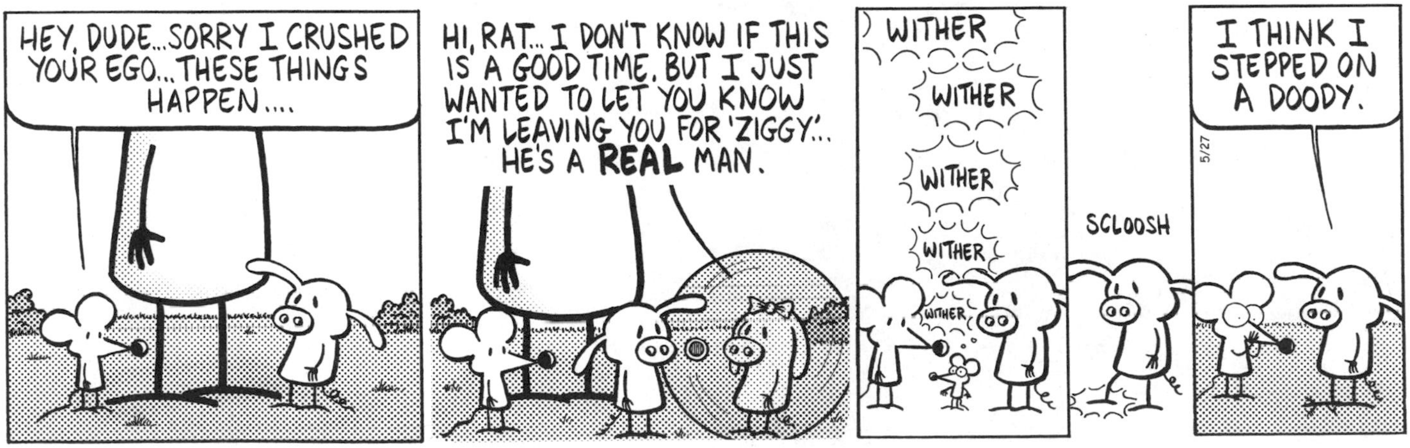
HEY, DUDE... SORRY I CRUSHED YOUR EGO... THESE THINGS HAPPEN....
HI, RAT... I DON'T KNOW IF THIS IS A GOOD TIME, BUT I JUST WANTED TO LET YOU KNOW I'M LEAVING YOU FOR 'ZIGGY'... HE'S A REAL MAN.
WITHER
WITHER
WITHER
WITHER
WITHER
SCLOOSH
5/27
I THINK I STEPPED ON A DOODY.

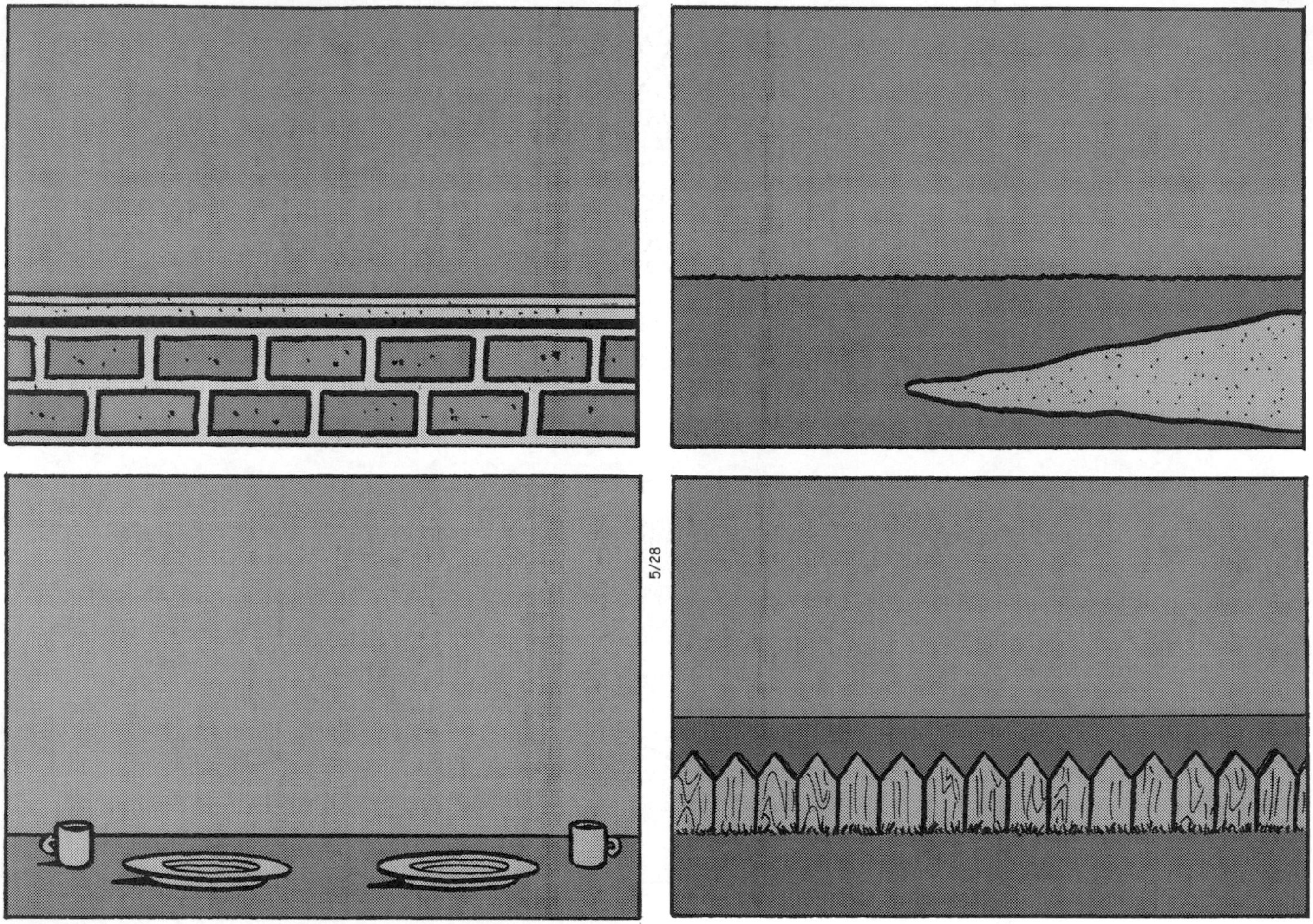
5/28

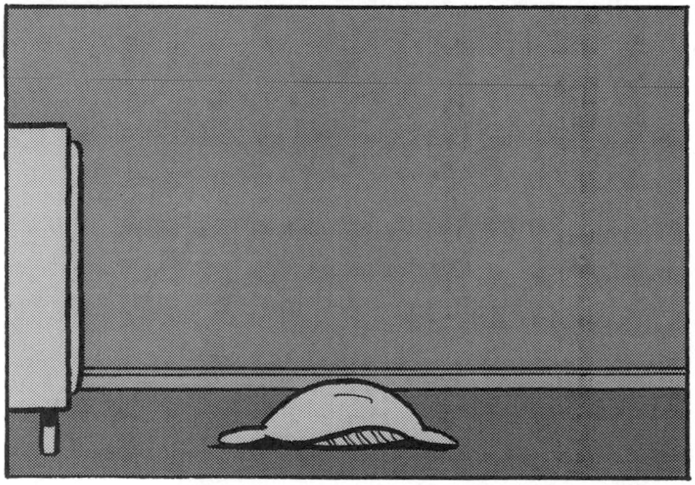

A moment of silence
in honor of the American
men and women killed
in Iraq and Afghanistan.

Memorial Day, 2006

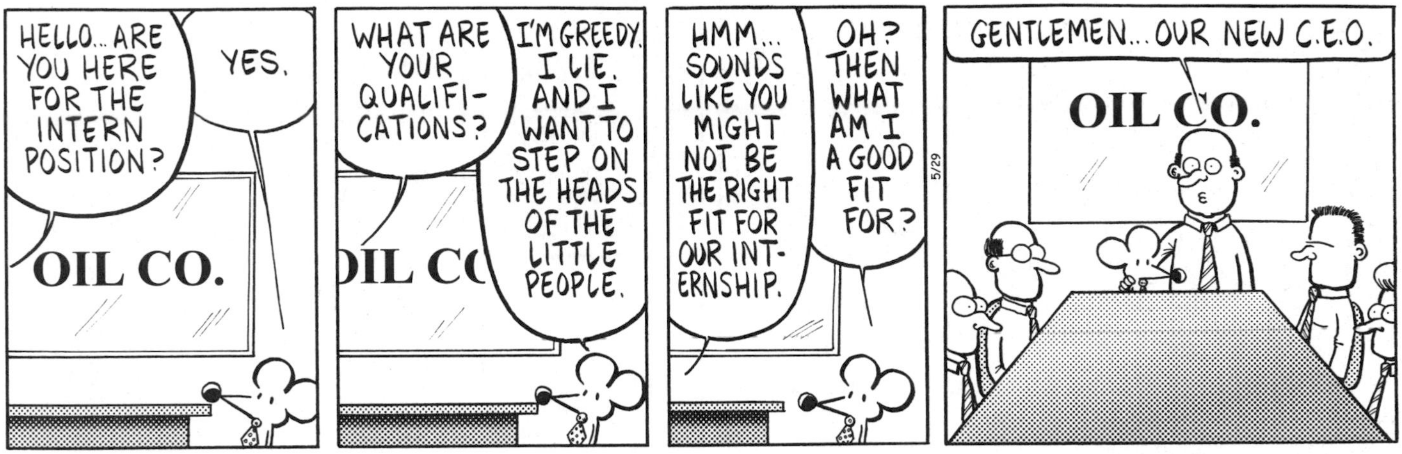
HELLO... ARE YOU HERE FOR THE INTERN POSITION?
YES.
OIL CO.
WHAT ARE YOUR QUALIFICATIONS?
I'M GREEDY. I LIE. AND I WANT TO STEP ON THE HEADS OF THE LITTLE PEOPLE.
HMM... SOUNDS LIKE YOU MIGHT NOT BE THE RIGHT FIT FOR OUR INTERNSHIP.
OH? THEN WHAT AM I A GOOD FIT FOR?
5/29
GENTLEMEN... OUR NEW C.E.O.
OIL CO.

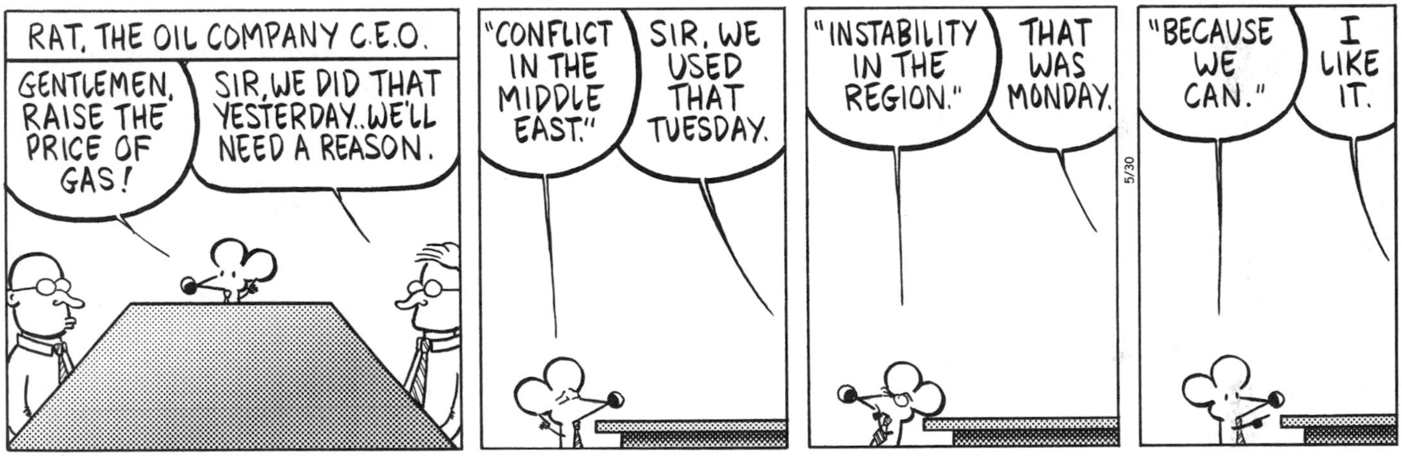
RAT, THE OIL COMPANY C.E.O.
GENTLEMEN, RAISE THE PRICE OF GAS!
SIR, WE DID THAT YESTERDAY.. WE'LL NEED A REASON.
"CONFLICT IN THE MIDDLE EAST."
SIR, WE USED THAT TUESDAY.
"INSTABILITY IN THE REGION."
THAT WAS MONDAY.
5/30
"BECAUSE WE CAN."
I LIKE IT.

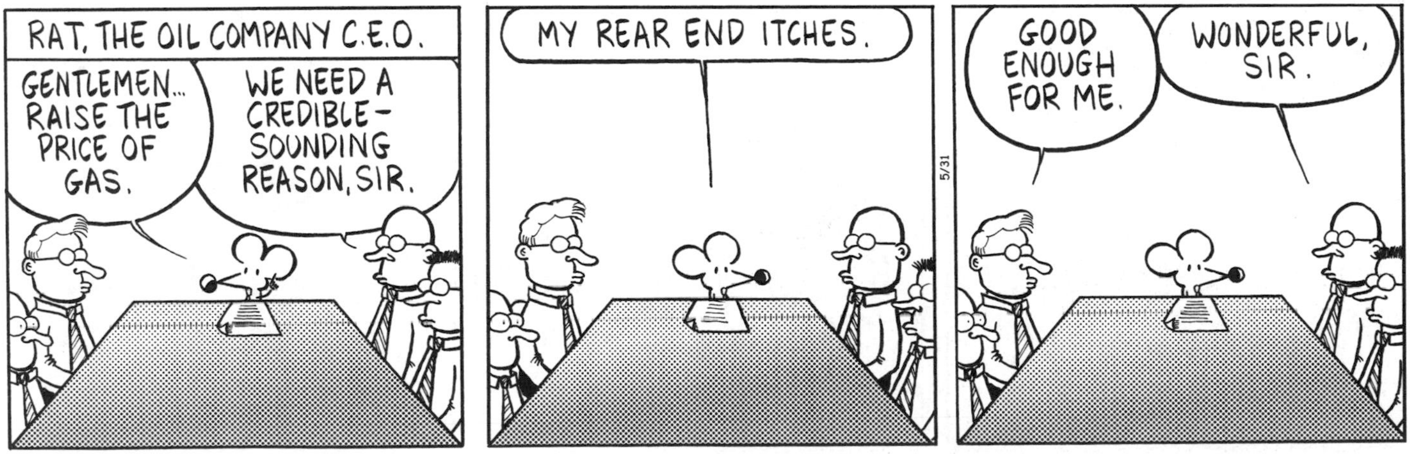
RAT, THE OIL COMPANY C.E.O.
GENTLEMEN... RAISE THE PRICE OF GAS.
WE NEED A CREDIBLE-SOUNDING REASON, SIR.
MY REAR END ITCHES.
5/31
GOOD ENOUGH FOR ME.
WONDERFUL, SIR.

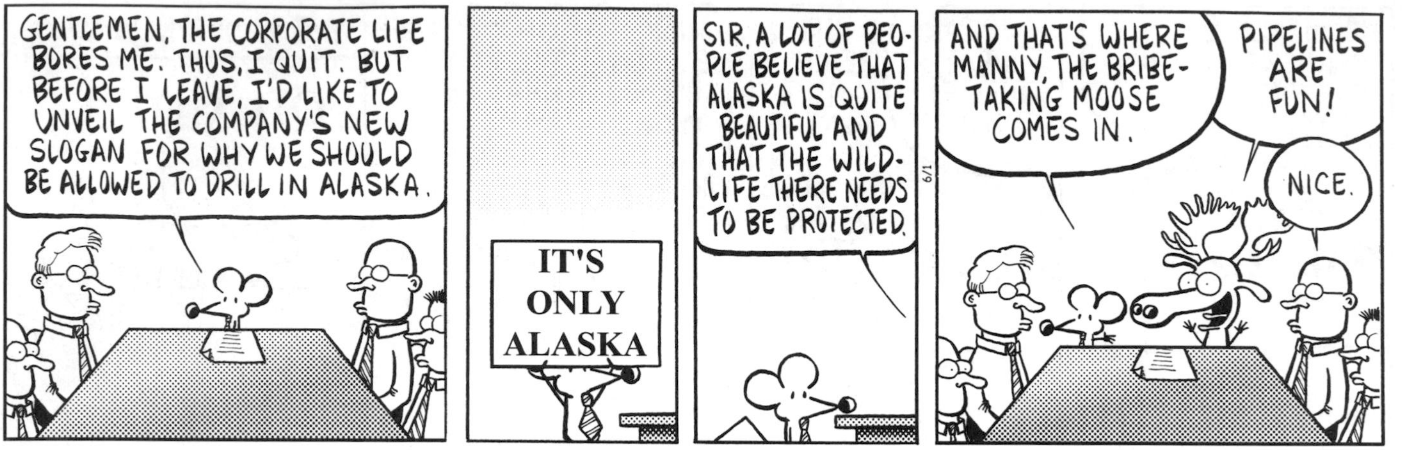
GENTLEMEN, THE CORPORATE LIFE BORES ME. THUS, I QUIT. BUT BEFORE I LEAVE, I'D LIKE TO UNVEIL THE COMPANY'S NEW SLOGAN FOR WHY WE SHOULD BE ALLOWED TO DRILL IN ALASKA.
IT'S ONLY ALASKA
SIR, A LOT OF PEOPLE BELIEVE THAT ALASKA IS QUITE BEAUTIFUL AND THAT THE WILDLIFE THERE NEEDS TO BE PROTECTED.
6/1
AND THAT'S WHERE MANNY, THE BRIBE-TAKING MOOSE COMES IN.
PIPELINES ARE FUN!
NICE.

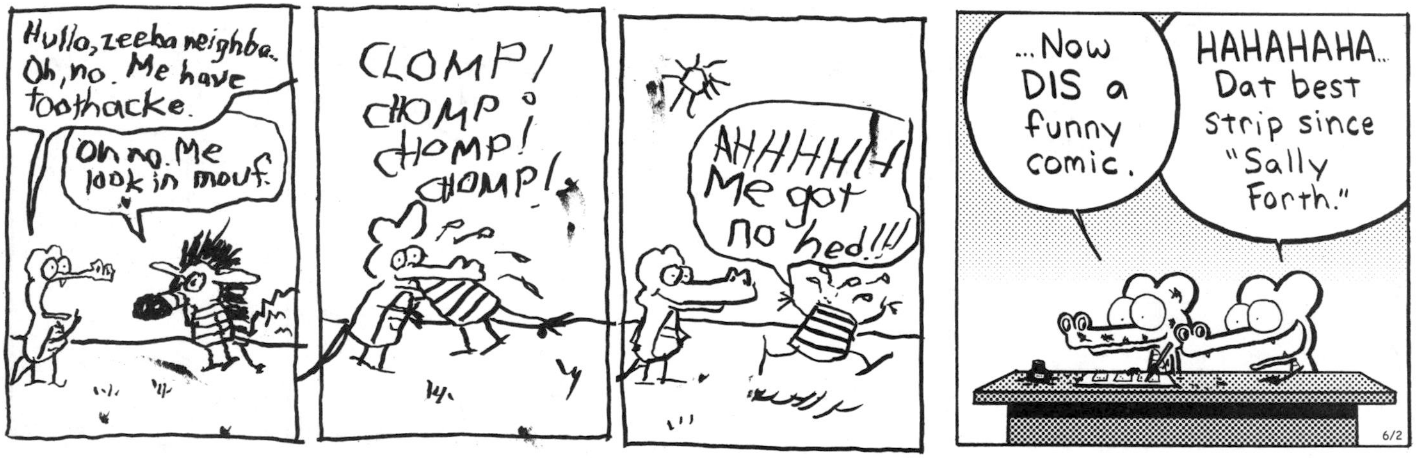
Hullo, zeeba neighba. Oh, no. Me have toothacke.
Oh no. Me look in mouf.
CLOMP! CHOMP CHOMP! CHOMP!
AHHHHH Me got no hed!!!
...Now DIS a funny comic.
HAHAHAHA... Dat best strip since "Sally Forth."
6/2

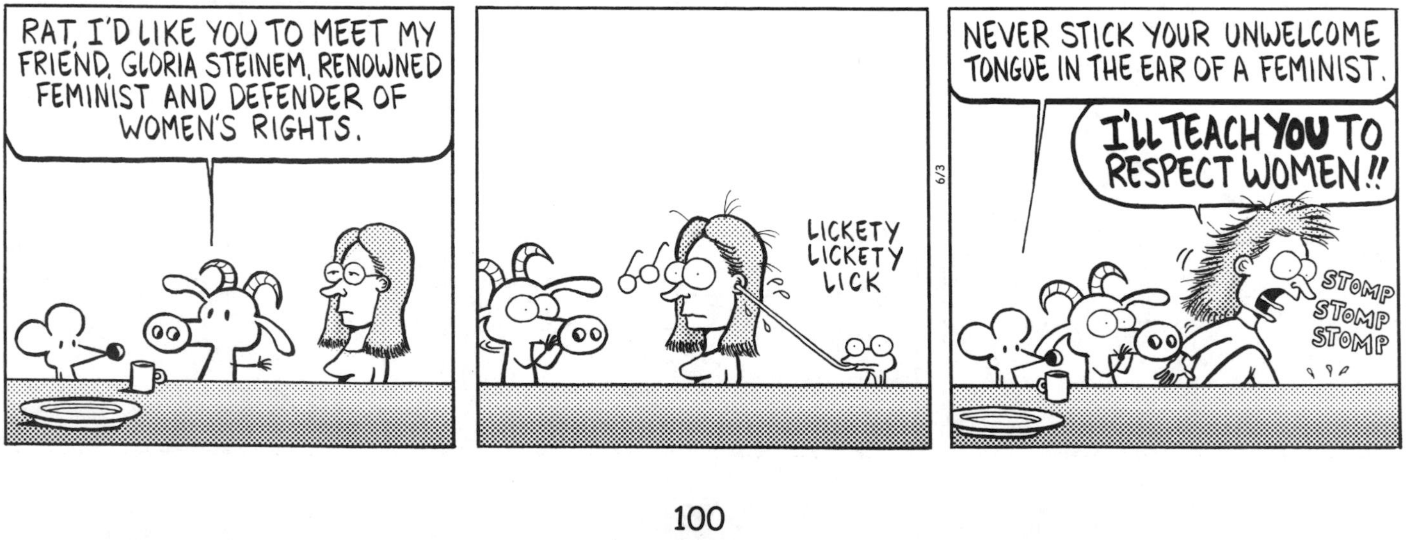
RAT, I'D LIKE YOU TO MEET MY FRIEND, GLORIA STEINEM, RENOWNED FEMINIST AND DEFENDER OF WOMEN'S RIGHTS.
6/3
LICKETY LICKETY LICK
NEVER STICK YOUR UNWELCOME TONGUE IN THE EAR OF A FEMINIST.
I'LL TEACH YOU TO RESPECT WOMEN!!
STOMP STOMP STOMP

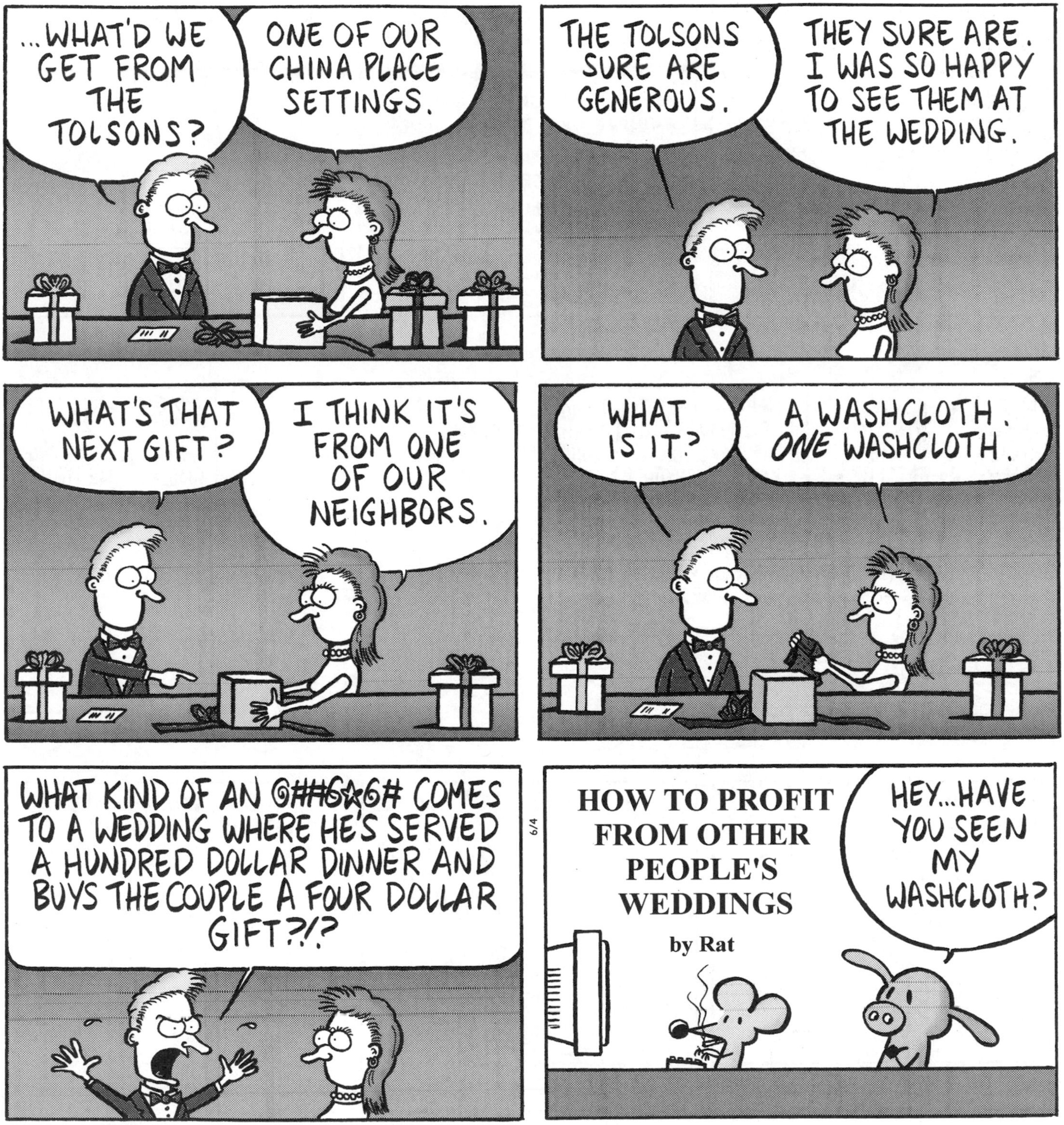
...WHAT'D WE GET FROM THE TOLSONS?
ONE OF OUR CHINA PLACE SETTINGS.
THE TOLSONS SURE ARE GENEROUS.
THEY SURE ARE. I WAS SO HAPPY TO SEE THEM AT THE WEDDING.
WHAT'S THAT NEXT GIFT?
I THINK IT'S FROM ONE OF OUR NEIGHBORS.
WHAT IS IT?
A WASHCLOTH. *ONE* WASHCLOTH.
WHAT KIND OF AN @##G☆G# COMES TO A WEDDING WHERE HE'S SERVED A HUNDRED DOLLAR DINNER AND BUYS THE COUPLE A FOUR DOLLAR GIFT?!?
6/4
HOW TO PROFIT FROM OTHER PEOPLE'S WEDDINGS
by Rat
HEY...HAVE YOU SEEN MY WASHCLOTH?

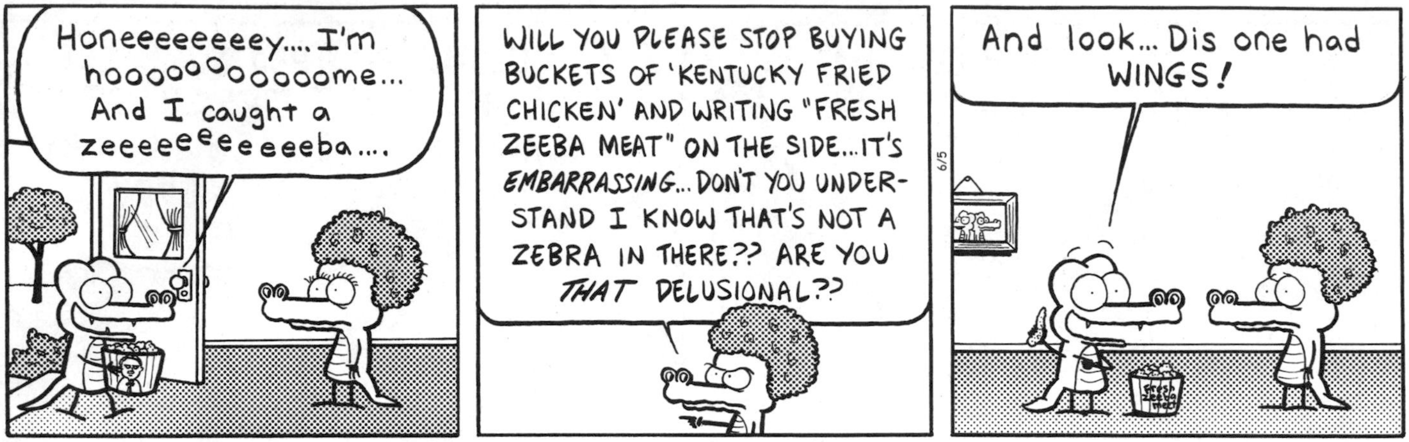
Honeeeeeeeey.... I'm hoooooooooome... And I caught a zeeeeeeeeeeeba....
WILL YOU PLEASE STOP BUYING BUCKETS OF 'KENTUCKY FRIED CHICKEN' AND WRITING "FRESH ZEEBA MEAT" ON THE SIDE... IT'S EMBARRASSING... DON'T YOU UNDERSTAND I KNOW THAT'S NOT A ZEBRA IN THERE?? ARE YOU THAT DELUSIONAL??
6/5
And look... Dis one had WINGS!

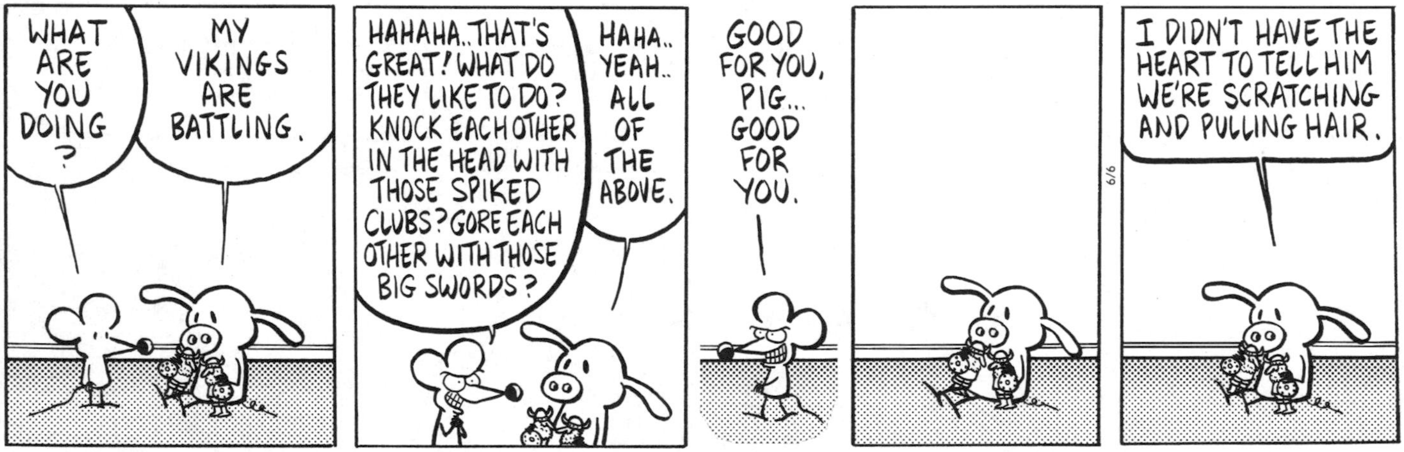
WHAT ARE YOU DOING ?
MY VIKINGS ARE BATTLING.
HAHAHA.. THAT'S GREAT! WHAT DO THEY LIKE TO DO? KNOCK EACH OTHER IN THE HEAD WITH THOSE SPIKED CLUBS? GORE EACH OTHER WITH THOSE BIG SWORDS?
HAHA.. YEAH.. ALL OF THE ABOVE.
GOOD FOR YOU, PIG... GOOD FOR YOU.
6/6
I DIDN'T HAVE THE HEART TO TELL HIM WE'RE SCRATCHING AND PULLING HAIR.

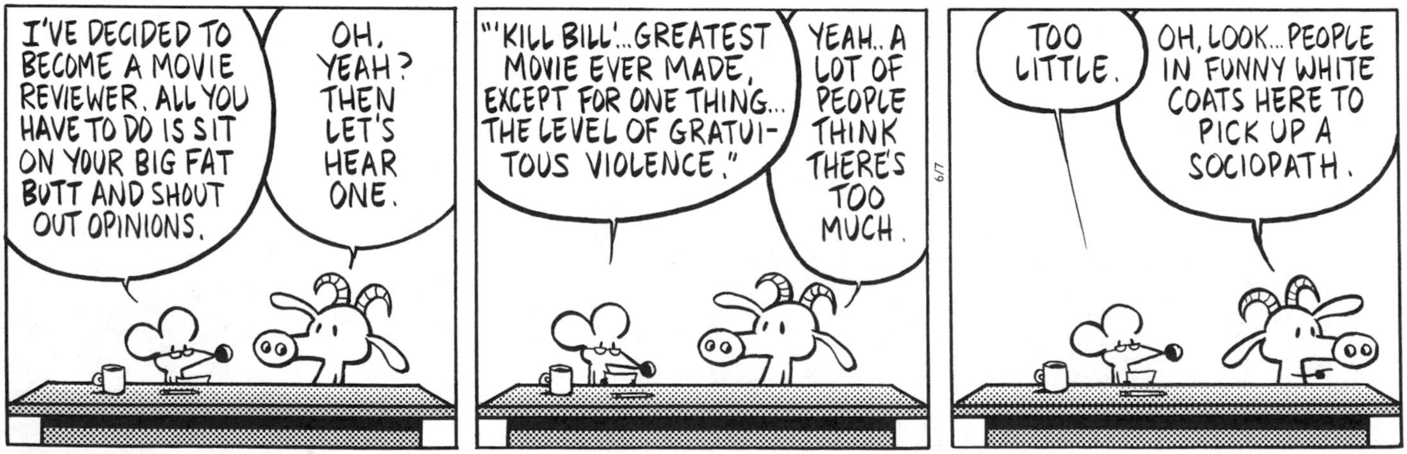
I'VE DECIDED TO BECOME A MOVIE REVIEWER. ALL YOU HAVE TO DO IS SIT ON YOUR BIG FAT BUTT AND SHOUT OUT OPINIONS.
OH, YEAH? THEN LET'S HEAR ONE.
"'KILL BILL'... GREATEST MOVIE EVER MADE, EXCEPT FOR ONE THING... THE LEVEL OF GRATUITOUS VIOLENCE."
YEAH.. A LOT OF PEOPLE THINK THERE'S TOO MUCH.
6/7
TOO LITTLE.
OH, LOOK... PEOPLE IN FUNNY WHITE COATS HERE TO PICK UP A SOCIOPATH.

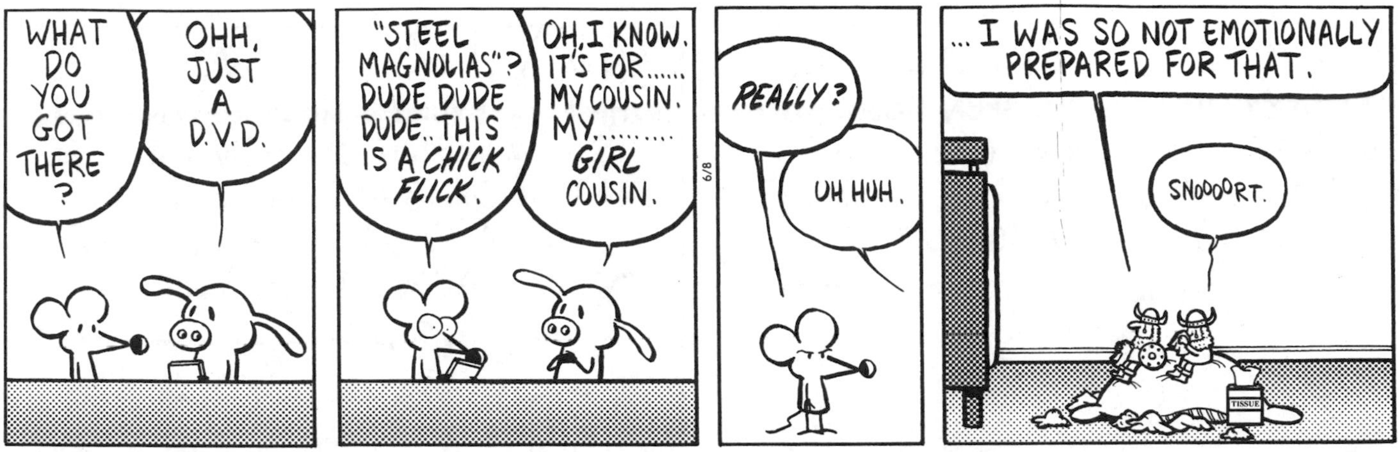
WHAT DO YOU GOT THERE?
OHH, JUST A D.V.D.
"STEEL MAGNOLIAS"? DUDE DUDE DUDE.. THIS IS A CHICK FLICK.
OH, I KNOW. IT'S FOR...... MY COUSIN. MY.......... GIRL COUSIN.
6/8
REALLY?
UH HUH.
... I WAS SO NOT EMOTIONALLY PREPARED FOR THAT.
SNOOOORT.
TISSUE

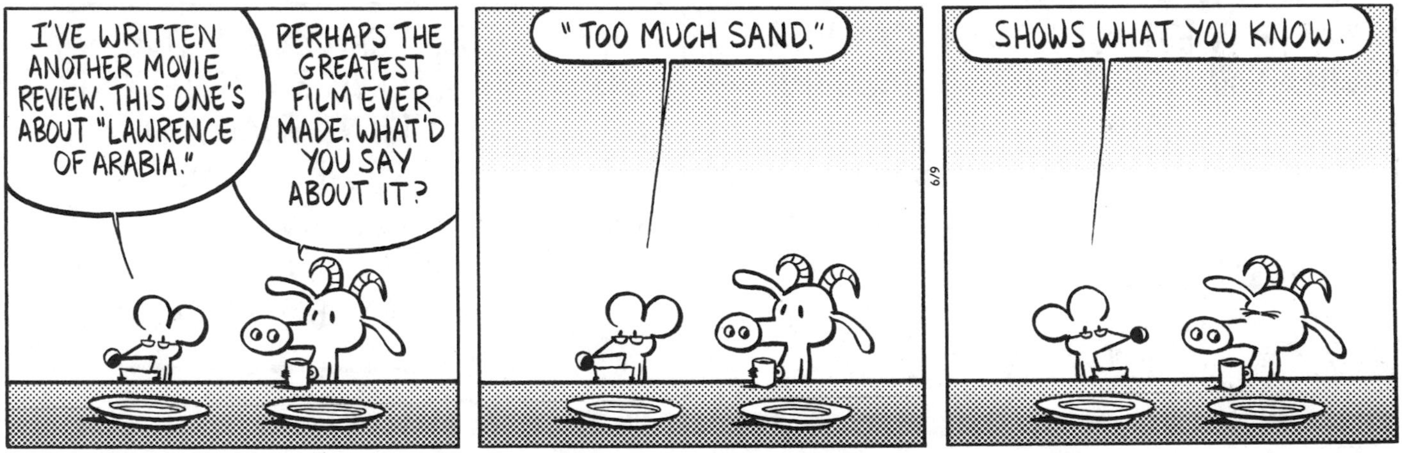
I'VE WRITTEN ANOTHER MOVIE REVIEW. THIS ONE'S ABOUT "LAWRENCE OF ARABIA."
PERHAPS THE GREATEST FILM EVER MADE. WHAT'D YOU SAY ABOUT IT?
"TOO MUCH SAND."
6/9
SHOWS WHAT YOU KNOW.

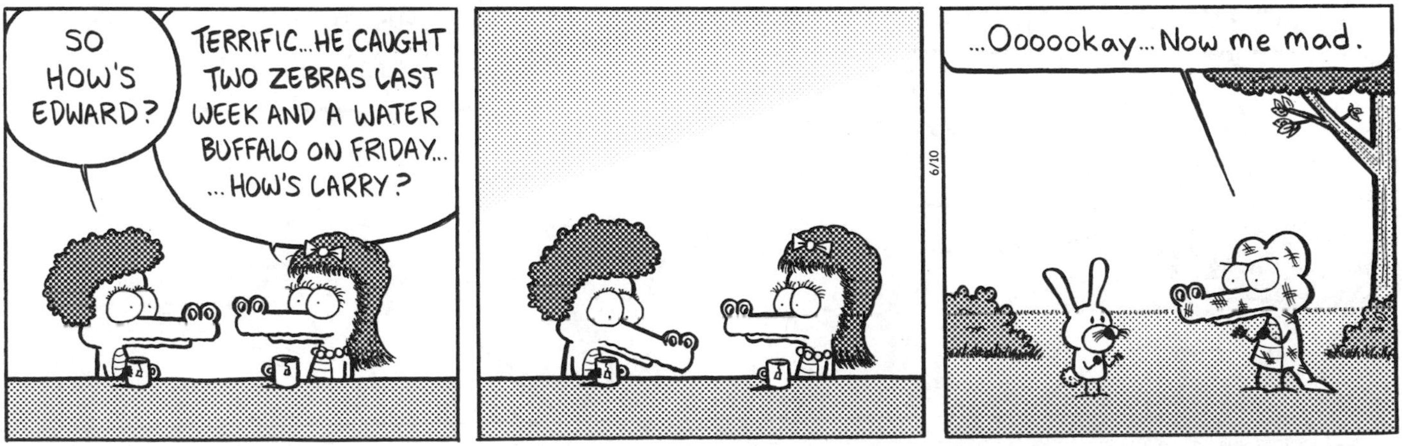
SO HOW'S EDWARD?
TERRIFIC...HE CAUGHT TWO ZEBRAS LAST WEEK AND A WATER BUFFALO ON FRIDAY... ...HOW'S LARRY?
6/10
...Oooookay... Now me mad.

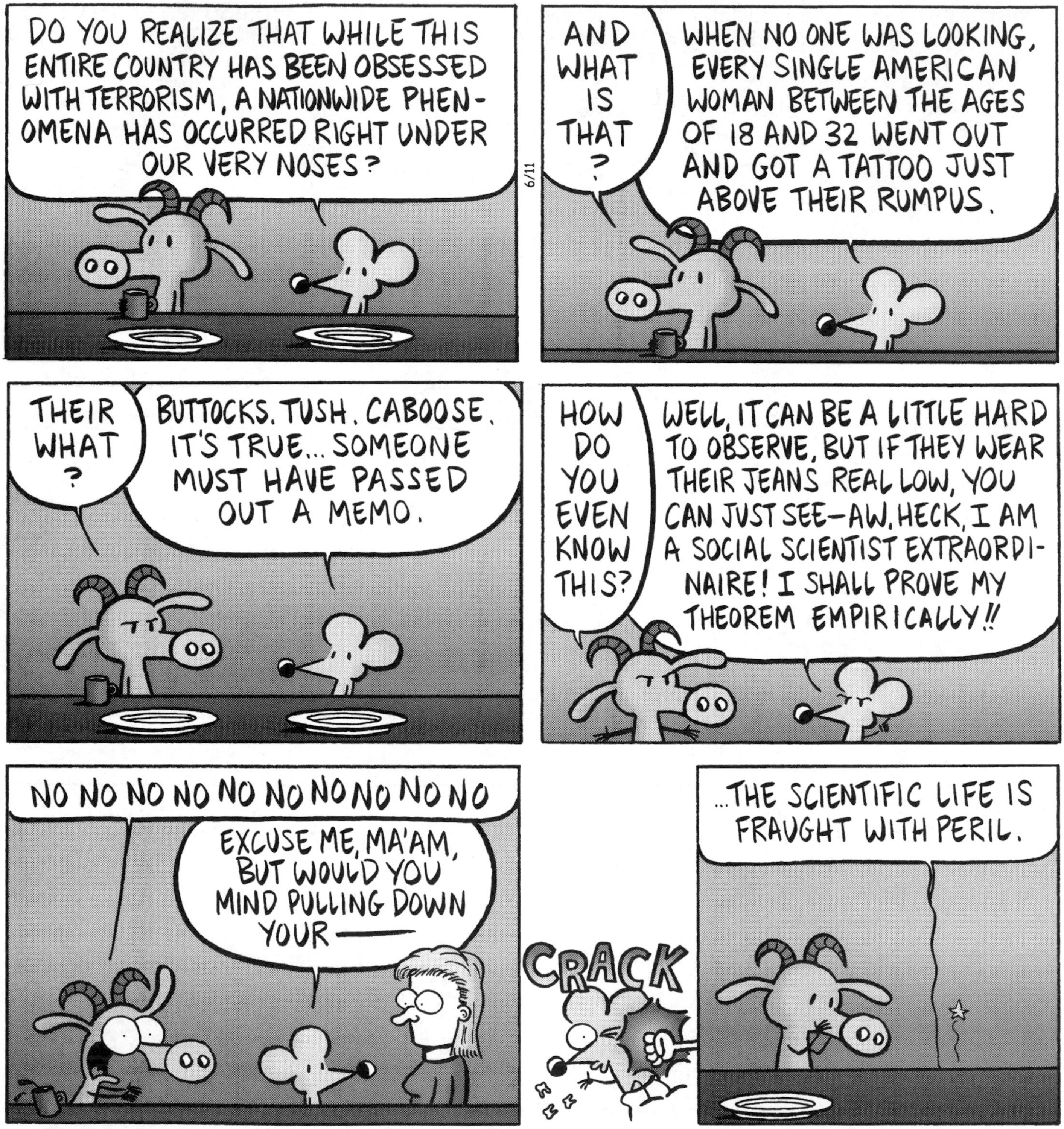
DO YOU REALIZE THAT WHILE THIS ENTIRE COUNTRY HAS BEEN OBSESSED WITH TERRORISM, A NATIONWIDE PHENOMENA HAS OCCURRED RIGHT UNDER OUR VERY NOSES?
6/11
AND WHAT IS THAT?
WHEN NO ONE WAS LOOKING, EVERY SINGLE AMERICAN WOMAN BETWEEN THE AGES OF 18 AND 32 WENT OUT AND GOT A TATTOO JUST ABOVE THEIR RUMPUS.
THEIR WHAT?
BUTTOCKS. TUSH. CABOOSE. IT'S TRUE... SOMEONE MUST HAVE PASSED OUT A MEMO.
HOW DO YOU EVEN KNOW THIS?
WELL, IT CAN BE A LITTLE HARD TO OBSERVE, BUT IF THEY WEAR THEIR JEANS REAL LOW, YOU CAN JUST SEE—AW, HECK, I AM A SOCIAL SCIENTIST EXTRAORDINAIRE! I SHALL PROVE MY THEOREM EMPIRICALLY!!
NO NO NO NO NO NO NO NO NO NO
EXCUSE ME, MA'AM, BUT WOULD YOU MIND PULLING DOWN YOUR——
CRACK
...THE SCIENTIFIC LIFE IS FRAUGHT WITH PERIL.

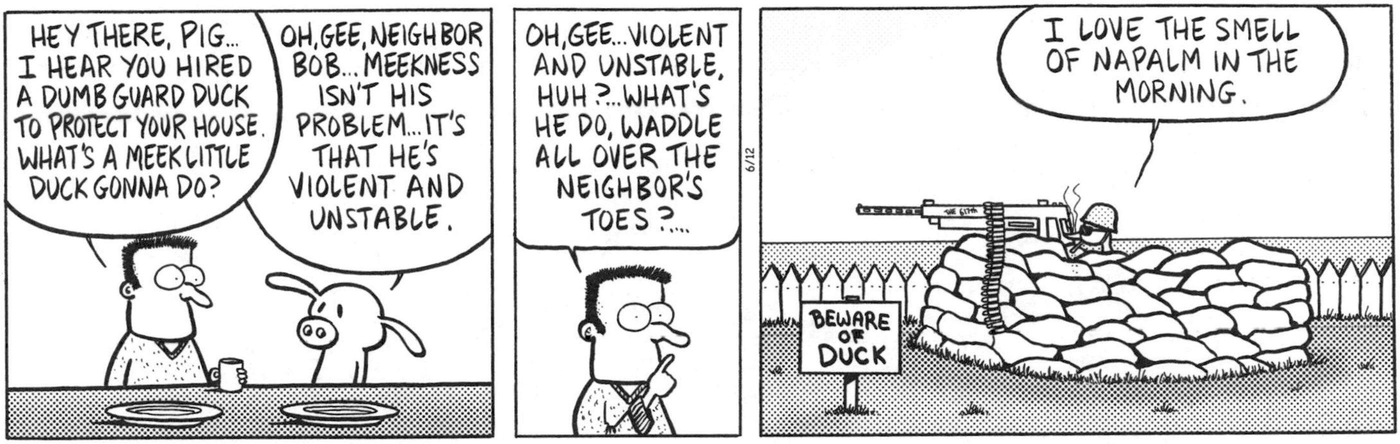
HEY THERE, PIG... I HEAR YOU HIRED A DUMB GUARD DUCK TO PROTECT YOUR HOUSE. WHAT'S A MEEK LITTLE DUCK GONNA DO?
OH, GEE, NEIGHBOR BOB... MEEKNESS ISN'T HIS PROBLEM... IT'S THAT HE'S VIOLENT AND UNSTABLE.
OH, GEE... VIOLENT AND UNSTABLE, HUH?... WHAT'S HE DO, WADDLE ALL OVER THE NEIGHBOR'S TOES?....
6/12
I LOVE THE SMELL OF NAPALM IN THE MORNING.
BEWARE OF DUCK

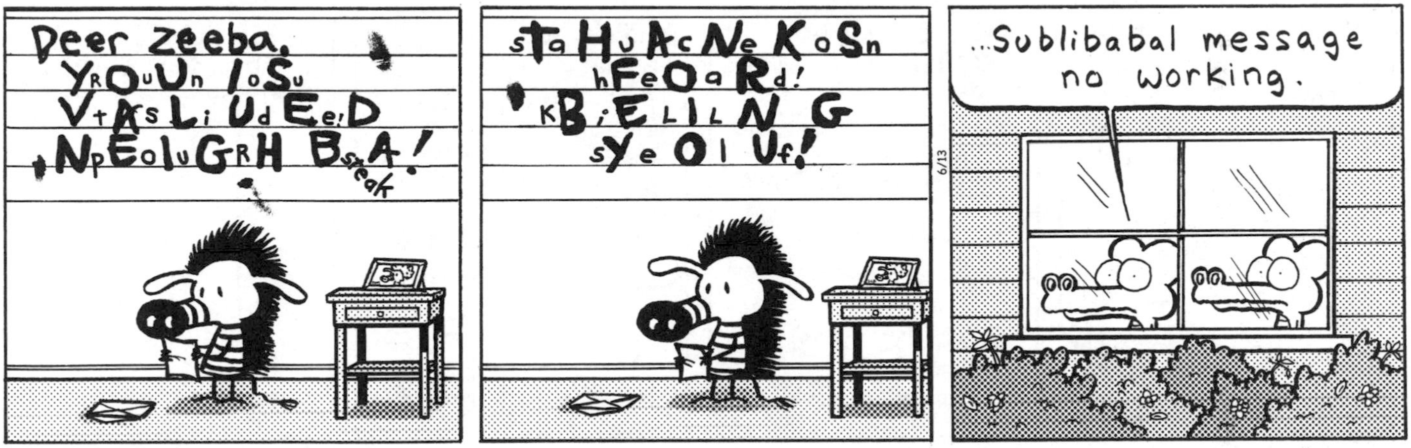
Deer zeeba,
YROUUn IoSu
VtAsLiUdEeiD
NpEoluGRH BsteakA!
sTaHuAcNeKoSn
hFeOaRd!
kBiELiLNG
syeOiUf!
6/13
...Sublibabal message no working.

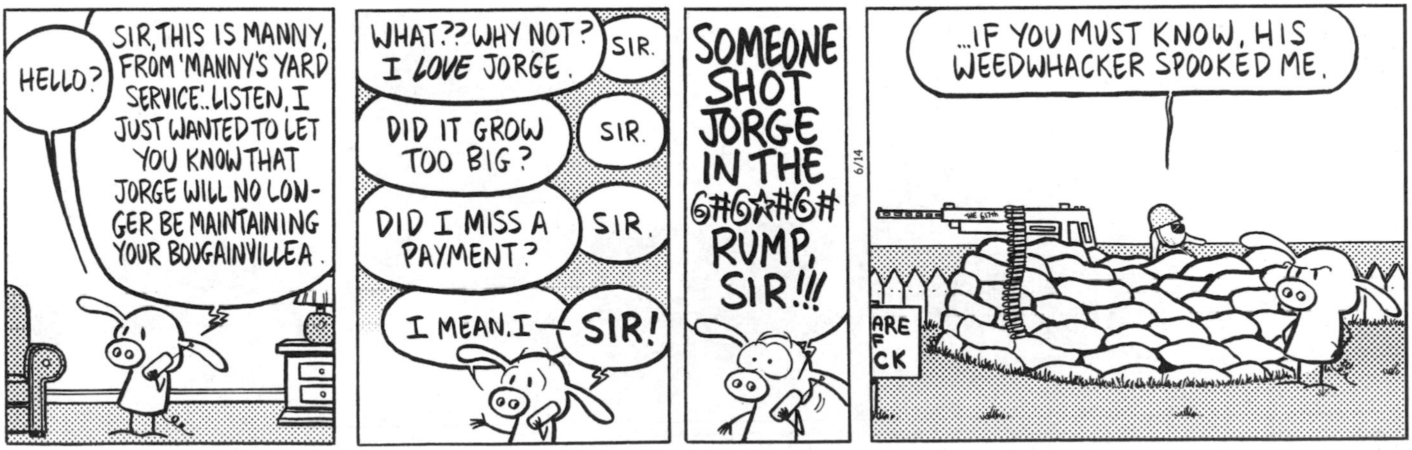
HELLO?
SIR, THIS IS MANNY, FROM 'MANNY'S YARD SERVICE'.. LISTEN, I JUST WANTED TO LET YOU KNOW THAT JORGE WILL NO LONGER BE MAINTAINING YOUR BOUGAINVILLEA.
WHAT?? WHY NOT? I LOVE JORGE.
SIR.
DID IT GROW TOO BIG?
SIR.
DID I MISS A PAYMENT?
SIR.
I MEAN, I—
SIR!
SOMEONE SHOT JORGE IN THE 6#G☆#G# RUMP, SIR!!!
6/14
...IF YOU MUST KNOW, HIS WEEDWHACKER SPOOKED ME.

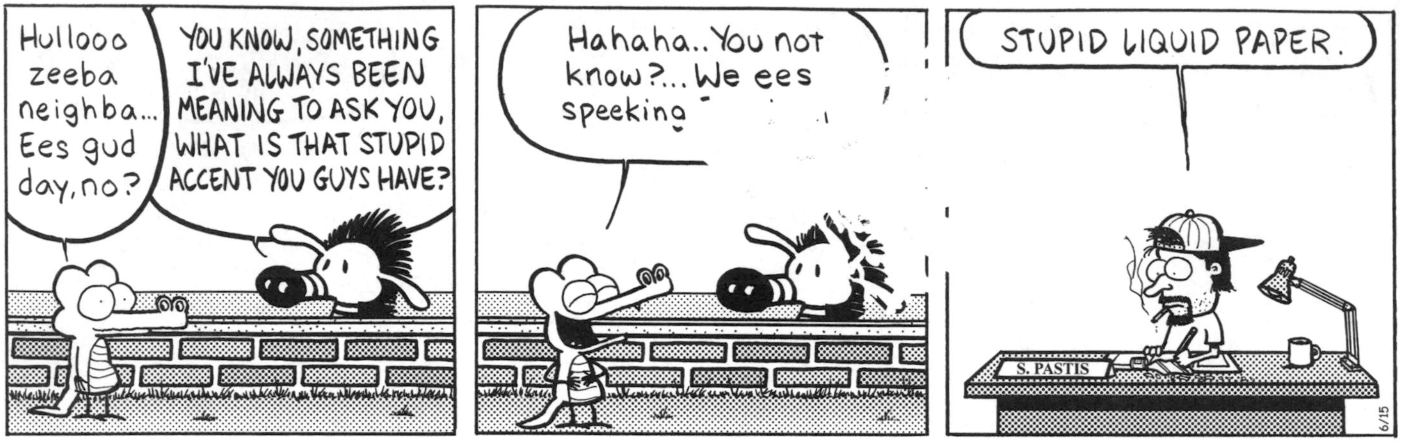

Hullooo zeeba neighba... Ees gud day, no?
YOU KNOW, SOMETHING I'VE ALWAYS BEEN MEANING TO ASK YOU, WHAT IS THAT STUPID ACCENT YOU GUYS HAVE?
Hahaha.. You not know?... We ees speeking
STUPID LIQUID PAPER.
S. PASTIS
6/15

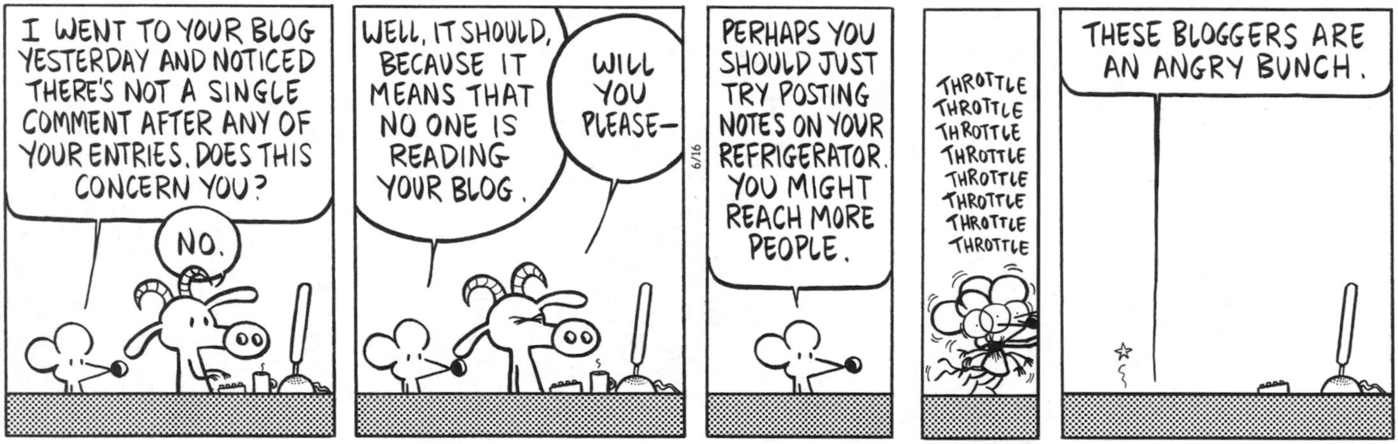

I WENT TO YOUR BLOG YESTERDAY AND NOTICED THERE'S NOT A SINGLE COMMENT AFTER ANY OF YOUR ENTRIES. DOES THIS CONCERN YOU?
NO.
WELL, IT SHOULD, BECAUSE IT MEANS THAT NO ONE IS READING YOUR BLOG.
WILL YOU PLEASE—
6/16
PERHAPS YOU SHOULD JUST TRY POSTING NOTES ON YOUR REFRIGERATOR. YOU MIGHT REACH MORE PEOPLE.
THROTTLE THROTTLE THROTTLE THROTTLE THROTTLE THROTTLE THROTTLE THROTTLE
THESE BLOGGERS ARE AN ANGRY BUNCH.

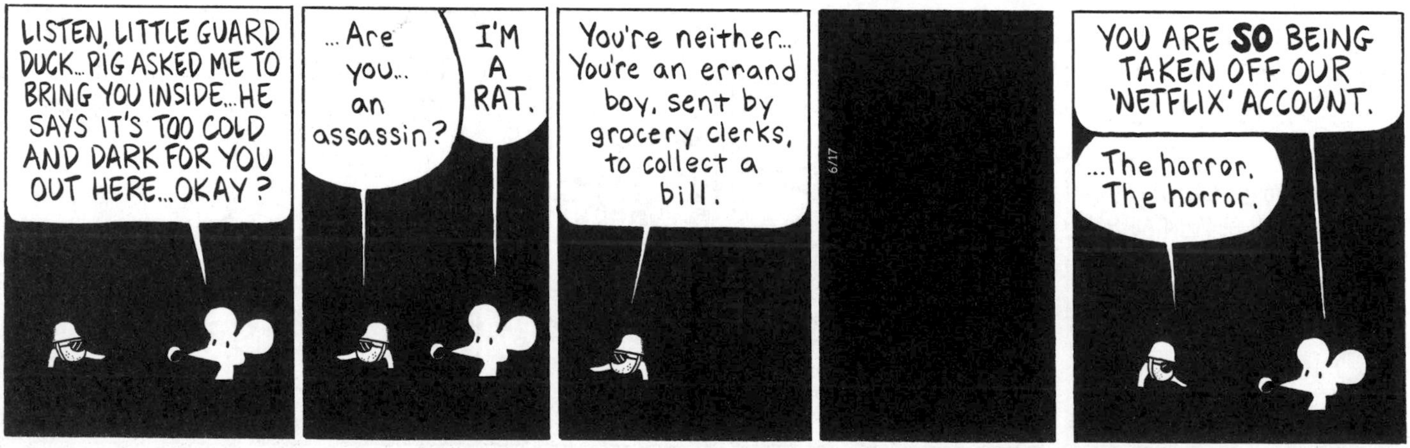

LISTEN, LITTLE GUARD DUCK... PIG ASKED ME TO BRING YOU INSIDE... HE SAYS IT'S TOO COLD AND DARK FOR YOU OUT HERE... OKAY?
... Are you... an assassin?
I'M A RAT.
You're neither... You're an errand boy, sent by grocery clerks, to collect a bill.
6/17
YOU ARE **SO** BEING TAKEN OFF OUR 'NETFLIX' ACCOUNT.
...The horror. The horror.

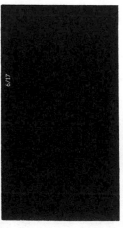

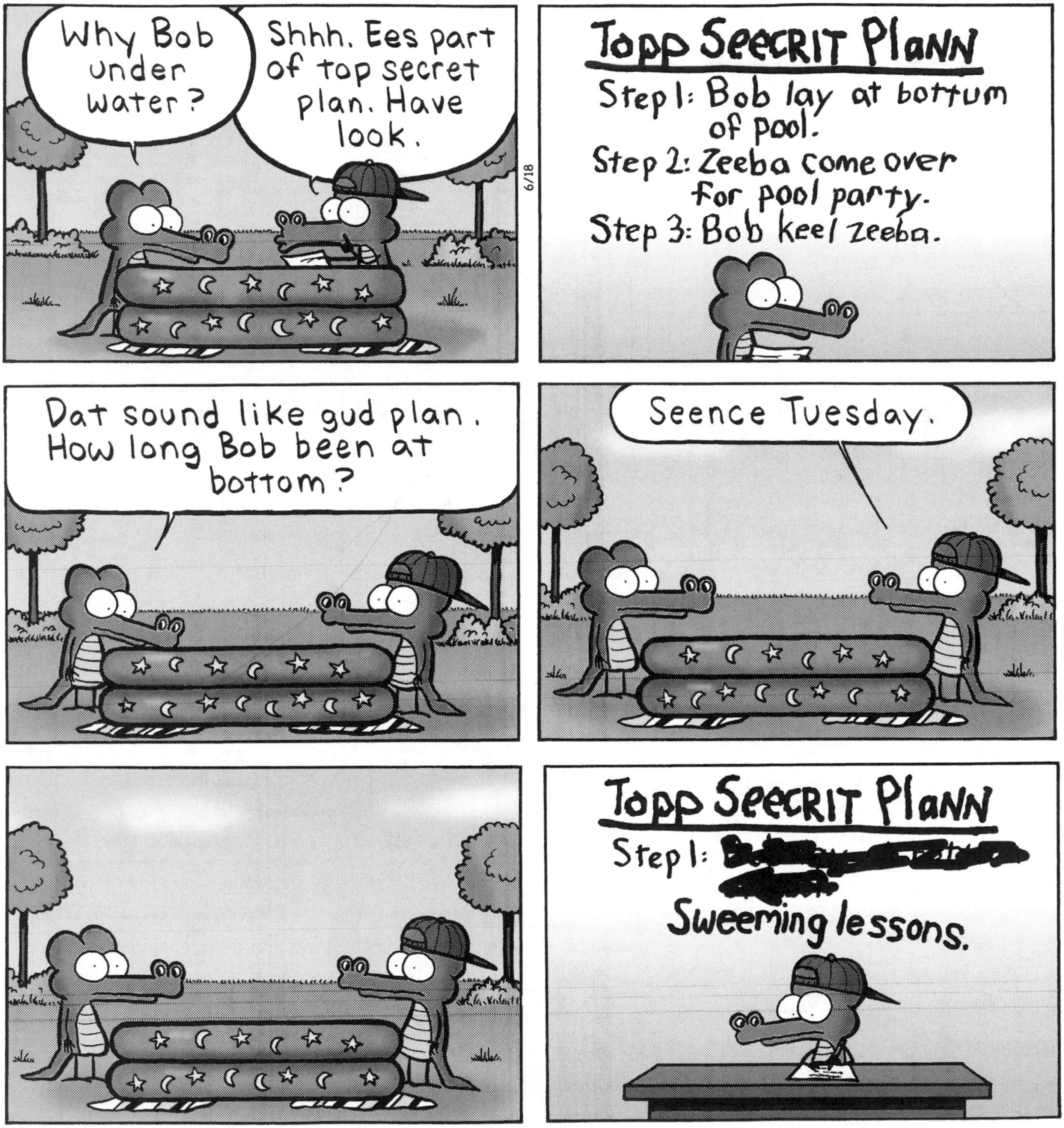

Why Bob under water?
Shhh. Ees part of top secret plan. Have look.
6/18
Topp Seecrit Plann
Step 1: Bob lay at bottum of pool.
Step 2: Zeeba come over for pool party.
Step 3: Bob keel zeeba.
Dat sound like gud plan. How long Bob been at bottom?
Seence Tuesday.
Topp Seecrit Plann
Step 1: [redacted]
Sweeming lessons.

Panel 1: SIR... GOOD EVENING, SIR.

CAN THIS WAIT 'TIL "DESPERATE HOUSEWIVES" IS OVER?

6/19

Panel 2: SIR, IF YOU LOOK OUT YOUR WINDOW, YOU'LL SEE THAT THE CIVILIAN ACROSS THE STREET HAS PAINTED HIS HOUSE A PARTICULARLY HEINOUS SHADE OF ORANGE... PERMISSION TO HANDLE THE SITUATION, SIR.

Panel 3: WELL, SURE, I GUESS YOU CAN TRY TO WORK IT OUT, BUT *PEACEFULLY*, OF COURSE.

Panel 4: PERMISSION TO SPEAK FREELY, SIR.

Panel 5: I NOTICED THAT YOUR BLOG ENTRY YESTERDAY WAS ONCE AGAIN FOLLOWED BY ZERO COMMENTS. THIS OBVIOUSLY MEANS THAT NO ONE IS READING IT... DOES THAT BOTHER YOU?

GO AWAY.

Panel 6: I WAS THINKING, MAYBE YOU COULD JUST SHOVE YOUR WRITING UNDER THIS BOX... THAT WAY, JUST AS MANY PEOPLE WOULD READ IT, BUT YOU'D SAVE A FORTUNE ON INTERNET CONNECTION FEES.

6/20

Panel 7: PERHAPS SAVING MONEY IS NOT A PRIORITY FOR YOU.

Panel 8: HI... I GOT A SPECIAL DELIVERY.

FLOWERS? WOW, NO ONE EVER SENDS ME FLOWERS!... THAT'S GREAT!... LET ME SEE THE CARD.

Panel 9: *Jo's Flowers*

Peese die.

1-800-555-5555

Panel 10: Is dere no pleasing dat guy?

6/21

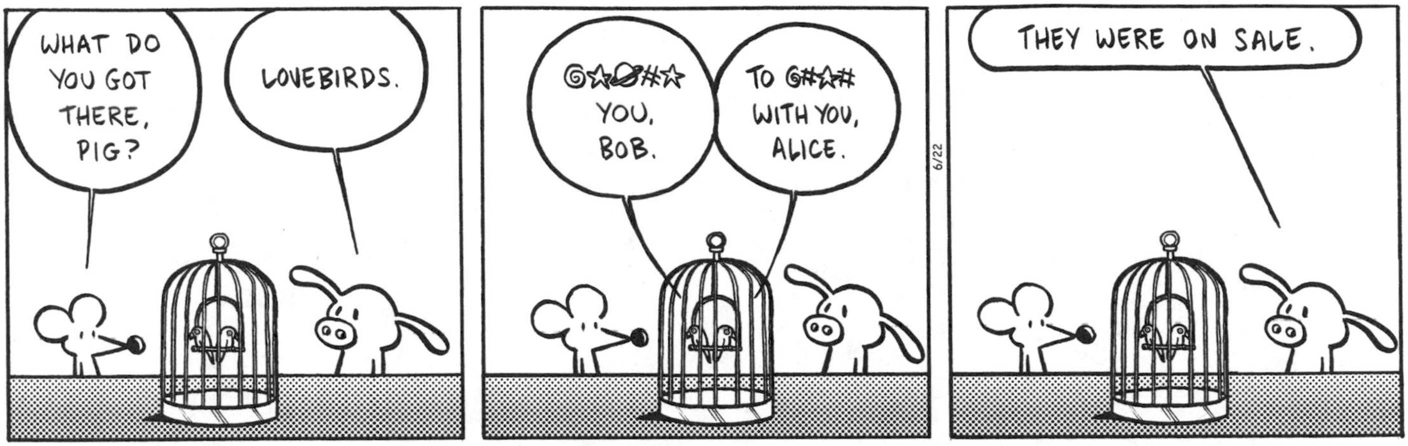
WHAT DO YOU GOT THERE, PIG?
LOVEBIRDS.
@☆@#☆ YOU, BOB.
TO @#☆# WITH YOU, ALICE.
6/22
THEY WERE ON SALE.

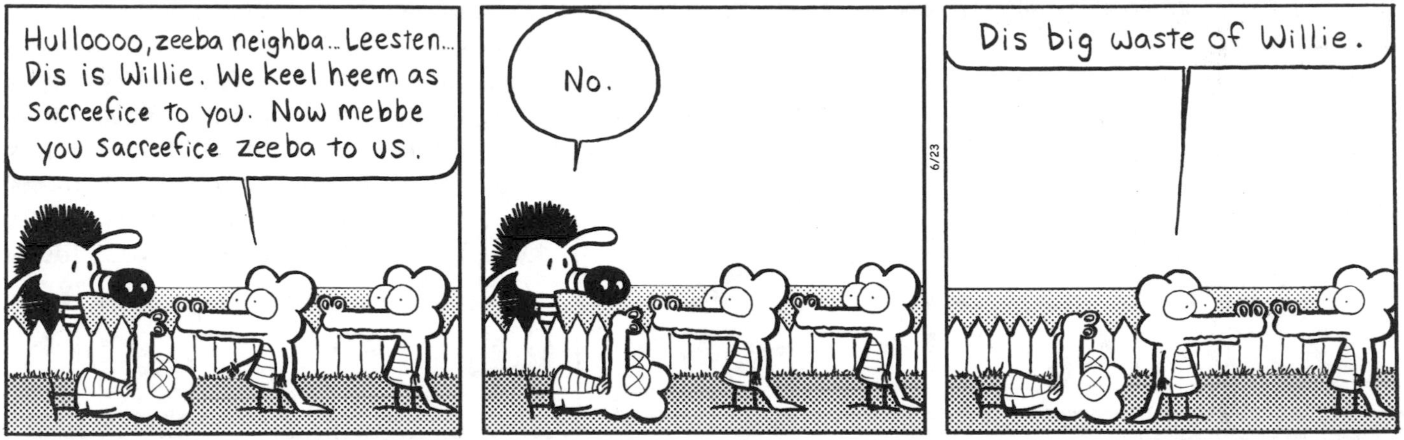
Hulloooo, zeeba neighba... Leesten... Dis is Willie. We keel heem as sacreefice to you. Now mebbe you sacreefice zeeba to us.
No.
6/23
Dis big waste of Willie.

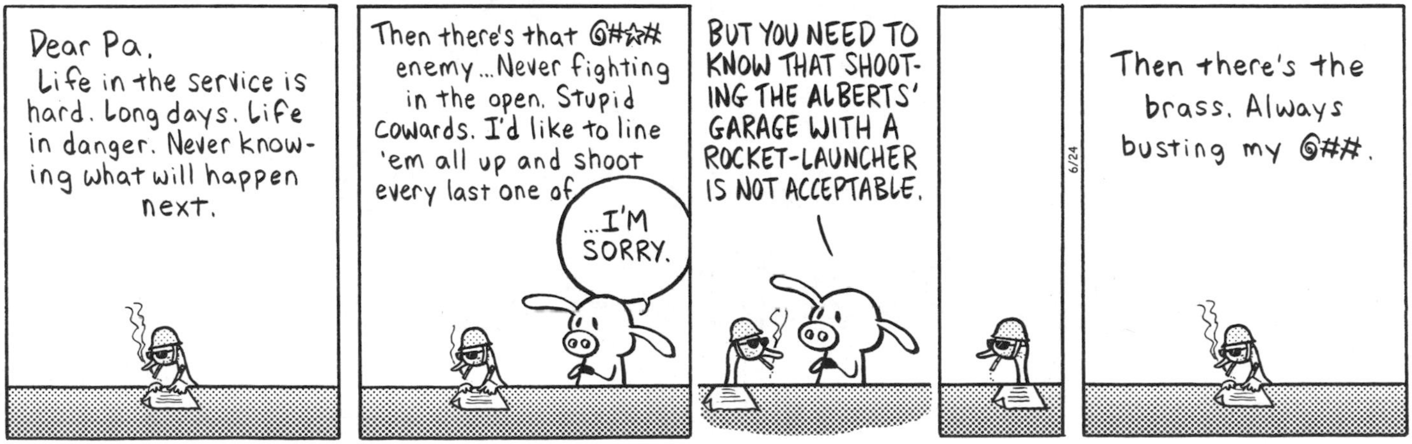
Dear Pa,
Life in the service is hard. Long days. Life in danger. Never knowing what will happen next.
Then there's that @#☆# enemy... Never fighting in the open. Stupid cowards. I'd like to line 'em all up and shoot every last one of
...I'M SORRY.
BUT YOU NEED TO KNOW THAT SHOOTING THE ALBERTS' GARAGE WITH A ROCKET-LAUNCHER IS NOT ACCEPTABLE.
6/24
Then there's the brass. Always busting my @##.

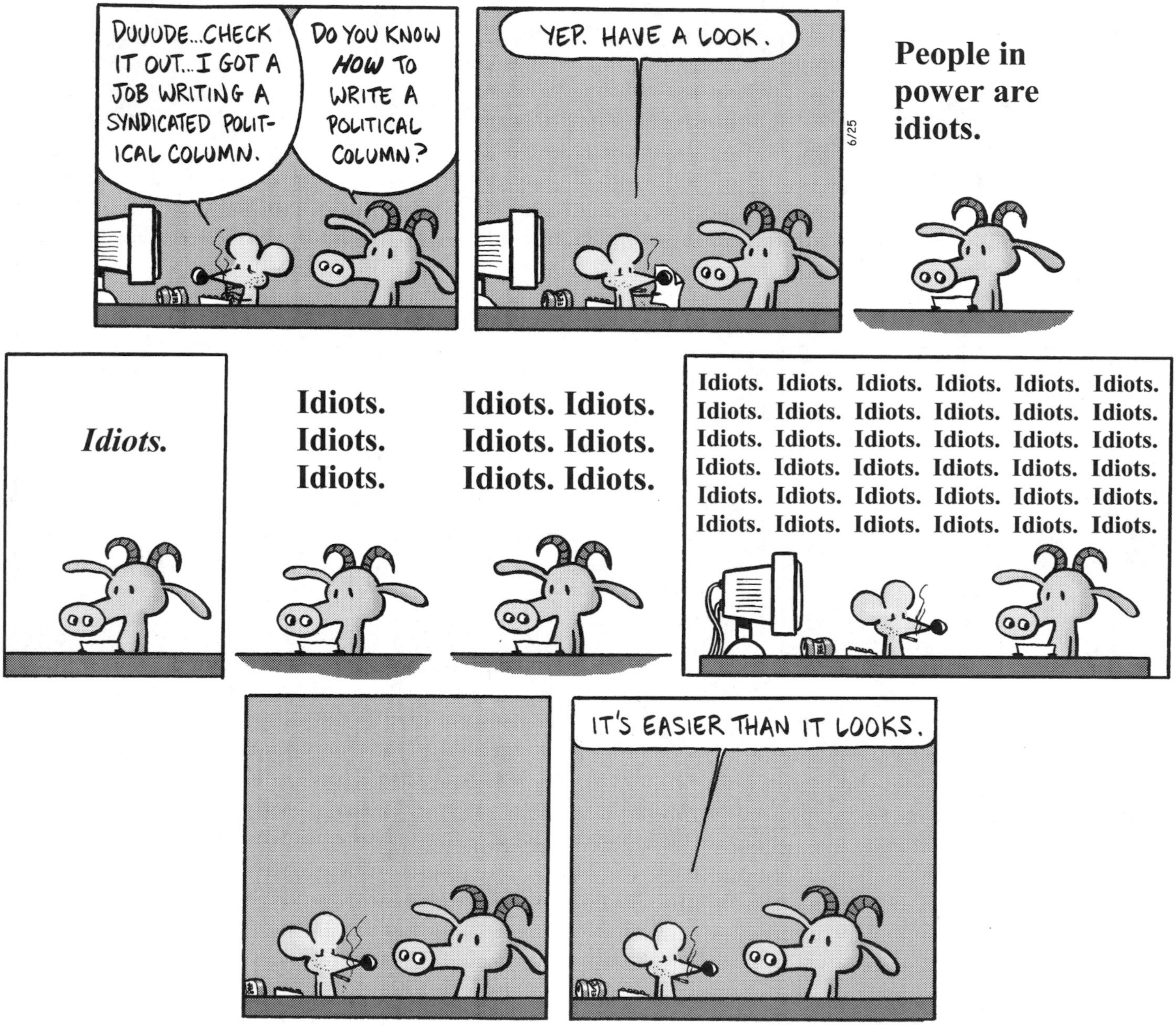
DUUUDE...CHECK IT OUT...I GOT A JOB WRITING A SYNDICATED POLITICAL COLUMN.
DO YOU KNOW HOW TO WRITE A POLITICAL COLUMN?
YEP. HAVE A LOOK.
6/25
People in power are idiots.
Idiots.
Idiots. Idiots. Idiots.
Idiots. Idiots. Idiots. Idiots. Idiots. Idiots.
Idiots. Idiots.
IT'S EASIER THAN IT LOOKS.

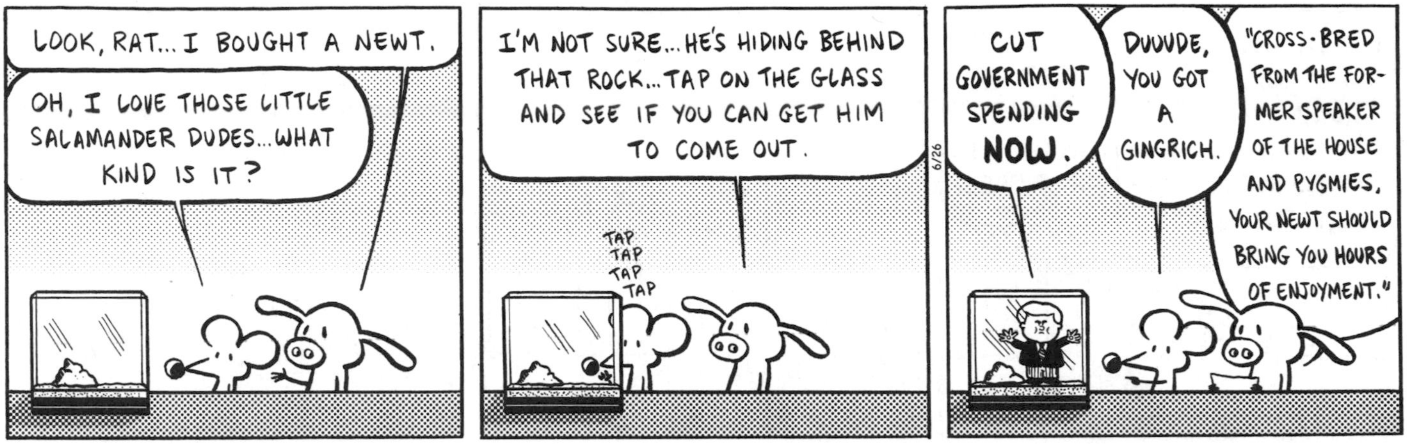
LOOK, RAT... I BOUGHT A NEWT.
OH, I LOVE THOSE LITTLE SALAMANDER DUDES... WHAT KIND IS IT?
I'M NOT SURE... HE'S HIDING BEHIND THAT ROCK... TAP ON THE GLASS AND SEE IF YOU CAN GET HIM TO COME OUT.
TAP TAP TAP TAP
6/26
CUT GOVERNMENT SPENDING NOW.
DUUUDE, YOU GOT A GINGRICH.
"CROSS-BRED FROM THE FORMER SPEAKER OF THE HOUSE AND PYGMIES, YOUR NEWT SHOULD BRING YOU HOURS OF ENJOYMENT."

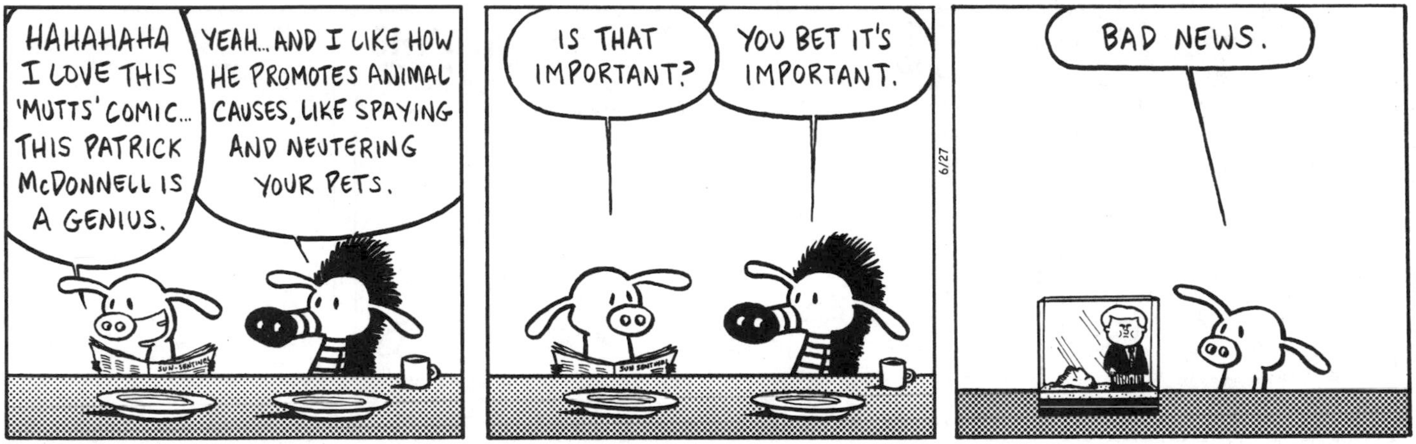
HAHAHAHA I LOVE THIS 'MUTTS' COMIC... THIS PATRICK McDONNELL IS A GENIUS.
YEAH... AND I LIKE HOW HE PROMOTES ANIMAL CAUSES, LIKE SPAYING AND NEUTERING YOUR PETS.
IS THAT IMPORTANT?
YOU BET IT'S IMPORTANT.
6/27
BAD NEWS.

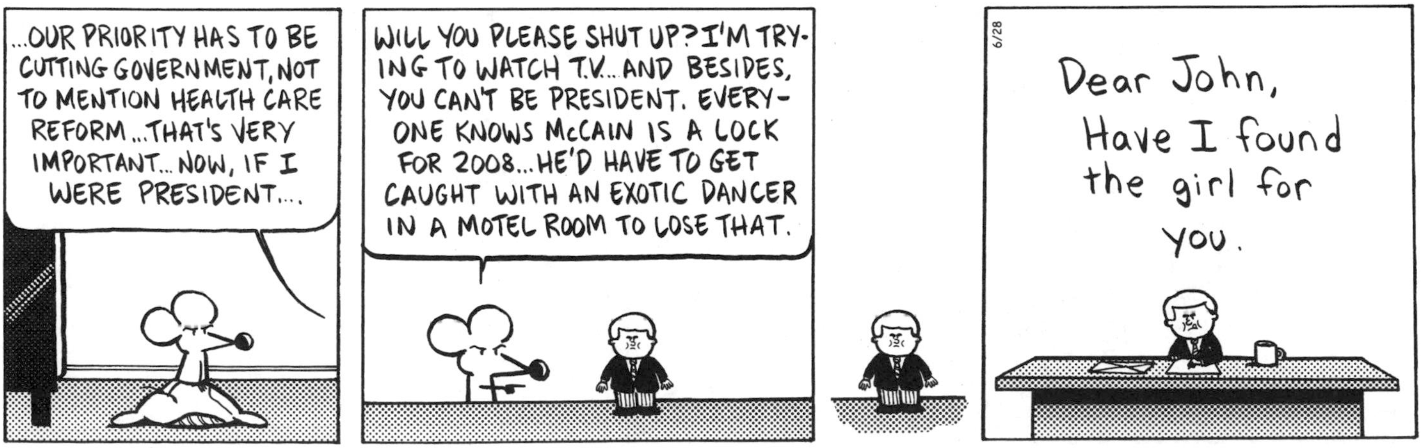
...OUR PRIORITY HAS TO BE CUTTING GOVERNMENT, NOT TO MENTION HEALTH CARE REFORM... THAT'S VERY IMPORTANT... NOW, IF I WERE PRESIDENT....
WILL YOU PLEASE SHUT UP? I'M TRYING TO WATCH T.V... AND BESIDES, YOU CAN'T BE PRESIDENT. EVERYONE KNOWS McCAIN IS A LOCK FOR 2008... HE'D HAVE TO GET CAUGHT WITH AN EXOTIC DANCER IN A MOTEL ROOM TO LOSE THAT.
6/28
Dear John,
Have I found the girl for you.

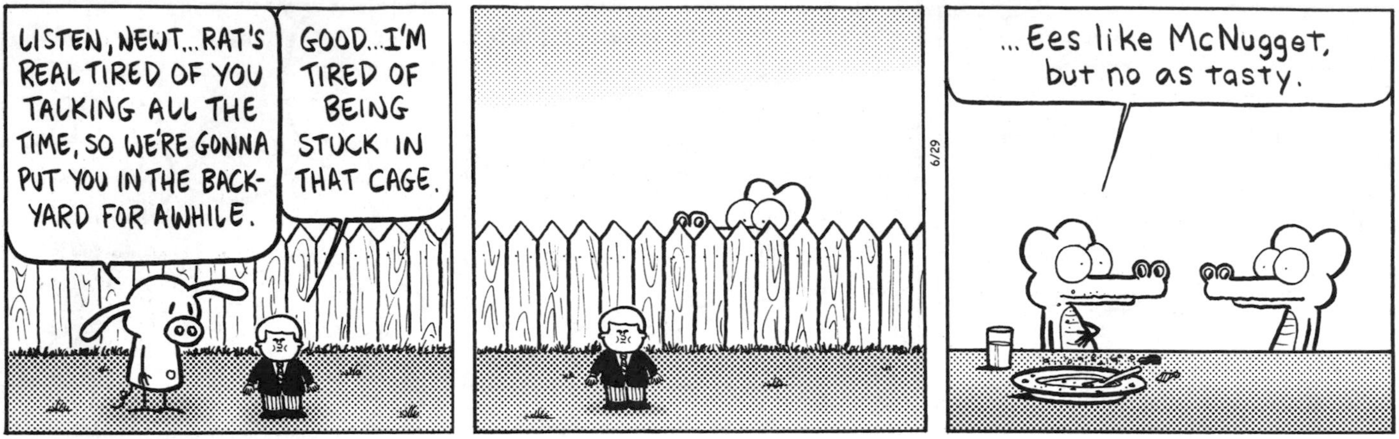
LISTEN, NEWT... RAT'S REAL TIRED OF YOU TALKING ALL THE TIME, SO WE'RE GONNA PUT YOU IN THE BACK-YARD FOR AWHILE.
GOOD... I'M TIRED OF BEING STUCK IN THAT CAGE.
6/29
... Ees like McNugget, but no as tasty.

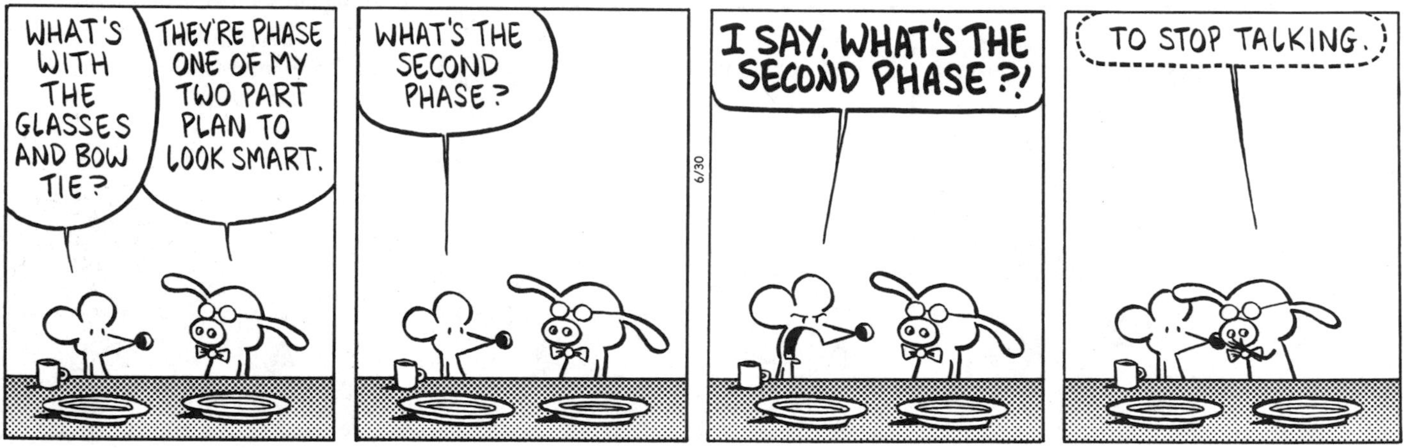
WHAT'S WITH THE GLASSES AND BOW TIE?
THEY'RE PHASE ONE OF MY TWO PART PLAN TO LOOK SMART.
WHAT'S THE SECOND PHASE?
6/30
I SAY, WHAT'S THE SECOND PHASE?!
TO STOP TALKING.

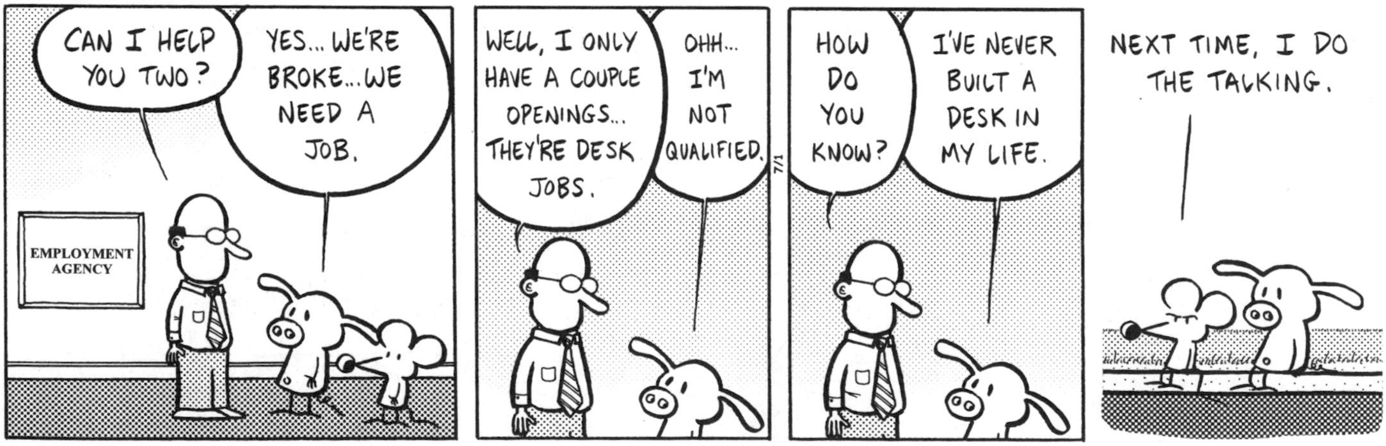
CAN I HELP YOU TWO?
YES... WE'RE BROKE... WE NEED A JOB.
EMPLOYMENT AGENCY
WELL, I ONLY HAVE A COUPLE OPENINGS... THEY'RE DESK JOBS.
OHH... I'M NOT QUALIFIED.
7/1
HOW DO YOU KNOW?
I'VE NEVER BUILT A DESK IN MY LIFE.
NEXT TIME, I DO THE TALKING.

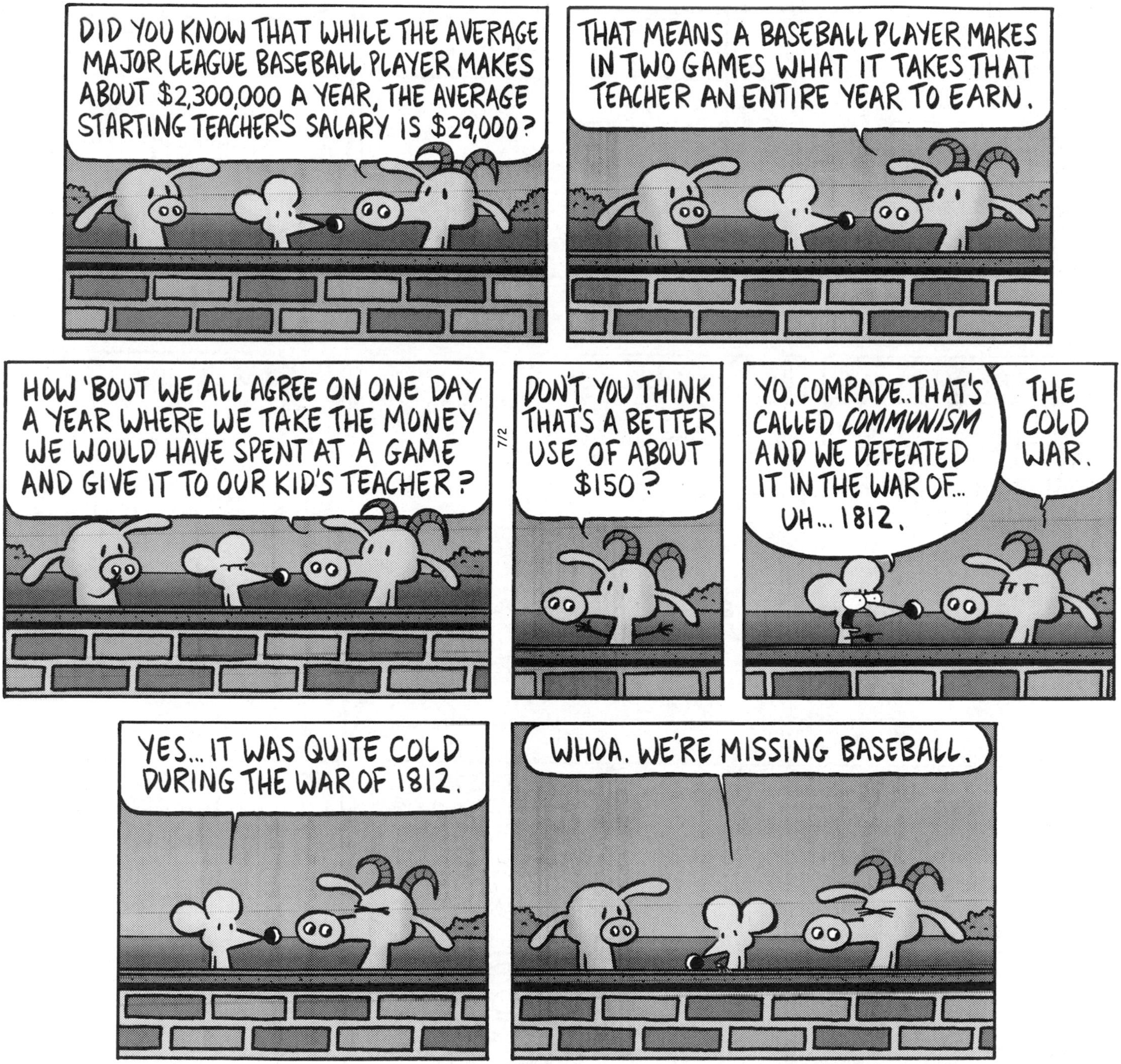
DID YOU KNOW THAT WHILE THE AVERAGE MAJOR LEAGUE BASEBALL PLAYER MAKES ABOUT $2,300,000 A YEAR, THE AVERAGE STARTING TEACHER'S SALARY IS $29,000?
THAT MEANS A BASEBALL PLAYER MAKES IN TWO GAMES WHAT IT TAKES THAT TEACHER AN ENTIRE YEAR TO EARN.
HOW 'BOUT WE ALL AGREE ON ONE DAY A YEAR WHERE WE TAKE THE MONEY WE WOULD HAVE SPENT AT A GAME AND GIVE IT TO OUR KID'S TEACHER?
7/2
DON'T YOU THINK THAT'S A BETTER USE OF ABOUT $150?
YO, COMRADE.. THAT'S CALLED *COMMUNISM* AND WE DEFEATED IT IN THE WAR OF... UH... 1812.
THE COLD WAR.
YES... IT WAS QUITE COLD DURING THE WAR OF 1812.
WHOA. WE'RE MISSING BASEBALL.

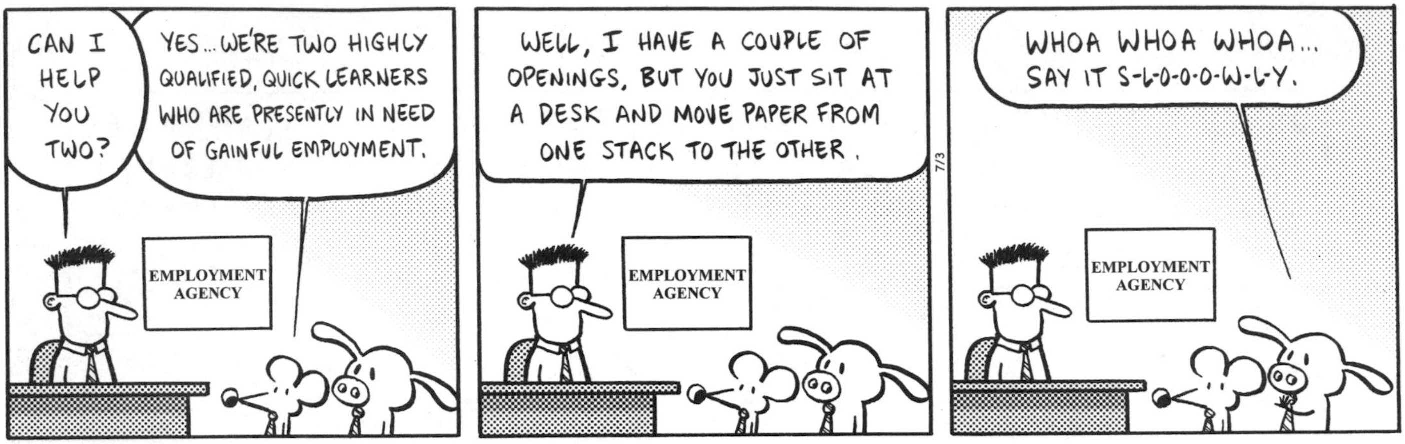
CAN I HELP YOU TWO?
YES... WE'RE TWO HIGHLY QUALIFIED, QUICK LEARNERS WHO ARE PRESENTLY IN NEED OF GAINFUL EMPLOYMENT.
EMPLOYMENT AGENCY
WELL, I HAVE A COUPLE OF OPENINGS, BUT YOU JUST SIT AT A DESK AND MOVE PAPER FROM ONE STACK TO THE OTHER.
EMPLOYMENT AGENCY
WHOA WHOA WHOA... SAY IT S-L-O-O-O-W-L-Y.
EMPLOYMENT AGENCY

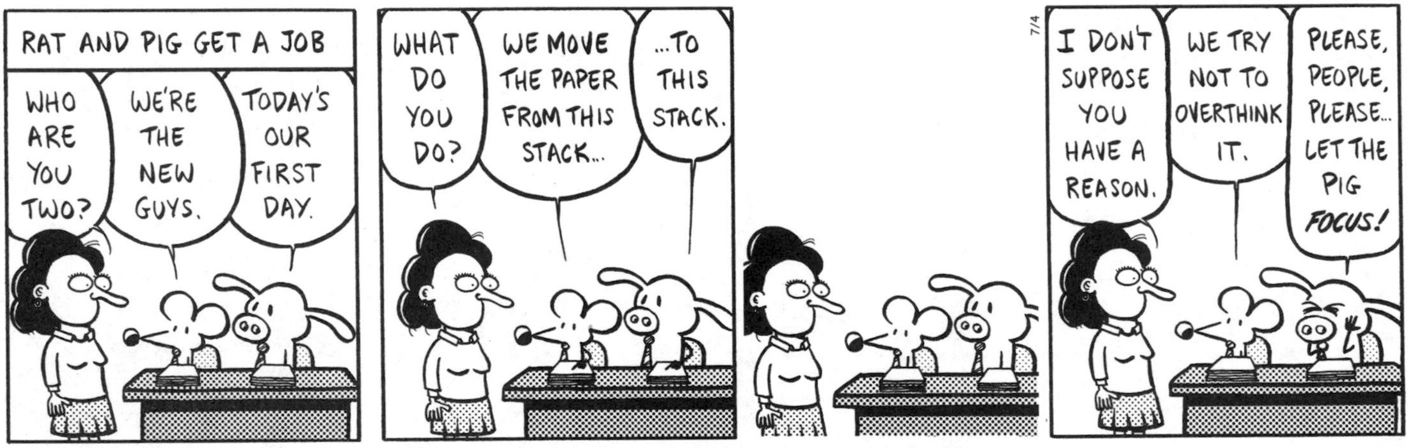
RAT AND PIG GET A JOB
WHO ARE YOU TWO?
WE'RE THE NEW GUYS.
TODAY'S OUR FIRST DAY.
WHAT DO YOU DO?
WE MOVE THE PAPER FROM THIS STACK...
...TO THIS STACK.
I DON'T SUPPOSE YOU HAVE A REASON.
WE TRY NOT TO OVERTHINK IT.
PLEASE, PEOPLE, PLEASE... LET THE PIG *FOCUS!*

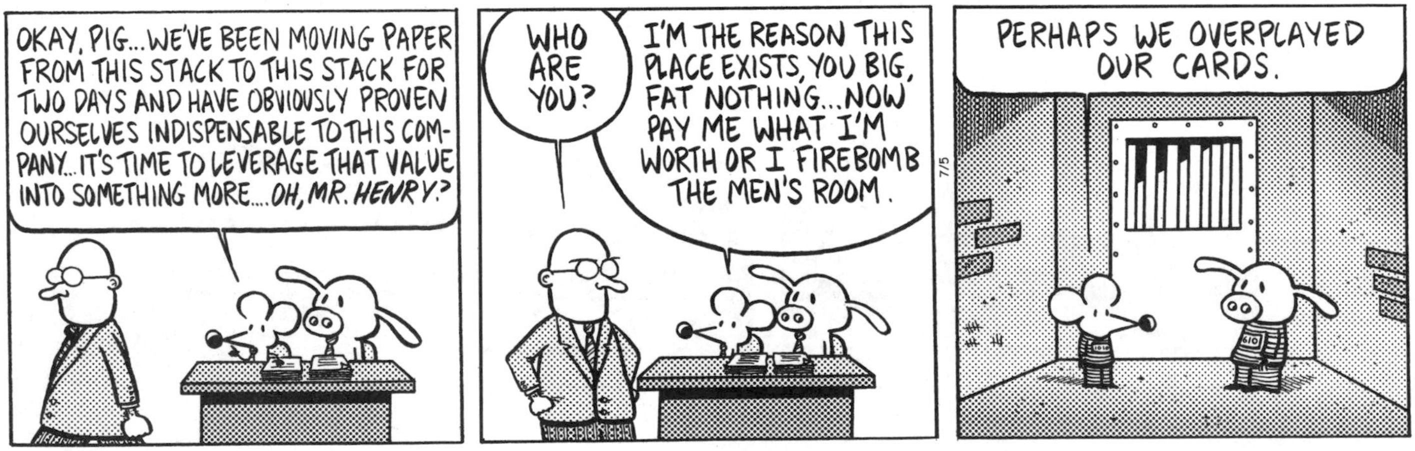
OKAY, PIG... WE'VE BEEN MOVING PAPER FROM THIS STACK TO THIS STACK FOR TWO DAYS AND HAVE OBVIOUSLY PROVEN OURSELVES INDISPENSABLE TO THIS COMPANY... IT'S TIME TO LEVERAGE THAT VALUE INTO SOMETHING MORE.... *OH, MR. HENRY?*
WHO ARE YOU?
I'M THE REASON THIS PLACE EXISTS, YOU BIG, FAT NOTHING... NOW PAY ME WHAT I'M WORTH OR I FIREBOMB THE MEN'S ROOM.
PERHAPS WE OVERPLAYED OUR CARDS.

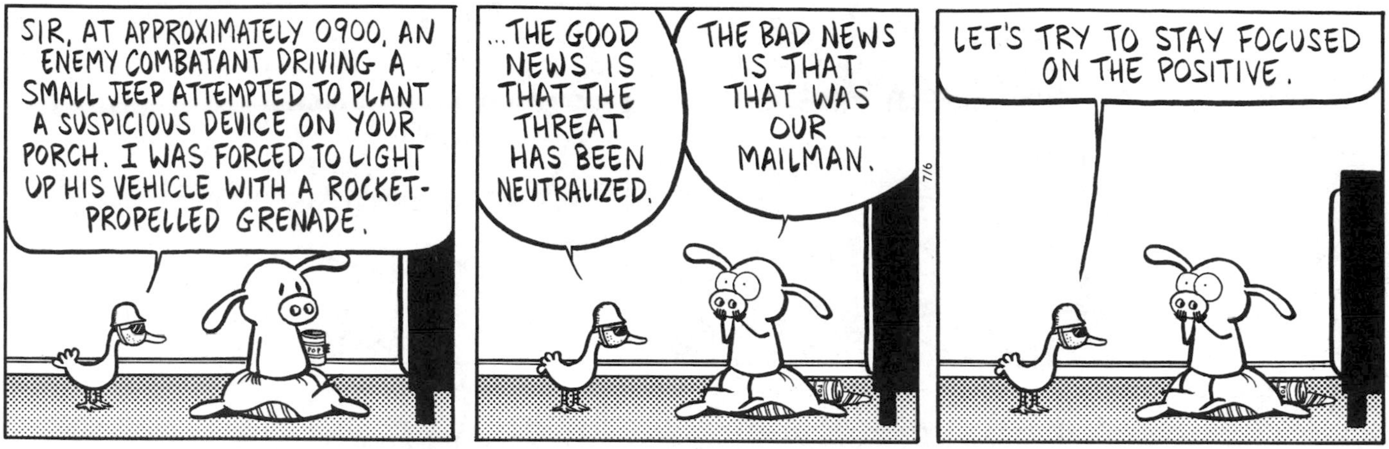
SIR, AT APPROXIMATELY 0900, AN ENEMY COMBATANT DRIVING A SMALL JEEP ATTEMPTED TO PLANT A SUSPICIOUS DEVICE ON YOUR PORCH. I WAS FORCED TO LIGHT UP HIS VEHICLE WITH A ROCKET-PROPELLED GRENADE.
POP
...THE GOOD NEWS IS THAT THE THREAT HAS BEEN NEUTRALIZED.
THE BAD NEWS IS THAT THAT WAS OUR MAILMAN.
7/6
LET'S TRY TO STAY FOCUSED ON THE POSITIVE.

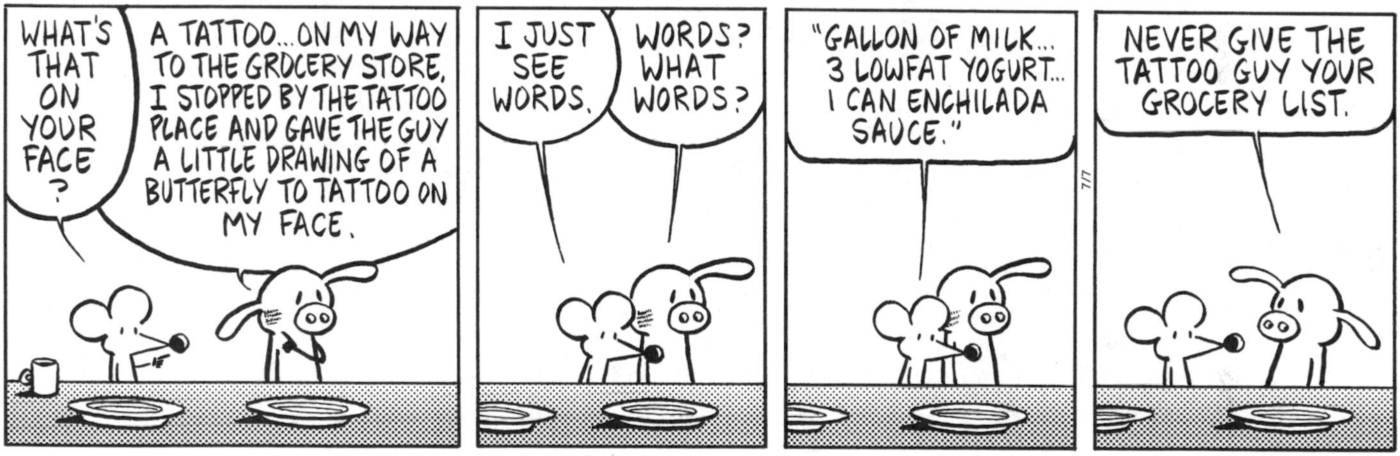
WHAT'S THAT ON YOUR FACE ?
A TATTOO...ON MY WAY TO THE GROCERY STORE, I STOPPED BY THE TATTOO PLACE AND GAVE THE GUY A LITTLE DRAWING OF A BUTTERFLY TO TATTOO ON MY FACE.
I JUST SEE WORDS.
WORDS? WHAT WORDS?
"GALLON OF MILK... 3 LOWFAT YOGURT... I CAN ENCHILADA SAUCE."
7/7
NEVER GIVE THE TATTOO GUY YOUR GROCERY LIST.

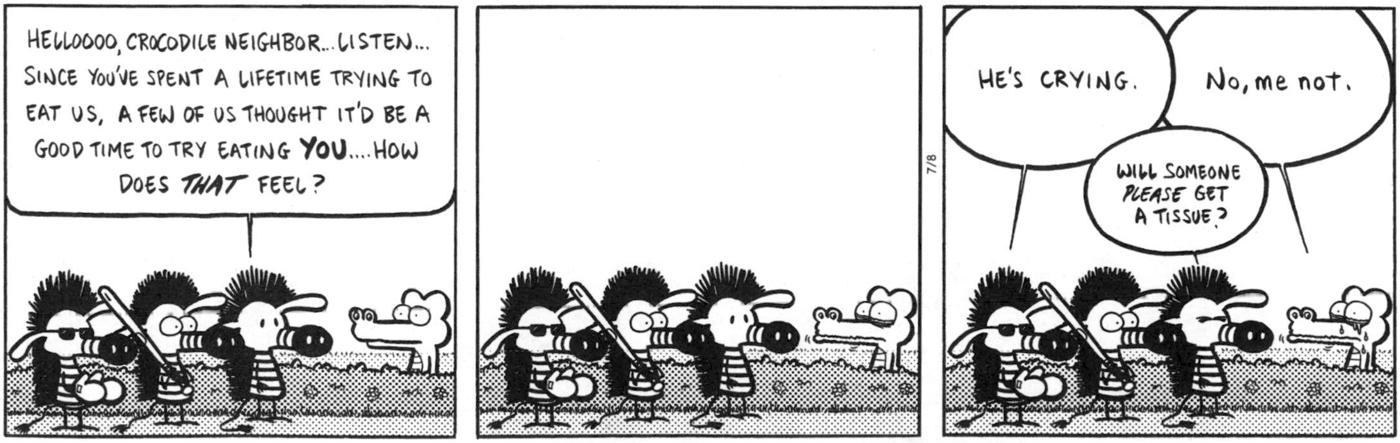
HELLOOOO, CROCODILE NEIGHBOR...LISTEN... SINCE YOU'VE SPENT A LIFETIME TRYING TO EAT US, A FEW OF US THOUGHT IT'D BE A GOOD TIME TO TRY EATING YOU....HOW DOES THAT FEEL?
7/8
HE'S CRYING.
No, me not.
WILL SOMEONE PLEASE GET A TISSUE?

SIR, GOOD EVENING, SIR...IF I COULD, SIR, I'D LIKE TO ADDRESS THE CURRENT R.O.E., SIR...

THE WHO?

THE RULES OF ENGAGEMENT, SIR... THE RULES GOVERNING WHEN I MAY FIRE MY WEAPON AT THE ENEMY, SIR.

OH. WHAT ARE THEY NOW?

WELL, SIR, TO QUOTE YOU, SIR, "YOU'RE A CRAZY LITTLE DUCK AND YOU MAY NEVER EVER EVER EVER FIRE YOUR WEAPON AT ANYTHING EVER."

OH, RIGHT. I REMEMBER.

WELL, IF I COULD, SIR, I'D LIKE TO PROPOSE A MINOR MODIFICATION.

OH...WHAT DO YOU WANT TO CHANGE IT TO?

"SHOOT LIKE THE DICKENS."

SIR, LOCKING ME IN THE CLOTHES HAMPER VIOLATES GENEVA, SIR.

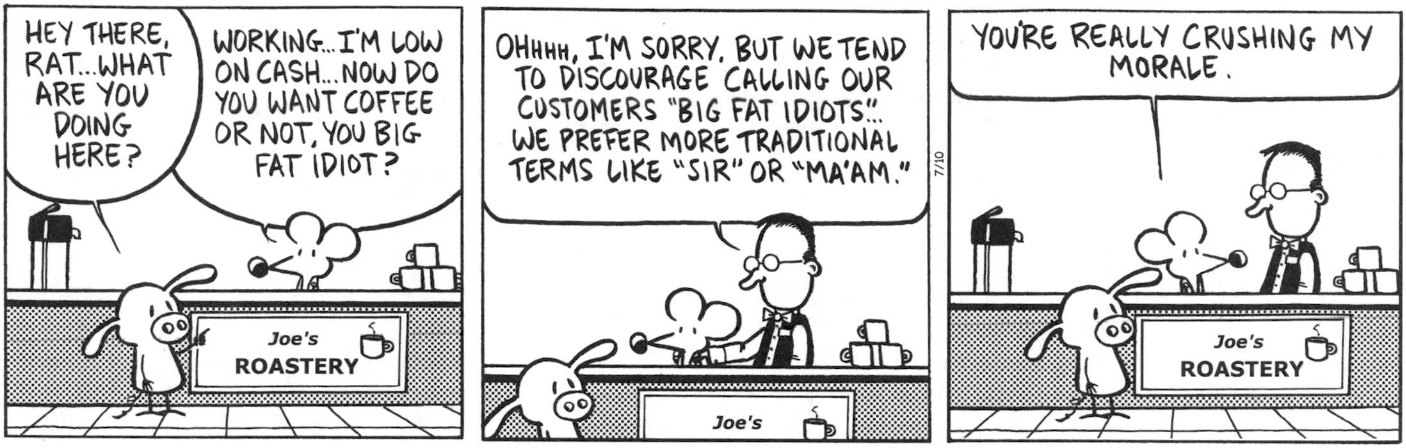
HEY THERE, RAT...WHAT ARE YOU DOING HERE?
WORKING...I'M LOW ON CASH...NOW DO YOU WANT COFFEE OR NOT, YOU BIG FAT IDIOT?
Joe's ROASTERY
OHHHH, I'M SORRY, BUT WE TEND TO DISCOURAGE CALLING OUR CUSTOMERS "BIG FAT IDIOTS"... WE PREFER MORE TRADITIONAL TERMS LIKE "SIR" OR "MA'AM."
7/10
YOU'RE REALLY CRUSHING MY MORALE.

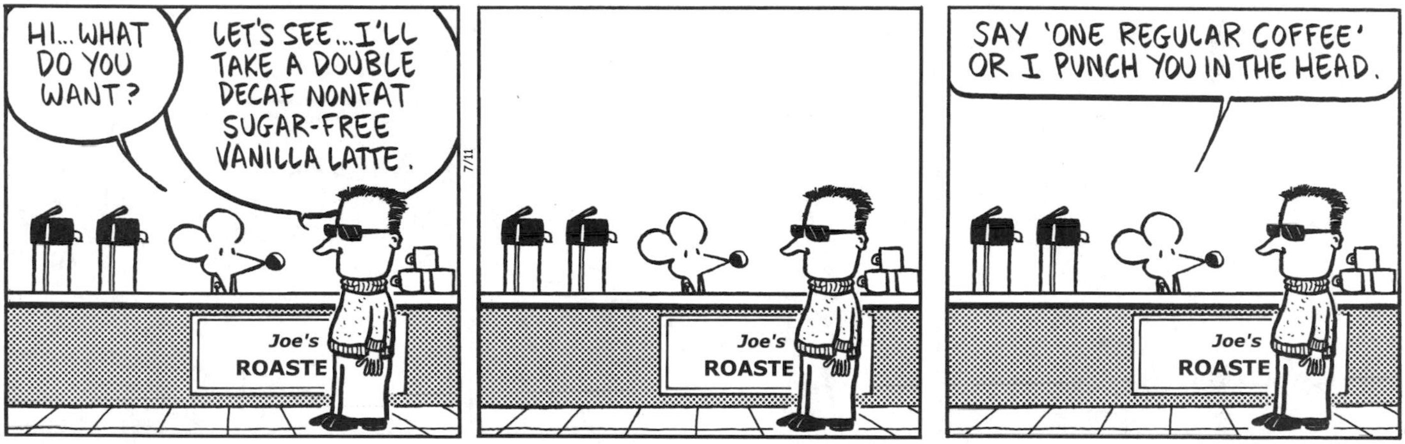
HI...WHAT DO YOU WANT?
LET'S SEE...I'LL TAKE A DOUBLE DECAF NONFAT SUGAR-FREE VANILLA LATTE.
7/11
SAY 'ONE REGULAR COFFEE' OR I PUNCH YOU IN THE HEAD.

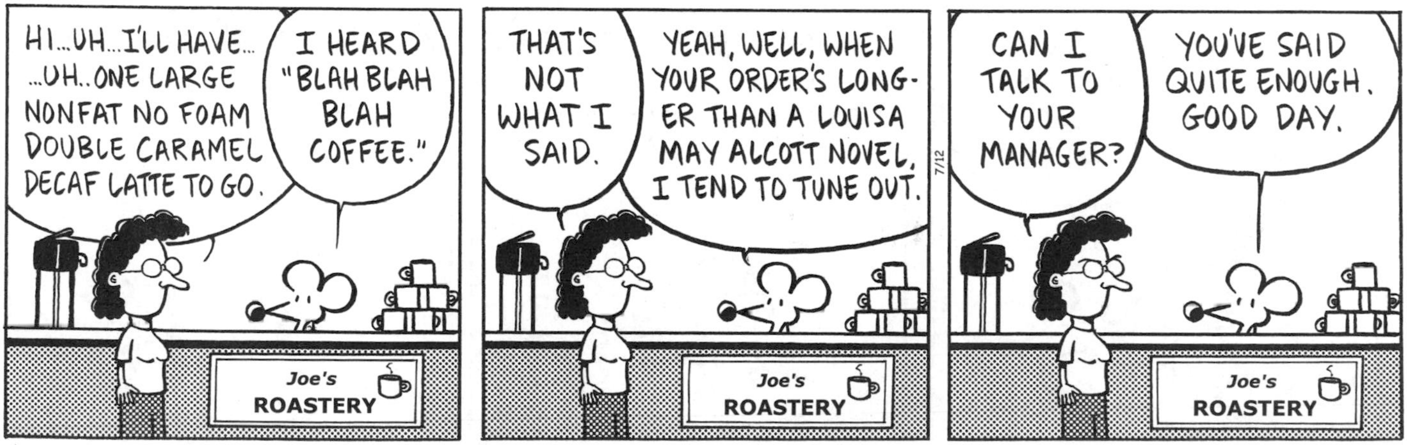
HI...UH...I'LL HAVE... ...UH..ONE LARGE NONFAT NO FOAM DOUBLE CARAMEL DECAF LATTE TO GO.
I HEARD "BLAH BLAH BLAH COFFEE."
THAT'S NOT WHAT I SAID.
YEAH, WELL, WHEN YOUR ORDER'S LONG-ER THAN A LOUISA MAY ALCOTT NOVEL, I TEND TO TUNE OUT.
7/12
CAN I TALK TO YOUR MANAGER?
YOU'VE SAID QUITE ENOUGH. GOOD DAY.

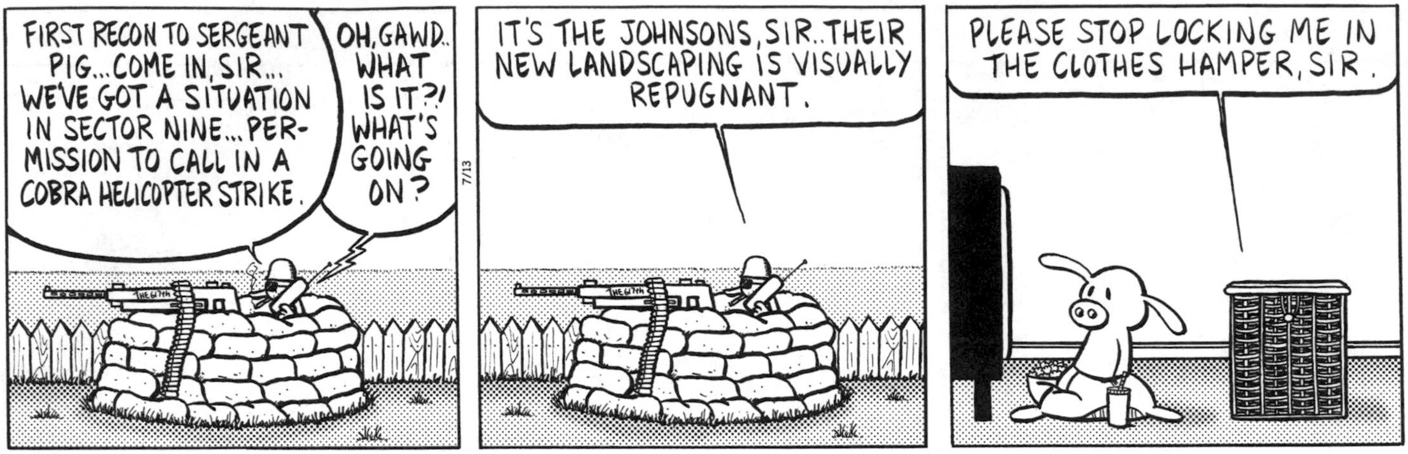
FIRST RECON TO SERGEANT PIG... COME IN, SIR... WE'VE GOT A SITUATION IN SECTOR NINE... PER-MISSION TO CALL IN A COBRA HELICOPTER STRIKE.
OH, GAWD.. WHAT IS IT?! WHAT'S GOING ON?
7/13
IT'S THE JOHNSONS, SIR.. THEIR NEW LANDSCAPING IS VISUALLY REPUGNANT.
PLEASE STOP LOCKING ME IN THE CLOTHES HAMPER, SIR.

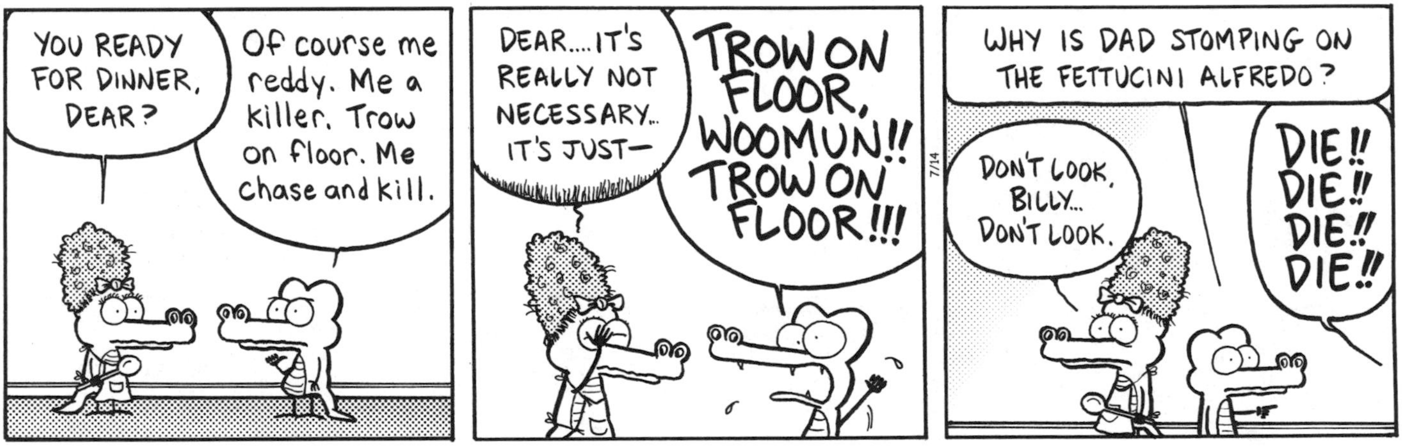
YOU READY FOR DINNER, DEAR?
Of course me reddy. Me a killer. Trow on floor. Me chase and kill.
7/14
DEAR.... IT'S REALLY NOT NECESSARY.. IT'S JUST—
TROW ON FLOOR, WOOMUN!! TROW ON FLOOR!!!
WHY IS DAD STOMPING ON THE FETTUCINI ALFREDO?
DON'T LOOK, BILLY... DON'T LOOK.
DIE!! DIE!! DIE!! DIE!!

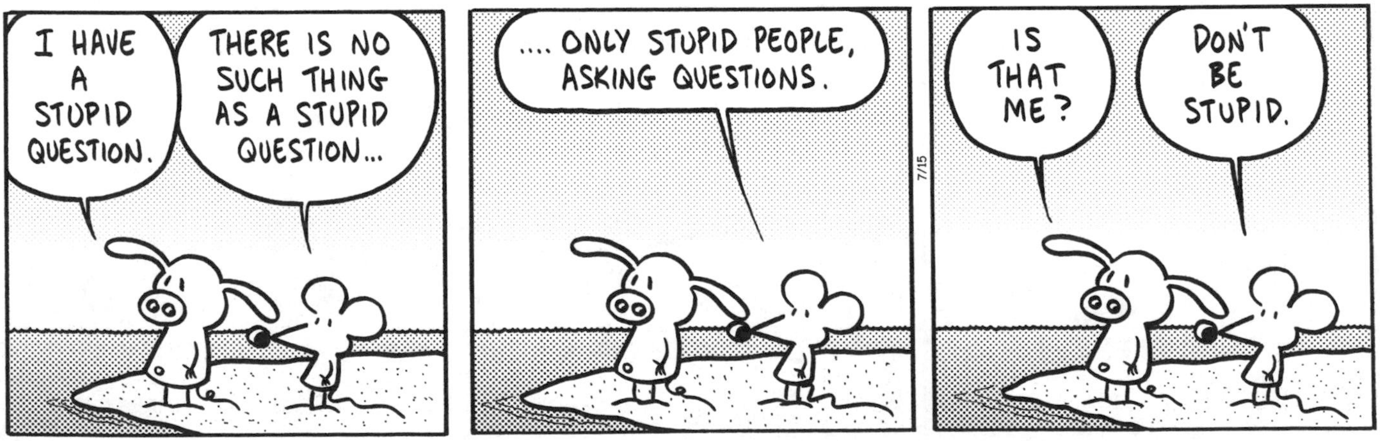
I HAVE A STUPID QUESTION.
THERE IS NO SUCH THING AS A STUPID QUESTION...
7/15
.... ONLY STUPID PEOPLE, ASKING QUESTIONS.
IS THAT ME?
DON'T BE STUPID.

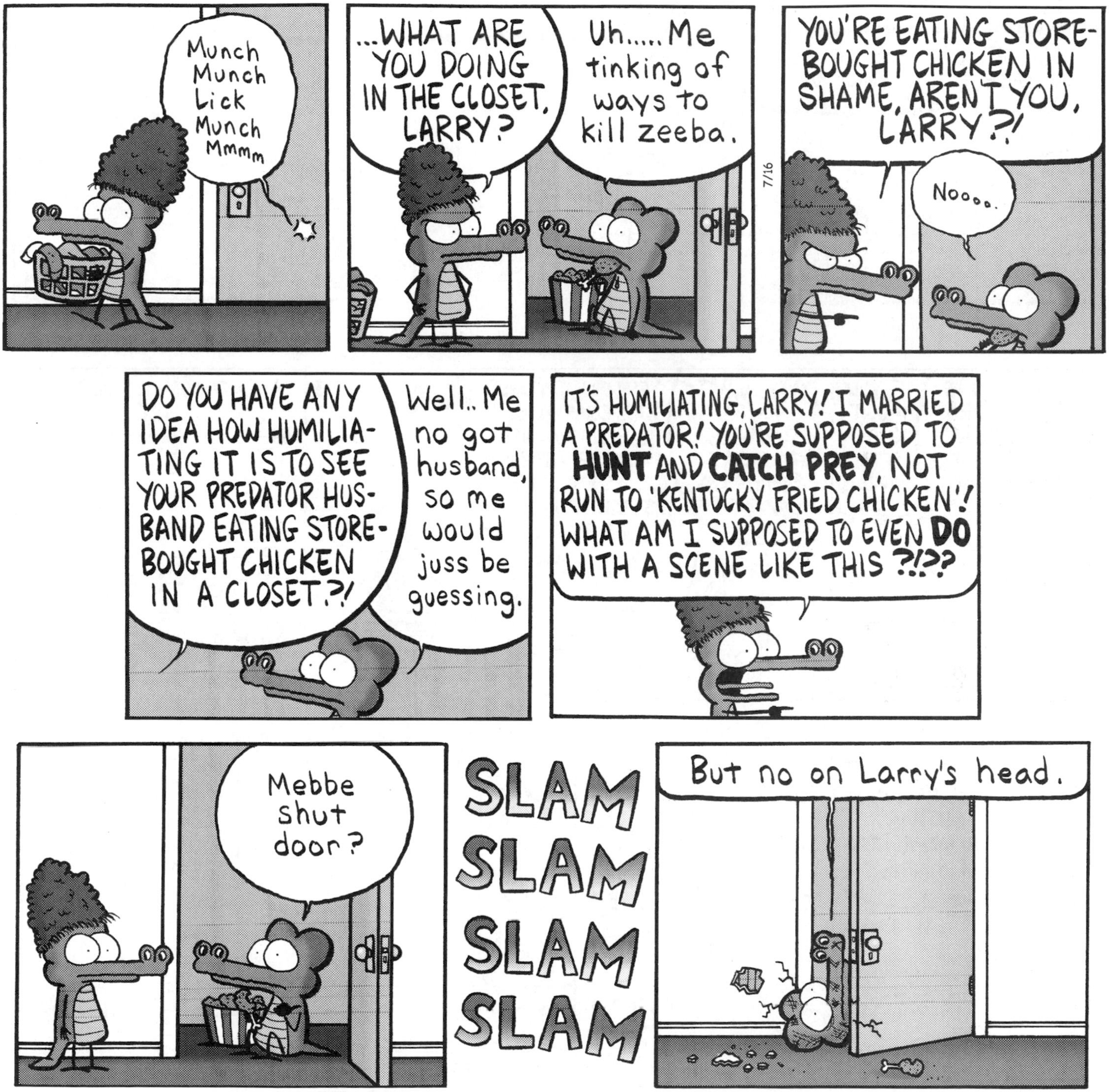
Munch Munch Lick Munch Mmmm
...WHAT ARE YOU DOING IN THE CLOSET, LARRY?
Uh..... Me tinking of ways to kill zeeba.
7/16
YOU'RE EATING STORE-BOUGHT CHICKEN IN SHAME, AREN'T YOU, LARRY?!
Noooo.
DO YOU HAVE ANY IDEA HOW HUMILIATING IT IS TO SEE YOUR PREDATOR HUSBAND EATING STORE-BOUGHT CHICKEN IN A CLOSET?!
Well.. Me no got husband, so me would juss be guessing.
IT'S HUMILIATING, LARRY! I MARRIED A PREDATOR! YOU'RE SUPPOSED TO HUNT AND CATCH PREY, NOT RUN TO 'KENTUCKY FRIED CHICKEN'! WHAT AM I SUPPOSED TO EVEN DO WITH A SCENE LIKE THIS?!?
Mebbe shut door?
SLAM
SLAM
SLAM
SLAM
But no on Larry's head.

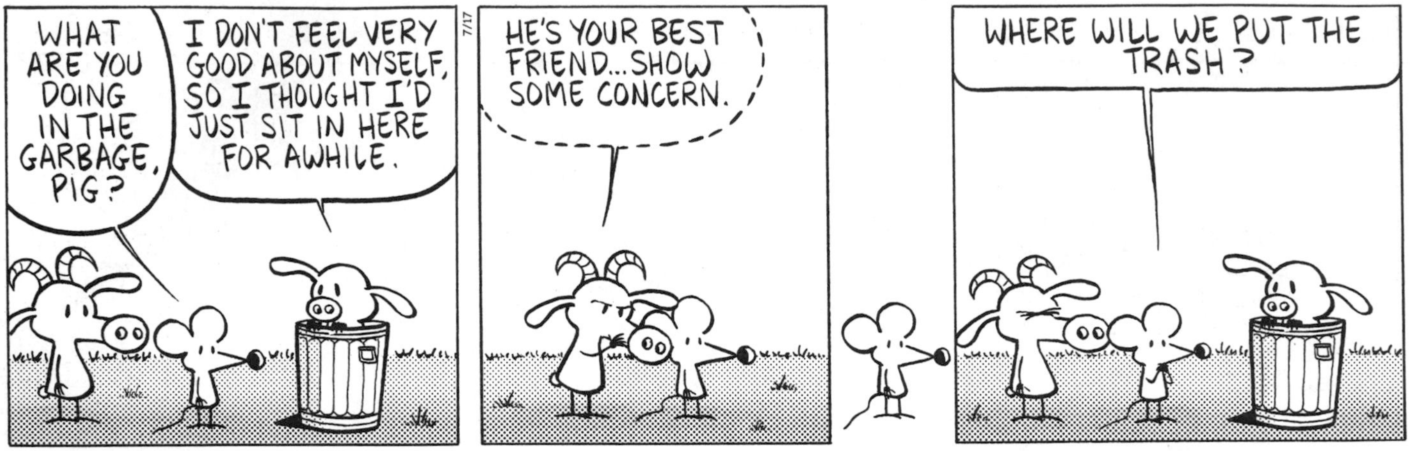
7/17
WHAT ARE YOU DOING IN THE GARBAGE, PIG?
I DON'T FEEL VERY GOOD ABOUT MYSELF, SO I THOUGHT I'D JUST SIT IN HERE FOR AWHILE.
HE'S YOUR BEST FRIEND...SHOW SOME CONCERN.
WHERE WILL WE PUT THE TRASH?

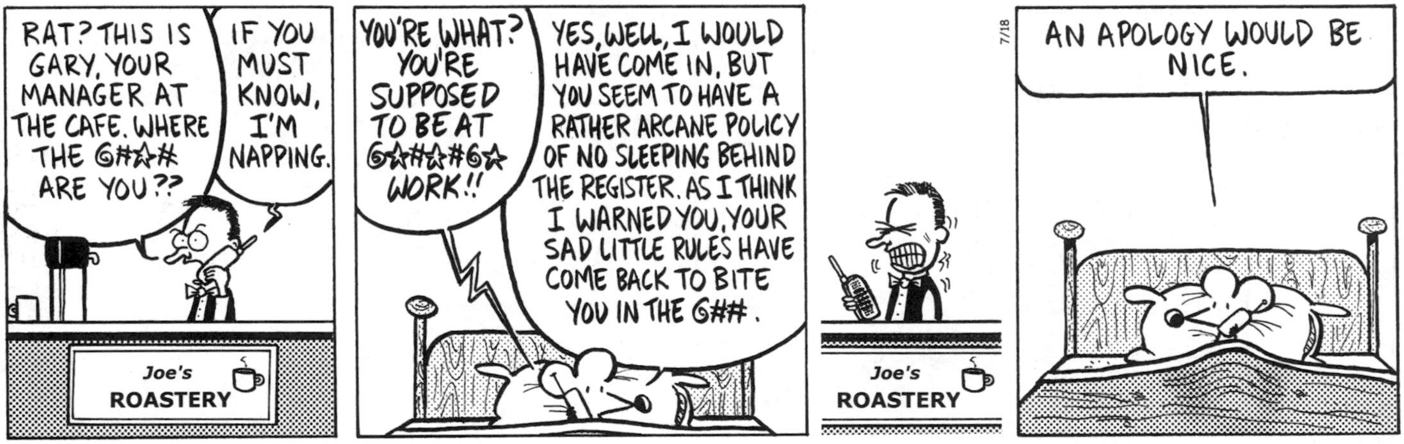
7/18
RAT? THIS IS GARY, YOUR MANAGER AT THE CAFE. WHERE THE @#☆# ARE YOU??
IF YOU MUST KNOW, I'M NAPPING.
Joe's ROASTERY
YOU'RE WHAT? YOU'RE SUPPOSED TO BE AT @☆#☆#@☆ WORK!!
YES, WELL, I WOULD HAVE COME IN, BUT YOU SEEM TO HAVE A RATHER ARCANE POLICY OF NO SLEEPING BEHIND THE REGISTER. AS I THINK I WARNED YOU, YOUR SAD LITTLE RULES HAVE COME BACK TO BITE YOU IN THE @##.
Joe's ROASTERY
AN APOLOGY WOULD BE NICE.

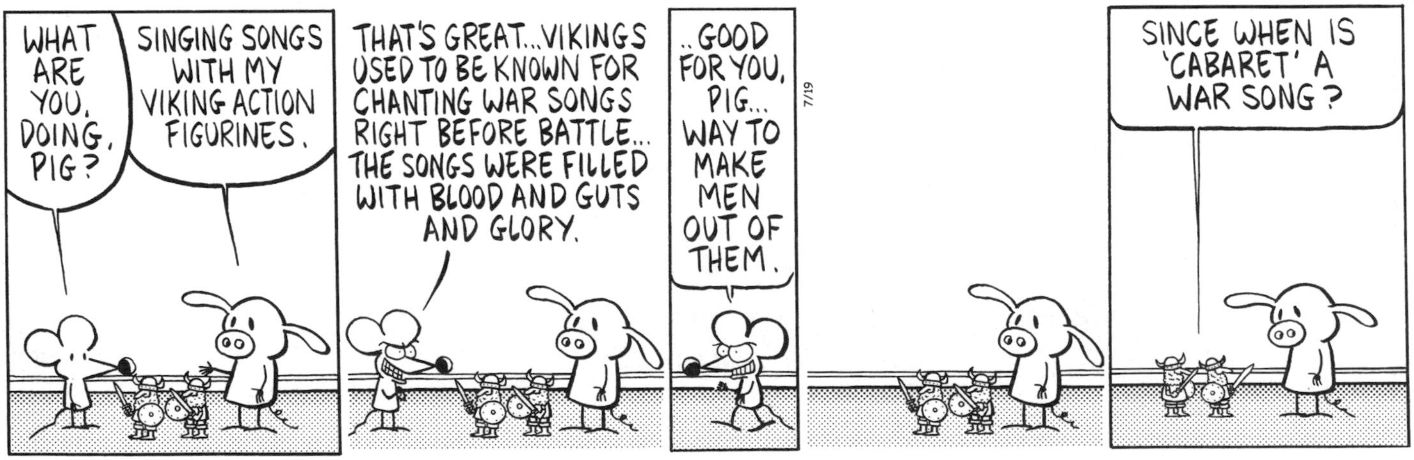
7/19
WHAT ARE YOU, DOING, PIG?
SINGING SONGS WITH MY VIKING ACTION FIGURINES.
THAT'S GREAT...VIKINGS USED TO BE KNOWN FOR CHANTING WAR SONGS RIGHT BEFORE BATTLE... THE SONGS WERE FILLED WITH BLOOD AND GUTS AND GLORY.
..GOOD FOR YOU, PIG... WAY TO MAKE MEN OUT OF THEM.
SINCE WHEN IS 'CABARET' A WAR SONG?

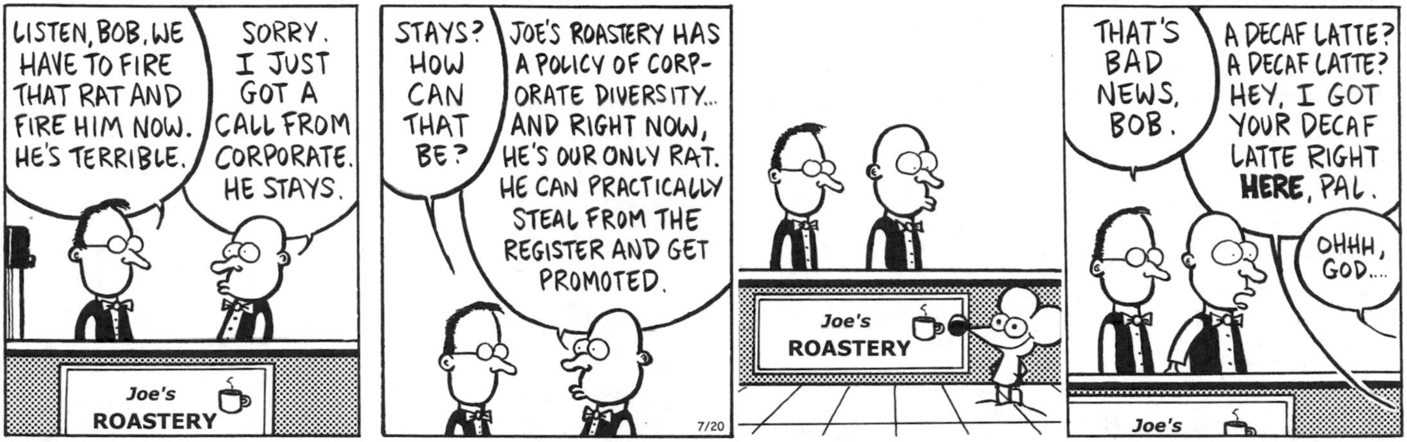
LISTEN, BOB, WE HAVE TO FIRE THAT RAT AND FIRE HIM NOW. HE'S TERRIBLE.
SORRY. I JUST GOT A CALL FROM CORPORATE. HE STAYS.
Joe's ROASTERY
STAYS? HOW CAN THAT BE?
JOE'S ROASTERY HAS A POLICY OF CORPORATE DIVERSITY... AND RIGHT NOW, HE'S OUR ONLY RAT. HE CAN PRACTICALLY STEAL FROM THE REGISTER AND GET PROMOTED.
7/20
Joe's ROASTERY
THAT'S BAD NEWS, BOB.
A DECAF LATTE? A DECAF LATTE? HEY, I GOT YOUR DECAF LATTE RIGHT **HERE**, PAL.
OHHH, GOD....
Joe's

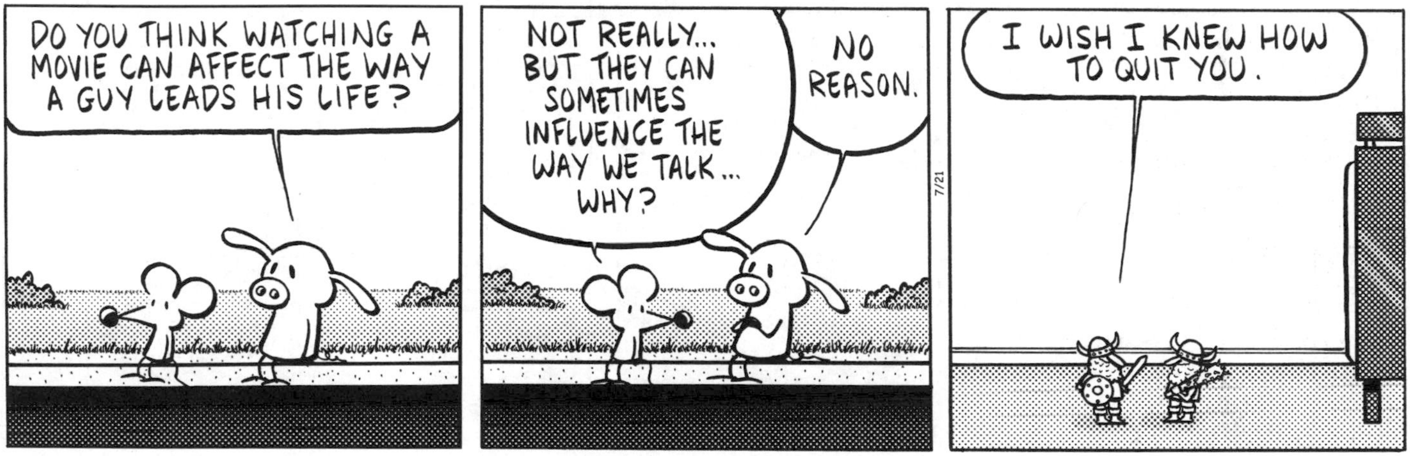
DO YOU THINK WATCHING A MOVIE CAN AFFECT THE WAY A GUY LEADS HIS LIFE?
NOT REALLY... BUT THEY CAN SOMETIMES INFLUENCE THE WAY WE TALK... WHY?
NO REASON.
7/21
I WISH I KNEW HOW TO QUIT YOU.

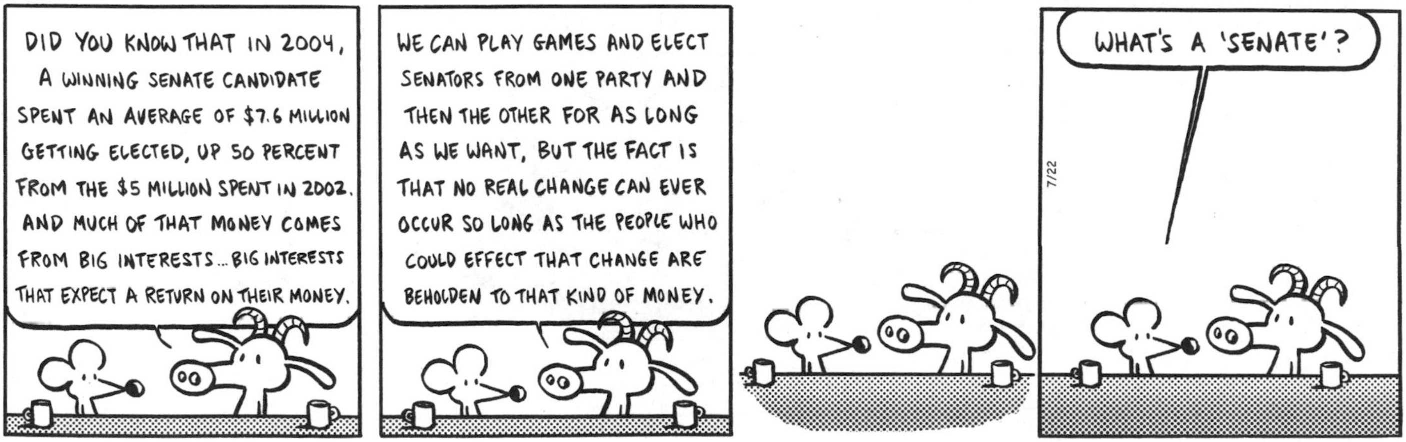
DID YOU KNOW THAT IN 2004, A WINNING SENATE CANDIDATE SPENT AN AVERAGE OF $7.6 MILLION GETTING ELECTED, UP 50 PERCENT FROM THE $5 MILLION SPENT IN 2002. AND MUCH OF THAT MONEY COMES FROM BIG INTERESTS... BIG INTERESTS THAT EXPECT A RETURN ON THEIR MONEY.
WE CAN PLAY GAMES AND ELECT SENATORS FROM ONE PARTY AND THEN THE OTHER FOR AS LONG AS WE WANT, BUT THE FACT IS THAT NO REAL CHANGE CAN EVER OCCUR SO LONG AS THE PEOPLE WHO COULD EFFECT THAT CHANGE ARE BEHOLDEN TO THAT KIND OF MONEY.
7/22
WHAT'S A 'SENATE'?

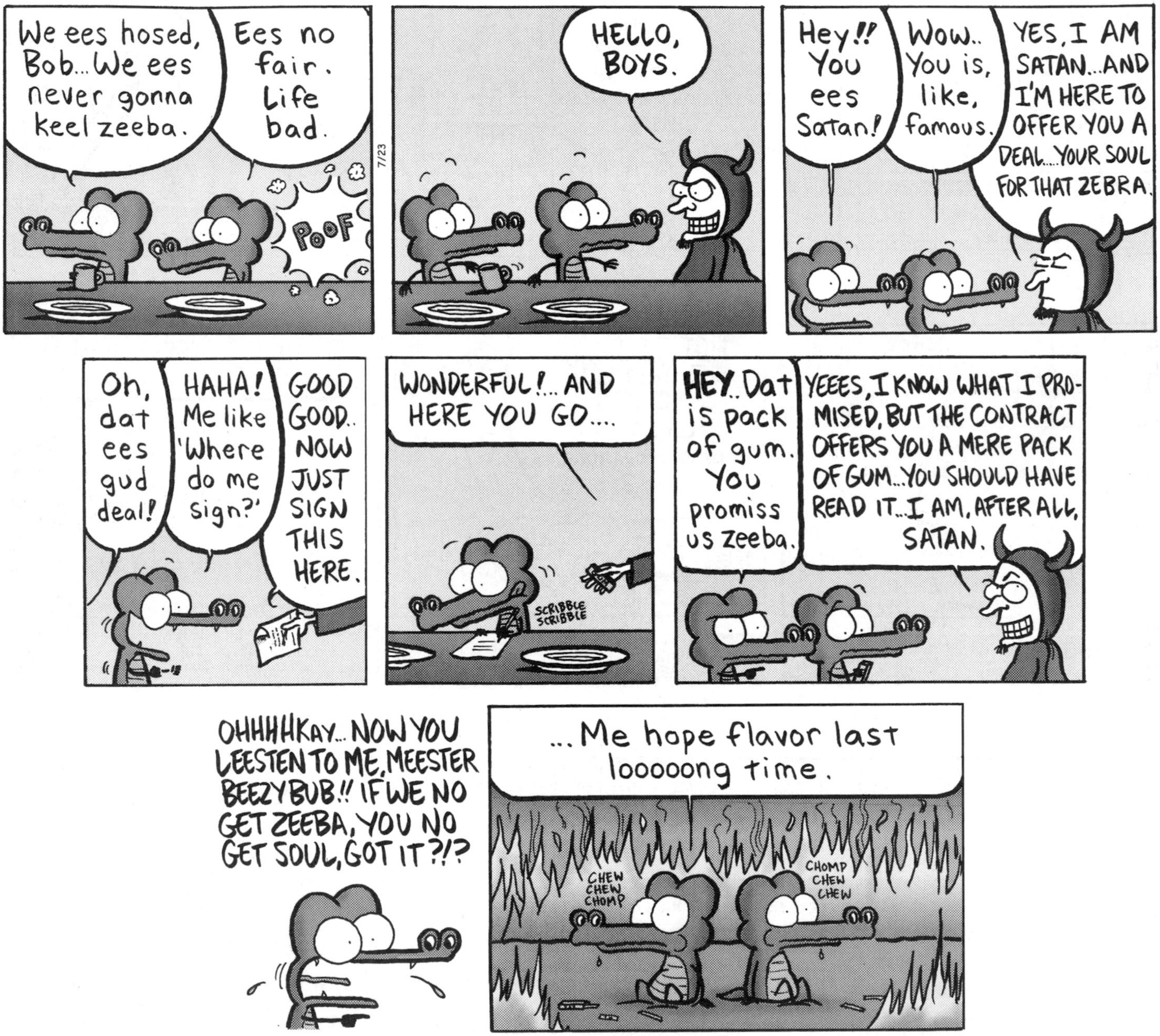
We ees hosed, Bob... We ees never gonna keel zeeba.
Ees no fair. Life bad.
POOF
7/23
HELLO, BOYS.
Hey!! You ees Satan!
Wow.. You is, like, famous.
YES, I AM SATAN... AND I'M HERE TO OFFER YOU A DEAL.... YOUR SOUL FOR THAT ZEBRA.
Oh, dat ees gud deal!
HAHA! Me like 'Where do me sign?'
GOOD GOOD.. NOW JUST SIGN THIS HERE.
WONDERFUL!... AND HERE YOU GO....
SCRIBBLE SCRIBBLE
HEY.. Dat is pack of gum. You promiss us zeeba.
YEEES, I KNOW WHAT I PROMISED, BUT THE CONTRACT OFFERS YOU A MERE PACK OF GUM... YOU SHOULD HAVE READ IT... I AM, AFTER ALL, SATAN.
OHHHHKAY... NOW YOU LEESTEN TO ME, MEESTER BEEZYBUB!! IF WE NO GET ZEEBA, YOU NO GET SOUL, GOT IT?!?
...Me hope flavor last loooooong time.
CHEW CHEW CHOMP
CHOMP CHEW CHEW

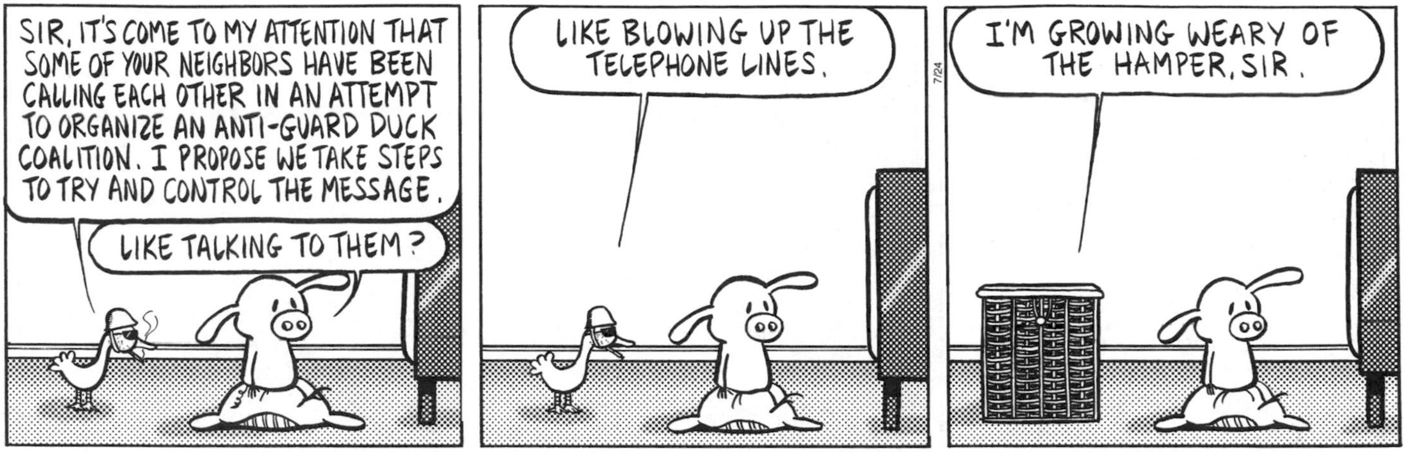
SIR, IT'S COME TO MY ATTENTION THAT SOME OF YOUR NEIGHBORS HAVE BEEN CALLING EACH OTHER IN AN ATTEMPT TO ORGANIZE AN ANTI-GUARD DUCK COALITION. I PROPOSE WE TAKE STEPS TO TRY AND CONTROL THE MESSAGE.
LIKE TALKING TO THEM?
LIKE BLOWING UP THE TELEPHONE LINES.
7/24
I'M GROWING WEARY OF THE HAMPER, SIR.

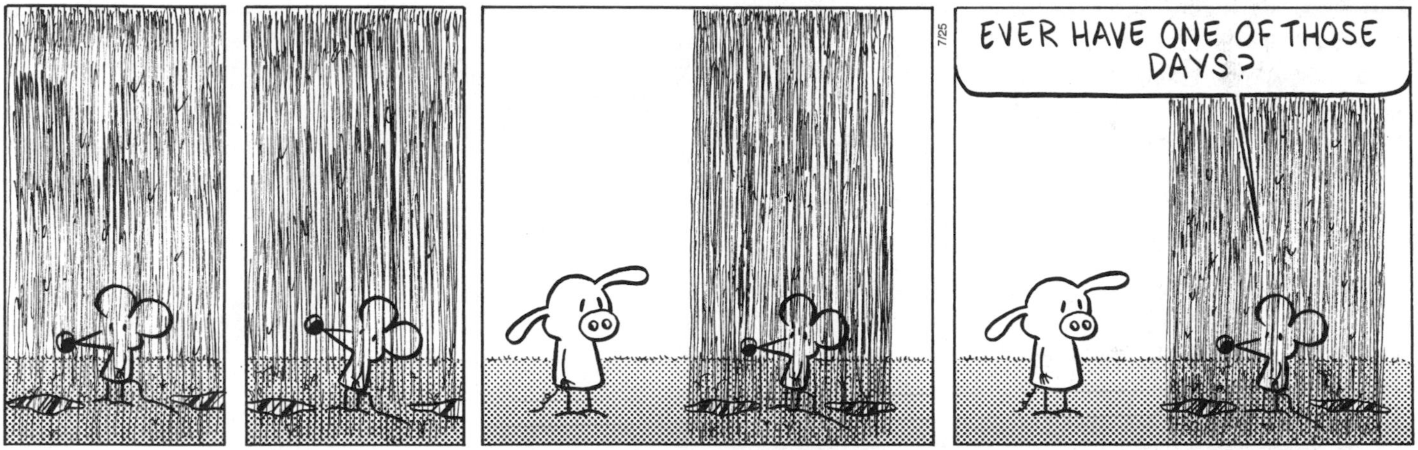
7/25
EVER HAVE ONE OF THOSE DAYS?

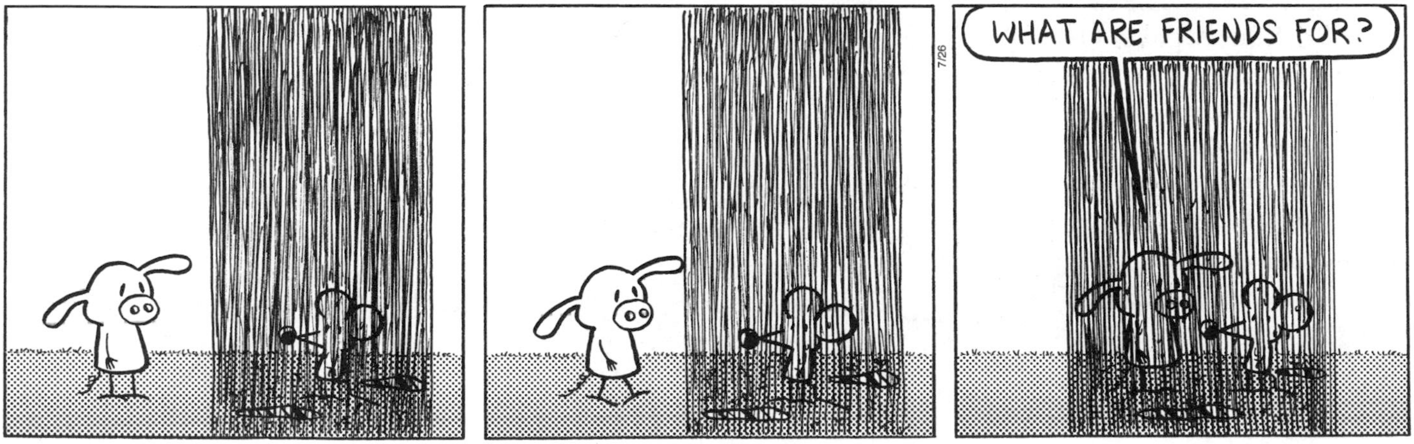
7/26
WHAT ARE FRIENDS FOR?

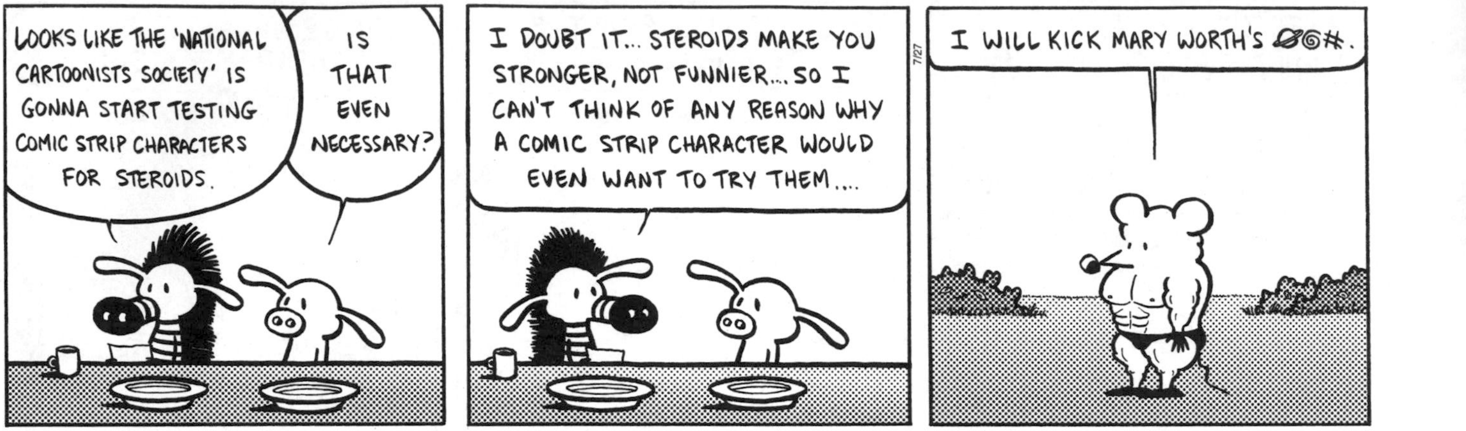
LOOKS LIKE THE 'NATIONAL CARTOONISTS SOCIETY' IS GONNA START TESTING COMIC STRIP CHARACTERS FOR STEROIDS.
IS THAT EVEN NECESSARY?
I DOUBT IT... STEROIDS MAKE YOU STRONGER, NOT FUNNIER... SO I CAN'T THINK OF ANY REASON WHY A COMIC STRIP CHARACTER WOULD EVEN WANT TO TRY THEM....
7/27
I WILL KICK MARY WORTH'S @@#.

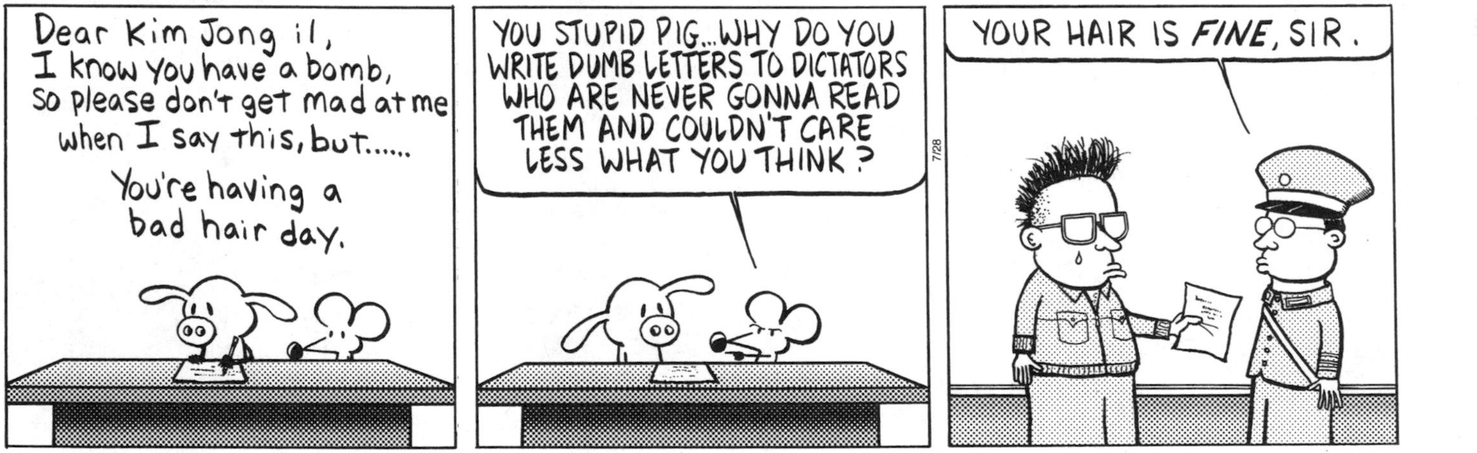
Dear Kim Jong il,
I know you have a bomb, so please don't get mad at me when I say this, but......
You're having a bad hair day.
YOU STUPID PIG... WHY DO YOU WRITE DUMB LETTERS TO DICTATORS WHO ARE NEVER GONNA READ THEM AND COULDN'T CARE LESS WHAT YOU THINK?
7/28
YOUR HAIR IS *FINE*, SIR.

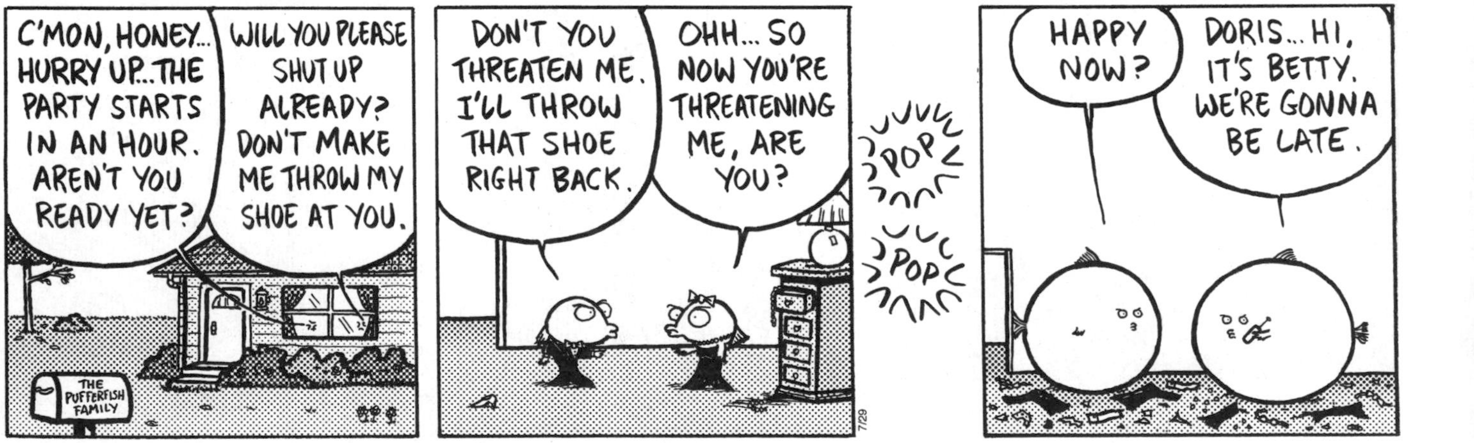
C'MON, HONEY... HURRY UP... THE PARTY STARTS IN AN HOUR. AREN'T YOU READY YET?
WILL YOU PLEASE SHUT UP ALREADY? DON'T MAKE ME THROW MY SHOE AT YOU.
THE PUFFERFISH FAMILY
DON'T YOU THREATEN ME. I'LL THROW THAT SHOE RIGHT BACK.
OHH... SO NOW YOU'RE THREATENING ME, ARE YOU?
7/29
POP
POP
HAPPY NOW?
DORIS... HI, IT'S BETTY. WE'RE GONNA BE LATE.

Rat's Travel Guide to the World's Great Cities

Chapter 1: Baghdad

Plusses:

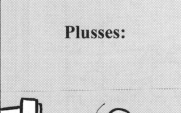

Warm. Cheap.

Not too touristy.

Minuses:

People with beards try to kill you.

7/30

This can ruin an otherwise wonderful vacation.

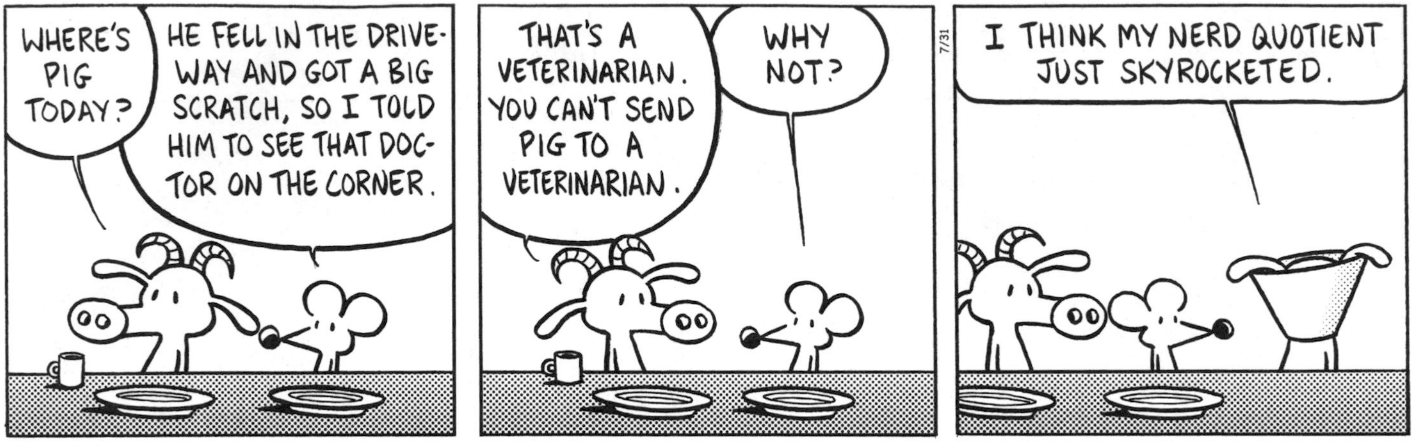
WHERE'S PIG TODAY?
HE FELL IN THE DRIVEWAY AND GOT A BIG SCRATCH, SO I TOLD HIM TO SEE THAT DOCTOR ON THE CORNER.
THAT'S A VETERINARIAN. YOU CAN'T SEND PIG TO A VETERINARIAN.
WHY NOT?
7/31
I THINK MY NERD QUOTIENT JUST SKYROCKETED.

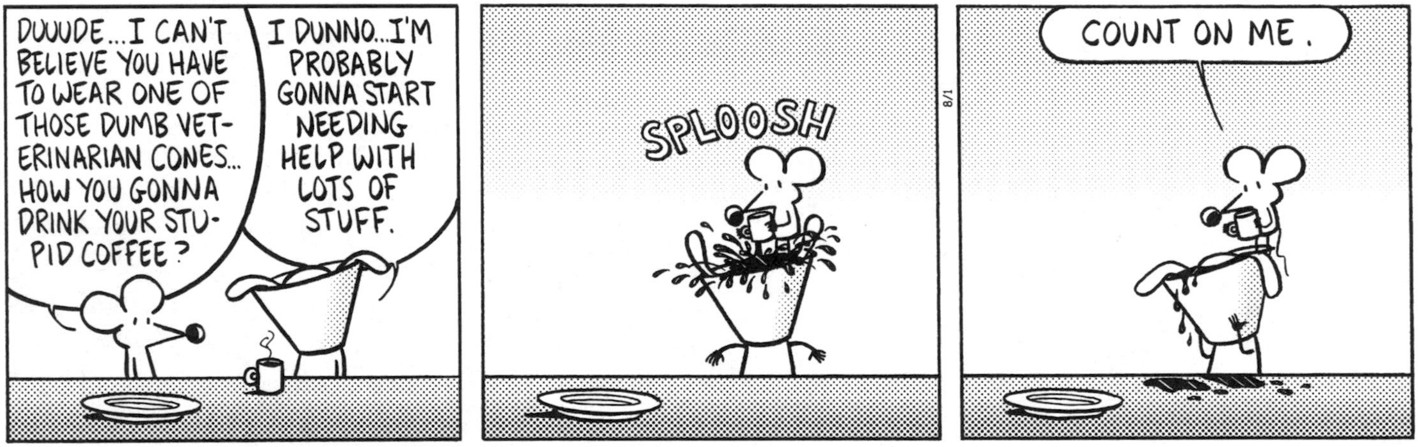
DUUUDE...I CAN'T BELIEVE YOU HAVE TO WEAR ONE OF THOSE DUMB VETERINARIAN CONES... HOW YOU GONNA DRINK YOUR STUPID COFFEE?
I DUNNO...I'M PROBABLY GONNA START NEEDING HELP WITH LOTS OF STUFF.
SPLOOSH
8/1
COUNT ON ME.

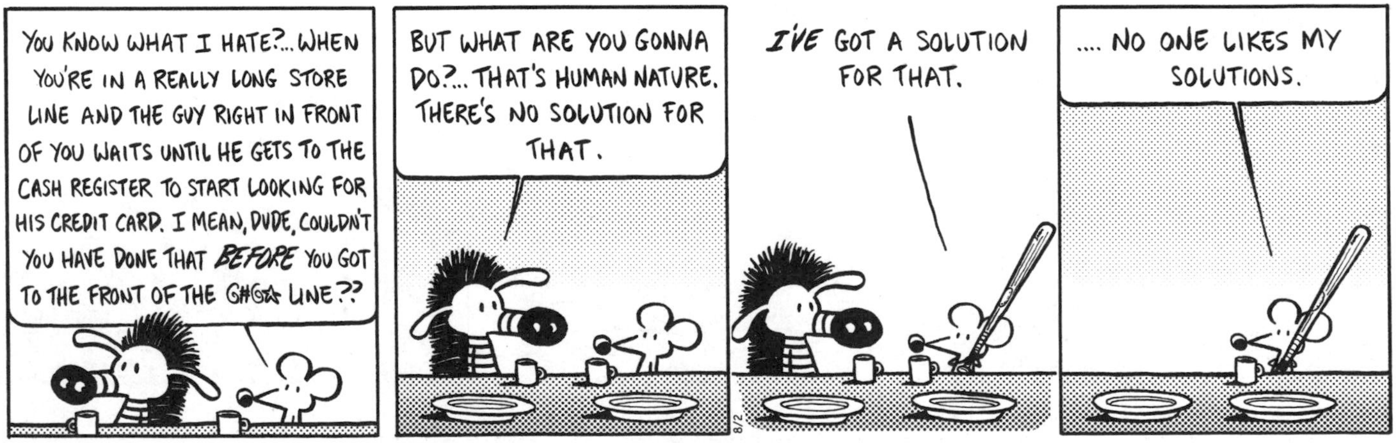
YOU KNOW WHAT I HATE?...WHEN YOU'RE IN A REALLY LONG STORE LINE AND THE GUY RIGHT IN FRONT OF YOU WAITS UNTIL HE GETS TO THE CASH REGISTER TO START LOOKING FOR HIS CREDIT CARD. I MEAN, DUDE, COULDN'T YOU HAVE DONE THAT BEFORE YOU GOT TO THE FRONT OF THE G#@☆ LINE??
BUT WHAT ARE YOU GONNA DO?... THAT'S HUMAN NATURE. THERE'S NO SOLUTION FOR THAT.
I'VE GOT A SOLUTION FOR THAT.
8/2
.... NO ONE LIKES MY SOLUTIONS.

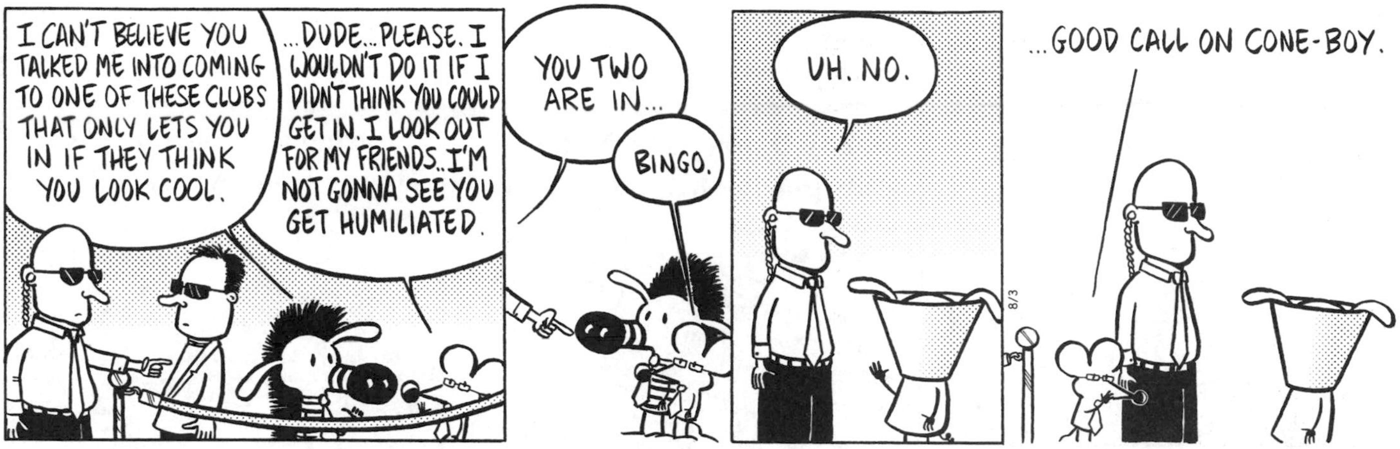
I CAN'T BELIEVE YOU TALKED ME INTO COMING TO ONE OF THESE CLUBS THAT ONLY LETS YOU IN IF THEY THINK YOU LOOK COOL.
...DUDE...PLEASE. I WOULDN'T DO IT IF I DIDN'T THINK YOU COULD GET IN. I LOOK OUT FOR MY FRIENDS..I'M NOT GONNA SEE YOU GET HUMILIATED.
YOU TWO ARE IN...
BINGO.
8/3
UH. NO.
...GOOD CALL ON CONE-BOY.

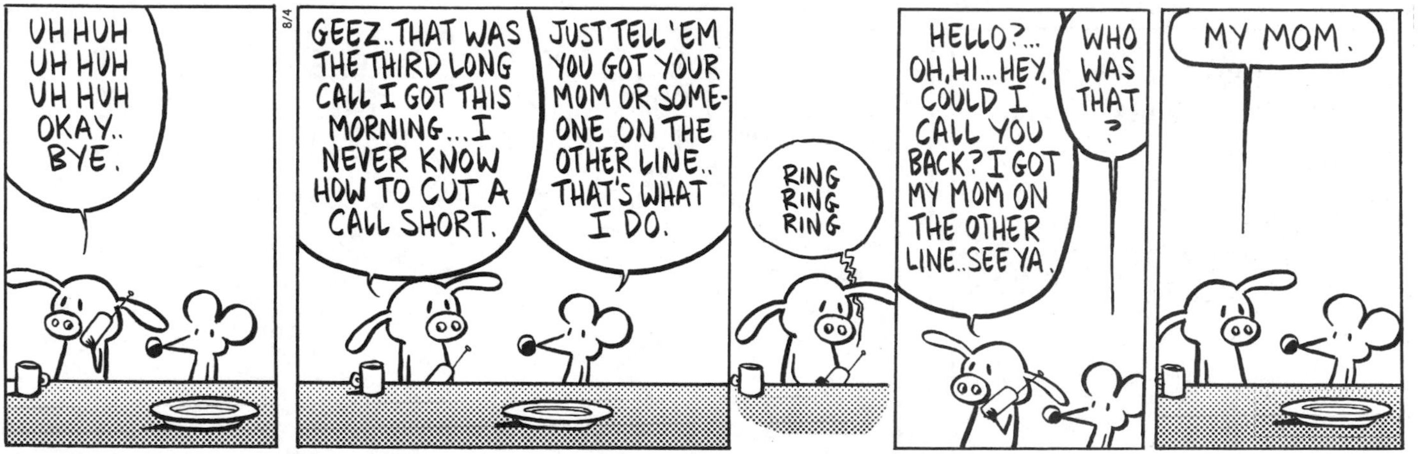
UH HUH UH HUH UH HUH OKAY.. BYE.
8/4
GEEZ..THAT WAS THE THIRD LONG CALL I GOT THIS MORNING...I NEVER KNOW HOW TO CUT A CALL SHORT.
JUST TELL 'EM YOU GOT YOUR MOM OR SOME-ONE ON THE OTHER LINE.. THAT'S WHAT I DO.
RING RING RING
HELLO?... OH,HI...HEY, COULD I CALL YOU BACK? I GOT MY MOM ON THE OTHER LINE..SEE YA.
WHO WAS THAT ?
MY MOM.

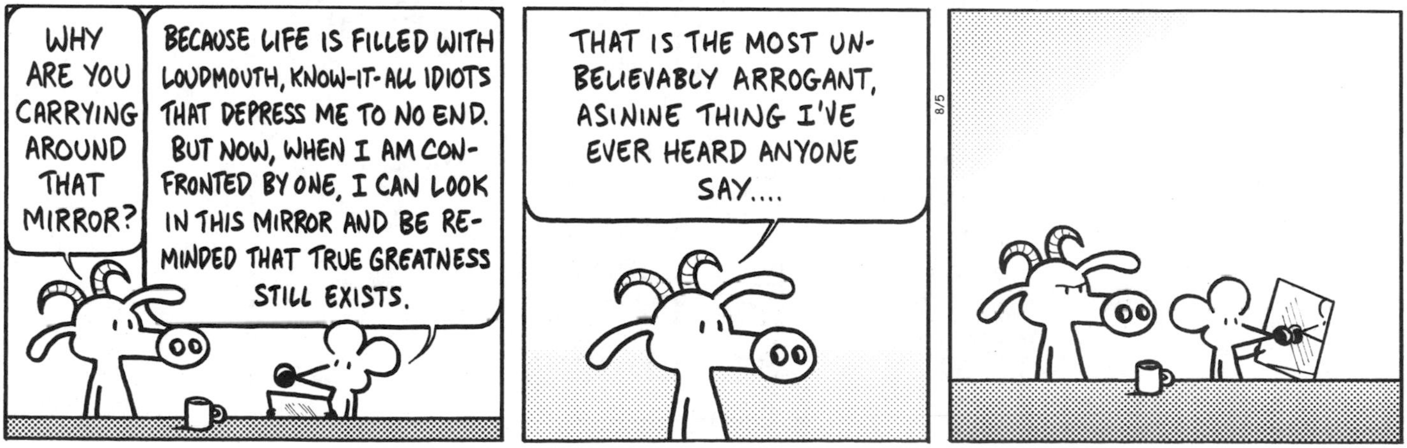
WHY ARE YOU CARRYING AROUND THAT MIRROR?
BECAUSE LIFE IS FILLED WITH LOUDMOUTH, KNOW-IT-ALL IDIOTS THAT DEPRESS ME TO NO END. BUT NOW, WHEN I AM CON-FRONTED BY ONE, I CAN LOOK IN THIS MIRROR AND BE RE-MINDED THAT TRUE GREATNESS STILL EXISTS.
8/5
THAT IS THE MOST UN-BELIEVABLY ARROGANT, ASININE THING I'VE EVER HEARD ANYONE SAY....

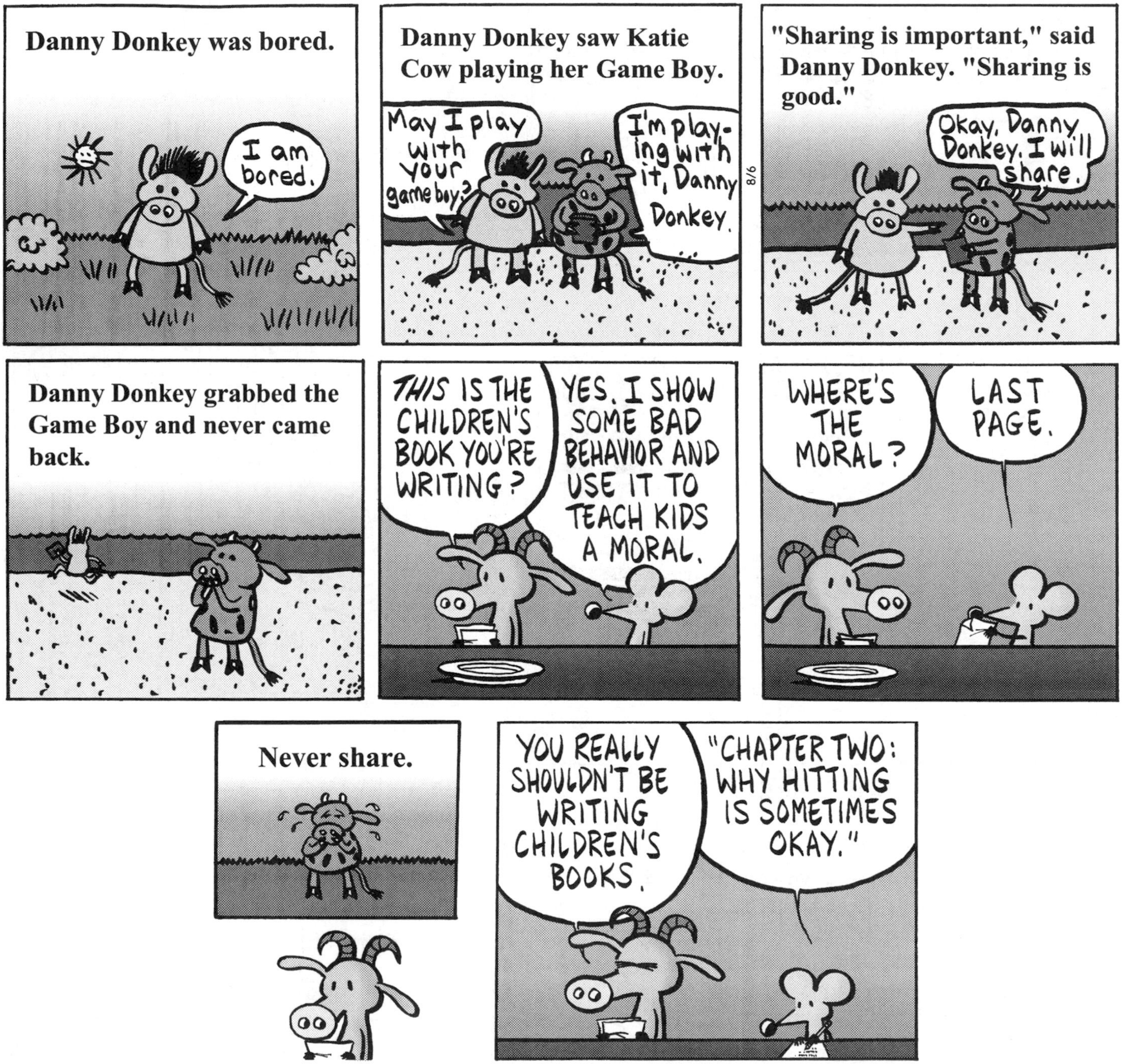

Danny Donkey was bored.
I am bored.
Danny Donkey saw Katie Cow playing her Game Boy.
May I play with your game boy?
I'm playing with it, Danny Donkey.
8/6
"Sharing is important," said Danny Donkey. "Sharing is good."
Okay, Danny Donkey. I will share.
Danny Donkey grabbed the Game Boy and never came back.
THIS IS THE CHILDREN'S BOOK YOU'RE WRITING?
YES. I SHOW SOME BAD BEHAVIOR AND USE IT TO TEACH KIDS A MORAL.
WHERE'S THE MORAL?
LAST PAGE.
Never share.
YOU REALLY SHOULDN'T BE WRITING CHILDREN'S BOOKS.
"CHAPTER TWO: WHY HITTING IS SOMETIMES OKAY."